CALL ME THE SEEKER

Listening to Religion in Popular Music

EDITED BY

Michael J. Gilmour

continuum

NEW YORK • LONDON

Copyright © 2005 by Michael J. Gilmour

The Continuum International Publishing Group
15 East 26th Street, New York, NY 10010

The Continuum International Publishing Group Ltd
The Tower Building, 11 York Road, London SE1 7NX

Unless otherwise indicated, Scripture quotations are taken from the New Revised Standard Version of the Bible, copyright 1989 by the Division of Christian Education of the National Council of the Churches of Christ in the USA. Used by permission. All rights reserved. Occasional quotations labeled KJV are from the King James Version; NIV, from the New International Version; RSV, from the Revised Standard Version.

Cover art courtesy of Corbis

Cover design by Corey Kent

Library of Congress Cataloging-in-Publication Data

Call me the seeker : listening to religion in popular music / Michael J. Gilmour, ed.
    p. cm.
  Includes bibliographical references (p.   ).
  ISBN 0-8264-1713-2 (pbk.) — ISBN 0-8264-1714-0 (hardcover)
  1. Popular music—Religious aspects. I. Gilmour, Michael J.
  ML3921.8.P67C35 2005
  781.64'112—dc22
                                    2004030921

Printed in the United States of America

05 06 07 08 09 10   10 9 8 7 6 5 4 3 2 1

Dedicated to the memory of
Anna Kessler, PhD

CONTENTS

INTRODUCTION

Radios in Religious Studies Departments

*Preliminary Reflections on the Study of
Religion in Popular Music*

—Michael J. Gilmour

THE STUDY OF RELIGION and popular culture has blossomed in the last decade. An increasing number of books, articles, and dissertations analyzing a wide array of topics—from comic books to movies—have been written, and there are more academic forums[1] where scholars of religion can present their research. We hope this book complements such ongoing work, focusing on an area receiving somewhat less attention than others do. There does not appear to be as much scholarly energy devoted to the links between religion and popular music compared to, say, television and movies.

In the fall of 2003, when I first asked people to write for this book, numerous chapter proposals were submitted, far more than could be included in a single volume. Why? What would compel busy scholars to turn their attention to popular music? There are a few reasons. First and foremost, each writer included here is a music fan. Even though we occasionally feel hints of embarrassment among colleagues in our primary fields of research,[2] we all welcomed the opportunity to look (listen) seriously and carefully at (to) the music we love. Also, as academics in various fields of religious studies, or as academics with an interest in religion, we share the conviction that spirituality is widely represented in popular music. Songwriters engage religions and their texts and explore grand theological questions, sometimes deliberately, sometimes not. At times they can be heard criticizing organized religion, and sometimes we hear them propagating their own views. Further, much can be learned about the large audiences that listen to this music, whose worldview is shaped in part by the songwriters they revere and the subcultures with which they identify. These reasons alone are sufficient to warrant a closer investigation.

Despite our best apology, there will always be those who view such an exercise with some condescension. How substantial can popular songs be? Harold Bloom defines reading as "the search for a difficult pleasure."[3] Reading involves work and risks, we are told. To open oneself to "a direct confrontation with Shakespeare at his strongest, as in *King Lear*, is never an easy pleasure, . . . and yet not to read *King Lear* fully . . . is to be cognitively as well as aesthetically defrauded."[4] In this prologue Bloom speaks specifically of "deep reading," and the authors treated throughout his book are among what he calls the traditional canon.[5] The reader's quest ought to be for a higher pleasure, and "a pleasurable difficulty seems to me a plausible definition of the Sublime."[6] This book is an exercise in "deep reading," though to introduce Bloom at the outset is somewhat ironic since he approaches the study of literature with a notion of canon that is rather exclusive. He would not look favorably—I suspect—on a book that celebrates the literary, artistic, and spiritual merits of popular music.[7] Nevertheless, the contributors have proceeded with the assumption that insight and profundity can be found not only in the traditional canons, religious or otherwise, but also in unexpected places.

Introducing a study of popular songwriters with an implied comparison with such English language luminaries as William Shakespeare, Emily Brontë, and Jane Austen—part of Bloom's traditional canon—is unabashedly presumptuous. One might respond that no pop musician has stood the test of time, a reasonable criteria for determining value and worthiness for serious study. Indeed, few of the artists treated in this book reach back more than, say, fifty years, whereas Shakespeare after four hundred years "is more pervasive than ever he was before [and] they will perform him in outer space, and on other worlds, if those worlds are reached."[8] Will U2 or Woody Guthrie still be heard on CD players (or whatever medium the future brings) when rockets carry music lovers to those other worlds? Of course, we can't know how future generations will receive our favorite artists' work, but we remain confident that the study of popular music is a worthy exercise. In many cases a sustained, careful, and "deep" reading of serious artists can prove rewarding, even pointing us beyond the music itself to something we might call "Sublime."

Each week Stuart McLean of CBC Radio visits Dave's Vinyl Cafe, the world's smallest record store. Despite its size, it provides listeners with endless variety for their listening pleasure. This book is similarly eclectic, bringing together studies on everything from folk to rap, country to metal. There is further diversity in the lines of inquiry pursued and the backgrounds of the contributors. Still, it is our hope that these chapters may provide clues for further research, whether by suggesting strategies for "listening" to religion in popular music or by pointing to artists whose work rewards sustained analysis.

As editor I express my thanks to the contributors and various colleagues at Providence College in Otterburne, Manitoba, Canada. Like the Vinyl Cafe—to press the analogy further—"We may not be big, but we're small." However, what we lack in size, when compared to larger institutions, we make up for in quality of personnel and students. Marla Williamson provided a great deal of assistance with the technical side of things, helping organize and format a scattered collection of electronic files. The idea for this book was largely born out of the lively discussions regularly enjoyed while carpooling and during coffee breaks. Here our musical tastes covered the spectrum, and yet we agreed that there is a remarkable and universal link between spirituality and music. In particular, I thank Drs. Brian Froese, Randy Holm, Cameron McKenzie, and Tim Perry for being supportive and enthusiastic about this project.

Notes

1. E.g., the *Journal of Religion and Popular Culture* (University of Saskatchewan; online: http://www.usask.ca/relst/jrpc/index.html).
2. "Many of us come to the analysis of popular culture with a particular special interest related to our own private enthusiasms, . . . and we sometimes hesitate to reveal our interest and even fandom to our more 'sophisticated' friends" (Bruce David Forbes, "Finding Religion in Unexpected Places," in *Religion and Popular Culture in America* [ed. Bruce David Forbes and Jeffrey H. Mahan; Berkeley: University of California Press, 2000], 17).
3. Harold Bloom, *How to Read and Why* (New York: Simon & Schuster, 2000), 29.
4. Ibid., 23.
5. That is, "the now much-abused traditional canon" (ibid., 29). See also Bloom's *The Western Canon: The Books and School of the Ages* (New York: Riverhead Books, 1994).
6. Bloom, *How to Read*, 29.
7. "There will always be (one hopes) incessant readers who will go on reading despite the proliferation of fresh technologies for distraction. Sometimes I try to visualize Dr. Johnson or George Eliot confronting MTV Rap or experiencing Virtual Reality and find

myself heartened by what I believe would be their ironical, strong refusal of such irrational entertainments. After a lifetime spent in teaching literature at one of our major universities, I have very little confidence that literary education will survive its current malaise. . . . Finding myself now surrounded by professors of hip-hop; by clones of Gallic-Germanic theory; by ideologues of gender and of various sexual persuasions; by multiculturalists unlimited, I realize that the Balkanization of literary studies is irreversible" (*Western Canon*, 483). "What are now called 'Departments of English' will be renamed departments of 'Cultural Studies' where *Batman* comics, Mormon theme parks, television, movies, and rock will replace Chaucer, Shakespeare, Milton, Wordsworth and Wallace Stevens" (ibid., 485). But can't we study both?

    8. Bloom, *How to Read*, 25.

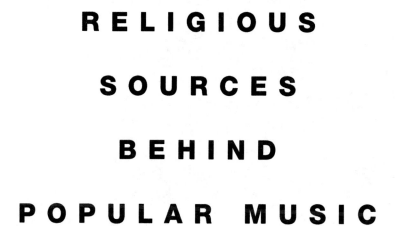

Section One

RELIGIOUS SOURCES BEHIND POPULAR MUSIC

Shekhinah as Woman

Kabbalistic References in Dylan's Infidels

—Daniel Maoz

The fierce power of imagination is a gift from G-d. Joined with the grandeur of the mind, the potency of inference, ethical depth, and the natural sense of the divine, imagination becomes an instrument for the holy spirit.[1]

The *Sefirot* and the Song

ON OCTOBER 27, 1983, Columbia Records released Bob Dylan's *Infidels*. I was living in France at the time. I picked up the cassette version some time in early November and, as in the early years of *Blonde on Blonde*, found myself playing the album over and over again, taking it all in through the earphones of my Sony Walkman, all the while walking along Strasbourg's ancient Julian canal system. One song in particular has haunted me from that moment on. As in my youth, there was no urgency to catch every word, let alone understand every song.[2] Yet something spoke to my deep inner being as Dylan's raspy voice crooned,

> I and I,
> In creation where one's nature neither honors nor forgives.
> I and I,
> One says to the other, no man sees my face and lives.

3

Some time between then and now I have come to think that *Infidels* holds the key to understanding what is the *crux interpretum* for Dylan's unique manner of expression and perception of life and afterlife. What seems clear in the lyrics of the songs of *Infidels* can at least be derived from the lyrics of his antecedent and subsequent works. I think it can be demonstrated that interpretive principles and methods of major kabbalistic interpreters have inspired Dylan, either directly or indirectly.[3] Yet Dylan continues to write, produce, revise, and direct his thoughts, both past and present. Dylan's canon is both loose and incomplete. *Infidels*, I propose, is the keystone in the arch of this ongoing structure.

The approach that I have adopted plays with four distinct considerations about the nature of poetry, which are subsequently applied to the lyrics of the eight songs included in Dylan's *Infidels*. These songs are viewed through the lens of the ten *Sefirot* of Kabbalah.[4] I have developed this methodology as much to offer a modern paradigm for understanding classical Jewish mystical thought as to hear Dylan's words in a way that invites unique reader response.[5]

Just as each song is the work of many things besides the author, so too the thoughts within each song are part of a complex and intricate process drawn from identifiable, supposed, and unknown sources.[6] Much like the wheels within wheels of Ezekiel's vision, the ideas of one song seem to provide backdrop, texture, or some other supporting role for the others. When we cannot trace the literary trail of an expressed thought, however, we may too quickly consider the author's originality,[7] although to consider the *genius*[8] of the author is yet another matter.[9]

Poems require the reader to assume a perceptual stance that is known to be untrue. And by the nature of literary process, the writer, the reader, and the poem itself are each interpreters and interpretations of what has preceded. Much in the way we allow ourselves to enter a movie theatre with a suspended sense of reality, permitting the film to introduce us to a world of hobbits and mysterious rings,[10] or of sorcerers and enchantment,[11] so we loosen our grip on reality, as it were, when listening to individual and composite compositions by Dylan.[12]

This essay considers ideas presented in the lyrics of *Infidels* in a modified reader-response critical manner. I claim neither to follow nor to invite any particular interpretive community. I simply respond to the texts, recreating a variety of details as viewed through the lens of the Sefirot, and trust that some level of understanding will fall perhaps halfway between Dylan's lyrics and the snapshots that I take of them. I have included two diagrams to indicate how the eight songs of *Infidels* can be understood to align with the ten Sefirot.[13]

Songs and Sefirot

Two overarching templates provide distinct paths of approach to the Sefirot.[14] They are derived from *Bereshit* (Hebrew for "creation," "In the beginning," Gen 1:1),[15] the first book of the Hebrew Bible, and from *Merkavah* (chariot-throne),[16] the text of the prophet Ezekiel. The ten Sefirot have been portrayed in a variety of ways, including a seven-branched menorah,[17] *Shivviti* (a calligraphic diagram),[18] geometric designs,[19] *Azilut* (the primordial man),[20] the Hebrew letter *Aleph*,[21] hands assuming the priestly posture,[22] an inverted tree,[23] and concentrically enclosed symbols,[24] to name the more familiar ones.[25]

The Upper Sefirot

The first three Sefirot have to do with primordial creation. They include *Keter* (Crown), *Khokhmah* (Wisdom), and *Binah* (Understanding). *Keter* is coeternal with the *Ain Sof* (the One who has no end/Infinity), the highest emanation of G-d. *Keter* is both *Ayin* (Nothingness) and the identity presented to Moses ("I") at the burning bush.[26] *Khokhmah* and *Binah* are the beginning of conceptualization and the boundary of intelligence, respectively. None of the "upper Sefirot" is analogous to human activity. These notions appear throughout the lyrics of "I and I." The listener is able to "hear" the dual manifestation of *Keter* in the title, which is repeated throughout the song: "*Ayin / Ehyeh*"—"*Nothingness / I*." Communication within these two emanations is conveyed in the familiar expression "One said to the other." As well, the three "upper Sefirot" dwell "in creation, where one's nature neither honors nor forgives"—where Moses could only regard the backside of G-d. Hence, "No man sees my face and lives." *Keter* is the dwelling place of—*nothing*. "Think I'll go out and go for a walk. Not much happenin' here, nothin' ever does." *Khokhmah* and *Binah*, father of fathers and mother of mothers, respectively, are portrayed as "two men [people] on a train platform," outside of which "there's nobody in sight." Nor can anyone be in the presence of these Sefirot, where noontime can indeed be "the darkest part," and where one removes the shoes from their feet in such creative Presence. "I've made shoes for everyone, even you, while I still go barefoot." The vast expanse of *Ayin*, where stumbling leads to *Binah* (Understanding), contrasts with the constrained setting of the material world: "Into the narrow lanes, I can't stumble or stay put."[27]

The Lower Sefirot

The remaining seven Sefirot include six "directional" divine emanations, *Khesed* (Lovingkindness"), *Gevurah/Din* (Power/Justice), *Tiferet* (Beauty), *Netsakh* (Eternity), *Hod* (Splendor), and *Yesod* (Foundation),[28] as well as G-d's female counterpart, *Shekhinah* (Presence). These are not a barefoot shoe-maker's Sefirot.[29] These divine emanations can be seen to correspond to dominant themes in each of *Infidels'* remaining seven songs (see diagram 2).

Khesed emanates compassion. It serves that which is in need of healing and restoration, bringing forth *tikkun olam* (repair of the world). It is the translation of knowledge to action, from hearing about a need to doing something about it. *Khesed* sees through the rhetoric of sociopolitical deception that is "opposed to fair play," beyond self-orbital greed that "wants it all and wants it his way." It is not enough for *Khesed* to notice how those who suffer are "trained and mismanaged, with great skill." *Khesed* demands of the listener to "leave no stone unturned . . . till your error you clearly learn." *Khesed* does not go away when ignored. "She just sits there as the night grows still, . . . facin' the hill . . . sitting there in a cold chill . . . as the night grows still." Until that which is wrong is righted, until that which is broken is repaired, *Khesed* sits with penetrating, in-your-face stillness, constantly asking, "Who's going to turn thought into action?" "Who's going to answer the call?" "Who's going to make the difference?"[30]

Gevurah, tempered by *Khesed*, confronts darkness in a nonviolent way. Just as *Gevurah* assures that *Khesed* will not set unrepentant criminals free, so *Khesed* assures that *Gevurah* will administer justice in fairness, "passing judgement with the fear of His strength."[31] Just as light displaces darkness, so *Gevurah* liberates that which is bound. *Gevurah* is "right action that leads to right vision to right results."[32] *Gevurah* elicits a fear for G-d that displaces even the greatest of "other" fears. Whether faced with the out-stretched arm of "Führer" or of "local Priest," the one who has placed all fear in G-d need not be overwhelmed by the "sweet gift of gab," "harmo-nious tongue," or being deceived by one who "knows every song of love that ever has been sung." *Gevurah* offers a path of elevation from lower to upper Sefirot, through the fear of G-d, which is the beginning of *Khokhmah*. *Khokhmah* produced by *Gevurah* knows that "good intentions can be evil," even when a velvet glove delivers its message.[33] *Gevurah*-produced fear of G-d allows its bearer to stand up to a demagogue, even warning others:

"You know that sometimes Satan will come as a man of peace." And *Gevurah* will not be distracted by those who are fascinating or dull, neither by those who play mind games[34] nor by those who attempt to employ humanitarian or philanthropic means to gain control. *Gevurah* will withstand Satan himself.

Tiferet emanates when *Khokhmah* and *Gevurah* are in balance. As indicated above, *Khesed* alone lacks the wherewithal to deter abuse of kindness, resulting in any number of related imbalances: vanity,[35] pride,[36] jealousy,[37] patriotism.[38] As one would expect, *Tiferet* cannot emanate where either *Khesed* or *Gevurah* lacks the other. In such a situation, one can only say to *Tiferet*: "What's a sweetheart like you doin' in a dump like this." To bring about such harmony would require that the "Boss" be around.[39] The emanating influence of the Sefirot results in elevation. It is contrary to the nature of the Sefirot to transcend, thus lowering that which their emanation influences. It follows, then, if *Khesed* and *Gevurah* do not maintain a perfect, *Tiferet*-producing balance, that the Boss has "gone North for awhile."

Netsakh is the seventh Sefirah, one step below *Tiferet*.[40] Rarely experienced in everyday life, enlightened beings alone speak of *Netsakh*.[41] With highest motive and most selfless intention as its fulfillment, *Netsakh* cannot settle for compromise, dilution, or diffusion. Where it sees such, it must awaken the higher inner self with a clarion call.[42] Good ideas replaced by lower thoughts too easily lead to acts of greed.[43]

Hod is natural splendor, but as has already been pointed out, when dealing with Kabbalah, "nothing of course is merely natural."[44] *Hod* is marked by abandonment of temporality.[45] Unobstructed by time-bound mental processes, *Hod* views with clarity that which cannot otherwise be seen.[46] *Hod* can be "standing on the water casting [one's] bread while the eyes of the idol with the iron head [are] glowing" and remain completely unaffected. All manner of activity can occur,[47] but *Hod* is fixed and has abandoned temporal engagement.[48] Small wonder that such disaffection could be attributed to the figure of a "Jokerman" and receive no end of pejorative slurs.[49] And it can rightly be asked, To what degree does the author identify with Jokerman?[50]

Yesod looks to the divine source from whence we came as well as recognizing that only by being grounded in a foundation that is established by the most exalted spiritual principles can right actions follow.[51] Historically, there can be no more obvious foundation within Judaism, Dylan's birth religion, than *Eretz Israel* (the land of Israel), which enjoys both the ancient mythical tradition of being called into being as a Holy Land by the Most Holy G-d as well as being a land (and people) that have endured the test of time.[52] If the Founder is righteous, holiness of the Foundation obtains.[53] As an analogy for *Yesod*, Eretz Israel is falsely perceived as trouble and troubler by the multitudes that surround it.[54] Yet as *Yesod*, despite any temporary twisting of justice, no charge can ultimately survive, no matter how many "enemies" rise up against it.[55] It is no wonder that the world labors as a pregnant woman, awaiting righteousness and justice from G-d while denying the very Foundation of that righteousness and justice here on earth.[56] To an unrighteous world, *Yesod* is merely a neighborhood bully.

Shekhinah is the tenth and final Sefirah. Though the lowest of the spheres, *Shekhinah* alone can encompass all of the Sefirot. The tenth Sefirah is also called *Malkhut* (kingdom), and when so is said to have inherited *Shekhinah*. As the "descent" of the *Shekhinah*, "*Malkhut* makes the world of emanation a pragmatic unity."[57] Talmudic literature knows no role of *Shekhinah* as a symbol of the feminine.[58] Yet in the Torah, Shekhinah is associated with women, albeit in limited contexts, and dwells both with men[59] and with women alone.[60] In kabbalistic literature, however, we find a reversal of this identification; it presents *Shekhinah* as woman.[61] If *Shekhinah* were to "fall apart," the entire structure of Sefirot would be unable to sustain itself due to the intricate connectivity between *Shekhinah* and *Khokhmah*.[62] Moreover, *Shekhinah* invites participation in the fullness of her position.[63] We have moved from Nothingness to Fullness, from Upper Sefirot to the lowest possible emanation of divine Presence. And yet we can see, even in this level of emanation,[64] the spiritually apogean height that can be achieved.[65] In the presence of *Shekhinah* one has lofty and yet pragmatic and attainable thoughts.[66] The practicality of *Shekhinah* is inescapable. Whereas other Sefirot could be portrayed as Nothingness, Inspiration, and Thought, *Shekhinah* is portrayed as positive action.[67] And her role is well beyond that which brought the worlds into being.[68]

Masked and Anonymous

"Alias"[69] is a well-suited epithet for one whose identity in various circles and at diverse times has included Shabtai Zisel ben Avraham v'Rachel Riva,[70] Robert (Bobby) Zimmerman,[71] Blind Boy Grunt,[72] Bob Dylan,[73] Billy ("Kick-Ass") Parker,[74] Lucky Wilbury,[75] Boo Wilbury,[76] Renaldo,[77] and Jack Fate.[78] And characteristically, Dylan is tight-lipped about himself. I have learned early on to be wary of self-revelatory "facts." For example, while admitting to his birthplace being Duluth, Minnesota, he added that he was raised in Gallop, New Mexico (not in Hibbing, Minnesota), where he learned many cowboy, Indian, and carnival songs, "vaudeville kind of stuff." From this fictitious childhood playground, he said that he joined different carnivals each year between the ages of about thirteen and nineteen.[79] None of this is true. Three years later, he teased reporters that he was a "song-and-dance man," later adding in an interview with a *Time* magazine journalist that he was "just as good a singer as Caruso."[80] When performing in New York at a dinner club, he spoke of leaving home at thirteen to join a circus and travel America.[81] If embellishing the truth about oneself makes one a liar, then perhaps completely reconstructing one's personal story makes that same person a poet the likes of a Bob Dylan.[82] It would seem plausible, however, that even a poet cannot but self-reveal through the medium of his or her creative product.[83] And so, *Infidels* marks the revealing of more than just a moving on from a clearly identifiable stage that Dylan went through, a phase popularly referred to as the Christian period of his life.[84] At the human level, Dylan could be reinventing himself as Jokerman, "shedding off one more layer of skin."

On another level entirely, *Infidels* provides a template for entrance into Jewish mysticism. The primary tenet of Jewish thought is that G-d is unknowable.[85] Soon thereafter, one learns to pursue G-d with all of one's heart, soul, and strength.[86] By encountering Dylan's lyrics through ordinary means, one may arrive at certain understandings, while being equally limited by certain parameters. Add to that the lens provided by Kabbalah, especially consideration of the Sefirot, and unfordable waters part.

I remember being in a bookstore no more than three years ago and looking up Dylan's name in a popular dictionary of quotations. Since then I have completely lost the piece of scrap paper onto which I dutifully copied the quote and its source. The setting was a small coffee shop somewhere in America. At a table were Bob Dylan, Joan Baez, and others whom I no longer remember, if they were even mentioned. Joan Baez, I think, was telling the story. Dylan asked if someone would pass him a device with which he could stir his coffee. They all sat before him, frozen in common thought: Did he mean a spoon? When mystical and familiar converge, even the steadiest hand can tremble.

There is a secular world and a holy world, secular worlds and holy worlds. These worlds contradict one another. The contradiction, of course, is subjective. In our limited perception we cannot reconcile the sacred and the secular, we cannot harmonize their contradictions. Yet at the pinnacle of the universe they are reconciled, at the site of the holy of holies.[87]

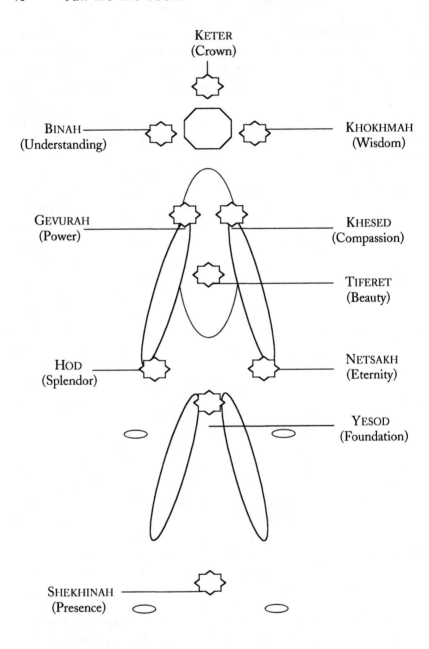

Fig. 1: This diagram portrays Azilut, the Primordial Person: "The Embodiment of the Sefirot and the most perfect image of Divinity" (adapted from Avram Davis and Manuela Dunn Mascetti, *Judaic Mysticism* [New York: Hyperion, 1997], 201).

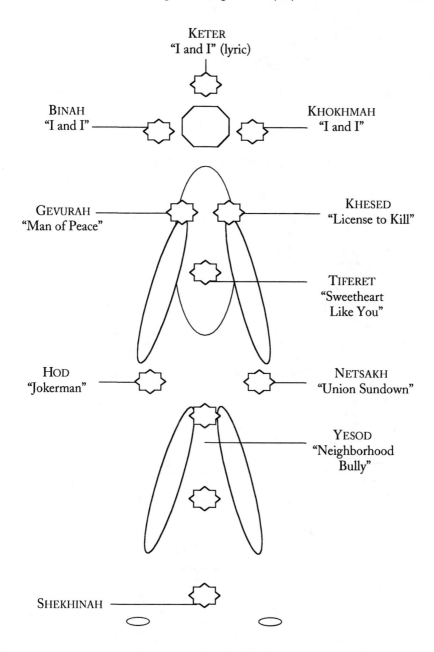

"Don't Fall Apart on Me Tonight"

Fig. 2: This diagram pairs each Sefirah with one of Bob Dylan's songs.

Notes

1. Abraham Isaac Kook, *Orot ha-Qodesh* [Lights of Holiness] (2 vols. in 3; Jerusalem: Masad ha-Rav Kuk, 1962/3–1963/4), 1:262; cited from Daniel C. Matt, *The Essential Kabbalah: The Heart of Jewish Mysticism* (San Francisco: HarperCollins, 1996), 116.

2. As we see below, the directional Sefirot are like poems, imaginative in function. Conversely, songs/poems can be understood through the language of the Sefirot.

3. Such attribution is not original to Dylan. Harold Bloom's "entire critical oeuvre either directly or indirectly has been inspired by the hermeneutical principles and methods of the major kabbalistic interpreters." Harold Bloom, *Kabbalah and Criticism* (New York: Seabury, 1975), cover blurb.

4. "Jewish mysticism in its various forms represents an attempt to interpret the religious values of Judaism in terms of mystical values. It concentrates upon the idea of the living G-d who manifests himself in the acts of Creation, Revelation, and Redemption. Pushed to its extreme, the mystical meditation of this idea gives birth to the conception of a sphere, a whole realm of divinity, which underlies the world of our sense-data and which is present and active in all that exists. This is the meaning of what the Kabbalists call the *world of the 'Sefiroth.'*" Gershom Scholem, *Major Trends in Jewish Mysticism* (1946; New York: Schocken Books, 1995), 10–11.

5. I accomplish this by merely fine-tuning the analogical identification of the Sefirot. See figures 1 and 2.

6. Paul Valéry, *Oeuvres*, vol. 2 (Paris: Pléiade, 1960), 629. "Les relations humaines sont fondées sur chiffres. Déchiffrer, c'est se brouiller. Ce chiffre a l'avantage de dire sans dire, et de garder suspendue, réversible, l'opinion réciproque. Il nous préserve de porter des jugements décisifs et définitifs qui ne sont jamais vrais que dans l'instant."

7. "We mean to say that the dependence on what he does on what others have done is excessively complex and irregular." Paul Valéry, "Letter About Mallarmé," in *Leonardo Poe Mallarmé* (trans. Malcolm Cowley and James R. Lawler; Collected Works 8; Princeton: Princeton University Press, 1972), 241.

8. Creative interplay with others' ideas may not be so much a mark of originality as it is an expression of one's spark of genius. Dylan himself once admitted: "Oh, if there's an original thought out there, I could use it right now." "Brownsville Girl," *Knocked Out Loaded* (Don Mills, Ontario: CBS Inc., 1986).

9. In instances where a particular source can be summoned, more often than not we tend to ask literary critical questions of the text. To what degree does the transmitted text align with an "original" text? Does the present work confuse the meaning of an "original" text? If not identical, to what degree does the present text stand in the likeness of its source(s)? Sometimes we even follow the "sources" of our text to their own "sources," knowing that any transmitted text has a variety of antecedent "sources" of its own. We soon realize, however, that such an exercise is both limited in scope and ultimately futile in comprehensiveness. Seldom can we identify a majority of influences that have shaped any present text, let alone the sources' own sources that shaped them. Reconstruction of any generation of source text is by nature complicated to elusive.

10. E.g., in J. R. R. Tolkien's *The Lord of the Rings* (part 1, *The Fellowship of the Ring*; part 2, *The Two Towers*; and part 3, *The Return of the King*; many editions).

11. E.g., the ongoing *Harry Potter* series.

12. Romanticism necessarily over-states mimetic representation in order to compensate for nature by generous exercise of the imagination. Misreading of a text alone permits

the text to continue in its own contradictions. "The fierce power of imagination is a gift from G-d. Joined with the grandeur of the mind, the potency of inference, ethical depth, and the natural sense of the divine, imagination becomes an instrument for the holy spirit." Abraham Isaac Kook, *Orot ha-Qodesh* 1:262 (Matt, *Essential Kabbalah*, 116).

13. The ten Sefirot represent ten names for G-d, or ten spheres of G-d's manifestation. Together they form the great unutterable Name of G-d, or the unified universe of G-d's life. See Scholem, *Major Trends*, 213; Bloom, *Criticism*, 71.

14. The two interpretive grids are not, however, always separated, resulting in a number of expressions of hermeneutical syncretism.

15. "Before the creation of the world, Ein Sof withdrew itself into its essence, from itself to itself within itself. It left an empty space within its essence, in which it could emanate and create." Attributed to the sixteenth–seventeenth-century Kabbalist Hayyim Vital, "On the World of Emanation," in *Liqqutim Hadashim* (Jerusalem: Mevaqqeshei ha-Shem, 1985), 17–23; Matt, *Essential Kabbalah*, 93.

16. I.e., a metalepsis for G-d, which Bloom identifies as "the transumptive trope-of-a-trope." Bloom, *Criticism*, 26.

17. Avram Davis and Manuela Dunn Mascetti, *Judaic Mysticism* (New York: Hyperion, 1997), 201.

18. *Shivviti* (I have set) refers to Ps 16:8, "I have set [Ha-Shem, the Tetragrammaton] always before me" (NIV). A pictorial representation of the *Shivviti* drawn in Iran (1855) is portrayed in the cover art of Matt, *Essential Kabbalah*. A thirteenth-century manuscript at the Bibliothèque nationale, Paris, France portrays a calligraphic diagram of the tree of life (sans *Shivviti*). See Davis and Mascetti, *Judaic Mysticism*, 190.

19. E.g., in an oriental kabbalistic scroll, The Bodleian Library, Oxford, England, ca. 1605. For a pictorial representation, see Davis and Mascetti, *Judaic Mysticism*, 184.

20. "The House of the Body," from Tobias Cohn, *Maaseh Tobiyyah* (Venice, 1707), is a more elaborate expression of this type of representation.

21. Moses Cordovero/Corduero, *Pardes Rimmonim* (Kraków, 1591/2).

22. Shabbathai Horowitz, *Shefa' Tal* (Hanau, 1612).

23. Traditional.

24. Cordovero, *Pardes Rimmonim.*

25. In many of the portraits, the ten Sefirot are joined by other kabbalistic symbols, including the twenty-two paths of the Tarot, and the Names of G-d.

26. Exod 3:14, where G-d's self-disclosure was given in terms of "'Ehyeh asher 'ehyeh [I am that I am]."

27. "Whoever delves into mysticism cannot help but stumble, as it is written: 'This stumbling block is in your hand' (Isa 3:6). You cannot grasp these things unless you stumble over them." Twelfth-century text, *Sefer ha-Bahir* 150.65 (Matt, *Essential Kabbalah*, 163). So too, one cannot understand the words of the Torah unless one has stumbled over them; *b. Git.* 43a.

28. As shown in figure 1, *Khesed* and *Netsakh* are on the right, *Gevurah* and *Hod* on the left, and *Tiferet* and *Yesod* are in the middle. As such, out of the "creative strife" of *Khesed* and *Gevurah* comes *Tiferet*. In similar manner *Yesod* comes out of *Netsakh* and *Hod*. Also, *Netsakh* emanates from *Khesed*, as does *Hod* from *Gevurah*.

29. "I make shoes for everyone else, even you, yet I still go barefoot" ("I and I," *Infidels*. Don Mills, Ontario: CBS Inc., 1983) identifies with the upper Sefirot of creation's domain, wherein the Creator ("the Shoemaker") must be satisfied to produce forms for all others while remaining formless (thus, a "barefoot Shoemaker").

30. "Who's gonna take away his license to kill?" ("License to Kill," *Infidels*).

31. Kenneth Hanson, *Kabbalah: Three Thousand Years of Mystic Tradition* (Tulsa, OK: Council Oak Books, 1998), 94.

32. Davis and Mascetti, *Judaic Mysticism*, 198.

33. I.e., "both hands can be full of grease" ("Man of Peace," *Infidels*).

34. I.e., "rid[ing] down Niagara Falls in the barrels of your skull" ("Man of Peace").

35. "They say that vanity got the best of him, but he sure left here in style. By the way, that's a cute hat, and that smile's so hard to resist" ("Sweetheart Like You," *Infidels*).

36. "You know, news of you has come down the line even before you came in the door. They say in your father's house, there's many mansions. Each one of them got a fireproof floor" ("Sweetheart Like You").

37. "Snap out of it, baby, people are jealous of you. They smile at your face, but behind your back they hiss" ("Sweetheart Like You").

38. "They say that patriotism is the last refuge to which a scoundrel clings. Steal a little and they throw you in jail. Steal a lot and they make you king" ("Sweetheart Like You").

39. The nature of the Sefirot is to work in harmony, with none emanating apart from the others.

40. And so one would expect *Tiferet* to know that "there's only one step down from here, baby. It's called the land of permanent bliss" ("Sweetheart Like You").

41. In other words, *Netsakh* "brings understanding that talks to our most enlightened self." Davis and Mascetti, *Judaic Mysticism*, 200.

42. Put another way, "Well, it's sundown on the Union" ("Sundown on the Union," *Infidels*).

43. "And what's made in the USA sure was a good idea till greed got in the way" ("Sundown on the Union").

44. Bloom, *Kabbalah and Criticism*, 31.

45. "The book of Leviticus and Deuteronomy, the law of the jungle and the sea are your only teachers" ("Jokerman," *Infidels*).

46. "Resting in the fields, far from the turbulent space. Half asleep 'neath the stars with a small dog licking your face" ("Jokerman").

47. Among common temporal distractions unnoticed by *Hod* are "distant ships sailing into the mist," "the rifleman's stalking the sick and the lame," "preacherman seek[ing] the same," "nightsticks and water cannons, tear gas, padlocks, Molotov cocktails and rocks behind every curtain, false-hearted judges dyin' in the webs that they spin" ("Jokerman").

48. "Oh, Jokerman, you know what he wants. Oh, Jokerman, you don't show any response" ("Jokerman").

49. "You're a man of the mountain, you can walk on the clouds, manipulator of crowds, you're a dream twister" ("Jokerman").

50. I owe this consideration to Howard Rotberg. During several "electric" dialogues in the months preceding research for this essay, he pointed out to me that Dylan, fated to be a public performer, was born in 1941, while the Holocaust raged on. Thus, "You were born with a snake [microphone] in both of your fists while a hurricane [the Holocaust] was blowin'" seemed to be autobiographical for him. Further, in the first draft of his own publication, *The Second Catastrophe* (Toronto: Mantua Books, 2003), Rotberg included a table of contents representing a study on Dylan and Kabbalah, done by one of the characters of his compelling historical fiction. Although the present study does not reflect the contents of the first draft of his book or much of what we discussed at that time, I have undoubtedly been inspired by his keen sense of accuracy and detail, combined with a rare expression of thought-provoking creativity.

51. Davis and Mascetti, *Judaic Mysticism*, 202.

52. "Every empire that's enslaved him is gone, Egypt and Rome, even the great Babylon. He's made a garden of paradise in the desert sand" ("Neighborhood Bully," *Infidels*).

53. "In bed with nobody, under no one's command" ("Neighborhood Bully").

54. "What's anybody indebted to him for? 'Nothin',' they say. 'He just likes to cause war.' Pride and prejudice and superstition indeed. They wait for this bully like a dog waits to feed" ("Neighborhood Bully").

55. "Seen his family scattered, people hounded and torn, he's always on trial for just being born. Well, he knocked out a lynch mob, he was criticized. Old women condemned him, said he should apologize. Then he destroyed a bomb factory, nobody was glad. The bombs were meant for him. He was supposed to feel bad. Well, the chances are against it, and the odds are slim that he'll live by the rules that the world makes for him. There's a noose at his neck and a gun at his back, and a license to kill him given out to every maniac" ("Neighborhood Bully").

56. "Well, he got no allies to really speak of. What he gets he must pay for, he don't get it out of love. He buys obsolete weapons, and he won't be denied. But no one sends flesh and blood to fight by his side" ("Neighborhood Bully").

57. Bloom, *Kabbalah and Criticism*, 31–32.

58. Gershom Sholem, *Origins of the Kabbalah* (trans. Allan Arkush from the German; Philadelphia: Jewish Publication Society, 1987), 163.

59. E.g., *Shekhinah* is said to dwell with husband and wife.

60. E.g., Lot's wife beheld *Shekhinah*.

61. See, for example, the detailed treatment of this topic in Gershom Scholem, *Origins of the Kabbalah* (trans. Allan Arkush; Princeton, NJ: Princeton University Press, 1987), 162–80.

62. *Na'utz tchiloson besofon, vesofen betchiloson* (Hebrew for "The beginning is embedded in the end, and the end is embedded in the beginning"); *Sefer Yetzirah* [Book of Creation] 1.7.

63. "Just a minute 'fore you leave, girl. Just a minute 'fore you touch the door. What is it that you're tryin' to achieve, girl? Do you think we can talk about it some more?" ("Don't Fall Apart on Me Tonight," *Infidels*).

64. For example, *Shekhinah* can be thought of as the Holy Spirit. Hanson, *Kabbalah*, 97.

65. "Come over here from over there, girl. Sit down here; you can have my chair. I can't see us goin' anywhere, girl. The only place open is a thousand miles away, and I can't take you there" ("Don't Fall Apart on Me Tonight").

66. "I wished I'd have been a doctor. Maybe I'd have saved some life that'd been lost. Maybe I'd have done some good in the world 'stead of burnin' every bridge I crossed" ("Don't Fall Apart on Me Tonight"). In other words, "*Shekhinah* is the form of enlightenment that demands to be given, to be shared, to be sowed as seeds of light into the human world." Davis and Mascetti, *Judaic Mysticism*, 203.

67. "Let's try to get beneath the surface waste, girl. No more booby traps and bombs. No more decadence and charm. No more affection that's misplaced, girl" ("Don't Fall Apart on Me Tonight").

68. "No more mudcake creatures lyin' in your arm" ("Don't Fall Apart on Me Tonight"). On this matter, Rabbi Yudel Rosenberg provided the Hans Grimm popularized legends of the Golem in nineteenth-century Germany. See B. Rosenfeld, "Die Golemsage und ihre Verwertung in der deutscher Literatur" (diss., Breslau, 1934), 41; in Gershon Winkler, *The Sacred Stones: The Return of the Golem* (New York: Judaica, 1991), xivn7. But

these "mudcake creatures" can be traced through the written folktales of Rabbi Judah Loew (Rabbi Judah Lowe of Prague [ca. 1525–1609], also known by the acronym MaHaRaL/Maharal; see Ira Robinson, Pierre Anctil, and Mervin Butovsky, eds., *An Everyday Miracle: Yiddish Culture in Montreal* [Montreal: Véhicule, 1990], 159) and the Golem to an oral tradition that may be as early as the sixteenth century. See Yudel Rosenberg, *Sefer Nifla'ot Maharal im ha-Golem* [Book of the Miraculous Deeds of Rabbi Loew with the Golem] (Warsaw, 1909). If the charge against Rosenberg—that he invented the Golem stories himself and merely attributed them to a sixteenth-century manuscript—is upheld, then he at least should be recognized for making a great creative literary contribution: the invention of the same Golem text.

69. *Pat Garrett and Billy the Kid* (Culver City, CA: Metro-Goldwyn Mayer, Inc., 1973). Soundtrack by Bob Dylan (Don Mills, Ontario: Sony Music Entertainment [Canada], Inc., 1973).

70. Given Hebrew name, according to www.jewhoo.com.

71. Born Robert Allen Zimmerman, May 24, 1941, Duluth, Minnesota.

72. Bootleg album (1961).

73. Self-titled (Toronto: Columbia Records of Canada Ltd., 1962).

74. *Hearts of Fire* (Don Mills, Ontario: Sony Music Entertainment [Canada], Inc., 1987); at one point "Parker" jokingly self-identifies as "Robin Hood."

75. Roy Orbison (Lefty), George Harrison (Nelson), Tom Petty (Charlie T., Jr.), Jeff Lynn (Otis), and Bob Dylan (Lucky) are the Traveling Wilburys on the cover of volume 1 (Scarborough, Ontario: WEA Music of Canada, 1988).

76. George Harrison (Spike), Tom Petty (Clayton), Jeff Lynn (Muddy), and Bob Dylan (Boo) are the Traveling Wilburys on the cover of volume 3 (Scarborough, Ontario: WEA Music of Canada, 1990), dedicated to Roy Orbison.

77. *Renaldo and Clara*, written and produced by Bob Dylan (bootleg, 1978).

78. *Masked and Anonymous*, DVD Video (Culver City, CA: Layout and Columbia Tri-Star Home Entertainment, 2003). Jack Fate is also listed for screenwriter credit as "Sergei Petrov."

79. New York Folk Song Festival, Sunday, October 29, 1961 (bootleg).

80. *Don't Look Back* VHS Documentary, Collector's Edition (New York: Pennebaker Hegedus Films, Inc., 1966; re-released New York: Medium Inc., 1999).

81. *Bob Dylan Sings for his Supper* (bootleg 1961; released 1993).

82. This reasoning follows Dylan's own logic: "Steal a little, and they throw you in jail; steal a lot, and they make you king." "Sweetheart Like You," *Infidels*.

83. "A poet's allegiance 'is to the notion that he is not bound to the world as given, that he can escape the painful arrangement of things as they are.'" Leonard Cohen, *Beautiful Losers* (Toronto: McClelland & Stewart, 1966, 1991), 267.

84. Three works limit this phase of Dylan's life: *Slow Train Coming* (1979), *Saved* (1980), and *Shot of Love* (1981). What preceded—*Desire* (1976), *Hard Rain* (1976), and *Street Legal* (1978)—as well as what followed—*Infidels* (1983), *Empire Burlesque* (1985), and *Knocked Out Loaded* (1986)—could not be identified "Christian" by any reasonable estimate. All albums are produced by CBS Inc.

85. "As Creator, G-d is absolutely different from anything else that exists. He is therefore totally unknowable." Aryeh Kaplan, *A Handbook of Jewish Thought* (2 vols.; Jerusalem: Maznaim Pubg. Corp., 1979–92), 1:8.

86. Deut 6:4–6.

87. Kook, *Orot ha-Qodesh* 2:311 (cited from Matt, *Essential Kabbalah*, 215).

"I Ain't Got No Home in This World Anymore"

Protest and Promise in Woody Guthrie and the Jesus Tradition

—James Knight

THE GOSPEL OF JOHN reminds us that at a particular point in time "the Word *became* flesh," yet it is also apparent that the incarnation of the Word is an ongoing process as people continue to bring Jesus into the realities of their everyday lives. It is as if an imaginary time machine exists, which enables people to magically transport Jesus (along with all that he stood for) from his first-century context to their era. This process of recontexualizing Jesus is an age-old practice, beginning, perhaps, with the word-of-mouth circulation of the stories of Jesus throughout the emerging Christian communities of the first-century world. The formation of the canonical Gospels demonstrates a further stage in this process as the evangelists shaped their accounts in order to address the concrete issues of their audiences. Yet the process did not end with the composition of the Gospels; throughout history, reflection upon and interpretation of the Gospels has enabled people to make the person of Jesus relevant for their age. This task, however, is not limited to Christian believers who earnestly seek to follow the Master; artists—specifically, musicians, film makers, and writers—have also been busy making the Word flesh. Furthermore, artistic depictions of Jesus and the Christian believer's contemplation of Christ share a common tendency in their attempts to bridge the gap between the world of the historical Jesus, as reflected in the Jesus tradition,[1] and that of the contemporary author/artist and audience.

An example of an artistic interpretation of Jesus can be found in the life and music of Woody Guthrie. His music emerged amid the grim realities of the 1930s and 40s, during the Great Depression and the rising tide of fascism. Born out of a time of extreme hardship, his music championed the cause of the poor and criticized the opulence of the rich. At the same time, Guthrie's lyrics expressed the hope for a better day, when the inequalities of the world would be erased. Into this setting of hardship and hope Guthrie brought the person of Jesus, manifested in two of his compositions: "Jesus Christ" (written and recorded by Guthrie) and "Christ for President" (written by Guthrie and recorded by Billy Bragg/Wilco). These songs reflect Guthrie's concern for social justice as they convey a vision of Jesus as a champion of the poor and a critic of the rich. While these songs explicitly show the reincarnation of Jesus within Guthrie's world, a look at the larger Guthrie canon reveals a number of interesting parallels with material from the Jesus tradition, such as sayings about itinerancy, possessions, and the coming utopia. Yet similarities between Guthrie and the Jesus tradition cannot be limited to his music alone; Guthrie's life and legacy has also taken on a Christ-life aura, giving a messianic quality to the whole protest music tradition.[2] For instance, both Guthrie and Jesus have become "human referent(s) for collective symbols and ideals,"[3] personifying a set of abstract values. To use biblical terminology, they incarnated the Word. In addition, both figures spoke of a future utopia that would triumph over the present system of evil and injustice. Guthrie dreamed of the "One Big Union"; Jesus anticipated the kingdom of God. Finally, the lasting legacy of Guthrie and Jesus has produced many followers, who cherish their words, follow their example, and long for their return to right the wrongs of the world.

Certainly, these parallels are interesting in terms of the correlation between messianic movements and protest music, but a far more important consideration has to do with the conclusions one draws from this comparison. While Guthrie and Jesus perceived the wrongs of the world and envisioned a better one, contemporary society is left with the dilemma of how to fix the poverty, suffering, and injustice in our world. Will the kingdom of God ever come? Is there, as Guthrie sang, "a better world a-comin'," or will things continue as they always have?

The Quest for Guthrie's Jesus: "Jesus Christ" and "Christ for President"

Guthrie's concept of Jesus grew out of his brief exposure to fundamentalist Christianity during his early twenties.[4] Organized religion, however, did not have a lasting impact upon Guthrie's religious thinking since he quickly lost interest in attending church.[5] Yet, the experience did foster a deep interest in reading the Bible.[6] He would often discuss biblical passages with friends and quote from Scripture "to fit virtually any situation."[7] Certainly, the Bible or, more broadly, religion had an enduring effect upon Guthrie's music. While Woody's radical politics propelled his music, biblical or religious language gave it expression. This is no more apparent than in his songs about Jesus.

Guthrie's outrage at the gross inequalities between the wealthy and the poor became the impetus for the song "Jesus Christ." On an early manuscript of this song he wrote:

> I wrote this song looking out of a rooming house in New York City in the winter of 1940. I saw how the poor lived, and then I saw how the rich folks lived, and the poor folks down and out and hungry, and the rich out drinking whiskey and celebrating and wasting handfuls of money on gambling and women, and I got [to] thinking about what Jesus said, and what if He was to walk into New York City and preach like he use[d] to. They'd lock Him back in Jail as sure as you're reading this. "Even as you've done it unto the least of these little ones, you have done it unto me."[8]

It is apparent that Guthrie's context, especially the great poverty in New York City, led him to reflect upon the life and preaching of Jesus. In this way, Guthrie recontextualized Jesus by envisioning him in the flesh, preaching in New York City as he did in Galilee.

The song itself gives a condensed version of the Jesus story, but with a distinctly Guthrie-esque quality. For instance, the song presents Jesus as a traveler, a quality that was valued by Guthrie, who loved being a rambling man. Also important is the presentation of Jesus as a common worker who was admired by other workers in keeping with Guthrie's sympathies with the cause of the working class. Jesus is described as "hard working and brave" and "a carpenter by hand," who becomes a hero for the "working folks" who "believed what he did say" and "follered him around, / Sung and shouted gay." Furthermore, Guthrie identifies Judas Iscariot, the rich, the preacher, the sheriff, the bankers, the cops, the soldiers, and the landlord as the ones who opposed Jesus and his working-class affiliation. These opponents rejected Jesus' message, "nailed him in the air" (or "on a cross" or "in the sky"), and "laid Jesus Christ in his grave." Clearly, Guthrie's opponents, the wealthy and their supporters—any who opposed the cause of workers—became Jesus' opponents.[9] Finally, the message of Jesus is completely centered on the antithesis between the wealthy and poor. Jesus commands the rich (and the preacher and the sheriff) to "give your goods to the poor," or to "sell all of your jewelry and give it to the poor." At the same time, Jesus' message to the poor (and the sick, the hungry, and the lame) was one of hope, centering on the great reversal that will soon happen when "the poor would one day win this world," and the rich will wish they had never been born.[10]

Certainly, the song "Jesus Christ" seems to tell us more about Guthrie than it does about Jesus. Some have even argued that Guthrie greatly misinterpreted Jesus. For instance, in his analysis of this song, Hampton writes, "Guthrie went so far as to proletarianize Christ."[11] Along similar lines Klein describes Guthrie's notion that Jesus Christ was a "socialist outlaw" as one of his "frequent ideological flights of fancy."[12] Yet how mistaken was Guthrie's interpretation of Jesus? On the one hand, it would be difficult to argue that Jesus was a Marxist or a socialist who fought for the rights of the proletariat. Such interpretations of Jesus take modern concepts and place them into the foreign soil of first-century Galilee. At the same time, Guthrie has emphasized several significant elements from the Jesus tradition.

The Gospels support the idea that Jesus was a traveling man (Matt 8:20/Luke 9:58),[13] a carpenter (Mark 6:3),[14] and one who preached about wealth and poverty. Guthrie's paraphrase of Jesus' preaching echoes the scene in the Synoptic Gospels where Jesus says to the rich man (ruler): "Go, sell your possessions, and give the money to the poor, and you will have treasure in heaven; then come, follow me" (Matt 19:21/Mark 10:21/Luke 18:22). In Luke's Gospel Jesus makes a similar pronouncement to his disciples: "Sell your possessions, and give alms. Make purses for yourselves that do not wear out, an unfailing treasure in heaven" (12:33). Interestingly enough, these accounts present the renunciation of one's possessions and charity to the poor as a sign of true discipleship, of becoming fully dependent upon God (Luke 12:22–31).[15]

Similarly, Guthrie's notion that the poor "would one day win this world," is congruent with the Gospel material where Jesus speaks of a great reversal of the rich and the poor, which was about to happen. In the passages listed above (Luke 12:32–34; Mark 10:21 et par), those who give up their possessions will be given the kingdom and "treasure in heaven" (Luke 12:32–33). The disciples who have left everything (homes, family, land) to follow Jesus will receive "a hundredfold" of these "now in this age" and in the "age to come eternal life." "The first will be last, and the last will be first" (Matt 19:27–30//Mark 10:28–31//Luke 18:28–30).[16] Furthermore, in the wider context of Luke 12:33, one finds Jesus' parable about the rich fool whose wealth and hubris results in the swift judgment of God (12:16–21). The story ends with the sobering reminder about the futility of earthly treasures: "So it is with those who store up treasures for themselves but are not rich toward God" (12:21).

Other Lukan passages emphasize the reversal of fortune between the rich and the poor. For instance, Mary praises God because "he has filled the hungry with good things and sent the rich away empty" (1:52–53). Luke's version of the Beatitudes (6:20–26) declares that the poor will receive the kingdom of God and the hungry will be filled; yet the rich will receive judgment and the full will become hungry. Finally, Jesus' parable of the rich man and Lazarus presents the great reversal in the postmortem existence of both men: the rich man is "in agony" and poor Lazarus is "comforted" (Luke 16:19–31). According to Luke, the essence of Jesus' ministry was preaching and enacting "good news to the poor" (4:18–19; 7:22–23).

The notion that Guthrie has proletarianized Jesus does not tell the whole story. Granted, Guthrie's political and social concerns did influence the elements of the Jesus tradition that he emphasized, but his portrait of Jesus is not completely inaccurate or fanciful since the song alludes to several Gospel texts. Guthrie was merely caught in the hermeneutical circle, that unavoidable tendency of all humans to analyze everything from their own perspective. But he should not be faulted for this; many Christians routinely apply Jesus' words to their own context, and Guthrie has done likewise.[17] It is important to observe, however, that Guthrie recognized this, as the final stanza of the song indicates. Here he names his context, the place of writing (New York City), makes reference to Jesus' context (his preaching ministry in Galilee), and ponders what would happen if Jesus was to preach like that again. He recontextualized Jesus by envisioning him in the flesh and preaching in New York City; yet, sadly, the result would be the same: Jesus would end up in the grave.

If "Jesus Christ" ends on a sad note, his other composition, "Christ for President" offers a much more hopeful vision.[18] Another striking difference between the two songs is their respective hermeneutical horizons. Stated plainly, "Jesus Christ" focuses on the past, whereas "Christ for President" looks to the present and the future. In "Jesus Christ" the story of Jesus is told as a *past* event, although Guthrie placed characters from his world into the song. The present implications of Jesus' preaching emerge when Guthrie pondered what would happen if Christ was to preach in New York City in 1940 like he did in first-century Palestine. The focus of "Christ for President," on the other hand, is completely on the *present* and the *future* (Guthrie's present and his foreseeable future). The song's lyrics are fixed on the problems with the political system of Guthrie's day (crooked politicians, unemployment, lack of social programs, economic inequalities, and rampant militarism), with Christ (and his presidency) as the solution to these problems.

The song exclaims, "Let's have Christ for President," and Jesus' original context fades into the background. He makes historical references, but they are in the service of addressing the modern context. For instance, in the second stanza of the song, Jesus' expulsion of the money changers from the temple (Matt 21:12–13//Mark 11:15–17//Luke 19:45–46//John 2:13–17) is likened to defeating "these crooked politician men." While the exact reasons why Jesus cast out the money changers remains a topic of discussion,[19] one can say that Guthrie's analogy between this event and voting out corrupt politicians is creative, but not exact. Also significant is Guthrie's constant reference to Christ as "the Carpenter" (three times),[20] undoubtedly emphasizing Jesus as a working-class hero. Yet, only Mark notes Jesus vocation as "the carpenter," and this is on the lips of his unbelieving neighbors, who fail to recognize him as God's agent.

Guthrie's intent, however, was not to flesh out a historical portrait of Jesus. He was expressing his hope that the problems with the political system of his day could somehow be remedied. According to Guthrie, with Christ as President, corrupt politicians would be gone. There would be full employment for the young and government pensions for the old, resources would be used to feed the starving and not wasted, and the destructive ways of war would be no more—the USA would be "prosperity bound." Christ, then becomes the embodiment of a number of political principles (government-funded social programs, economic equality, full employment, pacifism) that Guthrie championed. The song does not cite specific material from the Jesus tradition in support this political program. Instead, it embraces Christ as a ideal figure by imagining that his presence, meaning the enactment of particular political principles, would bring the kinds of changes outlined in the song's lyrics.

Guthrie's use of Christ as an ideal figure, however, is not completely divorced from the Jesus tradition. For instance, one could argue that Jesus' ethics of nonretaliation (Matt 5:38–48//Luke 6:27–36) and peacemaking (Matt 5:9) would support Guthrie's criticisms of warfare. At the same time, Guthrie's concern for the world's starving people ("Every year we waste enough to feed the ones who starve") echoes Christ's hope that the disparity between the rich and the poor would one day be rectified (Luke 6:20–26). Yet, even with possible allusions from the Jesus tradition, it is clear that Guthrie has thoroughly "incarnated" Jesus into modern America, having more concern for the ills of his day than for the historical Jesus.

Beyond Guthrie's direct references to Jesus in these two songs,[21] there are several interesting parallels between his lyrics and sayings in the Jesus tradition, especially those pertaining to the lifestyle of itinerancy. Interestingly enough, Guthrie's and Jesus' experience of life on the road has resulted in some shared themes and sayings.

"I Ain't Got No Home in This World Anymore": Guthrie and Jesus as Ramblin' Men

From 1937–39 Guthrie lived in Southern California and was involved in the effort to improve the wages and working conditions for migrant agricultural workers. Many of these migrant workers were, like Guthrie, refugees from the 1930s dust bowl. They had left or been evicted from their southern Plains farms during the Depression-era dust storms.[22] These migrants—or "Okies," as they were pejoratively called—fled to California, desperate for work, but they had a difficult time there. Many Californians were less than hospitable to them. The Los Angeles police set up illegal roadblocks at the California border to turn back "unemployables."[23] During the 1934 campaign for California governor, deep prejudices against "Okies" were fostered by a massive propaganda campaign that used phony newsreel footage.[24] Furthermore, the fruit growers could pay these migrant workers starvation wages since a great army of unemployed (four to ten workers for every job) were seeking work, and any efforts on the part of the workers to organize for better wages was suppressed with organized violence.[25]

In support of the migrant workers, Guthrie wrote political songs and sang at rallies in support of their cause. During one of his visits to a migrant camp, Guthrie discovered that one of the more popular songs with the workers was a bouncy Baptist hymn entitled "This World Is Not My Home." It promoted the notion of treasure in heaven and indifference to this world ("This world is not my home / I'm just a-passing through"). Guthrie disagreed with the song's message because it fostered a quiescent attitude among the migrants, encouraging them to accept the injustices meted out to them in this life since they would be rewarded in the next life. He responded by writing "I Ain't Got No Home in This World Anymore," a harsh criticism of the hymn's sentiments.[26] In Guthrie's words, "The reason why you can't feel at home in this world any more is mostly because you ain't got no home to feel at."[27]

Sung in the first person, "I Ain't Got No Home in This World Anymore" chronicles the immense hardship of the homeless, migrant worker. The story within the song is anything but happy. Already living in great poverty as sharecroppers, these workers were evicted by wealthy landowners and took the arduous and uncertain journey West. They traveled from town to town, desperately looking for work and often harassed by the police. In the final verse of the song Guthrie expresses the greatest irony within American society—the disparity between the rich and the poor: "The gamblin' man is rich, and the workin' man is poor." This makes the world a "funny place to be" and ultimately creates in him a sense that he is not at home in this world.

This song functions as Guthrie's renunciation of the world because of its great injustices. The world rejected him, so he rejected the world. Though the song speaks of the bitter experience of homelessness, in an ironic way the itinerant lifestyle becomes a concrete way of rejecting the world. Homelessness or itinerancy, or more broadly, asceticism, expresses an "estrangement from the normal structures of society,"[28] as also in the words of Bob Dylan: "When you got nothin', you got nothin to lose" ("Like a Rolling Stone").[29] These statements, however, should not be taken as an endorsement for the benefits of homelessness. There is no moral justification for the plight of the homeless or for society's indifference or hostility to street people. While the concept of choice is a murky one, with all the strange nuances of predetermination and human freedom, it does enable us to see that homelessness is a largely an involuntary situation.[30] At the same time, there is a type of homelessness exemplified in Jesus (and his followers) and in Guthrie that is completely voluntary.[31] In addition, this voluntary homelessness embodies a rejection of the present world in anticipation of another better world.[32]

Jesus and Guthrie are remembered as ramblin' men. The Jesus tradition provides a uniform picture of Jesus as one who adopted an itinerant lifestyle and asked his followers to do likewise (Matt 10:5–16//Mark 6:8–11//Luke 9:2–5). In one text (Matt 8:18–22//Luke 9:57–62) Jesus is met by a would-be disciple: "I will follow you wherever you go." Jesus replies by acknowledging his homeless existence: "Foxes have holes, and birds of the air have nests; but the Son of Man has nowhere to lay his head." With this response, Jesus speaks of his itinerancy and implies that to follow him, one must also embrace a similar way of life. In the same way, there is a rich tradition that celebrates Woody Guthrie's itinerant lifestyle.[33]

On one level, it is not an unusual coincidence that Jesus and Guthrie were itinerants; throughout human history people have embraced a transient existence. However, it is significant that one finds an interesting convergence of ideas between Guthrie's music and Jesus' sayings with respect to the itinerant life. Common to both is the relationship between itinerancy and renunciation of the world. In other words, in order to hit the road one must reject or give up the prevailing social order and all of its relationships. Rejection, however, is a two-way street. When individuals renounce society's dictated rules, they may, in turn, be rejected by the world.

For Jesus and Guthrie, the itinerant lifestyle constituted the renunciation of the foundational relationships of family and marriage. In "Ramblin' Round," Guthrie sings of leaving family ("My sweetheart and my parents / I left in my old hometown") and forsaking marriage ("I wish that I could marry") in order to "go ramblin' round." One of Guthrie's most-celebrated road songs, "Hard Travelin'," speaks of the demanding and low-paid jobs of the migrant worker, as well as the lack of intimate relationships ("Lookin' for a woman that's hard to find"). Beyond his music, however, there are many examples of Guthrie's own renunciation of family for life on the road. The most famous example was during his second marriage, when Woody went to the corner store for a paper and never came back.[34]

Similarly, the Jesus tradition stresses that Jesus and his followers abandoned traditional familial and marital relationships by becoming itinerants. Jesus' disciples left family and wives to follow him (Matt 4:22//Mark 1:20; Matt 19:29//Mark 10:29–30//Luke 18:29–30). Jesus emphatically states that those who wish to follow him must hate their family (Luke 14:25–27; cf. Matt 10:37–39), disregard family duties (e.g., burying the dead: Matt 8:21–22//Luke 9:59–60), and not even bid farewell to kin before hitting the road (Luke 9:61). Far from promoting "family values," Jesus came "to set a man against his father" (Matt 10:34–36//Luke 12:51–53). Furthermore, Jesus appears to have promoted celibacy ("eunuchs for the sake of the kingdom of heaven," Matt 19:11–12) and the curbing of sexual desire (Matt 5:27–28) as important virtues.[35]

Itinerancy also radically alters attitudes about worldly matters, particularly about earthly possessions and daily provisions. The Jesus tradition is rich with sayings that encourage the renunciation of earthly possessions in order to focus on God and his kingdom (Matt 6:19–21//Luke 12:33–34; Matt 6:24//Luke 16:13; Matt 6:33//Luke 12:15, 21; 12:31). Jesus' missionary instructions demonstrate this principle as he charges the disciples: "Take nothing for your journey" (Luke 9:3//Matt 10:9–10//Mark 6:8–9), implying that they were to be dependent upon God.[36] The Lord's Prayer typifies the concept of dependence upon God for daily needs: "Give us each day our daily bread" (Luke 11:3). In the famous "anxiety" pericope, Jesus declares that when people fully trust in God for their daily bread, they will be freed from the anxieties of life. "Do not worry about your life, what you will eat or what you will wear," Jesus proclaims, calling his disciples to trust in God, who feeds the ravens and clothes the lilies (Matt 6:25–33//Luke 12:22–31). At the conclusion of the "anxiety" pericope, Matthew notes, "So do not worry about tomorrow, for tomorrow will bring worries of its own. Today's trouble is enough for today" (6:34).

For the most part, Guthrie's music describes economic hardships of the migrant workers, who were "tryin' to make about a dollar a day" ("Hard Travelin'"). Yet, like Jesus, Guthrie also wished to ease the anxieties of these itinerants by telling them not to worry. In a serene song entitled "Hobo's Lullaby," Guthrie re-creates a typical scene from the Depression era—homeless men riding in a boxcar, traveling from place to place and looking for work. He lulls the hoboes to sleep with his song and the sound of the "steel rails hummin'." With words similar to Jesus', he calms their anxieties, singing, "Do not think about tomorrow. / Let tomorrow come and go." For the time being, according to Guthrie, the weary hobo has his basic need for shelter met within the "nice warm boxcar."

With all the hardships of life on the road, there was also a sense of freedom. On an unpublished manuscript of "Hobo's Lullaby," Guthrie wrote: "A hobo's life moves swiftly, broadly, talking and moving in terms of states, countries, seasons; instead of the narrow, suffocating, life of City Living so hemmed in on every side. . . . Friendless, and alone, he dwells among us, drifting like a tumbleweed across the earth, . . . seeking a freedom that you have only dimly felt at times."[37] For Guthrie, itinerants were "seeking a freedom" from being "hemmed in on every side." He describes the freedom of the itinerant worker with the image of one "drifting like a tumbleweed across the earth." A similar image is used to describe itinerant workers in his song "Pastures of Plenty": "We come with the dust and we go with the wind." Guthrie's link between itinerancy and freedom seems to capture the spirit of Jesus' charge to be freed from the anxieties of life.

Renouncing the present world through itinerancy, while typifying a life of freedom, also expresses the anticipation of the coming of a new and better world. Dale Allison uses the expression "eschatological asceticism" to describe Jesus' words and actions regarding itinerancy, celibacy, family, and earthly possessions.[38] He argues that Jesus' asceticism, his denial of worldly desires, emerged from his expectation of the passing of this world and the coming of the rule of God.[39] Jesus' asceticism, including his itinerancy, went hand in hand with his eschatological expectation and supported his eschatological beliefs in various ways. According to Allison, Jesus' asceticism facilitated his eschatological mission, emphasized his separation from the present world, demonstrated his commitment to his eschatological message, anticipated the coming judgment, and embodied the coming age.[40] What interests us here is the notion that asceticism acts as a way of separating oneself from the present world because of anticipating a new world. By renouncing the typical responsibilities of daily life (work, care for family and spouse, etc.), one is making a clear statement of the relative unimportance of these worldly matters in light of the approaching new age. Itinerancy, then, is temporary and anticipatory since the present world is wasting away and a new world is dawning. While there is no scholarly consensus on the eschatology of Jesus, Allison's observations on the link between asceticism and eschatology give us a context for Jesus' itinerant ethics.[41]

In a similar way, there seems to be a connection between Guthrie's itinerancy and his belief in the dawning of a better world. His "hard travelin'" life was in solidarity with the experiences of many migrant workers, becoming the creative force behind his music and politics. Guthrie's quiet rage at the immense gap between the rich and the poor exploded into lyrics laced with political radicalism.[42] Challenging the negative propaganda about the homeless, his songs serve as "grand testaments to the strength and perseverance of his 'brothers and sisters,' the homeless and the hungry, struggling to survive on the road."[43] His confidence in the strength of the homeless fueled his hope that they would unite and overcome the oppression of the wealthy.[44] "Pastures of Plenty" nicely illustrates this connection between itinerancy and the hope of a better world. The song itself describes the plight of the migrants, traveling on "a hot dusty road," sleeping on the ground, working hard, while envisioning the coming of an idyllic age: "Green pastures of plenty from dry desert ground."[45] For Guthrie, this future hope depended on the solidarity of the migrants in standing up for their principles: "We'll work in this fight, and we'll fight till we win." Guthrie especially promoted the view that the land belongs to everyone: "My land I'll defend with my life if need be / 'Cause my pastures of plenty must always be free."[46]

The shared experience of voluntary itinerancy has produced in Guthrie's music and Jesus' teachings an interesting convergence of ideas. For both, homelessness embodied a rejection of the present world and a forceful critique of its injustices. At the same time, the itinerant life anticipated the dawning of a better world. In this way, Guthrie's music spans the gap of time and space and incarnates the itinerant ethics of Jesus of Nazareth.

"Come Back, Woody Guthrie": The Legacy of Jesus and Guthrie

In his book *Guerrilla Minstrels*, Wayne Hampton makes the point that central figures within the protest music culture have taken on religious or messianic roles within the larger protest movements.[47] His study analyzes the music and the social impact of Woody Guthrie, along with other important members of the protest music fraternity: John Lennon, Joe Hill, Bob Dylan. The essence of his argument centers on the notion that heroism and hero-worship act as the "superglue" that joins "countless and diverse individuals" together under a banner of shared ideals.[48] The hero (e.g., Woody Guthrie) becomes what Hampton calls "a totalizer," "a public personage and a mythos around whom social unity and action crystallize."[49] Since political and social movements deal largely with abstract ideas and principles, they require a human agent, the hero, to bring these ideals to life within the "mythos of the hero."[50] In other words, "ideology is humanized" within a person, and people gravitate to that person and to the abstract ideals that the hero exemplifies, his utopian vision of a renewed world.[51] Beyond the sharing of the hero's ideals, this collective following engages in hero-worship by imitating the hero's example.[52] There is, then, a religious dimension within the culture of protest music.

By framing the impact of Woody Guthrie, and others, within these religious categories, Hampton is setting up a clear analogy between Guthrie and Jesus. At one point Hampton even uses religious language to describe the "messianic quality" of the hero, who is equipped with divine insight, rescues people from evil, and eventually dies for his principles.[53] Both Jesus and Guthrie serve as superglue for larger social movements by embodying a set of abstract principles around which diverse individuals have assembled. Guthrie, the hobo troubadour, exemplifies the struggle and the perseverance of the poor and the homeless, becoming a symbol of hope for a world of justice. Jesus, the Son of God, incarnates the love of God for humanity.

The ongoing legacy of the hero (e.g., Guthrie and Jesus) is the cult or "the loose, amorphous collective following formed in his name."[54] The cult cherishes and seeks to follow the hero's example since it typifies the ideals to which the group aspires. For instance, Bob Dylan, in his "Song to Woody," honors Woody's deeds ("'Cause there's not many men that done the things that you've done") and emulates his lifestyle ("I've been hittin' some hard travelin' too").[55] "Song to Woody," however, does not give the full picture of Guthrie's impact upon Dylan. Using religious terms, Robert Shelton has described Guthrie as Dylan's "spiritual father" and his influence on him as "Dylan's conversion, . . . a dramatic turning point, not unlike his later surrender to Jesus."[56]

Traces of Guthrie worship can also be observed in the Steve Earle composition, "Christmas in Washington."[57] The figure of Guthrie takes on messianic proportions as Earle laments on the sad state of the USA and longs for Woody Guthrie to rise from the grave ("So come back, Woody Guthrie") to challenge the country once more. In addition, Earle clearly emulates Guthrie's example ("I followed in your footsteps once, / Back in my travelin' days"), yet admits his failure "to find your [Guthrie's] trail." The worship of Guthrie is seen not only in following his example, but also in the longing for his return to set things right. Earle sees a broken system—the Democrats and the Republicans are playing power games, and the unions have been busted—and while the media conveys the message that everything is okay, he is filled with an uneasy feeling and the knowledge that "it's going straight to hell." So, he turns to Guthrie (along with other heroes of the past: Emma Goldman, Joe Hill, Malcolm X, Martin Luther King) to rise up and lead the people to freedom once again.

Guthrie's utopian hopes for "a better world a-comin' / When we'll all be union and we'll all be free" ("Better World A-Comin'") are hopes deferred. Similarly, those who cherish the words of Jesus and seek to emulate his example are caught in an eschatological never-never land, where the promises of the kingdom seem so distant. Have the poor inherited the kingdom, are the hungry filled, are the last first? A brief look around will give many examples to the contrary. Part of the problem is how we, the worshippers, selectively remember our heroes and their words. For instance, Hampton makes the point that once the hero-worshippers mythologize the hero, they attempt "to gloss over or ignore those aspects of the individual that do not fit neatly into the mold of the myth."[58] A couple of examples will suffice.

Perhaps the most familiar and widely sung song of the Guthrie canon is "This Land Is Your Land." Its celebration of redwood forests, wheat fields waving, and dust clouds rolling leaves it open to narrowly patriotic interpretations. Guthrie, however, intended the song not as a patriotic slogan, but as a critique of the sad state of the country.[59] Originally, the final line of each verse was, "God Blessed America for me," serving as an ironic jab at the popular tune "God Bless America" and the sentiments it expresses.[60] In two of the more unknown verses, Guthrie pointed out why America was not blessed for him and a great many people. In one verse he sings of "my people" standing hungry by the Relief Office, causing him to wonder "if God blessed America for me." In the other verse, he notes that the song's utopian vision of the land belonging to all ("This Land is your Land / this Land is my Land") was stopped by "a big high wall" with a sign saying "Private Property." Yet, these verses and the ideas behind the song have not filtered down into its popular renditions, giving us a nationalistic "This Land Is Your Land" minus its striking political radicalism.

In the same way, there is evidence that people have glossed over or ignored some of Jesus' more radical teaching. Jesus' command to "love your enemies" (Matt 5:44//Luke 6:27) is an example of such a tendency within the Christian tradition. Citing various Christian sources (e.g., Rom 2:1; 12:14, 17, 21; 1 Cor 4:12; 1 Thess 5:15; *1 Clem.* 13.2; Polycarp, *Ep.* 2.2–3; *Did.* 1.3–5), Allison argues that these writers have modified this radical saying of Jesus since they were "uncomfortable with the apparent implications of this radical imperative."[61] The examples cited by Allison appear to support his claim since they directly quote or allude to verses within the context of the imperative, while not citing the imperative itself. For instance, in Romans 12:14–21, one finds allusions to the context of Jesus' radical imperative (12:14 [Matt 5:44//Luke 6:28]; 12:17 [Matt 5:38–39]; 12:20 [Matt 5:39–42//Luke 6:29–30; 6:35]), yet the phrase "Love your enemies" is strangely absent. In the case of Rom 12, its absence is even more puzzling given that the immediate context explicitly talks about love (Rom 12:9–10; 13:8–10). While Paul, Clement, Polycarp, and the *Didache* have captured Jesus' commands to be nonjudgmental, forgiving, and kind to one's enemies, they have done so without recording "the most memorable and provocative phrase in the entire network of related texts."[62]

The point that I wish to make is that how we remember our heroes affects what we do in the name of our heroes. Jesus' most radical words about itinerancy, family, wealth, and nonretaliation seem impractical in our modern world, so we dismiss them as echoes of the past, as time-bound words from the dusty trails of Galilee. Yet, Woody Guthrie incarnated Jesus' itinerant ethics by standing in solidarity with the poor and dreaming of a better world, where the poor would be blessed and the hungry fed. In a world of immense poverty, with no apparent end in sight, the dream of Woody and Jesus is the one worth dreaming.[63]

Notes

1. The wording here reflects the notion that the "Jesus tradition," the four canonical Gospels, does not equal the "historical Jesus." Rather, the Gospels are a mixture of historical data and theological reflection. The aim of this paper is *not* to sort out the problem of the historical Jesus; instead, it is to give some reflections on the Gospel material as it pertains to Guthrie's music.

2. Wayne Hampton, *Guerrilla Minstrels* (Knoxville: University of Tennessee Press, 1986), 4–9, 42–59.

3. Ibid., 44.

4. Joe Klein, *Woody Guthrie: A Life* (New York: Dell, 1980), 58–59. Klein recounts Woody's friendship with a Church of Christ minister, Rev. Eulys McKenzie, and his eventual baptism by immersion.

5. Ibid., 59.

6. Ibid. Klein reports that although Guthrie stopped attending church, "he still loved the Bible."

7. Ibid.

8. Liner notes, *This Land Is Your Land*, vol. 1 of *The Asch Recordings*, 17–18.

9. The exception is Guthrie's mention of Judas Iscariot, an opponent of Jesus according to the Gospels.

10. Guthrie makes a direct allusion to Jesus' words about Judas Iscariot—"It would have been better for that one not to have been born" (Matt 26:24//Mark 14:21)—and reinterprets them as a condemnation upon the rich.

11. Hampton, *Guerrilla Minstrels*, 130.

12. Klein, *Woody Guthrie*, 163.

13. The Gospels clearly portray the itinerant ministry of Jesus and his disciples as they traveled from place to place. Matt 8:20//Luke 9:58 is an example of a Jesus saying that reflects this idea.

14. The parallel in Matt 13:55 refers to Jesus as "the carpenter son," not as "the carpenter." According to the 2DH (Markan priority + Q) this would be an interesting change on the part of Matthew, perhaps indicating that he did not want Jesus to be referred to as "the carpenter."

15. The story of Zacchaeus also illustrates this point as Zacchaeus gives half of his possessions to the poor and pays back those he defrauded (Luke 19:8). As a result salvation comes to his house (19:9).

16. Mark and Luke write that the disciples will receive houses, family, and land "in this time," whereas Matthew's version is more ambiguous, seemingly pointing to a future time ("will receive a hundredfold, and will inherit eternal life")

17. Witness the latest WWJD (what-would-Jesus-do) movement, where bracelet-wearing teens discern their moral options based on imagining what Jesus would do in their situation.

18. Billy Bragg and Wilco, *Mermaid Avenue*, vol. 1 (Elektra, 1998). This particular song is undated, representing a mass of unrecorded lyrics penned by Guthrie from 1947 until the onset of Huntington's disease rendered him unable to write. British folksinger, Billy Bragg, selected this song, along with many others, put them to music, and recorded this one with the country band Wilco.

19. Paula Fredriksen, *From Jesus to Christ* (2d ed.; New Haven: Yale University Press, 2000), xxi, 111–14, 129. Fredriksen has an excellent discussion that presents the different options and provides a plausible interpretation for the clearing of the temple.

20. Compared to the other titles for Jesus that Guthrie uses in the song, such as "Christ," "King," and "the Nazarene," "the carpenter" is the most frequent.

21. Klein (*Woody Guthrie*, 427–29) makes mention of an unpublished Guthrie song entitled "Jesus, My Doctor" which he penned during his final struggle with Huntington's. This song expressed Guthrie's hope that Jesus would heal him. Klein notes that Guthrie's image of Jesus shifted from a "socialist outlaw" to "a different, more fundamental Christ—the Savior, pure and simple."

22. Howard Zinn, *A People's History of the United States, 1492–Present* (rev. ed.; New York: HarperCollins, 1995), 379–80.

23. Klein, *Woody Guthrie*, 80.

24. Ibid., 82.

25. Ibid., 116.

26. Ibid., 119–20.

27. Liner notes, *Hard Travelin'*, vol. 3 of *The Asch Recordings*, 19. Guthrie's reflections on this song are taken from one of its four manuscript copies.

28. Dale Allison, *Jesus of Nazareth: Millenarian Prophet* (Minneapolis: Fortress, 1998), 204.

29. Bob Dylan, *Highway 61 Revisited* (Columbia Records, 1965).

30. Contrary to the opinion of some, most street people do not choose to be homeless. A number of factors, such as mental illness, the economic system, abuse, drug or alcohol addictions, family breakdown, and so on, lead to homelessness.

31. Although a number of external factors contributed to Guthrie's itinerant lifestyle, for the most part he took to the road out of his own free will. See Hampton, *Guerrilla Minstrels*, 100–101, 106, 112, 116; Klein, *Woody Guthrie*, 41, 73–76, 141, 180, 352, 377–78.

32. Allison, *Jesus of Nazareth*, 203–4.

33. The liner notes of the *Asch Recordings*, vols. 1–4, give a full summary of his travels. His traveling days began early, at age fourteen, when his family fell apart and he traveled from Okemah, Oklahoma, down to the Gulf of Mexico. His love for the open road would continue throughout his life, even after he married and fathered children.

34. Hampton, *Guerrilla Minstrels*, 116.

35. For an excellent discussion on celibacy in the Jesus tradition, see Allison, *Jesus of Nazareth*, 175–88.

36. Ibid., 205–6.

37. Liner notes, *This Land Is Your Land*, 14.

38. Allison, *Jesus of Nazareth*, 197.

39. Ibid., 188–97.

40. Ibid., 201–10.

41. Fredriksen (*From Jesus to Christ*, 98–101) makes a similar argument.

42. Hampton, *Guerrilla Minstrels*, 123.

43. Ibid., 124.

44. Ibid., 124.

45. Ibid., 132. "Pastures of Plenty" is one of the twenty-six songs that Guthrie wrote for the Bonneville Power Administration in 1941. This song in particular expresses Guthrie's notion that government projects, such as the Grand Coulee Dam, would guarantee the people's control of natural resources, as opposed to private companies.

46. The best known Guthrie song, "This Land Is Your Land," also celebrates the idea that the land belongs to everyone: "This Land was made for you and me."

47. Hampton, *Guerrilla Minstrels*, 6.

48. Ibid., 4.

49. Ibid., 5.

50. Ibid.

51. Ibid., 5, 52–54.

52. Ibid., 5.

53. Ibid., 6. Dying becomes a significant development in the myth of the hero as seen in the examples of Christ, John Lennon, Joe Hill, and Woody Guthrie.

54. Ibid., 6.

55. Bob Dylan, *Bob Dylan* (Columbia Records, 1962).

56. Robert Shelton, *No Direction Home: The Life and Music of Bob Dylan* (New York: Penguin, 1986), 74–75.

57. Steve Earle, *El Corazon* (Warner Bros., 1997). I would like to thank Daniel Smith, a friend and former Tyndale colleague, for bringing this song to my attention.

58. Hampton, *Guerrilla Minstrels*, 6.

59. Klein, *Woody Guthrie*, 141, 144–45; liner notes, *This Land Is Your Land*, 10.

60. Klein, *Woody Guthrie*, 140–41: "It was just another of those songs that told people not to worry, that God was in the driver's seat."

61. Allison, *Jesus of Nazareth*, 24.

62. Ibid., 24.

63. Ibid., 219. Allison's quite moving conclusion has served as an inspiration for these final thoughts.

The Prophet Jeremiah, Aung San Suu Kyi, and U2's *All That You Can't Leave Behind*

On Listening to Bono's Jeremiad

—Michael J. Gilmour

THERE IS NOTHING REMARKABLE about finding traces of biblical imagery and motifs in popular culture.* Less commonplace are examples of secular "texts" offering thoughtful readings and applications of Scripture. U2's recent album *All That You Can't Leave Behind* (2000) does just this, cleverly using various media—photographs, written text (nonlyric liner notes), appeals for participation in human rights organizations, and the songs themselves—to illustrate how Scripture can speak meaningfully to the needs of our world. The album tells a sad story of personal and corporate angst, yet one hopeful that there will be a happy ending—someday. But this is not uncontested faith, and a pervasive ambivalence is hard to miss. One moment the songwriter has enough confidence to pray: "Jesus, . . . throw a drowning man a line" ("Peace on Earth"). But at another moment he confesses that he "can't wait any longer" for the answer to that prayer, troubled by a world full of chaos and "everyone . . . walking lame" ("When I Look at the World"). Moments of despair are sandwiched between notes of joy as the album opens with the triumphal "Beautiful Day" and closes with the words "Grace makes beauty out of ugly things" ("Grace").[1] The songs acknowledge the presence of pain and injustice, yet offer words of comfort to the broken-hearted and hold out the promise of hope. How do they do this?

* This article was previously published in the *Journal of Religion and Society* 5 (2003): 1–8 (online: http://moses.creighton.edu/JRS/index.html) and is reprinted here with permission.

Throughout its career U2's message has had a political edge. Systemic injustice is an evil to be confronted.[2] Political oppression is part of the "darkness" (as in lyrics to "Walk On") that brings despair to the innocent. However, we are reminded that relief comes in two forms. Activism is encouraged in the liner notes to *All That You Can't Leave Behind* (specific human-rights groups are named). There is also an expectation that the prayers of the needy will be heard, as with "Reach me, I know I'm not a helpless case" ("Beautiful Day").[3] These weapons in the struggle for justice—nonviolent, grassroots, political action (activism) and religious hope (prayer)—are held together beautifully in Bono's writing.[4] He has captured the tension between faith and doubt experienced by all who have uttered prayer for deliverance from desperate situations (cf. Mark 9:24). Quite subtly, he has supplied two important clues that point us toward these themes.

Who Was Jeremiah?

The first of these clues is found on the album cover. A number of years ago Bob Dylan cited Jeremiah (31:31) in the liner notes to his 1980 album *Saved*, and by all appearances U2 has done the same on *All That You Can't Leave Behind*. The black-and-white picture shows the band standing in a nearly empty airport. A mother and child are walking in the blurred background near two other people standing at a counter. On what looks like a sign above the band members' heads, we read "J33-3→" which is clearly a biblical reference—Jer 33:3:

> Call to me and I will answer you,
> and will tell you great and hidden things
> that you have not known.

One biographer observes that during the 1970s "some members of charismatic prayer groups used those figures as a code for prayer, based on Jeremiah 33:3. . . . Confronted with this discovery by a journalist, Bono responded sheepishly, 'Yeah. It's, like, God's phone number.'"[5]

The Hebrew prophet Jeremiah was active in the late seventh and early sixth centuries BCE, a period of dramatic political change that culminated with the fall of Jerusalem in 586. His unpopular message of Judah's demise brought him into conflict with the political establishment that rejected his prophetic pronouncements (e.g., 36:17–32) and frequently imprisoned him (20:1–2; 32:2–3; 36:26; 37:11–21; 38:6–13, 28). But the picture of Jeremiah that emerges from the pages of the Bible is more than one of a strong, courageous prophet who carried out God's work without care for his own personal safety and well-being. He candidly reports an emotional frailty that sets him apart from many other biblical characters. Jeremiah seems to have wrestled with timidity (1:6), like Moses (Exod 4:1–17), especially when opponents to his message threatened his life (11:18–12:4). We even catch glimpses of extreme internal anguish (4:19; 9:1; 10:19–20; 23:9):

> O that my head were a spring of water,
>   and my eyes a fountain of tears,
> so that I might weep day and night
>   for the slain of my poor people! (9:1)

But despite the pain and sorrows he experienced and the doubts about his ability to complete his work (1:6), this weeping prophet never lost sight of his divinely appointed role (1:4–5, 17–19): "These tears are going nowhere, baby" ("Stuck in a Moment You Can't Get Out Of").

Who Is Aung San Suu Kyi?

The second clue helping us understand *All That You Can't Leave Behind* is the name Aung San Suu Kyi, mentioned two times in the liner notes.[6] Daw Aung San Suu Kyi is an author and one of the world's most famous political and social activists. The recipient of the Nobel Peace Prize in 1991, she has fought tirelessly for human rights and the restoration of democracy in Myanmar (formerly Burma) through nonviolent activism and has founded the National League for Democracy (NLD). Her struggle has frequently raised the ire of the military government of Myanmar, which placed her under house arrest at various times from 1989 to the present.[7]

Although Aung San Suu Kyi was given opportunity to leave Burma on the condition she agree never to return, she refused, choosing rather to remain in her homeland: "A singing bird in an open cage, / Who will only fly, only fly for freedom" ("Walk On").[8] This is an intriguing metaphor, and I wonder if Bono is here adapting words from Aung San Suu Kyi's own writing:

> [The children of prisoners] have known what it is like to be young
> birds fluttering helplessly outside the cages that shut their parents

away from them. They know that there will be no security for their families as long as freedom of thought and freedom of political action are not guaranteed by the law of the land.[9]

In U2's *All That You Can't Leave Behind*, the liner notes ask listeners to "remember Aung San Suu Kyi, under virtual house arrest in Burma since 1989" and encourage them to "Take Action!" on behalf of her country by contacting The Burma Campaign (address and website provided). She is also mentioned after the lyrics to "Walk On," a song "Dedicated to Aung San Suu Kyi." In what follows I argue that the relationship of these two clues—the biblical prophet Jeremiah, and this modern-day political "prophet" and social activist—is significant for understanding *All That You Can't Leave Behind*.[10]

How Are Aung San Suu Kyi and Jeremiah Alike?

Parallels between Jeremiah and Aung San Suu Kyi's careers can be observed, and I suggest that Bono was well aware of them. By incorporating the biblical text into the lyrics, he let it speak to a modern context. At least three similarities between these two prophets can be observed.

First, both Jeremiah and Aung San Suu Kyi announced political change and thus brought consternation to the establishment. For Jeremiah, this meant especially the reigns of Jehoiakim, Jehoiachin, and Zedekiah during the latter part of his prophetic activity (ca. 609–586 BCE). For Aung San Suu Kyi, it was the military regime in Burma that commenced in March 1962, following a military coup under the leadership of General Ne Win, "a xenophobic, eccentric and ruthless dictator."[11] The consequence for both was imprisonment. In Jer 32:3–5 we read that King Zedekiah of Judah imprisoned the prophet because of his announcement that Nebuchadnezzar, king of the Babylonians, would overtake Jerusalem and take the Judahite king into captivity (this eventually happened; 39:4–7). Captivity is a recurring theme in the book of Jeremiah. We have already seen that the prophet himself was frequently imprisoned for warning that the people of Judah and their king were facing captivity and exile (e.g., 10:17–18). This too eventually came to pass (39:9). I suspect this recurring motif was one reason why Bono was drawn to the book of Jeremiah for inspiration, and why he (or the band as a whole) flagged the significance of this text on the album's cover.[12]

Second, both prophets were active during their respective imprisonments. Aung San Suu Kyi was placed under house arrest on various occasions, though this did not put an end to her activities. She led the NLD to electoral victory in 1990 (though they were not allowed to take office), and her work continued to be published (e.g., her *Freedom from Fear and Other Writings* [1991; rev. 1995]). Yet, she admitted in an interview that she wrote little during her incarceration: "I didn't see the point in writing unless I could get my writing out to be published."[13] Similarly, arrest by the political establishment could not silence Jeremiah. The key chapter of his book (for Bono) begins with the reception of a revelation during the prophet's imprisonment: "The word of the LORD came to Jeremiah a second time, *while* he was still confined in the court of the guard" (Jeremiah 33:1; italics added). Again in 39:15: "The word of the LORD came to Jeremiah *while* he was confined in the court of the guard" (italics added). Significant for the album's message is that both prophets continued their work despite the deprivations and humiliation that come with imprisonment.

Related to this point, in both cases the captive "prophets" addressed the needs of their "captive" audiences. Aung San Suu Kyi once said, "We are . . . prisoners in our own country."[14] Much of Jeremiah's message was concerned to assure the soon-to-be captives of Judah that God would restore them following their own captivity (33:7, 11, 26).[15] The words *of* captives, addressed *to* captives.

Third, we have already commented on Jeremiah's emotional state. Bono's description of Aung San Suu Kyi suggests that she too (not surprisingly) experienced great anguish in her service to the cause of freedom. There are several touching phrases in "Walk On" that hint at the heroine's emotions. She is said to have a "glass heart" that might crack, and the songwriter knows that it aches and breaks, "and [she] can only take so much" (repeated twice).[16] The extraordinary cost of her service to her people is frequently recognized:

> Here is a woman who has already made some of the toughest decisions imaginable. At any time since her house arrest she could have taken an easy way out and left Burma to live in England with her husband and sons. Instead, she made a painful personal sacrifice, placing her belief in freedom and the love of her country first.[17]

When Jeremiah was decrying the ills of his own homeland, he lamented, "My heart is crushed within me" (23:9). Both prophets receive words of consolation and encouragement to press on with their missions. For Jeremiah, God provides this (1:18–19; 6:27; 15:20). For Aung San Suu

Kyi, such support is offered by U2's songs and the ideal audience to its album. This audience would not only echo the sentiments of the song but also—as required by the imperatives in the liner notes—"remember" her and "take Action!" in the fight for Burma's freedom.

Why Does Bono Use Jeremiah to Tell Aung San Suu Kyi's Story?

Bono stated that "J33-3→" was linked to prayer, but it is much more than this. The book of Jeremiah provides some of the backdrop for *All That You Can't Leave Behind*.[18] Why then did Bono use Jeremiah to tell Aung San Suu Kyi's story? One possibility is that for Bono, Jeremiah spoke words of comfort that modern-day victims of injustice need to hear. For example, in the key chapter of Jeremiah, the prophet announces: "Judah will be saved and Jerusalem will live in safety" (33:16). God "will restore their fortunes, and will have mercy upon them" (33:26).[19]

Further, most songs on *All That You Can't Leave Behind* involve some kind of travel motif.[20] In addition to the lyrics, the travel motif is unmistakable on the album cover (the band in an airport with suitcases) and various pictures in the liner notes. Examples are a suitcase with a heart on the side (inside front cover), the space shuttle orbiting the earth (with lyrics to "Beautiful Day"), a kite (with the lyrics to "Kite"), and a dove flying downward (with lyrics to "Grace").[21] This travel theme may be significant since Jeremiah frequently speaks of journeys the people of Judah would (and eventually did) embark on. They would travel to Babylon in captivity but would eventually make their way back to their homeland. Bono appears to liken the experiences of modern-day prisoners, like Aung San Suu Kyi, with the experience of the Israelites, whose captivity was brought to an end. The situation is desperate in the present time, Bono is saying, but a time of peace and restoration is on the horizon.

The book of Jeremiah also includes stories and language useful for the songwriter who has in mind the plight of political prisoners. Preexilic Israel and modern-day Burma attest to governments' determination to silence dissidents. The clearest picture of this in Jeremiah's writing is the occasion when he is literally thrown into a hole:

So they took Jeremiah and threw him into [a] cistern, . . . letting Jeremiah down by ropes. Now there was no water in the cistern, but only mud, and Jeremiah sank in the mud. (Jer 38:6)

Bono's language in "Elevation" picks up this image. The singer describes himself as a "mole, living in a hole," who needs the one addressed "to elevate" him and "lift me out of these blues." The first-person, prayer-like lyrics suggest that God is the one addressed; the needy narrator is speaking to "I and I in the sky" (cf. Exod 3:14)[22] and calls to "Love" to lift the singer out of his despair and speak words of truth. The image of someone in a hole is also found in the Psalms:

> For without cause they hid their net for me;
>   without cause they dug a pit for my life. (Ps 35:7)

> He drew me up from the desolate pit,
>   out of the miry bog,
> and set my feet upon a rock,
>   making my steps secure. (Ps 40:2)

Bono's choice of imagery not only recalls biblical poetry; it also echoes Aung San Suu Kyi's writing, in which readers can find the metaphor of rising out of painful circumstances. For example, in her essay "In Quest of Democracy," she describes the negative impact of authoritarianism on the spirit of the Burmese people:

> Intimidation and propaganda work in a duet of oppression, while the people, lapped in fear and distrust, learn to dissemble and to keep silent. And all the time the desire grows for a system which will *lift them* from the position of "rice-eating robots" to the status of human beings who can think and speak freely and hold their heads high in the security of their rights.[23]

Elsewhere, she speaks of the individual's efforts to transcend painful situations:

> Even under the most crushing state machinery courage *rises up* again and again, for fear is not the natural state of civilized man. . . . At the root of human responsibility is the concept of perfection, the urge to achieve it, the intelligence to find a path towards it, and the will to follow that path if not to the end at least the distance needed to *rise above* individual limitations and environmental impediments.[24]

This language of rising up or being lifted out of a hole well describes the plight of weak and powerless individuals. It was used effectively in ancient

Hebrew literature and also in descriptions of the situation facing victims of an unjust regime in Myanmar.[25]

The parallel Bono has created between Jeremiah and Aung San Suu Kyi serves to elevate the latter to the status of prophet. Both spoke out against the weaknesses of their political contemporaries and offered the promise of better times.[26] Further, if Aung San Suu Kyi is a prophet like Jeremiah, then those who oppress(ed) her—and by extension those who oppress others represented by the humanitarian organizations listed in the liner notes: Amnesty International, War Child, Jubilee 2000 Coalition, and The Burma Campaign—are equated with the unrepentant establishment that opposed Jeremiah, and the pagan armies of Babylon that took the Judahites into captivity.

Finally, in answer to the question why Bono used Jeremiah this way, it was a means of taking this ancient message of comfort addressed to Israel's captives and "recycling" them for a modern context. Difficult times are temporary, Jeremiah assures his readers (e.g., 25:11), and deliverance and justice will surely come (e.g., 25:12–14; 33:6–14). According to the ancient text (Jeremiah), this restoration is brought about by God. In U2's retelling of that message, restoration comes both through humanitarian efforts and divine intervention.[27] The promise and hope of both is that all will "live in safety" (Jer 33:16). Remember Aung San Suu Kyi.[28]

Notes

1. This contrast between ugliness and beauty recalls, and may be influenced by, Aung San Suu Kyi's writing, as in *Letters from Burma* (London: Penguin, 1997), 87–89. She will be introduced below.

2. This need not be exclusively political. Salman Rushdie offers some interesting reflections on his relationship with U2, including the following: "I think . . . the band's involvement in religion—as inescapable a subject in Ireland as it is in India—gave us, when we first met, a subject, and an enemy (fanaticism) in common" ("U2," in *Step across This Line: Collected Nonfiction 1992–2002* [Toronto: Knopf., 2002], 95).

3. "Beautiful Day" includes an unambiguous biblical allusion: "See the bird with a leaf in her mouth / After the flood" (cf. Gen 8:6–12). This provides some warrant for reading the words "Reach me" as a prayer.

4. Bono is the principal songwriter for U2. For three songs ("Stuck in a Moment You Can't Get Out Of," "Kite," and "When I Look at the World") the lyrics were cowritten by Bono and The Edge.

5. Mark Allan Powell, "U2," in *Encyclopedia of Contemporary Christian Music* (Peabody, MA: Hendrickson, 2002), 983.

6. During three songs on the *Elevation 2001: U2 Live from Boston* DVD ("Gone," "Wake Up, Dead Man," and "Walk On"), Bono wears a button on his guitar strap with a

picture of Aung San Suu Kyi. There is also a photograph in U2's *The Best of 1990–2000 and B-Sides* (2002) showing Bono wearing a T-shirt with her name and picture on it.

7. She was released on May 6, 2002, but was incarcerated again on May 30, 2003, following bloody clashes between NLD and government supporters. Four people were killed and many more injured during the most recent violence, according to Myanmar's military.

8. Alan Clements: "The [State Law and Order Restoration Council] offered you freedom to leave the country if you wanted on the condition that you remain in exile, but obviously you had a deeper conviction in staying in Burma to further the struggle for freedom." Aung San Suu Kyi: "I never forget that my colleagues who are in prison suffer not only physically, but [also] mentally for their families who have no security outside—in the larger prison of Burma under authoritarian rule. Prisoners know their families have no security at all. The authorities could take action against their families at any time. Because their sacrifices are so much bigger than mine I cannot think of mine as a sacrifice. I think of it as a choice. Obviously, it is not a choice that I made happily, but one that I made without any reservations or hesitation. But I would much rather not have missed all those years of my children's lives" (taken from Aung San Suu Kyi, *The Voice of Hope: Conversations with Alan Clements* [New York: Seven Stories, 1997], 132–33).

9. Aung San Suu Kyi, *Letters From Burma*, 25.

10. The arrow on the album cover symbol ("J33-3→") is taken here to be the equivalent of "and following"; hence, it refers not just to Jer 33:3 but also to the wider context of the following passage.

11. Alan Clements, in Aung San Suu Kyi, *Voice of Hope*, 10. The struggle for democracy in Burma continues to this day.

12. The band has taken up the cause of prisoners' rights and again, in the liner notes, invites fans to get involved: "Take a step to stamp out torture—join Amnesty International" (addresses are provided).

13. Aung San Suu Kyi, *Voice of Hope*, 146. One exception was a lecture entitled "Towards a True Refuge," composed during her house arrest and presented as the Eighth Joyce Pearce Memorial Lecture on May 19, 1993, at Oxford University. Her husband, the late Dr. Michael Aris of Oxford University, delivered the lecture on her behalf (ibid., 146n.). This lecture is included in Aung San Suu Kyi, *Freedom from Fear and Other Writings* (ed. Michael Aris; rev. ed.; Harmondsworth: Penguin, 1995).

14. Aung San Suu Kyi, *Voice of Hope*, 36.

15. Cf. Jer 29:14: "I will restore your fortunes and gather you from all the nations and all the places where I have driven you, says the LORD, and I will bring you back to the place from which I sent you into exile."

16. Cf., e.g., Alan Clements: "How would you characterize yourself as a person?" Aung San Suu Kyi: "Well, I see myself sometimes quite differently from how other people see me. For example, all this business about my being so brave . . . I had never thought of myself as a particularly brave person at all" (Aung San Suu Kyi, *Voice of Hope*, 67).

17. Fergal Keane, "Introduction," to Aung San Suu Kyi, *Letters from Burma*, xi.

18. The Edge, guitar player for U2, once described an album as "not just . . . a few songs you might have hanging around. For us in particular it's a collection that adds up to something more than just a few songs. It needs to have an overall logic that connects and complements and maybe not *resolves*, but has a beginning, middle, and end" (from Bill Flanagan, *U2 at the End of the World* [New York: Delta, 1995], 270; italics original). Given this approach to preparing albums, it seems reasonable to look for recurring themes.

19. The Christian perspective of U2's lyrics would not correspond theologically with Aung San Suu Kyi's Buddhist worldview. The point here is that Jeremiah describes a future

correction to a present-day crisis, and this general message of hope could be transferred meaningfully (in Bono's opinion) to the situation in Burma.

20. Examples are being on a road ("Beautiful Day"), flying ("Elevation"), walking ("Walk On"), being carried by the wind ("Kite"), a promise from someone absent that he will arrive soon ("In a Little While"), swinging from trees ("Wild Honey"), and the movement of immigrants ("New York"). The title of the album itself may be a play on Jesus' words in the Olivet Discourse, which urge followers to flee Jerusalem when calamity strikes, taking nothing with them (Matt 24:16–18//Mark 13:14–16//Luke 21:21; the crisis he describes is the fall of the city to the Romans in 70 CE). The album title makes it clear that some things (or something) cannot be left behind. This, we are told in "Walk On," is love, the "only baggage you can bring" and a possession that cannot be stolen, denied, sold, or bought.

21. A descending dove is a symbol of the Holy Spirit (see Matt 3:16//Mark 1:10//Luke 3:22). Both the suitcase and the dove also appear on the packaging of the 2001 DVD *Elevation 2001: U2 Live from Boston* (the tour that followed the release of *All That You Can't Leave Behind*).

22. There may also be an allusion here to Bob Dylan's song "I and I," from the album *Infidels* (1983). Cf. Daniel Maoz's article in this volume.

23. Aung San Suu Kyi, *Freedom from Fear*, 175 (italics added).

24. Ibid., 184–85 (italics added).

25. I am not suggesting Aung San Suu Kyi influenced Bono here, just that the notion of rising up out of pain is a universal way of expressing hope for a better future, as is the travel motif discussed above.

26. Aung San Suu Kyi's *Letters from Burma* includes short introductions of fellow members of the NLD who have suffered for the cause of freedom. One of these individuals is *Hsaya* (teacher) Maung Thaw Ka, who was, among other things, a poet who not only wrote original pieces but also translated English poems into Burmese. She provides an example of the latter, part of William Cowper's "The Solitude of Alexander Selkirk," which includes the following lines:

But the seafowl is gone to her nest,
      The beast is laid down in his lair:
Even here is a season of rest,
      And I to my cabin repair.

There is mercy in every place,
      And mercy, encouraging thought!
Gives affliction a grace
      And reconciles man to his lot.
(Aung San Suu Kyi, *Letters from Burma*, 153)

I call attention to this because it suggests that mercy is present everywhere, whether nest, lair, or "[mole's] hole." *All That You Can't Leave Behind*'s message of hope includes the theme that there is goodness in unexpected places (see, e.g., the lyrics to "Grace").

27. The lyrics to "Peace on Earth" and "Grace" are especially of interest on this point of divine intervention. U2's song lyrics are available at http://www.U2.com.

28. For more information on Daw Aung San Suu Kyi and up-to date news, see http://www.dassk.com.

Section Two

RELIGIOUS

THEMES

IN

POPULAR MUSIC

Suffering and Sacrifice in Context

Apocalypticism and Life beyond Les Misérables

—Karl J. McDaniel

MONEY—SPECTACLE—MCTHEATRE: the musical has indeed entered the realm of pop culture.[1] The Megamusical's success is frankly undeniable. One only need mention a crashing chandelier, a revolving stage, or barricades, and images of *The Phantom of the Opera* or *Les Misérables* (*Les Mis*) come to mind. Indeed, *Les Mis* alone has now been viewed by approximately forty-nine million people. "One Day More," the musical's climax song, was used by Bill Clinton in his 1992 U.S. presidential campaign, and the U.S. State Department had requested that "Bring Him Home" be used as background for Gulf War propaganda. Sales from the London-cast CD of *Les Mis* have surpassed one million copies.[2] Simply, it has been labeled the most successful musical in history.[3] This draw to *Les Mis* has generally been connected to its universal ideals of love, justice, and the utopian society.[4]

The quest of *Les Mis* toward this utopia is underlined with religious tendencies, particularly those related to the apocalyptic. Within its theatre-world,[5] one finds themes derived from the biblical texts of Daniel and Revelation, repeated images and references to suffering and martyrdom, with the ultimate conclusion—a heavenly paradise.

The Case of Daniel

Apocalypticism plays and has played a significant role in many cultures.[6] The manner in which it is to be defined is greatly debated,[7] but it is characterized as a genre for the suffering, encouraging them to persevere. At its heart, this type of writing is a response to theodicean questions: "Where is the justice of God?"[8] How am I to cope with suffering (rewards)? To what extent am I to suffer (martyrdom)? What are the rewards for this suffering (heavenly paradise)?

Many think the book of Daniel was written as reflection upon the events occurring around the time of Antiochus IV Epiphanes' persecution of the Jews (169–164 B.C.E.). The Jews represented in Daniel wished to remain faithful to Torah and were opposed to the Hellenistic policies of fellow Jews and Antiochus.[9] First Maccabees 1 summarizes some of the elements within this persecution: Jews were forced to participate in idolatry, they were not to circumcise their children, and they were to eat unclean animals. Daniel incorporates some of these aspects in its text. For example, Dan 1:8 states that Daniel did not want to defile himself with the king's food. The story then moves forward to a scene in which Shadrach, Meshach, and Abednego (Dan 3) refuse idol worship and are to be burned alive. Later, prayer must be given to the king alone and not to any other; Daniel's refusal to obey this decree results in his being sent to die in the mouth of lions (Dan 6).[10] Further, Dan 8:11 speaks of the removal of Jewish sacrifice.

In reaction to these instances of intense persecution in relation to the Jewish people of the time, Daniel's text contains encouragement for those who are suffering, offering a utopian kingdom in the afterlife, an indication that righteousness is not vain.[11] God will set up a kingdom that is to be eternal and that will transpire after the reign of numerous earthly kingdoms (2:44).[12] Daniel 7 speaks of God's judgment upon the unrighteous. This chapter also introduces readers to "one like a son of man," a glorious figure to whom God grants authority to rule over all (7:13–14 RSV). Later in the book, this figure is seen as a representative of the people, particularly the persecuted, bringing victory and vindication.[13] The audience is later promised: "Many of those who sleep in the dust of the earth shall awake, some to everlasting life, and some to shame and everlasting contempt. Those who are wise shall shine like the brightness of the sky, and those who lead many to righteousness, like the stars forever and ever" (12:2–3).[14] Daniel's text makes clear that the persecuted are to remain faithful to the law while suffering persecution, even to the point of death. Martyrdom, however, will not be a loss, for an eternal kingdom is ultimately coming, along with judgment for the wicked and reward for the righteous.

The Case of Revelation

Similar trends to that of Daniel exist also in the book of Revelation. The

Roman emperor cult recognized the emperor as divine. Domitian (81–96 C.E.) was called *dominus et deus noster* (our lord and god) and openly accepted such honors during his lifetime.[15] It is clear that the Christian church could not accept Caesar as God, for there was only one Lord and God within the book of Revelation. The emperor was involved in persecuting the Christians and had broad popular support: "From the viewpoint of the Roman world, Christians had 'lost their shelter of tradition' with Judaism, were recognized as atheists who did not worship the communal gods, were nonconformists adhering to a recently formed religion from the East, and possibly participated in sexual orgies and cannibalism."[16] The writer of Revelation was banished to Patmos for his witness to Jesus Christ (1:9), the same reason for which others were also persecuted (6:9; 20:4). Some were put to death for refusing to worship the emperor (2:13),[17] and the text speaks of the beast (Rome) who persecutes the saints (13:8, 12, 15). This "beast" in Rev 13 reminds one of the statue of Nebuchadnezzar in Dan 3. All were to worship this image, and they would die if they did not (Dan 3:6; Rev 13:15).[18] Yet, the book of Revelation exhorts its audience to remain faithful to the testimony of Jesus in spite of these threats, even unto death (2:10; 12:11).

Jesus himself was the example of the ideal martyr, the faithful and true witness (1:5; 3:14).[19] Jesus' death, however, extends beyond mere testimony since it was also a sacrifice providing the means to victory. The text makes this explicit in that those who praise Jesus declare:

You are worthy to take the scroll and to open its seals,
for you were slaughtered and by your blood you ransomed for God
    saints from every tribe and language and people and nation;
you have made them to be a kingdom and priests serving our God,
    and they will reign on earth. (5:9–10)[20]

In the end, there is a great judgment of the world (20:9, 11–15), and finally, the establishment of a utopian kingdom (21:1–7).[21]

Les Misérables and Apocalyptic

Daniel and Revelation were both written in times of persecution, for situations in which a lack of justice existed. From the perspective of Jews in Daniel and Christians in Revelation, their persecution was to be endured to the point of death. But they were not to fear, for the afterlife was promised along with the establishment of a new kingdom in which the righteous would reign. *Les Mis* generalizes the specifics: its protagonists die not as a testimony to the God of the Jews or to Jesus, but rather for a liberal ethic of equality and justice. Yet, many of the characters depicted within the work exist as the downtrodden, in need of a victory and a salvation; they need to be promised and reassured that a new and just world is surely coming.

The First Indication: Suffering

The texts of Daniel and Revelation emphasize the suffering caused through governmental persecution of Jews and Christians. Likewise, many of the lyrics in *Les Mis*[22] emphasize suffering due to social injustice for the poor. From the outset, the "Work Song" makes it clear that injustice flows through the land. The prisoners are in "hell"; they have "done no wrong," yet they are portrayed as slaves on the verge of death. Valjean himself is imprisoned five years for stealing a loaf of bread for his sister's dying child, a five years that ultimately becomes nineteen years. He is a "slave of the law," a prisoner in a social system of injustice. It is a system in which all hope is lost. One specific line in the song even states that Jesus does not care to hear the prayers of those in need. The suffering introduced in this song is carried throughout the musical. Valjean is released from prison only to have a farmer refuse to pay him properly for a day's labor and an innkeeper refuse to supply food and lodging.

The "Work Song" is followed shortly by "At the End of the Day." This number expresses the concerns of the poor. The poor see time as moving forward only to an inevitable death, in which there is no aid. "The righteous hurry past" as hunger and cold torment those in need. Within this song, Fantine is falsely accused of being a prostitute because she sends the money she has earned to individuals who are caring for her illegitimate daughter. She is subsequently dismissed by the factory manager as a pretense of propriety. The story progresses with "I Dreamed a Dream," in which Fantine has begun to move toward despair, ending her song with a lament:

> I had a dream that life would be
> So different from this hell I'm living,
> So different now from what it seemed;
> Now life has killed the dream I dreamed.

The despair continues in "Lovely Ladies," in which Fantine sells her necklace, hair, and ultimately herself in order to have the means to continue sending money to her daughter's caretakers. This piece finishes with Fantine singing:

Just as well they never see
the hate that's in your head!
Don't they know they're making love
    to one already dead?

This theme of social injustice and suffering recurs throughout the musical. To indicate individually each instance and its unique implications would be beyond the scope of this inquiry, though one last song must be mentioned: "Look Down." Pieces of this particular song (in some cases, in the form of the supporting music alone) resonate throughout the entire musical. The song itself expresses a culmination of the suffering that has occurred up until the point at which it appears in the musical, while resonating into the next act as well. It is associated with each of the major characters within the story. During the song itself, the audience is introduced to Gavroche, while the melody is later carried by Enjolras, members of the resistance, and Marius. The music that supports the lyrics, "Look down and see the beggars at your feet; / Look down and show some mercy if you can," also plays under the "Work Song" within Valjean and Javert's first conversation, and it is found again in their "Confrontation." It resonates as Valjean announces himself at the Thenardiers' inn, as Eponine arrives at the barricade, and as the students honor her death.[23] "Look Down" highlights the poverty and suffering that necessitates the revolution, thereby building the pressure and foreshadowing the climax: "Something's gotta happen now or something's gonna give." Enjolras sings:

With all the anger in the land,
How long before the judgment day?
Before we cut the fat ones down to size?
Before the barricades arise?

It is clear, then, that the social setting presented within *Les Mis* is similar to those contained within the apocalypses of Daniel and Revelation. In each, there indeed is persecution of the innocent, the poor, and the downcast. The law of the land seems to be motivated squarely against social justice.

The Second Indication: Martyrdom

Within this system of injustice, the question becomes, "How far will one go in the quest for what is right or in the quest to change the present situation?"

Here, one has to turn to Fantine, Gavroche, Enjolras, the students of the barricade, and ultimately to Valjean. Each of these individuals has a quest that he/she believes is worth dying for. *Les Mis*, in these characters, develops its martyrs.

Fantine is clearly portrayed as a victim in "At the End of the Day," falsely accused of being a prostitute. Thrown out onto the street when the factory manager fires her in a false stand of morality, Fantine is forced to survive on whatever she can. Driven to despair, she actually becomes a prostitute, sells her necklace, her hair, and herself. She only does these things because she had been deserted by her lover, who took her "childhood in his stride, but he was gone when autumn came" ("I Dreamed a Dream"). As a result, she was left alone with a daughter for whom she had to care. All of her sacrifice is undertaken for her daughter's survival and well-being. As a result of her harsh circumstances and working conditions, she becomes seriously ill. After Valjean has promised to care for her young daughter, Fantine eventually dies in a delirium, in which she sees her daughter playing ("Come to Me"). Fantine is never portrayed as a villain but rather as a martyr dedicated to maternal devotion. This devotion is transferred to Valjean.[24]

Gavroche, Enjolras, and the students of the barricade are moving forward the idea of the revolution. "Look Down" set the inspiration for their rebellion, and now it is time to move forward. "Red and Black" founds the ideology, the end of the present order, and Enjolras states:

> Who cares abut your lonely soul?
> We strive towards a larger goal;
> Our little lives don't count at all!

At the end of the song, Feuilly sings:

> Will you give all you can give
> So that our banner may advance?
> Some will fall and some will live—
> Will you come up and take your chance?
> The blood of the martyrs will water the meadows of France!

This verse, before the final chorus, leads the listener to understand that social injustice has forced a rebellion that will end in the death of many. The act 1 finale, "One Day More," is the final song before the rebellion commences. This song is a compilation of all the vocal lines that were sung by all of the lead characters to this point in the musical. It is the culmination of all the dreams of the singers, reflecting their greatest fears and hopes.[25] Javert predicts the defeat of the rebellion:

> One day more to revolution.
> We will nip it in the bud.
> We'll be ready for these schoolboys.
> They will wet themselves . . . with blood!

Two further comments are warranted on the recurring theme of martyrdom in *Les Mis*. Grantaire, in "Drink with Me," expresses some despair regarding the martyrdom of the rebels:

> Will the world remember
> When you fall?
> Could it be your death
> Means nothing at all?
> Is your life just one more lie?

The final conclusion of their deaths is summed up in "Empty Chairs at Empty Tables," in which Marius finally comments:

> Empty chairs at empty tables
> Where my friends will meet no more.
> Oh, my friends, my friends, don't ask me
> What your sacrifice was for.

Those of the revolution were martyrs for their cause. The cause was the great rebellion against social injustice: The Revolution. This effort, however, was crushed. As in "Turning," one is forced to ask:

> Fighting for a new world
>   that would rise up with the sun.
> Where's that new world
>   now the fighting's done?

Valjean is the final martyr in this epic musical. Interestingly, he is presented in the first act as an almost antichrist figure. When first introduced to him, the audience sees him as a prisoner who has just received his free-dom. Where Jesus is remembered on the cross for forgiving all those who had crucified him (Luke 23:34), Valjean states in the prologue, "Never for-get the years, the waste, nor forgive them." After moving into despair, being refused work and lodging, he is admitted and granted food and shel-ter by a bishop. Valjean betrays the bishop's kindness, stealing some of his silver place settings and running, though he is immediately captured and returned to the bishop. Instead of condemning him, the bishop grants him mercy, gives him two large silver candlesticks, and states:

> See in this some higher plan.
> You must use this precious silver
> To become an honest man.
> By the witness of the martyrs,
> By the Passion and the Blood,
> God has raised you out of darkness.
> I have bought your soul for God!

Valjean is now called to a righteous life. Indeed, after this event his life is full of sacrifice. He saves Fantine from the streets and, shortly afterward, saves a man being crushed by a runaway cart. The cart is "heavy as hell," and the onlookers state that it will kill Valjean if he attempts to save the man. Valjean, however, willingly risks his life and saves Mr. Fauchelevent. By this point, one realizes that Valjean has changed. In the words of Fauchelevent: "M'sieur le Mayor, I have no words. You come from God, you are a saint." This conclusion is further substantiated in the action that transpires shortly thereafter. Valjean has to reveal himself as a crimi-nal in order to save the life of another. He is compelled to do what is right and states:

> My soul belongs to God,
> I know I made that bargain long ago.
> He gave me hope when hope was gone.
> He gave me strength to journey on. ("Who Am I")

Right after this event, once Valjean has promised to care for Cosette, Fantine states, "Good M'sieur, you come from God in heaven." In his life with Cosette, Valjean is continually pursued by the law. After his false, innocent identity has been compromised, he states:

One day more! Another day, another destiny.
This never-ending road to Calvary.
These men who seem to know my crime
Will surely come a second time.

Here, the reference to his eventual martyrdom is explicit. His conversion
is complete: the once unforgiving is now a redeemer, a personification of
Jesus. He has dedicated his life to Cosette, and in order to let her live in
freedom, he gives her up to Marius (whose life he will also save by risking
his own later in the story). By letting Cosette go in this way, if Valjean is
found by the law, she will not be tarnished by his past. The "Finale" com-
pletes Valjean's martyrdom, and his depiction as a Christ-type continues.
In this final scene, Valjean is clothed in white while Fantine, also robed
completely in white, stands at his side. The scene is reminiscent of the
transfiguration of Jesus on the mountain, where Jesus stands with the dead
of the past, clothed in white, with bright light all around (Matt
17:1–4//Mark 9:2–5//Luke 9:28–30).[26] At this point, Valjean gives his last
confession. He indicates that he has given his life for Cosette. Valjean's
martyrdom for his daughter's sake seems then to usher in a new age, in the
same way that Jesus' transfiguration is related to themes of restoration and
change in the ruling governance.[27] Valjean's martyrdom indicates the com-
pleted redemption of himself and the beginning of the redemption of the
world ("The Finale").

The Third Indication: Utopian Kingdom

Apocalyptic material can be characterized by the establishment of a new
and ideal kingdom at the end of suffering and judgment. The ideal of new
governance was, as previously mentioned, the reason for the death of the
rebels and of Valjean. This theme also appeared in "Look Down," predict-
ing the coming of the revolution. Unfortunately, the rebellion was crushed.
No new world came into being, as indicated in the words of Marius
("Empty Chairs at Empty Tables").

That said, hints of a utopian, ideal society appear throughout the text
of the musical. Fantine's "I Dreamed a Dream" provides one example. In
her utopia, love is blind and the world is a song, though these fantasies are
crushed under the weight of an ever-present reality. The ideal appears
again in Cosette's "Castle on a Cloud," in which a heavenly reality is
clearly in view. Cosette, having vision of angels singing to her, states:

I know a place where no one's lost;
I know a place where no one cries;
Crying at all is not allowed;
Not in my castle on a cloud.

Later in the musical the relationship between Marius and Cosette seems to personify this ideal on earth. They begin to live a life of love and happiness (because of the sacrifices of Valjean), but the heavenly utopia is never established. The revolution ends in failure.[28]

The musical ends, however, with its inspirational finale. Here, the audience is faced with all of the revolutionaries and martyrs who died for their causes, among whom Fantine is included. She calls for the aged Valjean, who then dies, and on their lips is a powerful statement: "To love another person is to see the face of God." This is not yet the end, however. After Valjean's death, he sings, along with the other martyrs, a song of triumphant hope. The song is one of enlightenment and progress. The martyrs have returned on stage to deliver a final message:

Do you hear the people sing
Lost in the valley of the night?
It is the music of a people
Who are climbing to the light.
For the wretched for the earth
There is a flame that never dies.
Even the darkest night will end
And the sun will rise.
They will live again in freedom
In the garden of the Lord.
They will walk behind the plough-share,
They will put away the sword.
The chain will be broken,
And all men will have their reward.

The Finale announces a final judgment and the ultimate vindication of the righteous. There is also a return to utopia, the garden of creation in Genesis. It is a time of peace. The images of walking behind the plowshare and putting away the sword refer to Isa 2:1–4 and Mic 4:1–4, both of which speak of future peace and utopia.[29]

The summary of the life of Valjean,[30] undertaken as part of the Finale (from poor to prisoner to paradise), draws the listener into heaven with all of the martyrs. Indeed, the truth now is being explained by all the martyrs: their deeds have been justified, and now they call on all to continue the song of their lives. With this rapture into heaven, the apocalyptic journey is over as quickly as it began. It is significant, however, for how can the audience now argue with a voice that has come from the heavens? Gabriel reveals truth to Daniel in his apocalypse, and John is caught up in the spirit and also granted heavenly guides. Now, all who participate in *Les Mis* are caught in a heavenly experience.[31] The audience has journeyed through the suffering and the martyrdom; now it witnesses the glorification that calls for a change in governance and a future paradise.

The Finale

Daniel, Revelation, and *Les Mis* speak to their audiences of suffering, martyrdom, and eventually paradise. They move their audiences from loss to love and happiness, from sin to salvation, and from wretch to riches. The suffering portrayed in Daniel and Revelation seems to be primarily religiously focused rather than the pure social suffering reflected in *Les Mis*. And *Les Mis* offers general moral questions, maternal/paternal dedications, and personal honor, while the biblical texts are concerned more with the specifics of Torah and Christ. Nevertheless, the general themes of apocalypticism are undeniably evident within the musical. This climaxes with the final chorus, establishing hope and indeed a new and better life. Having overcome the beast, there is, without question, life beyond *Les Misérables*.

Notes

1. These ideas are discussed in Jonathan Burston: "Theatre Space as Virtual Place: Audio Technology, the Reconfigured Singing Body, and the Megamusical," *Popular Music* 17, no. 2 (1998): 205–6; also idem, "The Megamusical: New Forms and Relations in Global Cultural Production" (PhD diss., Goldsmiths College, University of London, 1998), 138–39, 231–32.

2. This information is readily available on the Internet home page for *Les Misérables*: www.lesmis.com/inspiration/facts/generalinfo.htm (accessed April 26, 2004).

3. Jessica Sternfeld, "The Megamusical: Revolution on Broadway in the 1970s and 80s" (2 vols.; PhD diss., Princeton University, 2002), iii.

4. Edward Behr, *Les Misérables: History in the Making* (New York: Arcade, 1996), 158; also Sternfeld, "Revolution on Broadway," 351.

5. The medium of the popular musical is particularly general in its message because it seeks a large audience. All comparisons must, then, follow as general, and some have wondered if the stage is able, in any way, to convey a religious message. St. Augustine has said it best: "I was captivated by theatrical shows. They were full of representations of my

own miseries and fuelled my fire. Why is it that a person should wish to experience suffering by watching grievous and tragic events which he himself would not wish to endure? Nevertheless he wants to suffer the pain given by being a spectator of these sufferings, and the pain itself is his pleasure. What is this but amazing folly? For the more anyone is moved by these scenes, the less free he is from similar passions. Only when he himself suffers, it is called misery; when he feels compassion for others, it is called mercy. But what quality of mercy is it in fictitious and theatrical inventions? A member of the audience is not excited to offer help, but invited on to grieve. The greater his pain, the greater his approval of the actors in these representations. If the human calamities, whether in ancient histories or fictitious myths, are so presented that the theatergoer is not caused pain, he walks out of the theatre disgusted and highly critical. But if he feels pain, he stays riveted in his seat enjoying himself." Augustine, *Confessions* (trans. Henry Chadwick; Oxford: Oxford University Press, 1991), 35–36. For further criticism of the impact of *Les Mis*, see Bruce Kirle, "Cultural Collaborations: Re-Historicizing the American Musical" (PhD diss., New York University, 2002), 357–61; as well as David Walsh and Len Platt, *Musical Theater and American Culture* (Westport, CT: Praeger, 2003), 117–19.

6. See Paul Boyer, "666 and All That: Bible Prophecy Belief in America from the Puritans to the Present," in *Millennial Perspectives: Lifeworlds and Utopias* (ed. Brigitte Georgi-Findlay and Hans-Ulrich Mohr; Heidelberg: Winter, 2003), 37–53. See also discussions in Bernard J. McGinn, John J. Collins, and Stephen J. Stein, eds., *The Continuum History of Apocalypticism* (New York: Continuum, 2003).

7. See the numerous essays in David Hellholm, ed., *Apocalypticism in the Mediterranean World and the Near East* (Tübingen: Mohr/Siebeck, 1983).

8. Michael E. Stone, "Reactions to Destructions of the Second Temple," *Journal for the Study of Judaism* 12, no. 2 (1981): 195–204. The view of apocalyptic as response to suffering is generally held but not without criticism; see David Sim, "The Social Setting of Ancient Apocalypticism: A Question of Method," *Journal for the Study of Pseudepigrapha* [*JSP*] 13 (1995): 5–16; also, John J. Collins, "The Sense of Ending in Pre-Christian Judaism," in *Fearful Hope: Approaching the New Millennium* (ed. Christopher Kleinhenz and Fannie J. LeMoine; Madison, WI: University of Wisconsin Press, 1999), 40–41.

9. Lester L. Grabbe, "A Dan(iel) for All Seasons: For Whom Was Daniel Important?" in *The Book of Daniel: Composition and Reception*, vol. 1 (ed. John J. Collins and Peter W. Flint; Leiden: Brill, 2001), 233–36.

10. John J. Collins, "Daniel and His Social World," *Interpretation* 39, no. 2 (1985): 135.

11. Thomas J. Sappington, "The Factor of Function in Defining Jewish Apocalyptic Literature," *JSP* 12 (1994): 87.

12. G. R. Beasley-Murray, "The Interpretation of Daniel 7," *Catholic Biblical Quarterly* 45, no. 1 (1983): 54.

13. For a thorough discussion of what the Son of Man may represent or be, see T. J. Meadowcroft, *Aramaic Daniel and Greek Daniel: A Literary Comparison* (ed. David J. A. Clines et al.; JSOTSup 198 (Sheffield: Sheffield Academic Press, 1995), 223–34.

14. Stefan Beyerle, "The Book of Daniel and Its Social Setting," in *Book of Daniel* (ed. J. Collins and P. Flint), 1:216–21.

15. Floyd O. Parker, "'Our Lord and God' in Rev 4.11: Evidence for the Late Date of Revelation?" *Biblica* 82, no. 2 (2001): 209–17.

16. Leonard Thompson, "A Sociological Analysis of Tribulation in the Apocalypse of John," in *Early Christian Apocalypticism* (ed. Adela Yarbro Collins; SemeiaSt 36 (Decatur, GA: Scholars Press, 1986), 169.

17. Adela Yarbro Collins, "Persecution and Vengeance in the Book of Revelation," in *Apocalypticism in the Mediterranean World* (ed. D. Hellholm), 729–36.

18. For further parallels, see Jan Willem van Henten, "Daniel 3 and 6 in Early Christian Literature," in *Book of Daniel* (ed. J Collins and P. Flint), 1:155–56.

19. B. Dehandschutter, "Example and Discipleship: Some Comments on the Biblical Background of the Early Christian Theology of Martyrdom," in *The Impact of Scripture in Early Christianity* (ed. J. Den Boeft and M. L. van Poll-van de Lisdonk; Leiden: Brill, 1999), 20–26.

20. For Jesus as martyr, see Mitchell G. Reddish, "Martyr Christology in the Apocalypse," *Journal for the Study of the New Testament* 33 (1988): 85–95; Kenneth Grayston, "Atonement and Martyrdom," in *Early Christian Thought in Its Jewish Context* (ed. John Barclay and John Sweet; Cambridge: Cambridge University Press, 1996), 260.

21. Numerous rewards are granted to those who endure the persecutions and trials: the tree of life (Rev 2:7), the crown of life (2:10), a new name (2:17), governance (2:26–27), the morning star (2:28), white garments (3:5), and inheritance of a new heaven and earth (21:7); Adela Yarbro Collins, "The Book of Revelation," in *Continuum History of Apocalypticism* (ed. B. McGinn et al.), 208–9.

22. The lyrics for the entire musical can be found in the back of Behr, *Les Misérables*, 165–91.

23. For a thorough examination, see Sternfeld, "Revolution on Broadway," 355–57, 388.

24. Here, the musical remains close to the ideas of the book by Victor Hugo. See Kathryn M. Grossman, *Figuring Transcendence in Les Misérables: Hugo's Romantic Sublime* (Carbondale, IL: Southern Illinois Press, 1994), 121.

25. Sternfeld, "Revolution on Broadway," 365–67.

26. In the Gospels is a clear relation between the transfiguration of Jesus and Dan 7, which, as mentioned above, was related to themes of judgment and retribution. Daniel 7 of the LXX is clearly related to Matt 17:1ff. (see A. D. A. Moses, *Matthew's Transfiguration Story and Jewish Christian Controversy* (ed. Stanley E. Porter; JSNTSup 122; Sheffield: Sheffield Academic Press, 1996], 100). For further similarity, see John Paul Heil, *The Transfiguration of Jesus: Narrative Meaning and Function of Mark 9:2–8, Matt 17:1–8 and Luke 9:28–36* (Rome: Editrice Pontificio Istituto Biblico, 2000), 217.

27. For Moses as a figure of restoration, see the pseudepigraphical *Exagoge* of Ezekiel the Tragedian and the discussion of J. J. Collins, "A Throne in the Heavens: Apotheosis in Pre-Christian Judaism," in *Death, Ecstasy, and Other Worldly Journeys* (ed. John J. Collins and Michael Fishbane; Albany, NY: State University of New York Press, 1995), 43–49. For expectation of Elijah and the coming kingdom, see Markus Ohler, "The Expectation of Elijah and the Presence of the Kingdom of God," *Journal of Biblical Literature* 118, no. 3 (1999): 461–76. The very word of God in Matt 17:5, affirming Jesus and calling people to "listen to him," reflects Deut 18:15, about the prophet like Moses who was to arise.

28. For the social audience and background to the musical, see Kirle, "Cultural Collaborations," 354–57.

29. On the relation between the Isaiah text and apocalypticism, see Donald C. Polaski, *Authorizing an End: The Isaiah Apocalypse and Intertextuality* (Leiden: Brill, 2001), 172–79; and on Micah's use of the Isaiah tradition, see William McKane, *The Book of Micah: Introduction and Commentary* (Edinburgh: T & T Clark, 1998), 117–27. The Isaiah and Micah texts are both related to the founding of a new kingdom.

30. The name Jean Valjean itself is symbolic, with *Val* being French for "valley," and the V-shape itself indicating a journey that moves down and comes once again to the top.

31. Here, one is within an apocalypse if one is to take J. J. Collins' definition: "'Apocalypse' is a genre of revelatory literature [here, oral song] with a narrative framework, in which a revelation is mediated by an otherworldly being [Valjean and others] to a human recipient [the audience], disclosing a transcendent reality which is both temporal, insofar as it envisages eschatological salvation ["the garden of the Lord"], and spatial, insofar as it involves another, supernatural world [the audience sees the martyrs in the heavens]." See John J. Collins, ed., *Apocalypse: The Morphology of a Genre* (SemeiaST 14; Missoula, MT: Scholars Press, 1979; reprint, 1998), 9.

Comic Endings

Spirit and Flesh in Bono's Apocalyptic Imagination,
1980–1983

—Brian Froese

THE STORY HARDLY NEEDS TO BE RETOLD, for, like a ritual incantation, it has been retold often. One day in 1976 in Dublin, Ireland, an adolescent student, Larry Mullen Jr., posted a note on a bulletin board at the progressive Mount Temple Comprehensive School that announced he wanted to start a rock band. Several young men responded to the query. As legend tells us, the lineup of Paul Hewson (Bono), Dave Evans (The Edge), Adam Clayton, and Larry Mullen Jr. was created.[1] Of special concern at that meeting was their general lack of musical talent. Bono presented a particularly interesting situation: as Mullen mentioned, despite being responsible for starting the band and Bono's inability to either play guitar or sing, within two days Bono was in charge of the band.[2]

Twenty-five years later U2 was one of the largest rock bands in the world. Unlike most predecessors and contemporaries, U2 overcame several long odds: they not only came from the then obscure musical locale of Dublin, but also sang passionately about typical adolescent angst informed by an obvious Christian spirituality. When U2 released their third album, *War* (1983), they integrated their overt Christian spirituality and questions of adulthood with social-political concerns. The result was at once earnest and pretentious, subtle and preachy, and both humble and messianic in its posturing. Yet they succeeded, and a quarter century has passed since the band formed an important popular cultural link between sexuality,

Christian spirituality, and social-political relevance. It is a convincing origin myth: out of the small comes something large, and from a place off the mainstream comes the future.[3] Nevertheless, this origin myth serves another purpose; it reads success back into time to hint at destiny, of a providential gathering of seemingly disparate parts to produce a charismatic whole.

In this essay, I explore the intersection of two broad themes in Bono's lyrics: first, the theme of masculinity, love, and sex; second, the theme of justice and prophetic conscience. Within these two thematic categories, Bono used, consciously or otherwise, historically timeless motifs that explore the intersection of the material world with the spiritual through the mediation of apocalyptic images. The use of historically significant thematic imagery, held together by chiliastic drama, may account for their ability to retain relevance in a youth-idolatrous industry even when at times slouching toward the banal.[4]

To define "apocalyptic" for this essay, Stephen D. O'Leary, a communications professor who has contributed greatly to the field of apocalyptic discourse, provides a helpful dichotomy based upon comic and tragic readings of the apocalyptic. The comic view of apocalypse is more an "exhortation to the saintly life and the aesthetic functioning of the text experienced as allegory."[5] The tragic view of the end, more common with North American evangelicalism, focuses on timelines, destruction, and historical determinism leading the world inexorably to a fiery end or purification—a time they and their coreligionists are extricated from at the last moment.[6] A comic reading of apocalypse does not negate suffering; instead, it understands suffering and potential destruction in terms of human agency. The "comic jeremiad," as O'Leary calls it, warns of trouble if humanity does not change its behavior. Within this rhetorical construct, history is not broken, as in a tragic reading, and failure to change often does not mean the end; rather, it is a painful lesson. In other words, a comic reading of apocalypse declares that the end is not so much near as it is a choice.[7]

As we move chronologically through the first phase of U2's career in the early 1980s, we find Bono introducing themes that will dominate his writing: sexuality, justice, and spirituality. Considering the length of U2's career, this study needs some boundaries. Despite the increasing video output of U2, this essay is concerned with Bono's lyrical writings in their major studio album releases, from 1980–83. During this time, when their first three albums were released, a popular following was established in

Europe and North America, followed by 1987's gigantic success, *The Joshua Tree*, which made them ubiquitous.[8] By 1987, Bono consistently articulated a worldview that combined apocalyptically informed Christian spirituality, a prophetic concern for social justice, and an initially ambiguous masculine heterosexuality.

One tendency in Bono's lyrics is an attention paid to his own station in life. For example, in terms of material success, he moved from "If I had anything"[9] to "Don't believe in riches / but you should see where I live,"[10] and confessing, "These hands never worked a day."[11] As Bono seems to have grown with his lyrics, his perspective on themes such as religion, politics, sex, and justice seem rather consistent. Though it is important not to confuse song lyrics with autobiography, one can still comment on the persistent use of certain images as reflective on the author's imagination. Throughout these albums the use of direction and movement dominate—with Bono often falling, trying to awaken, and—with varying levels of clarity—attempting to find an object of love, affection, meaning, or redemption.[12]

Boy, 1980

True to its name, U2's first album, *Boy*, explores typical late adolescent topics such as leaving childhood to become an adult. As Bono was quoted, "The songs are autobiographical."[13] Vocalist and principal lyricist for U2, Bono described *Boy* as "very picturesque; they don't tell a story as such, they're just various images in the album that link together to form one big picture."[14] The question, as framed by Bono, thus extends beyond the drama of teenage experience, told and retold over the course of an album. Instead, we must explore the images as a big picture presented. The recurring images of movement, ambiguous sexuality, liminal anxiety, and mortality expressed through family, nature, and escapism dominate the album. All of these themes and images, including one oblique biblical reference to paradise and judgment, become explicit in their later years.

As Bono mentioned in 1980, a primary theme of *Boy* was "meandering."[15] Tracing that theme in the lyrics, we find it expressed as following after a significant other who has left,[16] being in confusion while "running in the rain,"[17] having strong sexual ambiguity, and discovering that to "go back" to childhood is impossible.[18] At the conclusion of the album, however, the narrator is again walking, but not following anyone. The singer also has discovered that in adulthood, the mundane is prevalent: "Mrs. Brown's washing is always the same." As he walks along the street, wet with "rain" [water is a common image of Bono's], his disposition shifts from desperation, confusion, and alienation to "tragi comedy."[19] In this acceptance of contradiction, he goes home, as the wet street becomes "melody," indicating a shift from the mundane to the transcendent. At the conclusion of his meandering, where Bono, as we will see, discovers adults behaving badly, his body changing, and his sexuality maturing, he goes home and the path changes from earthy to transcendent.[20] The significance of holding apparent contradictions together is also found in the song title "Shadows and Tall Trees," a title borrowed from William Golding's novel *Lord of the Flies*, a parable of the dark human heart in children. Bono's picture of the boy's meanderings is not one of innocence lost; it is a picture of understanding what was always there.

One recurrent theme that forms the landscape of meandering is ambiguous or maturing sexuality, liminal anxiety, and mortality expressed through images of family, nature, and escapism. The maturing identity found in the opening song, "I Will Follow," finds its transformation not in the act of following, but in the act of entering into a new space. Moving out from an enclosure marked by four oppressive walls, the boy enters into a circle made from the eyes of an unnamed one to whom he sings. It is not a following after abandonment; it is finding someone stationary, forming a circle, a symbol of completeness. The liminal anxiety of entering the circle is also expressed in the relationship the boy had with his mother. Though trying to become a man, he was devastated and began to cry when his mother took "him by the hand."[21]

The liminal anxiety of maturity also has ambiguous sexual overtones in "Twilight," where the threshold is no longer a wall or an optical circle, but a shadow: "In the shadow, boy meets man." What confuses the nature of the shadow are the first two verses, where the boy struggles in relationships with older men: "I laugh when old men cry." In the second verse, the sexual confusion and even darkness is made stark, where his "body grows and grows." The boy is also "frightened" when "the old man tried to walk me home, / I thought he should have known."[22] As the sexual confusion is brought to the lyrical foreground, Bono's use of water imagery also emerges. He is "running in the rain," then "caught in a late night play," pointing to a simultaneous flight and restriction in a space of unreality, where he is "soaking through the skin."[23] The combination of water and clothing only appear on one other song on the album, "The Ocean," where youthful megalomania is contrasted with the ocean—to which he proclaims his messianic plan for the world—that soaks his shoes. The messianic posturing is poetically set, drawing from biblical images of the washing of Christ's feet, or the Christian practice of foot washing, "The sea / Washes my feet."[24] However, in "The Ocean" a typical Bono tension is articulated. In verse 1 he recalls Oscar Wilde's *The Picture of Dorian Gray*, the story of youthful decadence hid by a decaying painting. In verse 2 he reveals his messianic inclination to tell the world how to improve itself.

The liminal space in "Twilight" is described as a boy frightened with his growing body and the unwelcome presence of an old man wanting to walk him home. Other phrases used to describe this space include "darkened day," "lost my way," "night and day," and "can't find my way." This anxiety does not go away in Bono's writing. Thirteen years later he crooned, "I feel like I'm slowly . . . slipping under. / I feel like I'm holding onto nothing."[25] It is similar to "Twilight," where change happens in the dark: "Midnight is where the day begins."[26] In Bono's lyrics is also a gendered division between the pursuits of the male and the spirit of the female. The male finds agency through the creation of such markers of civilization as banks, cathedrals, cars, roads, and technology. In this material pursuit of meaning, Bono intones that such work "has come asunder," and it is time to "look for something other."[27]

Although the older male presence in "Twilight" creates anxiety in the young Bono, in "Stories for Boys" that confusion is contrasted with the seeming delight at being in the company of another male of unspecified age. The male other provides access to a variety of youthful escapes, including television, heroes, picture books, comics, laughter, and the radio.[28] In "Lemon," for example, spiritual meaning comes from a woman. The woman embodies the spirit of love Bono so often sings of, and she is both "imagination" and "destination." In a direct biblical parallel, the female spirit nurtures, "but when you're dry, / She draws water from a stone."[29] In "Twilight," when the other is male, the images are of flight through rain and a soaking to the skin; where the other is female, as in "Lemon," the female other is presented with water imagery that is life-giving.[30]

The meandering of *Boy* is cast in the images of movements of differing speeds, water that seems to both taunt and baptize him, and the dark imagery of the liminal space where relating to adult men is complicated. Thereby Bono admits to a lack of ultimate control over his life. Lack of control over life coincides with mortality, a theme rarely far from Bono's surface. In the song "Out of Control," Bono describes his young life through phases of birth, dawning adulthood, and death: "One dull morning / I woke the world with bawling." "Eighteen years are dawning." "One day I'll die. / The choice will not be mine."[31] Spacing these sentiments is the chorus, simply stating that he has both the "feeling" and "opinion" that "it was out of control."[32] When contrasted with the liminality of "Twilight," these thresholds in life carry less the sexual confusions and more a spiritual resignation to forces beyond him.

Bono claims to fight fate in the fourth verse, where his rebellion is conflated with postlapsarian blood on the garden gate. However, in "A Day without Me," a song about suicide, Bono describes the process as a "landslide in my ego," contrasting the imagery of sleep and wakefulness. Considering that death and sleep look the same, he asks, "If I was sleeping, what's at stake?" What Bono has discovered of the world is that to exercise his one alternative against fate, suicide, the world would go on and the people he knew would "wipe their eyes and then let go."[33] Yet, sleep is as much a sexual image as it is death. In "Another Time, Another Place," the lyric describes the need for limits on experience: the singer will "wipe the sleep / From another day's eye," akin to the biblical descriptions of wiping tears from the eyes in the last days.[34] Then he turns from a wall to an open space, described in stark vulnerability: "Being naked and afraid / In the open space of my bed."[35]

In "Another Time, Another Place," Bono uses another frequent image, of woman as spirit. Bono has no control over the situation, similar to major life transitions, and in a dream vaguely sexual, he describes, "In my sleep, I discovered the one / But she left with the morning sun." Having been transported to "a feeling of never before," the sexual insinuation is unmistakable, but here the power is with the female, for they will lie again, "on a cloud," but only in her time.[36] The song "Shadows and Tall Trees" concludes the album, and its importance to the overall picture of meandering is strong. Bono asks the listener a spiritual question, "Do you feel in me / Anything redeeming?" This is followed by the other question on the album: "Is love like a tightrope / Hanging on my ceiling?"[37] The juxtaposition of love and ceilings is made again in 1991, when Bono further develops his career-long idea that meaning and redemption are found in a spirituality informed by a nurturing female. "When I was all messed up and I heard opera in my head / Your love was a lightbulb hanging over my bed."[38] The person in this song is also called, "sugar," "child," and "baby." She has lit Bono's way, held power over him, and in turn, he describes her with diminutive expressions of affection.[39] In *Boy*, Bono expresses a reading of life that—while a part of something larger, sometimes called fate—is also affirming of a person's development. Though confused in its journey and frustrated by larger forces, this album was neither pessimistic nor fatalistic.

October, 1981

October is considered the most overtly "Christian" of all of U2's albums. The album was sold in Christian music stores, and evangelicals claimed U2 as their own.[40] *October* coincided with a real tension in the band that nearly broke it apart. Three of the four members were involved with Shalom, a charismatic evangelical group, which provided spiritual nourishment for the Christians in U2. Shalom leaders began asking Bono, Edge, and Mullen to leave U2 and commit fully to Christianity, considering the two as incompatible. Thus, a period of searching and tension descended upon the band. After some time, including a two-week period when the Edge broke off contact with his bandmates to seek God's purpose, they left Shalom and committed to U2. As Bono has explored the transition to manhood in *Boy*, in *October* the images of motion and nature continue. But this time certainty replaces angst, and the Christian spirituality explored here is openly apocalyptic; the second of his recurring themes is introduced—there will be a better time.

Bono himself has described *October* as "introspective," in contrast to *Boy* being "immediate."[41] The introspection of *October* mutes Bono's sexual expression and allows a degree of apocalyptic symbolism to emerge. In *October*, Bono explicitly wants to make his faith public.[42] Despite his desire to declare his faith, *October* suffers from religious tension within the band, threatening its survival, and from the theft of Bono's notebook of lyrics, forcing him to quickly create new ones, since the recording studio was booked.[43]

According to the Edge, the theme of the album is the reconciliation of Christianity with being in a rock band. The band was "nervous about the Christian label." They were in an "intense" phase in their spiritual lives and thought it responsible and important to put their Christianity "out-there," but in a way to avoid the epithet of "Christian music."[44] The religious intensity was due largely to the involvement of Bono, Larry, and the Edge in Shalom. Shalom preached baptism in the Holy Spirit, and both Bono and The Edge were baptized in the sea. Initially, the meetings were informal gatherings of singing, Bible studies, and speaking in tongues; most experienced some measure of "the Holy Spirit." What developed during a couple years was an increasing legalism and intrusion in the private lives of group members. Leaders within Shalom demanded that Bono, Edge, and Larry leave U2 and fully commit to their Christian faith. There was some soul-searching, but the three returned to U2.[45]

Though they chose U2 over Shalom, with the Edge in particular having struggled over the apparent "contradiction" between Christianity and rock music, they continued to embrace the spirituality of their youth. In his early thirties, the Edge commented while on tour in support of *Achtung Baby* and *Zooropa*: "The central faith and spirit of the band is the same. But I have less and less time for *legalism* now."[46] During the same tour Bono commented on religion: "Forget about the judgment of history. For those of you who are religious people, you have to think about the judgment of God."[47] Bono's understanding of art has a prophetic quality that borrows some technique from C. S. Lewis's book *The Screwtape Letters*. In *Screwtape Letters*, Lewis uses the devil as the mouthpiece for the Christian message of love, hope, and active religious faith.[48] Bono's concern to ignore the judgment of history for God's judgement is articulated clearly in *October*. Its imagery is haunting in its depictions of Christ, Bono's mother, and spiritual pilgrimages, using lyrics grounded in the Revelation of John.

In the first song, "Gloria," Bono declares his need for God. Bono's need comes from an inability to express himself: "I try to sing," and "I try to speak up, / But only in you I'm complete." Although this ambiguity could point again to a mysterious lover, the song's chorus petitions, "O Lord, loosen my lips." The desire to sing and speak is combined with another of Bono's recurring images, standing and walking: "I try to stand up, . . . can't find my feet."[49] However, he does stand and search for God when, subverting the image in Rev 3:20, "I am standing at the door, knocking," he searches for the door. He cannot find it until he realizes, "The door is open, / You're standing there, you let me in."[50] A reference to Rev 3:8 connects faith and struggle with an open door: "Look, I have set before you an open door, which no one is able to shut."

The open door of "Gloria" contrasts with the image of Jesus and the closed door in *Pop*, where Bono laments the barrier of organized religion: "Then they put Jesus in show business. / Now it's hard to get in the door."[51] Alternatively, in "The Playboy Mansion," Bono subverts the entire biblical apocalypse into a seemingly antinomian gospel song, again reminding us of the literary technique borrowed from *The Screwtape Letters*. Bono reverses "Gloria," where Christ waits at the door, with "It's who you know that gets you through / The gates of the playboy mansion."[52] However, Bono questions what will be found in the paradise beyond those gates: "Then will there be no time for sorrow. / Then will there be no time for shame. / . . . / Then will there be no time for pain."[53] Bono's religious searching, most clearly stated in "I Still Haven't Found What I'm Looking For," on *The Joshua Tree*, follows him to the playboy mansion. Bono asks if this is the place where the world will be put right.

Within "Gloria," Bono is still young, and on his search for God he is willing to commit himself: "O Lord, if I had anything, anything at all, / I'd give it to you."[54] Bono's search for a voice leads him to God, which leads to his submission. Nearing the end of the album, Bono not only has a voice to sing and talk with, but also a voice to shout out his new faith. In "Gloria," Bono wonders if he has anything to give; by the end of *October* he found that he can give his life. The directionless movements he describes have brought him to Mount Zion and Jerusalem.[55]

Like "Gloria," the song "I Fall Down" contains imagery frequently used by Bono. The juxtapositions of falling, walking, sleeping, and waking dominate the song. It has even been reported that the song is a metaphor of the biblical fall, using a couple from the Shalom group.[56] In "Gloria," Bono finds his voice to exalt the Lord; in "I Fall Down," a seemingly platonic couple desires to walk in the natural elements of sun, wind, and rain, but they are thwarted by one of the partners falling down. As they admit their mutual falling, the characters of the song express their commitment to each other, similar to the Hebrew story of Adam and Eve: "When you fall / I fall with you" and never find the place of sun, wind, and rain.[57] Bono also frequently uses the image of falling or sinking in order to find help.[58]

Wakefulness is another Bono image used to describe the intersection of spirituality and society. In "Rejoice," as the aforementioned couple struggles to wake up without falling down, Bono describes buildings falling down at the whim of children. Then he states: "He says he'll change the world some day. / I rejoice." This may refer to the child destroying buildings and the return of Christ to set the world right. After the mysterious male figure promises a changed world, Bono describes his day, beginning with him falling out of bed, waking to what the person said—indicating the song is a dream. Then Bono realizes that he himself cannot change the world, only "I can change the world in me."[59] Perhaps Bono is the child breaking things, holding to a messianic claim to change the world, and then rejoicing that he only needs to be responsible for his world.

These tropes are continued in "I Threw a Brick through a Window." The themes of searching for direction continue; falling is replaced with collision, where Bono "was walking into walls"—an image of restriction he often uses.[60] In *October*, attempts to find direction are always initially frustrated. In this song, Bono walks into a wall; he peers into windows, looking for his image, similar to the postapocalyptic prophet in "The Wanderer" on *Zooropa*.[61] These spiritual miscues are followed by the biblical injunction used by the Hebrew prophets and Jesus: those with eyes should see. Bono describes himself as the most blind for his unwillingness to see.[62] Again, Bono struggles to talk; here he speaks in his sleep, asking his brother to help him.[63]

In *October*, however, the search for God is constructed with an apocalyptic imagination. Four songs carry the apocalyptic theme: "Fire," "Tomorrow," "October," and "With a Shout." "Fire" is the most literal use of the New Testament book Revelation. The imagery includes "The sun is burning black," "The moon is running red," and "The stars are falling down."[64] Though the most literal use of Revelation imagery, Bono also sings of an inner dimension to the apocalyptic: the burning sun becomes "a fire inside," the falling stars are transformed into "I'm falling over," and "[the stars] knock me to the ground."[65] This is a poetic transformation of one of Bono's consistently used images—falling. Bono is now falling over in an inner transformation of apocalyptic proportions; he simply announces, "I'm going home."[66] Throughout *October*, Bono articulates a comic understanding of apocalyptic rhetoric.

The other three songs speak more directly to important human relationships, especially the haunting "Tomorrow," where the moving between Christ and Bono's mother transform the apocalyptic imagery with the deepest of human love. "Tomorrow" deals directly with the death of Bono's mother, which occurred when he was fourteen years old. He presents her death with a return to the image of knocking on a door; though we do not who is knocking, we do know that Bono and his family are inside. A stranger knocks at the door, prefiguring Christ's appearance later in the song. What we know is that on the street in front of the door is a black car. Bono pleads, "Don't go to the door." "I'm going outside, mother." The pathos of the chorus asks, "Will you be back tomorrow? / Can I sleep tonight?"[67] Bono speaking to his mother occurs one other time in U2's major studio releases, on "Mofo," where Bono asks her, "Mother, am I still your son?" Then he tells her, "Mother, you left and made me someone. / Now I'm still a child, but no one tells me no."[68]

Elsewhere Bono transposed Christ with other important people. For example, on *The Unforgettable Fire*, Bono moves between Christ and Martin Luther King Jr.[69] With "Tomorrow," the suffering and loss he experienced with his mother's death is cast in terms of Christ's suffering at the passion and with allusions to the second coming of Christ. Bono wonders why the window and door are broken and the curtain torn—a direct allusion to the torn curtain at Christ's crucifixion—and asks for the promised healing.[70] Bono's desire for his mother to return is conflated with a desire for Christ's return: "Will you be back tomorrow? / Open up, open up, to the Lamb of God." Bono opens up to the Lamb of God because it is God's love that has "made the blind to see." Recalling the end of Revelation, Bono ends the song: "He's coming back. / Oh, believe him."[71] This song of hope, returning, and love—wrapped up in the biblical story of Christ's return—is underscored in the song "October." "October" briefly restates "Tomorrow" by presenting Christ as standing outside of history: "October and kingdoms rise / And kingdoms fall, / But you go on."[72] These sentiments are echoed in "Until the End of the World." In this song Bono, playing the part of Judas, admits his complicity in betraying Christ, his desire to destroy Christ, and his need for Christ to save him. He acknowledges that, if necessary, the love of Christ will wait until the end of time.[73]

In *October*, Bono is not Judas, nor is he an apostle who has fled the passion; Bono is positioned at Christ's crucifixion.[74] Bono has moved from the blood at the gate of Eden, as found in *Boy*, to the blood of Christ's crucifixion and the city of Jerusalem. He wants to go "to the foot of Mount Zion" in order to be at "the foot of He [*sic*] who made me see" where "blood was spilt" and "we were filled with a love." The image of return is repeated: Bono declares his intention, "We're going to be there again."[75] In *October*, Bono has found his voice, footing, and sight. Though often searching for the right direction, the certainty of his mooring is assumed. By the end of the album, Bono has seen Christ's sacrifice, is filled with Christ's love, and is committed to return there. From the stage of "Gloria," where he has nothing to give Christ, in "With a Shout" he has found his life, to give it in pilgrimage. By the end of *October*, Bono has incorporated the apocalyptic themes of a world returned to right in the end, after suffering, and through the sacrifice and love of Christ, who stands outside of history. In so doing, Bono has provided, deliberately or otherwise, a comic reading of the biblical apocalypse narrative.

War, 1983

In *War*, Bono combines the lyrical themes of *Boy* and *October*. The themes of Christian faith and justice, mediated through apocalyptic and prophetic imagery, are combined with sexuality. The sexuality of *War* is tied less to the confusion of *Boy* and understood more as a category of redemption. The apocalyptic understanding of time, where history moves toward a final judgment, destination, or paradise, is an important aspect of *War*. As we read in several songs on *October*, the idea of there being a reality that stands outside of time, or that there is a second advent of Jesus to watch for, is present in *War*. Yet, here it is in the context of nuclear war, drowning, and in migrating to America.

In the song "Seconds," Bono incorporates two important New Testament expressions of Jesus' return. The first is in 1 Cor 15:51–52: "We will all be changed, in a moment, in the twinkling of an eye." The second is in 1 Thess 5:2: "The day of the Lord will come like a thief in the night." In "Seconds," Bono writes, "Takes a second to say good-bye," and "Like a thief in the night, see the world by candlelight." The candlelight recalls one of Jesus' parables concerning the coming kingdom of God (Matt 25:1–13). Ten virgins are asked to wait for the bridegroom. Five leave the waiting area to purchase oil for their lamps, to keep them lit. These five miss the wedding festivities because the groom arrives while they are gone. The five virgins who stay have enough oil in their lamps and join the celebration.

"Seconds" describes the proliferation of atomic weapons to the extent that anyone who wants one can have one. The song underscores the fragility of life in general with the repeated line that it only takes a second to say good-bye, or to "push the button and pull the plug."[76] Connecting nuclear proliferation with apocalyptic imagery is in itself not especially creative. What is intriguing about Bono's linking the two is his use of the biblical imagery of the twinkling of an eye, thief in the night, and candlelight. He thereby shifts the focus from tragic consequence to comic possibility, if the warning is heeded.[77] Bono also inserts an exceptionalist understanding of history in writing: "Lightning flashes across the sky, / East to West, do and die."[78] Lightning could simply be the nuclear blast feared in the song, with blame accorded to the Eastern Bloc. Alternatively, it could be read as an exceptionalist reading of history, where history moves east to west toward a culmination in America.[79] Later in the album, on the song "The Refugee," the end of history, or paradise, is America. Before the refugee migrates to America, however, Bono describes the scene: "In the evening / . . . / [she is] waiting for her man to come," and he will take her to the "promised land."[80] Again, if the effort is made to improve one's world, promised lands may be found.

On "Drowning Man," Bono brings in the lessons from *Boy* to add a layer of sexual maturity to the apocalyptic. He writes to a lover, "I'll cross the sky for your love," so that they will be together "for the time that will come." The uncertainty of events in the lives of these two people is contrasted with the strength of commitment: "This change of times / Won't drag you away." In fact, the one returning through the sky assures the other that all the "storms will pass" and "this love will last forever." As these actors cross through the sky, holding on tightly to each other, for each others' love, Bono references the Hebrew prophet Isaiah: "Rise up with wings like eagles, / . . . / run and not grow weary." Upon later reflection, Bono has described this song as psalmlike, perhaps from the perspective of God.[81]

The sexual theme continues in "Like a Song," where Bono implies that one brings sexual energy to the pursuit of social justice: "And in leather, lace, and chains we stake our claim." In so doing, an authenticity is found outside more fashionable expressions of revolution: "We love to wear a badge, a uniform, / And we love to fly a flag," while being "too right to be wrong."[82] Bono writes that revolution is to come from the heart, of which he asks, "God, make it bleed." Thus, he seemingly wants to reject the posturing of wearing it on his sleeve.[83]

All the major themes of Bono's writing come together most clearly in the opening two tracks that are among U2's more popular songs. In "Sunday Bloody Sunday," a song about sectarian violence, Bono paraphrases a line from Ps 6:3 as "How long must we sing this song," which reappears on the closing song, "40."[84] Then "40" paraphrases Ps 40:1–3 as a fitting benediction, describing the certainty of God's love. However, questions linger as to when the need to sing about hope in a violent world will end: "How long to sing this song?"[85] Bono brings together the victory of Christ in history—"The real battle just begun / To claim the victory Jesus won"—with a prophetic sense of justice in an unjust world, where families are torn apart and children play in the violence and destruction of religious warfare. Yet here Bono also expresses the human longing "We can be as one, tonight."[86] Though the situation is tragic, Bono's comic understanding of apocalyptic incorporates into its structures of meaning responses to suffering that involve such human action as claiming the victory of Jesus to build a sustainable society and meaningful human relationships.[87] A similar structuring of meaning and response occurs in "New Year's Day."

As "Sunday Bloody Sunday" is about sectarian violence in Ireland, "New Year's Day" is about the lifting of martial land in Poland in the early

1980s. It is a song where in an oppressed society hope remains: "We can break through." Mixed in with the biblical image of "the chosen few," who resist the powers, is the integrating of sexual desire. In both "Sunday Bloody Sunday" and "New Year's Day," he expresses such hope: "We can be as one." "Maybe tonight / I will be with you again."[88] These statements reflect a comic Christian sense of the apocalyptic, where a broken world will be set right, coinciding with sexual fulfillment in maturing human relationships that withstand the tempests of the day. Other images in "New Year's Day" underscore the apocalyptic imagination: the "world in white," a future utopia, and a "blood-red sky," recalling Revelation's imagery of the moon turning red.[89] "Sunday Bloody Sunday" connects to images often used by Bono in the wiping of tears from the eye and decadence dulling one's spiritual appreciation of the world situation.[90] "New Year's Day" presents the same comic problem. Despite the best of intentions, "nothing changes" with a new year where, if "this is the golden age," "gold is the reason for the wars we wage."[91] In its avarice, humanity chooses its violence.

From *Boy* to *War*, Bono has written about a world transcendent, where justice may be found, and of a spirituality that recognizes the spiritual and material, including sexual needs and desires.[92] The layers of meaning that Bono has incorporated in these first three major studio albums have a long history in Christian mysticism. There sexuality, justice, and spirituality are often understood together, especially through the Middle Ages.[93]

Exploring the lyrical imagery of Bono, we have seen an almost seamless incorporation of apocalyptic symbols with spirituality and sexuality. O'Leary provides a helpful perspective on apocalyptic rhetoric with his comic and tragic dichotomy. He also wrote that apocalypse is a "mythic narrative about power and authority, as affirmation of divine and spiritual power over and against the idolatrous claim of state authority."[94] Although O'Leary is exploring rhetorical uses of the biblical book Revelation, the subversive nature of apocalyptic is significant to this study. Bono consistently mixes themes of oppressive government, liberating sexuality, and transcendent spirituality with apocalyptic imagery. Through the course of U2's first three albums, Bono has articulated an almost mystical form of Christianity, appropriating the imagery of apocalypse in a rhetorically comic strategy to underscore hope, responsibility, and choice in how one may change his or her world. For Bono, that means working through suffering to find redemption; it also means being fully human and working for justice and healing as an integrated person, where spirituality and sexuality have both recognition and expression.[95]

To that end, in 2000 in the song "Walk On," Bono has subverted the determinism of a universe oblivious to human striving and longing depicted in the Pink Floyd song "Eclipse." With nearly identical lyrics, Bono exhorts his listeners to choose to return home, "where the hurt is," and to discard the works of their hands for the journey. They are to do this not because they are pointless, as in "Eclipse," but because they can be exchanged for a, hopefully, safer and newer tomorrow.[96]

Notes

1. Scott Isler, "Operation Uplift," *Trouser Press*, July 1, 1983, as reprinted in *The U2 Reader: A Quarter Century of Commentary, Criticism, and Review* [hereafter, *U2 Reader*] (ed. Hank Bordowitz; New York: Hal Leonard Corp., 2003), 13, 18.

2. Isler, "Operation Uplift," 13; Chris Heath, "Once upon a Time . . . ," *Star Hits*, January 1987, as reprinted in *U2 Reader*, 29; and Jay Cocks; reported by Elizabeth Bland, "Band on the Run: U2 Soars with a Top Album, a Hot Tour, and Songs of Spirit and Conscience," *Time*, April 27, 1987, as reprinted in *U2 Reader*, 53.

3. Bill Flanagan, *U2: At the End of the World* (New York: Delta, 1995), 87.

4. Although I am examining a particular aspect of Bono's lyrics, it is important to remember that there are a variety of literary influences to consider, not all of which are specifically Christian.

5. Stephen D. O'Leary, *Arguing the Apocalypse: A Theory of Millennial Rhetoric* (New York: Oxford University Press, 1994), 75.

6. Ibid., 76.

7. Ibid., 83–84.

8. The 1984 album *The Unforgettable Fire* was released between *War* and *The Joshua Tree* marking producer Brian Eno's inaugural appearance behind the boards. His style differed distinctly from former producer Steve Lillywhite's, effectively beginning a new era for the band and setting apart the 1980–83 Lillywhite albums.

9. "Gloria," *October* (Island Records, 1981). All lyrics are from the official U2 website: U2.com. Although their albums contain lyric sheets, it was not until 1987 that all songs were included. In their early period, of which this essay is concerned, there are only a few songs on each album where lyrics are printed. This is a study on the lyrical imagery of this early period, and there is no official published lyric book by U2. Hence, for consistency I have chosen to use the website.

10. "God Part II," *Rattle and Hum* (Island Records, 1988).

11. "Do You Feel Loved" *Pop* (Polygram International Music B.V., 1997).

12. The use of movement in the U2 album, *All That You Can't Leave Behind* (Universal International Music, 2000), is examined in Michael J. Gilmour, "The Prophet Jeremiah, Anung San Suu Kyi, and U2's *All That You Can't Leave Behind*" (in this volume).

13. Niall Stokes, *Into the Heart: The Stories behind Every U2 Song* (New York: Thunder's Mouth, 1996), 8.

14. Tim Sommer, "U2," *Trouser Press*, July 1, 1981, as reprinted in *U2 Reader*, 10. This reference also establishes Bono as the principal writer of the band.

15. Paulo Hewitt, "Getting into U2," *Melody Maker*, September 13, 1980, as reprinted in *U2 Reader*, 6

16. "I Will Follow," *Boy* (Island Records, 1980).

17. "Twilight," *Boy*.

18. "Into the Heart," *Boy*.

19. "Shadows and Tall Trees," *Boy*.

20. "Twilight."

21. "I Will Follow."

22. Two songs on *Boy*, "Twilight" and "Stories For Boys," were important to gay fans for expressing male sexuality beyond the rock music trope of "machismo." Though such homoerotic readings of the lyrics are understandable, they also subvert Bono's own reading of his lyrics as simply hetero-escapist; Stokes, *Into the Heart*, 10–11, 15.

23. "Twilight."

24. "The Ocean," *Boy*.

25. "Lemon," *Zooropa* (Island Records, 1993).

26. Ibid.

27. Ibid.

28. "Stories for Boys," *Boy*.

29. "Lemon."

30. Examples of other songs where women are described in terms of life or light: "Mysterious Ways" and "Who's Gonna Ride Your White Horses," *Achtung Baby* (Island Records, 1991); "If You Wear That Velvet Dress," *Pop*; and "Grace," *All That You Can't Leave Behind*. See also the penetrating examination of U2's theology through the lens of gender analysis, in Anna Bańkowska, "The 'Spirit Moves in Mysterious Ways': U2's Brand of Christian Theology in the 90's," *British Studies Web Pages*, http://elt.britcoun.org.pl/bank.htm (produced in Poland by The British Council, 2002).

31. "Out of Control," *Boy*.

32. Ibid.

33. "A Day without Me," *Boy*.

34. Rev 7:17: "God will wipe every tear from their eyes."

35. "Another Time, Another Place," *Boy*.

36. Ibid.

37. "Shadows and Tall Trees."

38. "Ultraviolet (Light My Way)," *Achtung Baby*.

39. This juxtaposition of male need and female deliverance occurs throughout *Achtung Baby*.

40. Mark Allan Powell, "U2," *Encyclopedia of Contemporary Christian Music* (Peabody, MA: Hendrickson, 2002), 978–79.

41. Scott Isler, "Operation Uplift," 15.

42. Ibid.

43. Flanagan, *U2*, 46.

44. Ibid., 47.

45. Eamon Dunphy, *Unforgettable Fire: The Story of U2* (London: Penguin, 1987), 184–86, 208–10. Dunphy's book has been criticized for a tendency to hagiography and for embellishing events. However, other sources have also remarked on this particular struggle; see Flanagan, *U2*, 47–49; Chris Heath, "Once upon a Time," 30–32; Jason White, "The Spiritual Journey of U2," *Religious News Service*, February 12, 2002, as reprinted in *U2 Reader*, 173–74; and Steve Stockman, *Walk On: The Spiritual Journey of U2* (Lake Mary, FL: Relevant Books, 2001), 25–27.

46. Flanagan, *U2*, 49. Italics in the original.

47. Terry Mattingly, "The Scripture According to Bono," *Scripps-Howard News Service*, June 20, 2001, as reprinted in, *U2 Reader*, 172.

48. Flanagan, *U2*, 434.

49. "Gloria." Later in life, Bono reflected upon "Gloria" as an attempt to talk about a woman in a "spiritual sense" and God in a "sexual sense"; Stokes, *Into the Heart*, 23.

50. "Gloria."

51. "If God Will Send His Angels," *Pop*.

52. "The Playboy Mansion," *Pop*.

53. Ibid.

54. "Gloria."

55. "With a Shout," *October*.

56. Stokes, *Into the Heart*, 24.

57. "I Fall Down," *October*; Gen 3:1–7; in 3:12 Adam betrays Eve before God.

58. We find this throughout Bono's career, as in these examples: falling, in "I Will Follow," *Boy*; tripping, in "Trip through Your Wires," *The Joshua Tree* (Island Records, 1987); stooping, in "Red Hill Mining Town," *The Joshua Tree*; falling, in "Stay (Far Away, So Close!)" and "Lemon," and crawling, in "One," *Zooropa*. In the song "Mysterious Ways," *Achtung Baby*, Bono sings, "She'll be there when you hit the ground."

59. "Rejoice," *October*.

60. Other examples of this trope include, "Where the Streets Have No Name," and "I Still Haven't Found What I'm Looking For," *The Joshua Tree*.

61. "The Wanderer, "*Zooropa*. Another example of the wandering prophet type is "Love Rescue Me," *Rattle and Hum*.

62. See Ezek 12:2; Matt 13:13–16.

63. Asking for help in the throes of sleep appears in other songs. He sings of heroin addiction in "Bad," *The Unforgettable Fire* (Island Records, 1984); and in "Running to Stand Still," *The Joshua Tree*. He identifies a general spiritual malaise in "Wake Up Dead Man," *Pop*.

64. See Joel 2:30–32; 3:15; Matt 24:29; Acts 2:20, and Rev 8:12. Other uses of these images include a funeral song where the dead and living will reunite in the future, "One Tree Hill," *The Joshua Tree*; in the paean to the rock star ego missing the signs of the end, "The Fly," *Achtung Baby*; and in mountains crumbling into the sea as a description of nuclear devastation, "The Unforgettable Fire," *The Unforgettable Fire*. Images of divine help expressed through falling occur in "Stay (Far Away, So Close!)" *Zooropa*. The first mixing of all the major themes in the early albums—justice, love, sexuality, and apocalyptic spirituality—is in "Drowning Man," *War* (Island Records, 1983), and will be discussed below.

65. "Fire," *October*.

66. Ibid.

67. "Tomorrow," *October*.

68. "Mofo," *Pop*.

69. "Pride (in the Name of Love)," *The Unforgettable Fire*.

70. See Matt 27:50–51.

71. "Tomorrow"; Rev 22:20.

72. "October," *October*.

73. "Until the End of the World," *Achtung Baby*.

74. Bono's presence at Jesus' crucifixion is repeated in "When Love Comes to Town," *Rattle and Hum*, where he is a soldier assisting in the execution and gambling at the foot of the cross.

75. "With a Shout."

76. "Seconds," *War*.

77. See O'Leary's discussion on this point, in *Apocalypse*, 218–24.

78. "Seconds."

79. For detailed background and analysis of this idea, see the classic essay by Loren Baritz, "The Idea of the West," *American Historical Review* 66, no. 3 (April 1961), 618–40.

80. "The Refugee," *War*.

81. "Drowning Man," *War*. See, Isa 40:31; and Powell, "U2," 979. Another biblical use of the eagle-in-flight metaphor that suits Bono's use is Exod 19:4: "You have seen what I did to the Egyptians, and how I bore you on eagles' wings and brought you to myself." See Stokes, *Into the Heart*, 43.

82. "Like a Song," *War*.

83. Ibid. Compare to "The Fly," *Achtung Baby*; and "Look, I gotta go, . . . I'm running outta change. / There's a lot of things, if I could I'd rearrange."

84. "Sunday Bloody Sunday," and "40," *War*. For a detailed and important analysis of "Sunday Bloody Sunday," see Susan Fast, "Music, Contexts, and Meaning in U2," *Expression in Pop-Rock Music: A Collection of Critical and Analytical Essays* (ed. Walter Everett; New York: Garland Pubg., 2000), 33–57.

85. "40."

86. "Sunday Bloody Sunday."

87. O'Leary, *Apocalypse*, 92.

88. "New Year's Day," *War*. See, Stokes, *Into the Heart*, 41.

89. "New Year's Day."

90. "Sunday Bloody Sunday." The same metaphor of television turning news into entertainment is found in "If God Will Send His Angels."

91. "New Year's Day." The theme of a better world coming is also found in "Van Diemen's Land," *Rattle and Hum*.

92. Bańkowska, "The 'Spirit Moves,'" par. 6.

93. Some important studies of this include Peter Brown, *The Body and Society: Men, Women, and Sexual Renunciation in Early Christianity* (New York: Columbia University Press, 1988); Caroline Walker Bynum, *Fragmentation and Redemption: Essays on Gender and the Human Body in Medieval Religion* (New York: Zone Books, 1991); Susanna Elm, *"Virgins of God": The Making of Asceticism in Late Antiquity* (Oxford: Clarendon, 1994); and Marcia L. Colish, *Medieval Foundations of the Western Intellectual Tradition, 400–1400* (New Haven: Yale University Press, 1997), passim.

94. O'Leary, *Apocalypse*, 55.

95. Nevertheless, the choice that Bono describes is not always for the spiritual. In "The First Time," *Zooropa*, the choice is between a lover and the father who gave him keys to the coming kingdom. At the end of the song the narrator throws the keys away, presumably choosing the lover over the future. "The First Time" contrasts with a similar leaving later in *Zooropa*, where the narrator in "The Wanderer" chooses messianic posturing over his/her partner in a postapocalyptic world.

96. Pink Floyd, "Eclipse," *Dark Side of the Moon* (Capitol Records, 1973); and U2, "Walk On," *All That You Can't Leave Behind* (Interscope Records, 2000).

Faith, Doubt, and the Imagination

Nick Cave on the Divine-Human Encounter

—Anna Kessler

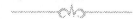

How can anyone be elevated spiritually if one is loaded up with the chains of religious jurisprudence? How can the imagination be told how to behave? How can inspiration or for that matter God be moral? The Letter kills, but the spirit brings life."

—Nick Cave

My faith is made up of doubts. Cognition of God includes a lot of beautiful and mysterious things; . . . that is why I think that my way to God is like the journey of lonely wanderer whose spiritual perception of the world is based on Doubt.

—Nick Cave

FOR THE LAST TWENTY YEARS rock artist Nick Cave (of the bands The Birthday Party, and Nick Cave and the Bad Seeds) has wrestled with profound biblical and philosophical themes. He admits ironically, "If I am a Christian, I am a very bad one." Yet he also acknowledges that there are "only two things I care about: love and God." Although widely known for his stark Goth look, discordant crescendos, macabre imagery, and often-gruesome murder ballads, his lyrics are suffused with religious content and biblical themes. Even his murder ballads are saturated with religious subject matter. Furthermore, he has explicitly expressed his interest and passion for religious and spiritual themes. Though such themes have been present throughout his entire music career, in his later, mature work his considered views become most lucid. In addition to numerous places in his music where Cave wrestles openly with spiritual concerns, he has made his religious thought explicit in his "Introduction to the Gospel according to Mark" and his lecture "The Flesh Made Word." In this essay, I intend to examine the influence that religion has had on Cave's work, and also to give his philosophical standpoint on God's relationship to humanity the treatment it richly deserves.

Cave's work addresses a wide range of religious themes and issues. However, the single area to which Cave has extended significant effort is the issue of the nature of the biblical God and how the divine and human spheres interact. Cave militates against the view of a directly intervention-ist God, who "makes people's lives better" by changing "the march of events." Nevertheless, he does insist that humanity and God can interact in a meaningful way. As he argues in his lecture "The Flesh Made Word," the medium through which this interaction occurs is the creative imagi-nation. Thus, Cave claims that it is through the process of the creative imagination taken flight that God both speaks *to* us and *through* us. Cave's exploration of the divine-human encounter ranges between firm devo-tional conviction, supplication, and active doubt. Such a view of faith thus necessarily oscillates between attitudes of doubt and certainty. However, despite the apparent ambivalence between doubt and confidence in Cave's treatment of the divine-human relationship—often punctuated by impas-sioned pleas for the divine presence—there is a fundamental certitude regarding the character of the faith at issue. As Cave clearly states: "Absence or presence, I still believe in Him."[1]

Here I assess Cave's model of the divine-human encounter as a rela-tionship that obtains through the medium of the creative imagination. When Cave says, "I don't believe in an interventionist God," this should not be taken as a passing remark or momentary ambivalence. Instead, Cave is firmly rejecting a strongly metaphysical picture of God as inter-ventionist, in favor of depicting the divine-human encounter as intrinsi-cally connected to the human perspective. On this view, then, there is a fundamental distinction between an interventionist model and what I call an *interactionist* model. The question is whether the divine-human rela-tionship is to be understood as entirely one-sided, with humans as grovel-ing supplicants, waiting for divine intervention to relieve us of the unrelenting gloom of everyday life. I maintain that Cave's work offers us a viable alternative understanding of divine-human rapport. This essay therefore looks critically at (1) Cave's exploration of the character of faith as involving an essential dialectical interplay between doubt and certainty, and (2) his claim that the medium through which humanity and God can truly interact is the creative imagination.

In part 1 of this essay, I discuss Cave's conception of the nature of faith at issue. I show that the essential and dialectically necessary relationship between doubt and certainty as constitutive of faith gives a clue as to how we should conceive of the encounter between humanity and the divine. The three main stances characteristic of Cave's configuration of faith—doubt, supplication, and devotion—point us to his focus on an interactive rather than interventionist model of the divine-human relationship.

Part 2 of the essay develops the alternative model that Cave presents, focusing intensively on Cave's radical claim that the creative imagination is the locus of the divine-human encounter. The path to the divine occurs, not in sterile religious services or pictures in books, but through an inward turn to the creative imagination. For the purposes of summary exegesis, I focus my attention on Cave's work from 1997 to 2004, where the themes in question are most lucidly and coherently crystallized.[2]

Doubt and Certitude: Cave's Phenomenology of Faith

Cave opens his 1997 album *The Boatman's Call* with the striking lyric "I don't believe in an interventionist God."[3] This may seem odd to the listener since the album is devoted almost exclusively to the exploration of various religious themes and adopts a devotional, questioning, and sometimes wry posture. The rejection of an interventionist God, however, is central to Cave's understanding of the relationship that human beings can have with the divine. Cave's entire project of advancing a subjectivist conception of the religious standpoint relies heavily on his dismissal of the interventionist model. It is not difficult to see why one would want to look for an alternative to the interventionist model. A cursory examination of philosophy of religion and theology reveals the myriad problems generated by the adoption of an interventionist picture of a metaphysical God. For example, the traditional interventionist depiction of God arguably presents us with a schizophrenic view of the divine both as a miracle-worker and yet as allowing—sometimes sanctioning—rampant suffering. Cave touches on the omnipresence of evil and cruelty explicitly in his murder ballads, but also implicitly in his more introspective work as well. His chief interest, however, is not with the philosophical baggage associated with the traditional conception of God as an all-powerful ruler capable of changing the march of events according to his will. Instead, he focuses on the way human beings subjectively experience and conceive of the world they inhabit. In the album *As I Sat Sadly by Her Side*, for example, he rails against the brutality of the world and the disinterestedness of human beings to each other's suffering:

> Then we pressed our different faces to the glass: "That may be very well," I said, "but watch the one falling in the street, see him gesture to his neighbours and see him trampled beneath their feet, all outward motion connects to nothing for each is concerned with their immediate need. When does the man reaching up from the gutter see the other one stumbling on who cannot see?"[4]

For our purposes, we should recognize that Cave is repudiating the interventionist model not for its reliance on metaphysically suspect notions, but for its failure to recognize the engagement of human subjectivity with the divine. Since the God in question is not the God of miracles or the smiting, vengeful, actively interventionist God of the Old Testament, the nature of faith on Cave's rapport-based picture will also be different. This is not to say that Cave's God is not the biblical God; Cave is not outright rejecting the God of the Old Testament.[5] If this were the case, Cave would simply be a Marcionite (Marcion, d. 160 C.E.). Cave, however, differs from the image of God represented in the traditional readings of both the Old and New Testaments. He distances himself from aspects of the Bible that portray God as a God of miracles—a smiting, vengeful, and actively interventionist God—without rejecting the biblical text as a medium through which the divine-human encounter can be engaged. Rather, as far as the personal, interactive, two-way relationship between humanity and the divine goes, he takes it that the New Testament has more to say in terms of the life of Jesus the sufferer.

What is the nature of religious faith for Cave? What does this conception indicate to us about the relational model that Cave is proposing as an alternative to the traditional model? The conception of faith at play in Cave's work presents a vacillation between doubt and certainty as central to religious experience.[6] As Cave succinctly puts it, "My faith is made up of doubts." In a sense, then, Cave's conception of faith is at least partially backstopped by an epistemology of doubt. The really interesting notion at work in this configuration of faith, however, is not the epistemological status of faith or belief as such, but the *phenomenological* character of a faith that is partly constituted by doubt. Cave's concern is with the personal face of religious experience. In Cave's treatment of faith, the work being done by the notion of doubt is at the level of one's own personal awareness of God, rather than functioning as a theoretical and philosophical skepticism about the existence of God as a metaphysical entity.

The metaphysical status of God as an existing entity and the epistemological status of belief in God are not at issue for Cave: they are not even "on the table" for discussion. Cave is concerned primarily with the personal and phenomenological nature of the divine-human encounter, and he sees doubt as a dialectical necessity in that relationship. For Cave, doubt is essential to faith. Rather than being inimical or antithetical to faith, Cave asserts that, in a deep sense, faith is *necessarily* underwritten by a certain misgiving about the object of belief. Doubt is a crucial and essential part of the subjective experience of faith. The key point is that Cave is presenting us with a conception of faith in which doubt is *phenomenologically constitutive*. This implies that the real experience of active doubt in the existence or presence of God is a necessary part of faith. When Cave says, "It seems that God lives only in our dreams,"[7] he is speaking to a profound skepticism that is constitutive of the human experience of the divine presence. The agnostic, almost mistrustful mood captured in statements like "There is a man who spoke wonders, well, I've never met him,"[8] is demonstrative of the deep human uncertainty about the presence of God. What Cave is trying to get at is the earnest questioning and doubting that is constitutive of the human experience of the divine.

The role that doubt plays in the dialectic of faith is not pejorative or negative, by Cave's lights. On this account, doubt is not a weaker or inferior form of faith, which the believer seeks to overcome or extirpate, nor does it represent a less sophisticated relationship of the human to the divine. On the contrary, Cave is advancing doubt as a positive and essential part of faith's dynamic. Doubt and faith, rather than being two antithetical concepts, go hand in hand. In fact, doubt is constitutive of faith itself. Doubt does not undermine belief in God: it is simply another face or moment of faith, of no less personal value to religious experience than the certitude Cave expresses elsewhere. Hence, doubt is essential and fundamental to faith: the dialectical interplay between doubt and certitude is the condition making a divine-human encounter possible.

Two existential and phenomenological implications of Cave's view are highly significant. First, as the practical outcome of such a position on faith, doubt is a recurring, if not continual, part of religious subjectivity. It is part of the personal experience of the believer and integrally linked to the stance of faith itself. Second, despite the thematic presence of doubt in the believer's personal experience of God, belief itself is never deeply at risk. Although doubt may loom more urgently in the phenomenology of faith at times, the fundamental character of faith as *belief* is never truly in question. Thus, on this issue Cave's position matches Kant's: "Faith can waver, but never fall into unbelief."[9] The belief can be cashed out attitudinally in quite different ways, but it is no less a touchstone to the divine when questioning as when petitioning. In his lyrics and writings, Cave expresses attitudes of doubt and agnosticism, supplication and petitioning, as well as love and devotion. Yet each of these subjective positions is as much a true and genuine moment of faith and experience of the divine. Hence, the experience of the believer as a doubter is no less valuable than the experience of supplication, petition, devotion, or love. God is to be found in the painful experience of longing and loneliness—even of forsakenness—as much as in contemplative wonderment of the lovely and amazing.

The phenomenology of faith that Cave supplies us with gives a clue to understanding the sort of model he has in mind. Because the experiential nature of the subjective religious experience takes pride of place over sterile proofs for God's existence, Cave is recommending that the divine be found through an inward turn. When we make the inward turn suggested by Cave's writings, we are truly able to communicate with the divine and find a medium through which we can experience and relate to God. This conception of the divine-human encounter is highly revelatory and deeply connected with individual human experience, more than with the world itself. Our looking without may stimulate questioning about God, but ultimately God is revealed more by the looking within. As Cave makes clear in one of his most purely devotional songs, God's kingdom is both without and within us:

Just like a bird that sends up the sun, so very dark, . . . such is my faith for you, such is my faith. All the world's darkness can't swallow up a single spark, such is my love for you, such is my love. There is a kingdom, there is a king and he lives without and he lives within. The starry heavens above me, the moral law within, so the world appears.[10]

Apart from the simple devotional themes of faith and love expressed in this song, the explicit reference to Kant is instructive. Cave directly quotes

Kant's famous comment in the *Critique of Practical Reason* that the two things moving him deeply are the starry heavens above and the moral law within. It is clear that Cave intends the comment in much the same way as Kant does: it is a reflection on the firmness and security of belief, while facing the rigid inflexibility of the natural world, and on the reality of the moral realm we encounter within ourselves. Kant wants to have morality, freedom, and human agency always be supported by our consciousness of the moral law within. Cave's gloss on the notion of the moral law within emphasizes the inwardness and "within-edness" of the presence of the divine. For our understanding of Cave, it thus is critical that we focus on the inward turn as the channel for experiencing the divine. The purpose of Cave's appeal to the Kantian reference is to denote the importance and immediacy of the human experience of the divine presence within ourselves. We encounter God by looking both outwardly at the world—at the starry heavens above—but also directly and inwardly, by accessing the divine world within. So, Cave is indicating the immanence of God in our own personal experience: God is not just an object of metaphysical speculation or philosophical discourse, but a live presence in our inner lives. As such, the kingdom of God is both within and without, and the consciousness of this kingdom is alienable, despite the darkness and brutality of the world.

In "Bless His Ever Loving Heart" and "He Wants You," Cave articulates the personal, interactive, and living nature of God in human life. Far from being an abstract entity or distant presence, the God described in these songs is "straight and true," the only one who truly knows each individual. The relationship depicted here is of a highly caring, personal nature, with a gentle, loving God who knows the depths of the human heart and is intimately present in human life. In "He Wants You," Cave describes a God who speaks gently to us in our dreams and in our everyday experiences, whose presence is immanent in our lives, and who wants us to enter into a personal relationship with him. In "Bless His Ever Loving Heart," Cave addresses the suffering endemic to human life and appeals to the loving and comforting nature of a benevolent God who truly knows the depths of the human heart. Even when God seems "so very far," he always knows who we are and is ever loving. Far from being a model of an austere or distant, purely theoretical God in a heaven above, Cave is clearly advancing a notion of an interactive, relational God, with whom it is possible to have a real and personal rapport. The confidence in the "hand that protects me . . . with every breath that I breathe and everything I know"[11] expresses the other face of faith's dialectic: confidence in the presence of God. Just as doubt is a real and urgent part of religious experience for Cave, a profound and ultimately secure belief in the immanence and active presence of God in human life is equally real and constitutive of religious subjectivity. The clearest example of the two seemingly opposing themes of doubt and confident devotion are expressed on the 1997 album *The Boatman's Call*, in which Cave works at many religious themes and adopts both stances described above. Oscillating between skeptical questioning and deep devotion, the attitude of *The Boatman's Call* is profoundly religious and philosophical, crystallizing Cave's various positions on religious phenomenology.

These two moments of faith, doubt and certitude, are punctuated throughout Cave's work by an attitude of supplication, which is cashed out both in terms of petition and impassioned pleas. In "No More Shall We Part," Cave entreats, "Lord, stay by me,"[12] in an attitude of patient and respectful prayer. In "Oh My Lord," Cave is abject and supplicant: "How have I offended thee? Wrap your tender arms around me, Oh Lord, Oh my Lord."[13] These are two of Cave's most intense and passionate songs and express an attitude of petitionary submission to God, as well as a desire and yearning for the divine presence. Cave takes loss, longing, and sorrow as intrinsic parts of human existence and fundamentally as appeals to God. He argues that all songs of love, despair, praise, rage, and so on truly address God. These songs speak to the deepest yearning and need of human beings, "the desire to be transported from darkness into light, to be touched by the hand of that which is not of this world, . . . the light of God."[14] As such, longing for the divine expressed in petition, prayer, and supplication is a constitutive part of religious phenomenology and subjectivity—in fact, according to Cave's conception of the nature of human life, longing for the divine is a necessary component of *any* human experience.

The longing to feel the presence of the divine is what motivates us to look for answers, whether we do so doubtingly, trustingly, or in fervent supplication. We saw that Cave rejects the interventionist model of the divine-human encounter because it radically disconnects God from our personal experience of him. Rather than waiting for a miracle-working God to strike us with his presence, we need to look for him. When we gaze passively for answers in the starry heavens above, we fundamentally mistake the world he created. We miss his presence when we focus intently on the outside world, with its attendant miseries and sufferings, being governed by natural laws. The inward turn represents where our focus should be in our search for the divine touchpoint; it is only our subjective experience that is profoundly revelatory for us. Although both the starry skies above and the moral law within are part of the divine, it is only the inner world that is specifically designed for the divine-human encounter. We can sometimes see God at work in the world, yet it is in the turn to inner experience that we encounter a living, breathing God present within the phenomenology of subjective experience. The wonders of the world are "out there," but there are more immanent and immediate truths about the divine to be found through inwardness. What distinguishes the outward look from the inward look is that the latter supplies us with a dialogue, a two-way organic relationship, in which both God and human beings participate actively. Thus, the model depicted on this reading is relational and interactive.

The Inward Turn and the Creative Imagination

As we have seen, what occupies pride of place in Cave's treatment of the divine-human encounter is the personal, subjective, and relational attitude of faith. His depiction of the model of divine-human rapport is best described as interactionist rather than interventionist. I take this to be the primary motivation for his statement "I don't believe in an interventionist God." Cave is simply drawing attention to the fact that the import of belief in God is not about metaphysics, but about subjectivity. He does this rather than advancing a metaphysical deus ex machina position about the extent to which God intervenes in human affairs or the mechanics of a world inhabited by beings with free will. Hence, his assertion that God is not an interventionist God and "does not change the march of events" is not to be read as a rejection of the robust relationship of the divine to the human. Instead, it is a vigorous restatement of his fundamental thesis that the divine-human encounter is relational and interactive. Because faith for Cave is ultimately a very personal connection to a living God, he does not think it can be adequately cashed out in terms of catechism or ritual, and it cannot be buttressed by traditional religious beliefs in the Trinity or the incarnation. The incarnation, for example, is instructive for human beings only insofar as the life of Jesus qua man is the life of the lonely sufferer. As we see more explicitly in the next section, Cave makes it quite clear that the loneliness and rejection felt by Jesus is what connects him so tightly with the experience of human beings. The thrust of the Gospels is to portray the life of Jesus as man, as lonely, misunderstood sufferer in a world of mediocrity. Cave interprets the biblical narrative of Christ as man as a call

to the imagination, to elevate ourselves above the mundanity and mediocrity of human existence: "to become Godlike."

In his lecture "The Flesh Made Word," Cave argues vigorously for the
novel and startlingly heterodox thesis that the medium through which
humanity and God interact is the creative imagination. Through the
creative process itself individuals can access and truly experience the presence of the divine. Cave's radical claim is that the locus of the divine-
human encounter is the creative imagination, and that the imagination
thus provides the critical link between the human and the divine. He
draws on the Gospels as evidence that the life of Jesus is instructive for us
primarily because that life is a flight of the imagination that then appeals
to our own imaginations as a way of accessing God.

Cave provocatively asserts: "There is a God. God is a product of the
creative imagination, and God is that imagination taken flight."[15] This
bold statement can easily be misread as stating that God is *merely* a product of the imagination, a sort of constructivist or psychological fiction.[16]
Hence, one might read this as an argument reducing belief in God to a
psychological fiction or construct, while denying that there is any metaphysical validity to the concept of God. With the interpretation given
here, it is not difficult to see why this statement might give one pause. This
is not Cave's position, however.[17] It is not in question for Cave that there is
a God and that this God is a real, living, existent entity with whom we can
have a meaningful relationship. His concern, as recognized above, is not
with the *metaphysics* of divine existence but with the nature of the divine-
human encounter itself. Cave is not doing metaphysics; he is chiefly concerned with the *phenomenology* of the subjective religious experience.[18] So
when Cave advances the claim that God is a product of creative imagination, this ought not to be read as a metaphysical thesis about the existence
or nonexistence of God. Instead, Cave is making a point about human subjectivity in its relationship to the divine. The thrust of Cave's position is that
it is through the creative process—the imagination taken flight—that
humanity and God can encounter one another and communicate.

Cave argues that the imagination is the place where a human being and
God meet: the language of creative inspiration is the tongue with which a
person and God can communicate. Hence, through the creative process one
can access and experience God. Cave's treatment of the role of the imagination in the divine-human encounter gives pride of place to the creative
process as both the locus and language that link humanity and the divine.
However, his basic thesis is that creative activity does not "construct" God

but instead provides the language and channel for God to be brought into immanent reality. As he explains, the creative process allows us direct access to the imagination and "ultimately to God": "I found that through the use of language I was writing God into existence, . . . the actualizing of God through the medium of the love song remains my prime motivation as an artist."[19]

The idea at play here is that God "needs" us to become immanent in our reality: this is part of what Cave means when he argues that he does not believe in an interventionist God. God does not intervene in human life. Instead, he speaks through us only if we allow him to, through a flight of the creative imagination, which transports us from the human—the mundane—to the divine. Thus, there is an interdependence between humanity and God, in that God requires the creative activity of human beings to find a voice in the world.

It is important to understand exactly what Cave is saying here. He is not claiming that without human imagination, God would have no metaphysical existence; but he is declaring that the focal point of religion is the place where humanity and God meet. The chief concern here is with the interrelationship between humanity and God and that there is an interdependence at the level of expression in a human world. As Cave elucidates:

> Just as we are divine creations, so we must in turn create. Divinity must be given its freedom to flow, through us, through language, through communication, through imagination. . . . Through us God finds His voice, for just as we need God, He in turn needs us.[20]

What Cave is driving at is that the meaningfulness of God in human life occurs at the level of creative expression, because it is through us that God finds a voice in the world. Thus, through communication and communion with other human beings, through love, language, and the imagination, God finds a foothold in a human world. The divine can meaningfully interact with the human through language and creativity, because the imagination functions as an avenue where God and human beings can share a voice. Without human acts of creative expression, without the activity of the imagination as the critical link between heaven and earth, God does not lose existence, but loses immanence and presence: He loses his voice. Our activity of creative expression allows God to speak to us and through us: without that channel, God would have no medium through which to reach human beings. As Cave explains: "Rather than praising a personal supernatural God as an almighty, all-knowing, all-seeing force existing somewhere in the great beyond, the emphasis is placed clearly on man, that without him as a channel God has nowhere to go."[21]

Cave buttresses his arguments concerning the role of the creative imagination in the divine-human encounter with a reading of the New Testament that places Jesus' life as the "man of sorrows" at the center. Cave takes the chief message of the life of Christ to be an appeal to the imagination, an invitation to take up the inspiration brought to humanity by the divine. The thrust of Cave's reading is that the main message of Christ's life on earth is an appeal to humanity to rise above the shackles of mundanity and mediocrity so characteristic of human existence. Thus, the divine command enjoins us to be Christlike by taking flight from the world of earthly things to the divine, through the active use of the imagination. He makes much of the story of Jesus stooping to write in the sand and then declaring, "Let anyone among you who is without sin be the first to throw a stone at her" (John 8:6–8). Cave interprets the act of stooping and writing in the sand as Jesus engaging his own creative imagination as a way of reaching out to God.

Although Cave is explicit about the fact that he despises the church, he is drawn to the Bible and in particular the Gospels and the example set of Christ's life. The really relevant aspect of the Gospels that backstops Cave's interpretation is the humanness of Christ: Christ the man, the lonely sufferer. So, it is Christ's "creative potent sorrow" and his "boiling anger"[22] that really entreat us and speak to us on a level that we can comprehend. This humanness gives us a touchpoint into the divine. Christ is not some abstract or serene portrait on a church wall. As Cave puts it, rather than revering Christ on pitifully bent knees, we ought to be "aspiring to" reach God through the active use of the creative imagination, which frees us from "the mundanity of our existences." Cave takes the main message of the life of Christ to be an example of the creative imagination taken flight. He sees it as a message of liberation for human beings chained to a mediocre life of loneliness and misunderstanding.

> Christ came as a liberator. Christ understood that we as humans were forever held to the ground by the pull of gravity—our ordinariness, our mediocrity—and it was through His example that He gave our imaginations the freedom to rise and to fly. In short, to be Christ-like.[23]

> He came with the gift of language, or love, of imagination. Said Jesus, the Gospel of John, "The words that I speak unto you, they

are spirit and they are life" [John 6:63], and it is these words, His language, the *logos*, that sings so eloquently and mysteriously from the Gospels. Christ is the imagination, at times terrible, irrational, incendiary and beautiful—in short, God-like.[24]

Put simply, Cave argues that the creative imagination enables the individual and God to interact directly, precisely because it is the active use of the imagination that allows human beings to rise above existence and aspire to reach upward toward the divine. The ability to communicate and to create—through language, love, and the imagination—is part of what enables human beings experience and access God. Through our creative acts of imagination and expression, through our communion and interaction with other human beings, we allow God to speak through us by giving him a voice that would otherwise be silenced. So, the interactive model described in section 1 involves an interdependence between an individual and God. Humanity and God can meaningfully interact, and the divine can be present to us in our lives, but we must be active in the process for the process to be actual. This means that there is an active human component to the divine-human encounter. Not only must the human subject be open to the presence of the divine; it is also up to the human being to bring God into immanence by giving him a voice, by creating, by accessing the imagination. Without that voice, God can only speak to us in our dreams and remain a voiceless, silent, shapeless presence in the world.

As observed in the previous section, the focus is again on the interrelationship between the human subject, rather than merely on divine majesty or the gap between a wretched humanity and a brutal, all-powerful God. The real burden of Cave's discussion addresses the human subject as one who experiences the divine, encountering the realm of the divine through the active use of one's own creative powers. Rather than accentuating the vast differences between human and God, Cave's position enacts a rapprochement between the human and the divine—with the life of Christ as the critical link—by locating an avenue where the divine and the human can meaningfully interact.

In light of this understanding of the divine-human encounter, let us look at back at the aforementioned lyric from "Are You the One That I've Been Waiting For?" It states: "There's a man who spoke wonders, well, I've never met him, he said 'he who seeks finds and who knocks will be let in.'" Notice that it is the man who spoke wonders whom the lyricist has not met in experience. The God of miracles is not the sense of the divine present to us; instead, it is the God we find when we seek and petition actively, the God we access though the creative imagination. In the song "Into My Arms," Cave begins with his statement that he does not believe in an interventionist God, then concludes by claiming that "we can choose our path and walk like Christ in grace and love." Cave's injunction in *As I Sat Sadly by Her Side* also instructs us that God "does not care for you to sit in judgment of the world he created, while sorrows pile up around you: ugly, useless and overinflated."[25] The view of the divine-human encounter Cave carves out enjoins an attitude of activity and engagement, not passivity, inertia, or pessimism toward ourselves, the world, and God. Rather, it entreats us to search for and bring about the wondrous in life that is there if we strive for it. Thereby we truly experience God as present to us. We are called not solely to gaze up to the starry heavens above, wishing for relief from the loss, longing, and harshness of this life, but to turn to the moral law within, to God's voice within us. To remain entrenched in the mediocrity and mundanity of existence is to fail to reach out to God, to misunderstand the world he has created, and to ignore the demands of human subjectivity: the yearning of the human subject for the divine.[26]

Conclusion

What is highly revelatory about the inward turn Cave suggests is that it offers us a conception of the divine-human encounter that is decisively and definitively linked to human subjectivity. The inward turn is an embracing of human subjectivity in its relationship both to the world and to the divine. What is front and center on this view is what we can contribute to the God relationship, not merely what we can get from it. In short, we are active in creating a space for God to be present to us. The force and insight of this active rapport-based model of the divine-human relationship is that it asks us to look at the world differently, which in turn allows us to meet God in our lives. No distant, austere metaphysical entity, the relational God of the subjective human experience is engaged, present, immanent, and part of an organic relationship with humanity. Hence, the "haunted premise of the love song" that ultimately addresses God is not a "cry in the void," for God is always with us.[27] To look at the mediocrity of the world is to fail to understand God, for he is part of both the miserable and the wonderful. The inward turn reveals God to us through our active use the imagination. When we do look within, we see that God has been here all along. We just needed to give him a voice.

Notes

1. Nick Cave, interviewed by Mick Brown, "Cave's New World," *The Age* (Australia), May 31, 1998; online: http://www.bad-seed.org/~cave/interviews/98-05-31_theage.html.

2. Mick Harvey, Nick Cave's longtime friend and comember of the bands The Birthday Party and The Bad Seeds, calls the early work the "fire and brimstone Nick" and the later Cave the "newly humanitarian Nick." I shall focus on the latter, without ignoring or rejecting the former.

3. Cave, "Into my arms," in Nick Cave, *The Complete Lyrics, 1978–2001* (London: Penguin Books, 2001), 271.

4. Cave, *As I Sat Sadly by Her Side*, in *Complete Lyrics*, 303–4.

5. In his lecture "The Flesh Made Word" (in *King Ink II* [London: Black Spring, 1997], 137–42), Cave devotes some time to developing the thesis that the Old Testament represents God improving himself through the life of Jesus. Thus, he claims that "Jesus came to right the wrongs of the Father."

6. Cave points out that part of what motivates this apparent ambivalence in his depiction of the stance of faith is the Bible itself, especially the Psalms: "What I found, time and time again in the Bible, especially in the Old Testament, was that the verses of rapture, of ecstasy and love could hold within them apparently opposite sentiments—hate, revenge, bloody-mindedness, etc.—these sentiments were not mutually exclusive. This idea has left an enduring impression upon my song-writing." Nick Cave, *The Secret Life of the Love Song*, in *Complete Lyrics*, 10–11.

7. Nick Cave and the Bad Seeds, "There Is a Town," *Nocturama* (recorded, 2002; London: Mute Records, 2003).

8. Cave, "Are You the One That I've Been Waiting For?" in *Complete Lyrics*, 271.

9. I. Kant, *Critique of Pure Reason* (many editions).

10. Cave, "There Is a Kingdom," in *Complete Lyrics*, 271.

11. Cave, "Lime-Tree Arbour," in *Complete Lyrics*, 267.

12. Cave, "No More Shall We Part," in *Complete Lyrics*, 305.

13. Cave, "Oh My Lord," in *Complete Lyrics*, 316–18.

14. Nick Cave, "Secret Life," in *Complete Lyrics*, 7.

15. Nick Cave, lecture, "The Flesh Made Word," in *King Ink II*, 137.

16. Nietzsche and Freud, for examples, both argue for versions of constructivism and psychological reductionism about religion and theism that reduce belief in God to a psychological creation or fiction.

17. This is not to say that the sociology and psychology of belief has no purchase in Cave's position. Cave makes perfectly clear the influence that the death of his father and his own feelings of anger, loss, loneliness, and longing have profoundly influenced his relationship to God and his reading of the Bible. However, although he takes stock of the biographical influences on his personal belief in God and his biblical interpretation, he by no means maintains that religious belief is merely a matter of sociology.

18. On this point, the positions of Cave and Kierkegaard are of a piece.

19. Nick Cave, "Secret Life," in *Complete Lyrics*, 6.

20. Cave, "The Flesh Made Word," in *King Ink II*, 142.

21. Ibid.

22. Nick Cave, "Introduction to the Gospel according to Mark," in *Mark's Gospel* (KJV; Pocket Canon; Edinburgh: Canongate, 1998), xi; online: http://members.fortunecity.com/vanessa77/index700.html.

23. Ibid., xii.

24. Cave, "The Flesh Made Word," 140–41.

25. Cave, *As I Sat Sadly by Her Side*, in *Complete Lyrics*, 303–4.

26. Again, Cave's view is of a piece with Kierkegaard's claim that to despair is to fail to will the eternal.

27. Nick Cave, "Secret Life," in *Complete Lyrics*, 6.

Metallica and the God That Failed

An Unfinished Tragedy in Three Acts

—Paul Martens

Fall to your knees
And bow to the Phantom Lord.[1]

—Metallica

THE PURPOSE OF THE FOLLOWING ESSAY is to analyze the significance and development of Metallica's entanglement with Christianity, or to state it another way, to analyze Metallica as an emphatically religious band. In short, my thesis is that the notions of sin, guilt, forgiveness, and especially evil perpetually haunt Metallica's lyrics, shaping the lyrical corpus into a tragedy. It is a tragedy properly construed through a theologically sensitive perspective alone. Metallica is a San Francisco–based heavy metal band formed in the early 1980s around guitarist/vocalist James Hetfield and drummer Lars Ulrich. It is shaped by punk and New Wave of British Heavy Metal musical influences (Iron Maiden, Diamond Head).[2]

With the ambitious, self-referential choice of "Metallica," this young group attempted to stylize themselves as the quintessence of metal. The name assumes, however, what is usually uncertain or misconstrued: an accurate understanding of the nature of heavy metal. Some clarity may help to diffuse immediate visceral responses that might be predisposed to foreclose the following discussion concerning Metallica before it even begins. To some, heavy metal is, in all cases, "ugly guys singing ugly things to ugly music."[3] To some, it embodies a shameless attack on the "central values of Western civilization."[4] Robert Duncan penned the following frequently cited censure of heavy metal that imposingly stands before any attempt to take an example from the genre seriously:

> Heavy metal: pimply, prole, putrid, unchic, unsophisticated, anti-intellectual (but impossibly pretentious), dismal, abysmal, terrible, horrible, and stupid music, barely music at all; death music, dead music, the beaten boogie, the dance of defeat and decay; the *huh?* sound, the *duh* sound, . . . music made *by* slack-jawed, alpaca-haired, bulbous-inseamed imbeciles in jackboots and leather and chrome *for* slack-jawed, alpaca-haired, downy-mustachioed imbeciles in cheap, too-large T-shirts with pictures of comic-book Armageddon ironed on the front.[5]

A closer look at heavy metal, however, illuminates and corrects the overblown, comical, and simply misguided nature of the above rhetoric.

To begin, heavy metal is, and is not, a unified genre.[6] Yes, it is music that emphasizes volume, power, and intensity.[7] Yes, one could say it is "energetic and highly amplified electronic rock music having a hard beat."[8] And yes, perhaps the one feature that underpins the coherence of heavy metal is the power chord.[9] However, none of these notoriously facile definitions provides any insight into the vast difference between the classically inspired guitar virtuosity of Yngwie Malmsteen, the frantic ranting of Anthrax, and the simplistic anthems of Twisted Sister and early Bon Jovi.

If a musical family resemblance still remains, attention to lyrical content further convolutes the picture. For example, it is virtually impossible to distill any sort of coherent unity from the diverse lyrics of Stryper's "In God We Trust," Mötley Crüe's "Girls, Girls, Girls," Guns N' Roses' "Civil War," and Megadeth's "Symphony of Destruction."[10] And, apparently easily identifiable shared themes (death, war, and violence) derived from a literal reading of lyrical fragments usually miss the individuating techniques of sarcasm, irony, metaphoric or hyperbolic language, or contextualization within lyrical wholes (meaning entire songs, albums, or groups of albums). As the ensuing essay methodologically examines the development of Metallica's lyrical corpus, recognizing and deconstructing tendencies toward artificial generalizations on this level are fundamentally important to opening the way for letting their lyrics speak for themselves, on their own terms, within their own context.

What then can one say about heavy metal? At least, one can begin with the historical connotations of the term "heavy metal": military references to large guns carrying balls of a large size (1828) and figurative references to power, influence, and great ability, as in "he is a man of heavy metal" (1882).[11] Certainly, these meanings are enfolded in all the positive and negative contemporary attributions of the term to the genre. By most accounts, this music style originated sometime in the late 1960s or early 1970s with founding bands such as Led Zeppelin and Black Sabbath.[12] One can then identify the musical family resemblance discussed above. To move further in a general way, however, is difficult. More honest than most, Robert Walser rightly observes that any precise definition of heavy metal depends on the ongoing arguments of those involved, and like all culture, it is "a site of struggle over definitions, dreams, behaviors, and resources."[13]

Surely, Metallica fits musically within the family of heavy metal; their lyrics also constitute a site of struggle over definitions, dreams, behaviors, and resources. Metallica, however, is not merely a generic heavy metal band. First, not only did Metallica pioneer thrash/speed metal in the early 1980s; they also went on to become the most commercially successful heavy metal band in history, and they show no signs of stopping. As of 2003, Metallica had sold over eighty-five million CDs and albums. This feat may provide some hindsight into the ambitions lying behind the initial arrogance of their self-referential name choice. They are currently the seventh biggest-selling group of artists in U.S. recording history. Even their closest competitors within the genre—such as Iron Maiden, Guns N' Roses, and Korn—do not come close in commercial terms.[14]

Second, Metallica is unique in its lyrical content and development. Admittedly, they follow some of the more familiar provocations by offending their detractors with repeatedly misunderstood lyrics about hatred and rage, about death, and about alcohol and drug use. Nonetheless, their frequently polemical engagement with Christianity is perhaps their most individuating characteristic. For this reason, they strike fear into the hearts of their critics. According to Barbara Wyatt, the president of the politically influential Parents' Music Resource Center (PMRC), this constitutes a direct attack on the values of Western (or at least American) civilization.[15] Following her appeal to the United States Senate Commerce Committee to enforce labeling of music for indecent and immoral content on June 16, 1998, she closed with the following statement:

> We are all familiar with the words from the Bible which state
> "Bring up a child in the way he should go and when he is old he
> will not depart from it." The [recording] industry is constantly cap-
> turing our next generation. Morality, civility and virtues have made
> civilizations prosper and have been the basis for noble leadership.
> Today that is lacking in America. We can either be the beacon on
> the hill for good or the Sodom and Gomorrah of the next century.[16]

Clearly, a particular theological orientation lies behind the moral and civil
virtues that Wyatt and the PMRC champion, an orientation that not only
assumes a belief in God, but also a conviction that belief in God corresponds
to particular moral and civil virtues that undergird the health of American
civilization. Deena Weinstein sums up the obvious when she concludes that
"fundamentalists" like Wyatt are convinced that music is a tool of the
antichrist.[17] Fulfilling Wyatt's worst fears, select atheists openly embrace
Metallica's lyrics (especially "Leper Messiah," but also "The God That
Failed") on such websites as "Alabama Atheist"[18] and "The Secular Web."[19]

The difficulty with this atheistic description and appropriation is that
Metallica does not neatly fit the expected nonreligious heavy metal pro-
file,[20] nor do they uniformly fulfill the anti-Christian, anti-American pro-
file expected by critics such as Wyatt. As this essay illustrates, the story is
much more complex. It demonstrates that if Metallica's lyrics amount to
atheism (and this is certainly up for grabs), they amount to a theological
or religious atheism. To my mind, this is not an oxymoron: I mean that
despite Metallica's explicit questioning and criticism of Christianity and
its God, conceptions of God, along with theologically informed notions of
sin, guilt, forgiveness, and especially evil, continue to haunt their lives and
lyrics. As stated at the outset, the persistence of these notions shapes the
lyrical corpus as a tragedy, a tragedy properly construed from a theologically sensitive perspective alone. To support and illuminate this claim, the
remainder of the chapter traces the tripartite theological development of
Metallica's lyrical corpus. It begins with their early rejection of God,
moves through their later introspective recognition of sin and need for forgiveness, and concludes with their recent failing attempts to reassert independent control over themselves.[21]

Act 1: Death, Madness, and the God That Failed

Many of Metallica's lyrics owe their existence to a history that precedes
Metallica itself. After all, how can one write or sing about rejecting God

if one does not know about God, or has not initially accepted God? How can one write about God's failure unless there is some expectation of what it would mean for God to succeed? These questions find many of their answers in the early life of James Hetfield, Metallica's lead singer and sole lyrical composer.[22] Hetfield has starkly summed up the scarring experiences of his early life as follows:

> I was raised as a Christian Scientist, which is a strange religion. The main rule is, God will fix everything. Your body is just a shell, you don't need doctors. It was alienating and hard to understand. I couldn't get a physical to play football. It was weird having to leave health class during school, and all the kids saying, "Why do you have to leave? Are you some kind of freak?" As a kid, you want to be part of the team. They're always whispering about you and thinking you're weird. That was very upsetting. My dad taught Sunday school—he was into it. It was pretty much forced upon me. We had these little testimonials, and there was a girl that had her arm broken. She stood up and said, "I broke my arm but now, look, it's all better." But it was just, like, mangled. Now that I think about it, it was pretty disturbing.[23]

Nursing and nurturing these experiences, Hetfield therapeutically spit out nihilistic lyrics filled with anger, hatred, and condemnation over the first decade of Metallica's existence.

In these early years, war is one of the most prevalent and obvious metaphors of chaos and existential meaninglessness. "For Whom the Bell Tolls"[24] gives the perspective of someone observing an unknown army storming an unknown hill in the early morning; it poignantly captures Metallica's not yet fully articulated point of view. The bleak cold and gray imagery of twilight reiterates the explicit questioning: "On they fight, for they are right, yes, but who's to say?" The song then sharpens this question while simultaneously broadening it beyond the limits of war by turning to focus on a single mortally wounded soldier, staring blindly up at the sky through blackened eyes before fading to the chorus of "For whom the bell tolls, Time marches on."[25] Innocence is lost. The brutal reality of war is chaos, undifferentiated meaningless chaos.

Two years later, "Disposable Heroes"[26] echoed similar themes more pointedly by attacking the notion that young men are merely empty shells for military or governmental authorities to manipulate at will. Written from the dual perspectives of a young soldier and his superior, the barked lyrics attributable to a superior—"Back to the front, You will die when I say, you must die"[27]—exemplify the connection between arbitrary authority and meaninglessness. Innocence is not even lost, since it has never existed; the soldier boy is merely a lump of clay to be molded into a disposable fighting machine. It is impossible not to shudder before the almost remorseless cry, "I was born for dying."[28] The soldier is blind though perfectly healthy. Returning to the tragic horror of "For Whom the Bell Tolls," "One"[29] imaginatively recounts the thoughts of a soldier who has lost all his limbs, his eyes, his ears, and his ability to speak in a land-mine explosion. The heartrending final chorus echoes the pathetic unfulfillable hopes of the damaged man: "Now the world is gone I'm just one / Oh God, help me hold my breath as I wish for death / Oh please God, help me."[30]

Is "One," with its overpowering empathetic appeal, an antiwar song? No. In the face of increasing antiwar interests in 1991, Hetfield personally addressed a group of activists while on tour in Italy and emphatically stated, "All it is, is a big fucking song about a guy who steps on a land mine!"[31] But, of course, this is not all it is. So, what is this (and the other similarly themed war songs)[32] about then? Tentatively, I suggest that they graphically depict Hetfield's view of life: meaningless blind chaos, inevitable death, and helplessness in the avoidance or bringing about of death. To support this conclusion, however, one must also attend to the other pertinent themes of madness, hypocrisy, and religion.

From the point of view of a sane resident of an asylum, "Welcome Home (Sanitarium)"[33] blames the artificial constraints and expectations of the sanitarium (which may or may not be taken literally) for the creation of the "mentally deranged" protagonist. In the beginning the protagonist appears to be wholly sane, but the imposed protective cage of restrictions, fear, and whisperings eventually creates the insanity, creates the hell that it allegedly seeks to diminish. Despite the protagonist's cries of "Sanitarium, leave me be," the pressure builds until the protagonist finally resolves to release himself: "'Kill,' it's such a friendly word / Seems the only way / For reaching out again."[34] The problem is tragic, the solution equally so. Most terrible of all is that the song is, in truth, about "the real-life horrors of the world at large."[35]

What "Welcome Home (Sanitarium)" describes metaphorically, Metallica specifies in a variety of ways. In these early years, external arbitrary and hypocritical limitations and confinements in "the world at large" are a recurring source of anger and hatred. On one hand, aside from the allusions already present in the lyrics discussed above, the internal organizational structures and policies of America take a beating. "Blackened," with its bleak prognostication of nuclear holocaust, attacks the cold war proliferation of nuclear weapons. ". . . And Justice for All" laments the hypocritical state of justice in America: "Justice is lost / Justice is raped / Justice is gone."[36] And "Eye of the Beholder" bitterly decries the arbitrary and fear-motivated censorship enforced by parents and such groups as the PMRC, which, according to Metallica, does little more than stifle choice, imagination, and freedom. All of these songs appeared on . . . And Justice for All, and Hetfield later admitted that on that particular album "we stayed to the shitty side—not 'America sucks' but we pointed out the scary parts."[37]

On the other hand, Hetfield also specifies God as a source of his anger and hatred. Metallica's critique of God, however, is not as straightforward as their critique of America simply because Hetfield's God was so powerfully mediated to him through his parents and his early experiences as a Christian Scientist. He first implicates God in the arbitrary chaos of war, then in the hypocrisy of those in power; finally, he attacks God directly . . . through his parents.

The first oblique critique of God appears in "Creeping Death,"[38] a song recounting God's rescue of the Israelites from Egypt through multiple plagues, and most importantly, the slaughter of Egypt's firstborn sons. Defiantly, Hetfield wrote the lyrics through the eyes of the destroyer sent by God to fulfill the killing. In trying to make sense of this song, Chris Ingham, editor of the magazine Metal Hammer, begins his assessment as follows: "Rather strangely, this tale of murder most foul is set in ancient Egypt; maybe James had been watching one too many re-runs of Charlton Heston in The Ten Commandments before entering the studio?"[39] Ingham is right to link "Creeping Death" with Moses and the plagues that the song addresses;[40] Ingham is probably wrong to attribute the inspiration of this song to The Ten Commandments. Rather, it makes more sense to read this song as the first intentional shot in Hetfield's battle with the Christianity of his past, and it is not merely a shot over the bow. The more mature Hetfield is fascinated, and horrified, by a God who can command this kind of murder. The critique lies in the intensified irony of the youth who used to believe that God will fix everything, but now writing of a messenger of God who sings: "Die by my hand. . . . I shall soon be there, deadly mass," and then goes on to self-righteously proclaim: "I'm creeping death."[41] Already, it is clear that God cannot be the source of salvation from the chaos and arbitrary meaningless of violence and war; God is inextricably part of it, thereby divinely sanctioning its meaninglessness while heightening the tragic power of fate.[42]

Another oblique attack on God occurs through Metallica's mockery of hypocritical purveyors of Christianity. First, in "Leper Messiah,"[43] Hetfield's object of scorn is the (stereotypical) lying, money-hungry preacher who seeks fame and power through his "tricks." This is the abominable work of the leper messiah. Giving in to him is another way to lose one's life, to become blind in a new way. Likewise, "Holier than Thou"[44] challenges the excesses present in "Leper Messiah" and yet shows that the true object of Hetfield's scorn is judgmental arrogance. Speaking in the first person, he rancorously taunts: "Before you judge me, take a look at you / Can't you find something better to do?"[45] Certainly, one cannot help but be amused by the fact that after almost a decade of judging and blaming others, Metallica's own introspective self-examination is still a few years away. This fact, however, does not detract from the existential angst dripping from the lyrics, lyrics that do, in fact, appear to recognize and respect the difference between God and the excesses of certain prose-lytizers. Analogous to Hetfield's summation of their attitude to America, these two songs do not necessarily say "God sucks," but they do "stay to the shitty side," pointing out the scary parts of contemporary Christianity. For this reason, "Creeping Death" is a much more damning song than the apparently more obvious "Leper Messiah" and "Holier than Thou."

Finally, directly developing the increasingly irrational rage and hatred described above in "Welcome Home (Sanitarium)," Hetfield links the moral and spiritual boundaries—another kind of cage of restrictions, fear, and whispering—imposed by his parents with God's failure. With its pregnant title, "Dyer's Eve"[46] is Hetfield's earliest first-person desperate cry for—and therefore against—his parents. Here Hetfield immerses his listener in his visceral rage directed toward his parents (simultaneously believers and deceivers) who sheltered him within the false innocence and shelter of their Christian Scientism. He rants about getting his wings clipped before he learned to fly, about not being given a chance to think for himself; he rants about being unprepared, unable to cope with the horrors of the world. He rants: "I'm in hell without you / Cannot cope without you two / Shocked at the world that I see."[47] Though claiming to see the world beyond innocence, Hetfield admits that he is really "living blindly" in shock, again invoking the imagery of the land-mine victim in "One": hearing nothing, seeing nothing, saying nothing, paralyzed by the chaos of reality.[48]

Three years later, his parents again appear as believers and deceivers . . . and the deceived. "The God That Failed"[49] directly addresses the death of Hetfield's mother, who died of cancer when he was only seventeen. As a Christian Scientist, she refused treatment. Her son believes that had she not done so, she could have beaten the cancer and still be alive today.[50] It is not surprising, then, that Hetfield makes the parallels between death-dealing cancer and Christian Scientism. He acknowledges that his mother had faith; he acknowledges that she trusted she would be healed. He also demands that her cloudy mind, colonized by falsehoods, could not discern truth from lie. Her physical death points back to the greater hopelessness and meaningless, not only for her, but also for her son, James: "Trust you gave / A child to save / Left you cold and him in grave."[51] The specific divine failure is his mother's death; the general divine failure is the mad world that is nothing other than pride, betrayal, deceit, and death.

In 1882, Friedrich Nietzsche, through a literary character named "the madman," famously announced that "God is dead!"[52] Nietzsche clearly saw that this was not an occasion to celebrate, but an earthshaking event. The madman calls out:

What were we doing when we unchained the earth from its sun? Where is it moving to now? Where are we moving to? Are we not continually falling? And backwards, sideways, forwards, in all directions? Is there still an up and a down? Aren't we straying as though through an infinite nothing? Isn't empty space breathing at us?[53]

Like Nietzsche before him, Hetfield does not celebrate the God that failed. He grim-facedly dares to confront the mosaic of reality discernable through the lyrical samples examined above. He has blamed violence and war, society, his parents, and even God for contributing to the chaotic meaninglessness in the world. With no one left to blame, he is left alone, "dying to live,"[54] empty "to the point of agony."[55] Resignedly, Metallica's first decade ends with the hopelessly nihilistic "Who we are / Ask forever / Twisting / Turning / Through the never."[56]

Act 2: Sin, Guilt, and the Specter of Christianity

Robert Walser, on good grounds, rejects nihilism as the primary theme of heavy metal. On the contrary, he argues that heavy metal is nearly always concerned with making sense of the world: "If [heavy metal] offers opportunities for expressing individual rage, it is largely devoted to creating communal bonds that will help fans weather the strains of modernity."[57] Sociologically, this may be a by-product of Metallica's nihilistic, angst-ridden lyrics. Many comments on Metallica-dedicated websites attest to this.[58] Nonetheless, any attempt to describe Metallica's idiosyncratic "making sense of the world" must begin internally, with Metallica's own music and lyrics.

In 1996 and 1997, Metallica released *Load* and *Reload*. A contemplative, more-mature Metallica emerged, both musically and lyrically. The lyrics reveal Hetfield's turn from blaming the world to introspective self-examination: the meaningless, arbitrary chaos "out there" is no longer the sole problem; the evils within emerge, assuming their own responsibility. From a later perspective, Hetfield candidly admits his own historical hypocrisy, projection, and denial.[59] Ingham, with only slight exaggeration, points out that these newer songs are "all about James, about his anger, his pain, his loss and not about a second or third person standing in for him."[60] The question left hanging at the conclusion of the early years—"Who we are / Ask forever"—is engaged in earnest.

Surprisingly, or perhaps not, the albums of the late 1990s are saturated with biblical imagery. The two songs that illuminate the symbolic agenda for these two albums are "Until It Sleeps" and "Slither." "Until It Sleeps," alluding to Gen 4:11, introduces an internalized notion of the stained world. Ostensibly referring to his father's cancer,[61] Hetfield croons: "Just like the curse, just like the stray / You feed it once and now it stays."[62] He begs for comfort from the pain; he begs to be held until it stops, until it sleeps. Perhaps unconsciously, or perhaps consciously, the invocation of the curse also provokes the possibility of interpreting "Until It Sleeps" as a song about original sin. Given the content of several other songs on *Load*, this interpretation certainly seems plausible. After all, cancer and religion have already been linked once. "Slither" invokes another, more-expected heavy metal image, the image of the snake. Unlike the snake's connotations found, for example, in Mötley Crüe's "Rattlesnake Shake,"[63] sexual innuendo is absent in "Slither." Like the account of pain discovered in "Until It Sleeps," it also recounts another discovery: the power of temptation, the powerlessness before temptation. Again, idiosyncratically invoking Genesis, Hetfield strikingly confesses the loss of innocence, the loss of Eden: "We're standing in this jungle / With serpents I have found."[64] And, contra Metallica's infamous contemporaries, Guns N' Roses, the jungle is not "fun and games;"[65] the inverted, labyrinthine garden of Eden is not the world of racial violence and dangerous governments.[66] No, the jungle is inside.

Together, these images—the curse and the snake—intimate the complex background for the later lyrics; these images create a theologically inflected horizon for lyrical interpretation. The serpent signifies temptation, animates the presence of evil, and occasionally facilitates demonic inferences. The curse, the pain of life, the result of seeking and finding the snakes—all this takes on a life of its own. According to "Bad Seed,"[67] biting the forbidden apple entails consequences: the veil hiding the knowledge of good and evil has been thrown off, and humanity stands naked before God. Continuing the associated biblical imagery, "Bad Seed" also poses two possible responses to the knowledge of good and evil, and nearly all the rest of the lyrics explore either one of these options. The first alternative is to embrace fallenness and defiantly challenge God to the end. To this end, urging on the apocalyptic endgame, Hetfield screams, "Bring it on, break the seal."[68] The second alternative is to attempt to understand and then reject (or escape) evil in any way possible. To this end, metaphorically identifying evil with the bad seed embedded underneath the apple skin, Hetfield demands: "Spit it up, spit it out."[69] In either case, the situation is urgent since Hetfield, presumably speaking in the first person, claims to be choking on the bad seed.

So amenable to the lyrics of the early years, the first alternative—defiantly challenging God—loses its conviction and convincingness in the later years. For example, "Prince Charming," "2 x 4," and "Carpe Diem Baby," with their nihilistic, irrational antimorality (complete with the closing jab at Hetfield's parents—"Hey, Ma / Hey Ma! Look it's me"[70]—in the former) are laden with Nietzschean will to power and could have been written ten years earlier. In another vein, and more interestingly, the evil within that evokes and animates the image of the snake is also personified as the devil. The kitsch, antiestablishment transvaluation of values of "So come on in / Jump in the fire" found on *Kill 'Em All* has become more serious. Contra Weinstein, "Devil's Dance"—written from the devil's point of view—exposes the devil as more than merely an antiestablishment or anti-Christian symbol.[71] Hetfield identifies the devil as the deceiver, the tempter, the one who understands the evil yearnings of the human heart, the one who confidently urges, "One day you will see / And dare to come down to me."[72] Yet, at this stage in Hetfield's lyrical development, not even the devil can be blamed for all the evil yearnings of the human heart. Therefore, it quickly becomes obvious that the listener is forced to consider the second alternative.

Running against the current of the early lyrics, the second alternative—attempting to understand and escape evil—poignantly punctuates the later lyrics. Logically, this attempt leads, first, to a general understanding and admission of responsibility, and second, to an increasingly articulate plea for forgiveness. Proleptically, "Low Man's Lyric"[73] narrates the story of a downtrodden man seeking forgiveness for his life, for his life spent running from reality through drugs and/or religion. The low man lives a recognizably low life, but the fact that he feels he needs to confess and ask forgiveness for it is genuinely new for Hetfield. Further developing this theme, "Thorn Within" formally and materially places forgiveness in a specifically Christian context. Taking responsibility for his own sin, his own guilt, his own thorn within, Hetfield sincerely requests: "Forgive me, Father, for I have sinned / Find me guilty when true guilt is from within."[74] Although American excess, religious corruption, and his parents' failings are not absolved, Hetfield has illustrated why and how he believes personal absolution might be obtained.

Although popular Christianity and his parents are not absolved, Hetfield's critique has been shifted and moderated. Certainly, a comparison between alcoholism and religious addiction is not flattering for either, yet in "Cure" Hetfield designates both as apparent "cures" for an unspecified sickness, a perceived "hollow" in one's existence. Yes, he still maintains a passionate dislike for purveyors of deceptions, but he has shifted the blame to the foolish, insecure seeker, the one who gives in too easily to temptation, the one who irresponsibly bets on the cure because it must be better than the "sickness."[75] Concerning his relationship with his parents, he again reiterates their overbearing tendencies. Unexpectedly, he adds a negation to the critique; he acknowledges his own rebellious contribution to the disharmony, his own tendency to take their love for granted.[76] It is certainly understandable why McIvor would write that, by this time, many of the astute listeners were praying that Hetfield would "get some counseling, overcome his demons and stop plaguing us with sob-stories about his upbringing."[77] What McIvor passes over too quickly, however, is the non-identical repetition in the sob stories. Not only is Hetfield's confession a significant step in his relation to the parental adversaries; it is also a potentially reconciling development in his relationship to the God that failed.

Finally, on the fringes of the second alternative, remnants of the early lyrics remain, those lyrics fixated on the symbiotic relation between life and death. For example, "Fixxxer" acutely acknowledges the need to heal the broken world within, the need to start over again, and in so doing, it roughly parallels "Until It Sleeps." Rather than seeking forgiveness, however, another means is needed to the end, another means to break the curse and fall in love with life again. The answer: "To break this curse a ritual's due / . . . Shell of shotgun, pint of gin."[78] Whatever Hetfield is referring to here, it appears to have little to do with confessing one's sins and asking for forgiveness.

By now, it is clear that these two albums are as lyrically unfocused as they are musically unfocused, and that they are as lyrically diffuse as the preceding four albums are uniform.[79] The lack of uniformity is, however, a mixed blessing. On one hand, no consistent point of view represents these albums, leaving fans and critics alike with little traction to make confident claims or conclusions. On the other hand, the conflicted lyrics provide a vulnerable, unvarnished portrait of Hetfield's conflicted soul: a soul struggling with evil, responsibility, and incapability; a soul struggling to find meaning in life; a soul struggling about who is, or should be, in control.

On one of the forums found on the *Encyclopedia Metallica* website, "Rasmus" insightfully responds to the query of what he would ask of Hetfield if given the opportunity. He wrote: "I would ask him if he still walks behind a god that fails."[80] The three parts to this question are (1) Does Hetfield *walk?* (2) Does he walk *behind?* and (3) Does God still fail? Certainly, *Load* and *Reload* illustrate that Hetfield has changed and developed immensely in his relation with God, so the answer to the first part could be yes. Responding to the other two parts is more difficult. Although Hetfield has changed, it is still not clear he is walking behind (inferring movement in the same direction as) God. In truth, Hetfield's evident vacillation apparently indicates that if he is walking behind God, he is alternately running toward God, trying to catch up; and running away, in the opposite direction. Finally, the question of whether God still fails appears, at least, to be reopened, allowing other explanations for chaotic and calamitous events previously laid damningly at God's feet. A few years after *Reload*, Hetfield gratefully and openly acknowledged his therapeutic, "God-given gift" of music and lyrics, further suggesting a possible rapprochement.[81] Whatever the case may be, Metallica appears to be making no attempt to escape its multifaceted entanglement with the specter of the Christian God, which pervasively haunts these lyrics.

Therefore, the 1990s close with the possibility that Metallica's lyrical corpus need not necessarily end as a tragedy. It has opened the possibility for resolution between Hetfield as protagonist and God. Hetfield himself neither assists nor forecloses this option, stating, "We're a selfish band, we just write what we wanna and people can take it as they want."[82]

Act 3: The Tragic Return for the Future

After several years of touring, bassist Jason Newsted's departure, many music-industry related distractions, and a year of alcohol-related rehab for Hetfield, Metallica reinvented itself and released *St. Anger*.[83] *St. Anger* inaugurates the unfinished third era of Metallica's lyrics and signals a musical and lyrical return to its angry, angst-ridden roots.[84] Nothing signals this more acutely than the opening track, "Frantic."[85] "Frantic" hypothetically asks "Could I have my wasted days back / Would I use them to get back on track?" Like *Load* and *Reload*, this introspective questioning opens innumerable possible responses. Unlike *Load* and *Reload*, "Frantic" quickly concludes with the impossibility of finding an answer, slipping back to the old nihilistic resignation that since birth, life, and death are pain, "it's all the same." The rest of the album, with a few exceptions, develops the ascending interplay between Metallica's willful embrace and sanctification of anger and rage, and helplessness before these very demons, the latter proving to be more powerful.

Choosing the easy path, since it is "easier to find something to hate than something to like,"[86] *St. Anger* discovers and sanctifies the new source of freedom: anger. Likewise, "The Unnamed Feeling" provides the new pragmatic program: hating it all away. In doing so, Metallica has again turned its back on God. Metallica implicitly reaffirms God as an irrelevant failure and a new, more-powerful figure takes God's place—Saint Anger—with dubious results.

In 1943, Jean-Paul Sartre published *The Flies*, a modern, post-Christian interpretation of Aeschylus's *Oresteia*. Near the end of the play, Orestes, the protagonist, claims his independence on the basis of his despair. Recognizing Zeus's impotence and failure, he announces his freedom, his break with Zeus:

> I knew myself alone, utterly alone in the midst of this well-meaning universe of yours. I was like a man who's lost his shadow. And there was nothing left in heaven, no right or wrong, nor anyone to give me orders. . . . But I shall not return under your law; I am doomed to have no other law but mine.[87]

Orestes boldly proclaims his ability to have no other law but his own. Yet, in an ironic twist that foreshadows Metallica's dilemma, the tormenting Furies, formerly held in check by Zeus, cannot be held at bay merely by one's own law. As the curtain falls on *The Flies*, the Furies fling themselves after Orestes in shrieks of terror.

Metallica also articulates this two-edged effect of rejecting God, of making their own law. "St. Anger" cryptically refers to a Saint Anger medallion hanging around one's neck as a "medallion noose." Saint Anger has the power to set one free and, simultaneously, to kill. Less cryptically, more overtly, "My World"—if the scrawled liner notes are an accurate indication—is about demons taking hold of the "heaven" in Hetfield's head: "Who's in charge of my head today / Dancin' devils in angel's way." Pleadingly, James repeatedly commands them to get out, to let him be himself. Reinforcing this image, "The Unnamed Feeling" recounts the recurring nightmare of another demon, "the unnamed feeling": "It comes alive / And I die a little more." Finally, "Some Kind of Monster"—after repeating so much of the above, asking whether we are who we think we are, attributing an otherworldly and godlike character to these monsters— pitifully avows: "Ominous / I'm in us." No longer facing Nietzsche's infinite nothing, not even Hetfield's valiant vulgarity and volubility can chase the demons away. With youthful insolence dissipating, purification returns to the death theme, to stripping away the past, to stripping away the dirt, to stripping away life; unsurprisingly, Hetfield's wish is "Wanna be skeleton."[88]

So what is left for the future? If there is another album, what direction will it take? Will it echo the torment and hopelessness of *St. Anger*? Will it find hope and resolution? Although these questions cannot be determined in advance, one thing is almost certain: it will invoke and employ some version of the theological and religious themes that have haunted Metallica for over two decades. Granted, they may not be Christian, they may be anti-Christian, and some might even argue that they are atheistic. Yet, at the end of the day, God undeniably plays a central, defining role in their lyrical corpus.

Over the years, Metallica has developed the reputation of being the "Thinking Man's Heavy Metal band,"[89] and this attribution certainly can be justified in a variety of ways. After attending carefully to Metallica's lyrical development, however, there is also a sense in which Socrates' summation of the poets—"what they composed they composed not by wisdom, . . . for these also say many fine things, but know none of the things they say"[90]—also applies to Metallica. Whether they know it or not, they are the protagonists in an unfinished drama. No longer struggling directly with God, who is (by their own admission) the only way out of sin and guilt, they are struggling against their demons, against the result of rejecting God. Too proud to give up control to parents or other authorities, to God or demons, *St. Anger* draws to a conclusion with the only perceived possible outcome, the anonymous, ambiguously tragic "Kill Kill Kill Kill Kill."[91]

Notes

1. Metallica, "Phantom Lord," *Kill 'Em All* (1983), in *Metallica: The Complete Lyrics* [hereafter, *MCL*] (New York: Cherry Lane Music, 2002), 13.

2. Other current band members include Kirk Hammett (lead guitar) and Robert Trujillo (bass). Former band members include, in chronological order of their departure, Ron McGoveny (bass), Dave Mustaine (lead guitar), Cliff Burton (bass), and Jason Newsted (bass).

3. Metallica's guitarist, Kirk Hammett, made this summation in reference to Metallica's reputation in the mainstream rock press. See Chris Crocker, *Metallica: The Frayed Ends of Metal* (New York: St. Martin's Press, 1993), 67.

4. Deena Weinstein, *Heavy Metal: A Cultural Sociology* (New York: Lexington Books, 1991), 3.

5. Robert Duncan, *The Noise: Notes from a Rock 'n' Roll Era* (New York: Ticknor & Fields, 1984), 36–37.

6. For example, a few recognizable derivatives and subgenres within the generic ascription "heavy metal" are speed/thrash metal (Megadeth, Slayer), lite/glam metal (Poison, Ratt), white—Christian—metal (Stryper, Vengeance), black metal (Mercyful Fate), death metal (Coroner, Sepultura), and nu-metal (Limp Bizkit, Korn). Each has its own musical and/or lyrical idiosyncrasies. Admittedly, the lines are blurry, and bands frequently transgress the boundaries in various songs or albums, but metal performers and avid fans generally recognize the self-imposed rules of heavy metal's unique and complicated discourse.

7. Jeffrey Jensen Arnett, *Metalheads: Heavy Metal Music and Adolescent Alienation* (Boulder, CO: Westview, 1996), 10.

8. *Merriam-Webster's Collegiate Dictionary* (11th ed.; Springfield, MA: Merriam-Webster, 2003), 576, "heavy metal."

9. Robert Walser, *Running with the Devil: Power, Gender, and Madness in Heavy Metal Music* (Hanover, NH: University Press of New England, 1993), 2.

10. "In God We Trust" is a pro-Christian, pro-America anthem calling for a return to trusting God and accepting Jesus (*In God We Trust* [1988]). "Girls, Girls, Girls" is what it sounds like, an objectifying, sexualizing "tribute" to women (*Girls, Girls, Girls* [1987]). "Civil War" is a critique of the meaningless, self-perpetuating cycle of violence (i.e., assassination of Kennedy) and war (i.e., Vietnam War and Latin American guerilla warfare), "with no love of God or human rights" (*Use Your Illusion II* [1991]). And "Symphony of Destruction" is an ironic critique of the corrupting and controlling effects of power that lead inevitably to mechanized inhumanity and war (*Countdown to Extinction* [1992]).

11. Walser, *Running with the Devil*, 1 (citing the *Oxford English Dictionary*).

12. See Weinstein, *Heavy Metal*, 14–18.

13. Walser, *Running with the Devil*, 3.

14. Joel McIvor, *Justice for All: The Truth about Metallica* (New York: Omnibus, 2004), xiii.

15. The Parents' Music Resource Center (PMRC) was formed in 1985 by the wives of several congressmen and senators, including Tipper Gore, Susan Baker, and Nancy Thurmond, and it spearheaded the attack on heavy metal and rap lyrics in the mid 1980s. Under pressure from the PMRC, the United States Senate Commerce, Technology, and Transportation committee began an investigation into the pornographic content of rock music on September 19, 1985. On November 1 of the same year, the Recording Industry Association of America (RIAA) voluntarily agreed to put parental advisory labels on albums containing what the PMRC considered objectionable content.

James Hetfield's (Metallica's lead vocalist) summation of the PRMC is clear, even if simplistic: "They'd look for bad shit and find it. 'Cause you're gonna find what you're looking for, even if it ain't there to someone else. Or ain't there at all." Quoted in K. J. Doughton, *Metallica Unbound: The Unofficial Biography* (New York: Warner Books, 1993), 164.

16. Barbara P. Wyatt, online: www.massmic.com/testwyat.html (accessed May 30, 2004).

17. Weinstein, *Heavy Metal*, 261–62.

18. Online: www.alabamaatheist.org/awareness/music/metallica.html (accessed May 30, 2004).

19. Clark Adams comments in "My Cup Is Half-Full—Why I Am Optimistic about the Rights of Nonbelievers": "Bands such as Godsmack, Nine Inch Nails, . . . [and] Metallica . . . feature atheistic lyrics." Online: www.secweb.org/asset.asp?AssetID=207 (accessed May 30, 2004).

20. Supporting the general perception, Arnett confidently claims that metalheads (those who listen to heavy metal) are the vanguard of the decline of religion's importance. See *Metalheads*, 122–23.

21. The years indicated here roughly correspond to the appearance of Metallica's albums. The first era includes *Kill 'Em All* (Megaforce/Elektra, 1983), *Ride the Lightning* (Elektra, 1984), *Master of Puppets* (Elektra, 1986), . . . *And Justice for All* (Elektra, 1988), and *Metallica* (Elektra, 1991); the second era contains *Load* (Elektra, 1996) and *Reload* (Elektra, 1997); the third, unfinished, era contains only *St. Anger* (Elektra, 2003). To be clear, the appearances of the albums are determinative for the delimitation of the stages. I do not account for various videos, live albums, or covers that Metallica released intermittently during these years. Also, because of space constraints, no attempt will be made to engage or examine every song written.

22. Because it is clearly documented that Hetfield is solely responsible for Metallica's lyrics up until 2003, the case for unity and development is easier than if this task had been shared among the band members. This entails that (1) Hetfield's personal history is relevant, and (2) the other band members may not understand or they may interpret the lyrics differently. See McIvor, *Justice for All*, 317–39.

23. Ibid., 10.

24. *Ride The Lightning*.

25. *MCL*, 20.

26. *Master of Puppets*.

27. *MCL*, 32.

28. Ibid., 33.

29. . . . *And Justice For All*.

30. *MCL*, 42.

31. Cited in Mark Putterford, *Metallica: In Their Own Words* (New York: Omnibus, 2000), p. 36. On the other hand, however, songs like "Don't Tread on Me" (*Metallica*)—borrowing the phrase from the Christopher Gadsden flag (online: http://www.interesting.com/stories/gadsden/index.html#standard), also adapted by the Culpepper County, Virginia, Minutemen (revolutionaries)—are not to be interpreted as pro-war either. Kirk Hammett, the lead guitarist, comments on "Don't Tread on Me": "That tune was around a long time before anybody even knew who Saddam Hussein was. A lot of people misinterpreted that as being a pro-war song like, 'Let's go out there and kick some ass.' . . . It was a huge misunderstanding based on a very wrong assumption. People are quick to assume things." See Chris Ingham, *Metallica: Nothing Else Matters: The Stories behind the Biggest Songs* (New York: Thunder's Mouth, 2003), 101.

32. In addition to the lyrics discussed above, see also, "No Remorse" (*Kill 'Em All*), "Fight Fire with Fire" (*Ride the Lightning*), and "Blackened" (*. . . And Justice for All*).

33. *Master of Puppets*.

34. *MCL*, 31.

35. Ingham, *Nothing Else Matters*, 65. Returning to the theme of madness first present in "Welcome Home (Sanitarium)," "The Frayed Ends of Sanity" (*. . . And Justice for All*) allows dementia to rule the protagonist from the start; it narrates the power of fear and terror to shatter sanity. Ingham rightly suggests that, in the mind of the narrator, there are demons—personifications of fear and terror—at work ripping apart all sense of the normal. The lines "Into ruin / I am sinking / Hostage of this nameless feeling" presciently foreshadow one of the most important themes in their later albums.

36. *MCL*, 39.

37. Cited in Ingham, *Nothing Else Matters*, 101.

38. *Ride the Lightning*.

39. Ingham, *Nothing Else Matters*, 58.

40. See Exod 7–12 for the account of Moses and the plagues.

41. *MCL*, 24.

42. Weinstein's conclusion that religion, especially the Judeo-Christian tradition, is heavy metal's major source for imagery and rhetoric of chaos is also applicable to Metallica (*Heavy Metal*). Nonetheless, there is a sense that the imagery more appropriate to this perceived reality is their early fascination (owed to Cliff Burton) with horror writer H. P. Lovecraft's mythos. This is explicitly referred to in "The Thing That Should Not Be" (*Master of Puppets*), and is the inspiration between the instrumental "Orion" (*Master of Puppets*) and "The Call of Ktulu" (*Ride the Lightning*). See Ingham, *Nothing Else Matters*, 59. After Burton's death in 1986, references to Lovecraft's work disappear and therefore will not be further considered in this context.

43. *Master of Puppets*.

44. *Metallica*.

45. *MCL*, 53.

46. *. . . And Justice for All*.

47. *MCL*, 48.

48. See ibid., 48. Another equally disturbing song also deserves mention here. "Unforgiven" (*Metallica*) recounts Hetfield's bitterness at his parents, who continually attempted to run his life. Weary from this fight, the son has become old prematurely, prepared "to die regretfully." His final parting words to his parents, who have already passed away, are disturbingly left hanging: "So I dub thee 'Unforgiven'" (*MCL*, 54).

49. *Metallica*.

50. Ingham, *Nothing Else Matters*, 108.

51. *MCL*, 60.

52. Friedrich Nietzsche, *The Gay Science* (trans. Josephine Nauchkoff; Cambridge: Cambridge University Press, 2001), 120.

53. Ibid.

54. "Trapped under Ice," *Ride the Lightning*; *MCL*, 22.

55. "Fade to Black," *Ride the Lightning*; *MCL*, 21.

56. "Through the Never," *Metallica*; *MCL*, 57.

57. Walser, *Running with the Devil*, 162.

58. For example, the Web forum of www.encycmet.com is often replete with fans' daily personal testimonies to meaning found in Metallica's lyrics. The following are examples, all posted on June 5, 2004. Referring to "The Outlaw Torn" (*Load*), "Raze the Tornado" writes: "i don't wanna get into it, but it's kinda bout me and I really understand what James is singing. i too sometimes have unwilling tears when i listen to it." "Hero of the day" writes: "Unnamed feeling means one hell of a lot to me. Especially the last verses from 'get the fuck out of here' to 'I wanna hate it all away' that's exactly how I felt, some time ago. Something inside me was screaming. I was depressed, and I hated everyone and everything." Finally, in response to another's plaintive query—"Anyone else here in high school wannakill their mom?"—"Metal-Assmonkey" responds: "Hey, i have huge arguments with my parents every night but seriously, if you wanna kill your mom go listen to mamma said [*Load*] and then post back" [all *sic*].

59. See "Dirty Window," *St. Anger*. All lyrics for *St. Anger* are cited from the CD jacket.

60. Ingham, *Nothing Else Matters*, 116.

61. Yes, both Hetfield's parents succumbed to cancer. His father's later death was less of a surprise than his mother's. Hetfield had an opportunity to rebuild bridges with his father before his death, and through this coming together again, Hetfield came to appreciate his father's influence on his life. See Ingham, *Nothing Else Matters*, 229–30.

62. *MCL*, 68.

63. *Dr. Feelgood* (Elektra, 1989).

64. *MCL*, 88; see Gen 3.

65. See "Welcome to the Jungle," *Appetite for Destruction* (Geffen, 1987).

66. See "Garden of Eden," *Use Your Illusion I* (Geffen, 1991).

67. *Reload*.

68. See Rev 8–9.

69. "Bad Seed," *Reload*; *MCL*, 90.

70. "Carpe Diem Baby," *Reload*; "Prince Charming," *Reload*; *MCL*, 93.

71. Weinstein, mistakenly, adamantly maintains the universality of the following assessment: "Heavy metal's embrace of deviltry is not a religious statement. It is a criticism of the phoney heaven of respectable society where no one boogies and everyone goes to ice-cream socials. It is not a countertheology. Metal lyrics do not attack God and certainly do not malign Jesus. They just appeal to the devil as a principle of chaos (*Heavy Metal*, 260).

72. "Devil's Dance," *Reload*; *MCL*, 84.

73. *Reload*.

74. *Load*; *MCL*, 76.

75. *Load*; see *MCL*, 72.

76. See "Mama Said," *Load*; *MCL*, 75.

77. McIvor, *Justice for All*, 234.

78. *Reload*; MCL, 97.

79. Admittedly, the earliest, *Kill 'Em All*, does not neatly fit into this analysis, not least because of its inchoate, lengthy creation, the changing personnel of the band during the songwriting, and the young age of the members at the time. Lars Ulrich, the drummer, acknowledges the banality of these earliest lyrics: "The lyrics were all written in the plural/ 'we' form and dealt with subjects such as 'rock 'n' roll all night,' 'kick ass,' and 'let's party.'" See Putterford, *Metallica*, 52.

80. Online: www.encycmet.com (accessed June 7, 2004).

81. McIvor, *Justice for All*, 311.

82. Putterford, *Metallica*, 53.

83. For the purposes of clarity, *St. Anger* refers to the album, "St. Anger" refers to the title track of the album, and Saint Anger refers to the artificially created personification of anger referred to in "St. Anger."

84. Lyrically, *St. Anger* is more of a collaboration than previous albums, with the other members of the band providing occasional ideas and lines. In the end, however, Hetfield's personal stamp is evident on all the tracks. See Ingham, *Nothing Else Matters*, 139.

85. All subsequent lyrics are from *St. Anger* and cited from the CD jacket.

86. Putterford, *Metallica*, 100.

87. Jean-Paul Sartre, *The Flies* (trans. Stuart Gilbert), in *No Exit and Three Other Plays* (New York: Vintage International, 1989), 118–19.

88. "Purify," *St. Anger*.

89. Putterford, *Metallica*, 52.

90. Plato, *The Apology* 22C, in *Euthyphro, Apology, Crito, Phaedo, Phaedrus* (trans. Harold North Flower; Loeb Classical Library; 1914; Cambridge, MA: Harvard University Press, 2001), 85.

91. "All within My Hands," *St. Anger*.

The Nature of His Game

A Textual Analysis of "Sympathy for the Devil"

—Harold Penner

"What the devil!" the Master exclaimed suddenly. "Why, just think of it. . . ." He stamped out his cigarette in the ash tray and pressed his head with his hands. "No, listen, you are an intelligent woman, and you were not mad. . . . Are you quite certain that we visited Satan the other night?" "Quite," answered Margarita.[1]
                                                        —*Mikhail Bulgakov*

THIS ESSAY IS A TEXTUAL ANALYSIS of "Sympathy for the Devil," a song that explores the drama of history from a rarely seen perspective. In these words we see history through the devil's peremptory lens. Who is responsible for the atrocities soaking the canvas of history? Is it a personal devil or a principle of evil that brought Jesus before Pilate, initiated the Russian Revolution, and killed the Kennedys?

After a historical introduction and the Rolling Stones' performance history of "Sympathy for the Devil," we investigate various textual elements of the song: (1) the unknown or unguessed name, (2) "the nature of [the devil's] game," the devil's "name," and "in need of some restraint." This draws us nearer to the meaning of this "mad samba." The essay then underscores "Sympathy for the Devil" as a historical and a reflexive theodicy.

Historical Introduction

The Rolling Stones entered the studio to record "The Devil Is My Name." Jean-Luc Godard's[2] camera caught Mick Jagger teaching Brian Jones the chords to the song. Keith Richards took his shoes off, and Charlie Watts loosened his tie. As the hours passed through cigarette-smoke filled air,[3] "The Devil Is My Name" developed from a Dylanesque folk song into "Sympathy for the Devil." Mick Jagger:

> I think that ["Sympathy for the Devil"] was taken from an old idea of Baudelaire's, I think, but I could be wrong. Sometimes when I look at my Baudelaire books, I can't see it in there. But it was an idea I got from French writing. And I just took a couple of lines and expanded on it. I wrote it as sort of like a Bob Dylan song. And you can see it in this movie Godard shot called *Sympathy for the Devil*, which is very fortuitous, because Godard wanted to do a film of us in the studio. I mean, it would never happen now, to get someone as interesting as Godard. . . . We just happened to be recording that song. We could have been recording *My Obsession*. But it was *Sympathy for the Devil*, and it became the track that we used.[4]

Keith Richards: "'Sympathy for the Devil' . . . ended up as a kind of mad samba, with me playing bass and overdubbing the guitar later."[5]

Marianne Faithfull was the instrument by which Lucifer made his appearance. She handed Jagger Mikhail Bulgakov's *The Master and Margarita*, a novel that supplied Jagger with some of his ideas for the lyrics to "Sympathy." In the novel, Satan visits 1930s Russia as a smooth-talking gentleman, a type visible in other novels and films. We may look at such films as Francis Ford Coppola's 1992 adaptation of *Bram Stoker's Dracula*,[6] a seductive lover at one moment and a horrendous ghoul the next. The movie *Legend*[7] portrays Satan as a large somewhat stereotypical devil with horns, strangely seductive and erudite. *Time Bandits*[8] is not too serious a film, but the portrayal of both Satan and God are worth examining. In this sketch neither are very typical. Both botch up their plans: God's creation has serious flaws, including the people who assist in his creation. And the evil creatures who do Satan's bidding would rather be somewhere else and usually end up as sows rather than efficient agents of evil.

C. S. Lewis, a Christian writer, tries to get into the mind of the devil as he schools a neophyte demon in the ways of tempting humans and the problems God poses for hell.[9] J. R. R. Tolkien mythically explores the sin of desire for power among those who "hunger" for the ring: "One Ring to bring them all and in the darkness bind them."[10]

At the time "Sympathy" was written, the Stones were involved in black magic and the occult. Keith Richards and Anita Pallenberg (whose knowledge of the black arts was rumored to be extensive) contemplated a pagan marriage ceremony, to be officiated by Kenneth Anger, a connoisseur of the occult and disciple of Britain's most notorious black magician, Aleister Crowley.[11] But they were deterred "by an unmistakable warning from 'the other side' not to meddle in realms they did not understand."[12] Jagger, too, flirted with black magic but only insofar as it was prudent. "For something like a year after working with Kenneth Anger on a film *Invocation of My Demon Brother*,[13] Mick wore a large wooden crucifix.[14] "His experiments with the black arts . . . did not proceed one step further than was quite prudent."[15]

Altamont: The Concert to End the Sixties

Although we often reflect on the 1960s as a perforce utopia, it was simultaneously a decade of tumult; in one concert drama *Gimmie Shelter* signified both. Inside this drama, at the concert, we have people "freaking out" at a free concert juxtaposed against the threatening behavior of the Hell's Angels, which resulted in murder. The *Rolling Stone* magazine treated Altamont unfairly, joining with those who placed the blame for its eruption squarely on the shoulders of the Stones.[16] On hindsight, Jagger realized it was all about control, and control had definitely been lost.[17] The Grateful Dead previously used the Hell's Angels for concerts, without incident. On the day of the Altamont concert, the Grateful Dead's helicopter landed, and Jerry Garcia and the others ran into Santana's drummer, who told them what was "going down."[18] The Grateful Dead did not play that day.

The Unknown or Unguessed Name

"Sympathy for the Devil" has endured an enigmatic mythology. On the Christian evangelical front, it has been treated as an "Ode to the Devil," and rumors of malevolence have charmed the song with its foreboding mystique. Let us not so easily pin the rap on a religious audience; its hearers, who do not understand the dialectical rhythm of these lyrics, have constructed the mistaken identity of "Sympathy." While some claim

"Sympathy" is only about the devil, others believe this song speaks only of humankind. Keno (of keno.org): "I hope that you understand that the song isn't about the Devil. The devil Mick Jagger sings about here (and what he wrote the song about), is mankind, which is in part why the 'who who' backing vocal keeps coming up in the song."[19] Keno has a good point; in this song Mick is not primarily concerned with the devil as a spiritual entity or as a personification of evil. He wants to use this only as a foil, to get us to look deep within ourselves, at our own capacity for evil. Mick Jagger captures this Christian preoccupation with blaming the devil for all things evil. It is an erroneous predilection to claim that the devil is behind every evil deed, from the crucifixion of Jesus to the Russian Revolution, to the assassination of John F. Kennedy.

The beautiful rhythm of thought, engineered complicity, that Jagger is posing cuts to the quick; the devil shouts knowingly, "Who killed the Kennedys?" and the lyric adds, "When after all, it was you and me." There have been suggestions that the background vocals, the "woo woo's," with the samba element, give "Sympathy" its mystique. Mick Jagger:

> It has a very hypnotic groove, a samba, which has a tremendous hypnotic power, rather like good dance music. It doesn't speed up or down. It keeps this constant groove. Plus, the actual samba rhythm is a great one to sing on, but it's also got some other suggestions in it, an undercurrent of being primitive—because it is a primitive African, South American, Afro-whatever-you-call-that rhythm. So to white people, it has a very sinister thing about it. But forgetting the cultural colors, it is a very good vehicle for producing a powerful piece. It becomes less pretentious because it's a very unpretentious groove. If it had been done as a ballad, it wouldn't have been as good.[20]

Some suggest that these background vocals are "who who's" pointing to the unknown actor in the history of humankind. Keno observes that the "who who's" refer to the undisclosed actor of history. However, it is my contention we need to see this as a dialectical movement. A pure atheist may be able to see history moving without the handiwork of God involved; in like manner, we can hardly understand history without acknowledging a principle of evil also at work.

As Jagger inflected the words to "Sympathy," the "woo woo's" broke out in an impromptu fashion among Anita Pallenberg and her friends in the control room. "Played back, it seemed indivisible from the song: a sound-track from a coven of sarcastic witches."[21] Jimmy Miller: "Anita was the epitome of what was happening at the time. She was very Chelsea. She'd arrive with the elite film crowd. During "Sympathy for the Devil" when I started going 'whoo, whoo' in the control room, so did they. I had the engineer set up a mike so they could go out in the studio and 'whoo, whoo.'"[22] This inveighs against the argument that these are calculated "Who Who's" asking "Who is responsible for the evil in the world," with the implied answer being humankind. Instead, it is a chorus of witches pulling us into the mystique of the mad samba.

This song therefore has nothing to do with the devil. That is, it has little or nothing to do with a personal devil. But it does have something to do with a principle of evil personified by the devil. We cannot lay everything at the foot of humankind in act, but maybe in thought, in imagination.

Placing this in the context of Altamont, a place and time when many will argue that the devil did play an ironic jest on the Rolling Stones, we need to look at this "moment" a little closer. The first issue is the Hell's Angels. Why did they use the Hell's Angels as security? This goes back to a Hyde Park concert for which the Stones employed the London chapter of the Hell's Angels as stewards. This concert of 250,000–300,000, which went smoothly, should not have set a precedent in anyone's mind, because the Angels of London were mere pretenders to their California name-sakes.[23] While the Stones were aware of their British Angels, the event organizers should have been and were *also* aware of the risks involved with inviting the California branch of the Angels. For California events, the Hell's Angels were usually invited as guests to avoid ugly scenes such as Altamont. Several chapters of the Angels were given a nominal official status (as bodyguards for the performers) to assuage their violent tendencies, or to channel it into constructive directions. Exactly who hired the Hell's Angels is not known, but the Grateful Dead management is suggested more than once. "The Oakland, San Jose and Frisco chapters of the Hell's Angels were invited by the Grateful Dead's organization to protect the stage, much as they had done, peacefully, at previous San Francisco festivals. This was no big deal. Payment was said to have been a busload of beer, but this was later indignantly denied"[24] by the Angels. We appropriately see factors such as poor decision making at work rather than supernatural conspiracy. In addition, the concert was moved from Golden Gate Park to another venue, Sears Park Raceway. Three days before it was to happen, greedy promoters—who wanted film rights to what would become the movie *Gimmie Shelter*—forced a quick uprooting of the entire set to a new facility named Altamont.

This is a year before the release of the *Beggar's Banquet* album, which included "Sympathy for the Devil." Brian Jones had died just before the Hyde Park concert, and the Stones were immersed in the worst controversy of their careers. There were drugs, calls for peace, and beatings from pool cues at the front of the stage. A member of the Jefferson Airplane was knocked unconscious twice, and a person was killed. Evil, yes; but as Mick so aptly crooned in "Sympathy," "I tell you one time, you're to blame."[25]

The Nature of His Game

The nature of the devil's game is enduringly enigmatic, to which varying degrees of attention are paid. C. S. Lewis wrote that to "admire Satan . . . is to give one's vote not only for a world of misery, but also for a world of lies and propaganda, of wishful thinking, of incessant autobiography. Yet," insists Lewis, "the choice is possible. Hardly a day passes without some slight movement towards it in each of us."[26] Lewis explains that Adam, though "locally confined to a small park on a small planet, has interests that embrace 'all the choir of heaven and all the furniture of earth.' Satan has been in the Heaven of Heavens and in the abyss of Hell, and surveyed all that lies between them, and in that whole immensity has found only one thing that interests him. . . . He has chosen to have no choice. He has wished to be himself and his wish has been granted."[27] From the biblical story, we know that Satan led a revolt of angels from heaven because he wished to have equality with God (Isa 14:12–15). So it is not so much that Satan chose not to have a choice but that choice was taken from him. He simply lost free will, which Adam and Eve retained.

Jagger offers us another perspective, a view that sees us as lords on earth and movers in and of history. However, if we are good theologians, we realize that we too are moved. God, who transcends history and yet is immanent in it, creates humankind who moves within history only to rediscover the Creator. In the duration of our search for ultimate meaning—that we find only in God—we often become too enamored with ourselves. Yet, when we uproot what we term evil, we turn the blame upon another: we find someone to take the blame, even our share. In effect, the nature of the devil's game is the nature of our game, which includes placing the final blame on God. How can a good God allow evil?

The Devil's Name

Pleased to meet you,
hope you guess my name. . . .
. . . .
Tell me, baby, what's my name?
Tell me, honey, can you guess my name?
Tell me, baby, what's my name? (from "Sympathy")

There is a population within Christianity that takes the person and the actions of the devil too seriously. "There are two equal and opposite errors into which our race can fall about the devils," C. S. Lewis explains. "One is to disbelieve in their existence. The other is to believe, and to feel an excessive and unhealthy interest in them."[28] This figure, if we are honest with ourselves, is at best speculative, and the speculative nature is asserted in the lyrics of "Sympathy." The name "Lucifer" (cf. Isa 14:12 KJV) appears once in "Sympathy" and the name "Satan" not at all. Some may point to Isa 14 and the king of Tyre as a type or a metaphor of the devil; this answers my argument. The king of Tyre may have borne all the humanly quantifiable characteristics to make him a useful metaphor for the devil, but we must not make this monarch qualitatively the same as the devil (monarch qua devil). This is not a useful way to find either the nature or the origin of evil.

> According to the myth of the Fall, evil came into the world through human responsibility. It was neither ordained in the counsels of God nor the inevitable consequence of temporal existence. . . . The origin of evil is attributed to an act of rebellion on the part of man. Responsibility for the evil which threatens the unity of existence is laid upon mankind, but this responsibility is slightly qualified by the suggestion that man was tempted. The serpent, symbol of the principle of evil, in the story of the Fall, does justice to the idea that human rebellion is not the first cause and source of evil in the world.[29]

Participating in the debates surrounding the person and nature of the devil that certain more allegedly literal groups entertain bears little fruit and does not lead us closer to an answer for a question that has been posited in ancient poetic and mythic literature. Paul Ricoeur explains that evil is involved in "interhuman relationships, like language, tools, institutions; it is transmitted; it is tradition, and not only something that happens. There is thus an anteriority of evil to itself, as if evil were that which always precedes itself." That is why, "in the Garden of Eden, the serpent is already there; he is the other side of that which begins."[30]

Mick Jagger is espousing what humanity has been afraid to admit. When Margarita says she is quite sure she visited the devil, whom did she see but a handsome gentleman. More important, Jagger has offered us a view of the collective human psyche, but it only hearkens back to something Ludwig Feuerbach observed in his *Essence of Christianity*,[31] that God is a reflexive image of humanity. So too, we deduce that the devil is a reflexive image of the other side of humanity.

One of the more intriguing parts of "Sympathy" is when Mick sings: "Just as every cop is a criminal / And all the sinners saints, / As heads is tails, / Just call me Lucifer / 'Cause I'm in need of some restraint." Jagger would not consider himself a biblical historian or a Reformation scholar. Yet, he captures two significant elements of Christian history: *simul iustus et peccator* (justified and sinner at the same time; see Rom 7–8) and the more esoteric concept of restraining the devil (here Jagger refers to himself as Lucifer for the only time in the song).

In 2 Thess 2:3–9, the one wreaking havoc is not the devil but the mysterious man of lawlessness. We are harassed by this image of a human doing the work attributed to the devil (this figure exalts itself above every object of worship and takes a seat in the temple of God and claims to be God). We have on the one hand a symbol of evil and the other hand a present reality of evil—or do we admit we have a symbol of a symbol? It is the genius of prophetic religion to insist on the organic relation between historic existence and that which is the ground and fulfillment of this, the transcendent.[32] In this passage we see the dialectical relationship between humanity and the principle of evil—both of which must not be taken literally but seriously.[33]

John F. Kennedy was assassinated over forty years ago, and the saga as to who and how many people were responsible continues. Like many of the lyrics to "Sympathy," Mick picks on particular historic events to draw out larger conceptual and even cosmic implications. Jagger is not saying that we are all to blame for putting several bullets in JFK. But on a larger scale he is saying that we all eventually slay our leaders. On another more cosmic level, we are all good and yet have the evil within us to hold the gun that the assassin(s) held. That is, we are all "righteous yet sinners," a point made by Martin Luther.[34] We are all capable of rising to the level of general in an army, to do heinous atrocities in the name of national pride or security.

In Need of Some Restraint

Just as every cop is a criminal
And all the sinners saints,
As heads is tails,
Just call me Lucifer
'Cause I'm in need of some restraint.

There is nothing like the sway of a Rolling Stones concert. Likewise, one can make few musical comparisons to "Sympathy": the flaming lips, the sometimes taunting and other times enchanting lyrics, painting a deep horizon around often historically poignant and challenging lyrics. Who wrote the chronicles of Jesus? Who recounted the blitzkrieg's devastation? Who shot the Kennedys? Yes, we also had faith in Jesus, put an end to the Nazi threat, and sifted through the evidence regarding JFK ad nauseum. We "made damn sure that Pilate / Washed his hands, and sealed his fate." Now we wonder (with a safe and distanced moral purity) how any one person can be this evil—no one person can be this evil; the social and political forces that led Pilate into the decision were overwhelming.

Martin Luther might have assented to the sentiment of the aforementioned lines from "Sympathy." Gerhard Ebeling elucidates: "There is such a thing as righteousness brought about by man himself through his works. . . . Christian righteousness is the very opposite: not the righteousness of works but the righteousness of faith."[35] Legal or forensic righteousness is no righteousness at all, but the righteousness given to us freely, by no effort of ourselves, is salvific.

As heads is tails,
Just call me Lucifer
'Cause I'm in need of some restraint.
So if you meet me,
Have some courtesy,
Have some sympathy, and some taste.
Use all your well-learned politesse
Or I'll lay your soul to waste.

A few things happen in these final words. After the paradoxical statement concerning cops and criminals, sinners and saints, Jagger sings "as heads is tails," so my confused audience can "just call me Lucifer / 'Cause I'm in need of some restraint." We also learn how to behave around the devil, who is in need of some restraint. We need to practice courtesy and politesse or suffer dire consequences. Jagger does not paint the devil as someone we should feel sorry for and respect. He is not hard done by; the devil got what he deserved.

Theodicy

"Sympathy for the Devil" is a historical theodicy, concentrating on things below rather than above, on the devil and humankind, rather than on God. God, the Prime Mover, bears responsibility for the devil and his crown of creation, humanity. But is God also responsible for the actions of these beings? This is a long-disputed question that has set Augustine against Pelagius, Luther against Erasmus, and Calvin against Arminius.[36]

"Sympathy" does not ask who is responsible for evil in the world; it tells us who is responsible for evil in the world. Then again, Jagger tells us and in a sense leaves the answer unspoken.

> Pleased to meet you,
> Hope you guess my name,
> But what's confusing you
> Is just the nature of my game.

We have comfortably attributed evil to the devil. When the flip side of good reveals its confusing visage, we quickly lay the responsibility at the foot of the devil and his minions. We could pose this admittedly abstract question: Exactly when do we lose control of our "selves," and when does the devil gain control of us? This puts us on a slope that can only be subjectively or mystically analyzed. Some people have more self-control than others. Does this mean some are more spiritually self-aware than others? One facet of the devil's game is to throw us into a state of confusion.

Reflexive Theodicy

Because a historical theodicy focuses on things below and encompasses humankind, we cannot place entire blame elsewhere. The line of responsibility is a fine one when we are blaming a principle of evil for things we do wrong. After all, from the blitzkrieg to the Kennedy assassinations, the blame does not lie far from us. The final taunt—after Jagger has begged us to guess "his" name and to puzzle over and to muse at "his" game—reveals not so much the devil's disdain for the audience, but rather gets us to swallow the kernel of the song: "I tell you one time, you're to blame."

In the end, we must take full responsibility; for what do we take responsibility? In the end, we are ultimately responsible to God, the Ground of All Being. But I think the song is referring us more to an existential responsibility. We need to be responsible to our fellow persons, as Mick sings: "When after all it was you and me." We are to blame for the harm we have caused and are causing one another.[37] At the same time, the devil revels in taking none of the responsibility;[38] after all, this is a principle of evil that mythically explains the etiology and endurance of evil. My argument, then, which has been used to relinquish humans of all responsibility for their actions, proves their liability. If we do not have a devil on which to cast the blame, where does the blame fall? If we continue to look at this historical theodicy from below, we cannot bring the narrowly defined God of "ultimate transcendence only"[39] or special revelation into the picture. But I posit that there is always a dialectic between our responsibility to God and our responsibility to our fellow humans.

The Place of "Sympathy for the Devil" in Theodicy

Feuerbach concludes that anthropology is the mystery of theology,[40] an anthropology that is exalted into theology.[41] As I have listened to "Sympathy" and read the lyrics written by Mick Jagger in 1969, I have gained more respect for the mystery involved in the subject matter. Evil is manifested phenomenologically; but it is more than a thing to be investigated. It often impairs judgment and impedes justice. "Anastasia screamed in vain."

"Sympathy for the Devil" does not offer an ode or a tribute to the devil. This misses the important dialectic of the text. Such paradoxical suasion of "Sympathy" and other Rolling Stones songs such as "You Can't Always Get What You Want" and "Gimmie Shelter" reveal the paradoxical wit of Mick Jagger and Keith Richards in their lyrical collaborations. Ron Rosenbaum is not out of step when he places Mick Jagger among our most underrated songwriters.[42]

During the period in which "Sympathy" was written, certain people influenced the Rolling Stones to dabble in the occult, but the down-to-earth Keith and the pragmatic Mick never did.[43]

After completing this essay, I reviewed the DVD *Sympathy for the Devil*, by Jean-Luc Godard, which includes the Neptune mix video.[44] This "text" puts all the blame on the devil for being the destroyer of homes, families, and our world—which is interesting because this secular interpretation is akin to several religious interpretations. But this is not where the lyrics of "Sympathy" point us. The "Sympathy" place in theodicy is marked by several choice lines:

[I] made damn sure that Pilate
Washed his hands and sealed his fate.

Anastasia screamed in vain.

I shouted out,
"Who killed the Kennedys?"
When after all it was you and me.

I'll tell you one time, you're to blame.

When we speak of the devil, we are using religious language. Jagger and the Stones make "Sympathy" work as a theodicy for precisely the reason that we believe in Mick as the devil incarnate who, when we least expect it, drawls out: "I tell you one time, you're to blame" for the evil in the world. A useful theodicy should problematize the question for which we have too simple a solution. The question posed to us in this historical theodicy is the name and nature of the devil's game.

Notes

1. Mikhail Bulgakov, *The Master and Margarita* (trans. Mirra Ginsburg; New York: Grove, 1967), 372.

2. *Sympathy for the Devil* (Cupid Productions, 1970; ABKCO Music & Records, 2003). Ironically, it would be Brian Jones's guitar that would be unplugged for the larger duration of the session; Stephen Davis, *Old Gods Almost Dead* (New York: Broadway Books, 2001), 240.

3. Davis, *Old Gods*, 240.

4. Mick Jagger, quoted from Ian McPherson's *Track Talk* (1995), online: http://www.timeisonourside.com/SOSympathy.html.

5. Keith Richards, quoted from Ian McPherson's *Track Talk* (1977), ibid.

6. *Bram Stoker's Dracula* (produced and directed by Francis Ford Coppola; 130 min.; Columbia Pictures, 1992).

7. *Legend* (produced by Tim Hampton and Arnon Milchan and directed by Ridley Scott; 94 min.; Twentieth Century Fox, 1985).

8. *Time Bandits* (produced and directed by Terry Gilliam; 116 min.; Handmade Films, 1981).

9. C. S. Lewis, *The Screwtape Letters* (London: Geoffrey Bles, 1942).

10. J. R. R. Tolkien, *The Lord of the Rings* (London: HarperCollins, 1991), 49.

11. See Philip Norman, *The Stones* (London: Pan Books, 2002), 312–13. For a charitable view of Aleister Crowley, see Christopher M. Moreman, "Devil Music and the Great Beast: Ozzy Osbourne, Aleister Crowley, and the Christian Right," *Journal of Religion and Popular Culture* 5 (Fall 2003): paragraphs 1–34.

12. Ibid., 313.

13. *Invocation of My Demon Brother* (directed by Kenneth Anger; 12 min.; Fantoma Films, 1969).

14. Norman, *The Stones*, 313.

15. Ibid.

16. Michael Sragow, "*Gimmie Shelter:* The True Story," online: http://www.Salon.com (August 10, 2000): 2f. Making an appearance as a young camera operator for *Gimmie Shelter* was George Lucas, progenitor of the *Star Wars* mythos.

17. Alan Lysaght, *An Oral History of the Stones* (London: McArthur & Co., 2003), 136–37.

18. Davis, *Old Gods*, 319.

19. Keno, author of the Rolling Stones Web page online: http://www.keno.org.

20. Mick Jagger, quoted from Ian McPherson's *Track Talk* (1995), online: http://www.timeisonourside.com/SOSympathy.html.

21. Norman, *The Stones*, 314.

22. Jimmy Miller, The Rolling Stones' producer (1968–73), quoted from Ian McPherson's *Track Talk* (1977), online: http://www.timeisonourside.com/SOSympathy.html.

23. Davis, *Old Gods*, 296. Davis describes the local Hell's Angels as a "bunch of yobs in studded leather costumes."

24. Norman, *The Stones*, 384; Davis, *Old Gods*, 317.

25. Contrary to urban myth, The Stones were playing "Under My Thumb" when the murder of Meredith Hunter occurred, not "Sympathy for the Devil." Douglas Cruickshank, "Sympathy for the Devil," online: http://salon.com/ent/masterpiece/2002/01/14/sympathy/, 1.

26. C. S. Lewis, *A Preface to Paradise Lost* (London: Oxford University Press, 1942), 100.

27. Ibid.

28. C. S. Lewis, *Screwtape Letters*, 9.

29. Reinhold Niebuhr, *An Interpretation of Christian Ethics* (San Francisco: HarperCollins, 1963), 44.

30. Paul Ricoeur, *The Symbolism of Evil* (New York: Harper & Row, 1967), 258.

31. Ludwig Feuerbach, *The Essence of Christianity* (trans. George Eliot; Amherst, NY: Prometheus Books, 1989).

32. Reinhold Niebuhr, *An Interpretation of Christian Ethics* (New York: Charles Scribner's Sons, 1935), 105.

33. For an instructive phrase by Reinhold Niebuhr, see *The Nature and Destiny of Man* (New York: Charles Scribner's Sons, 1943), 2:50; cf. Gary J. Dorrien, *The Making of American Theology: Idealism, Realism, and Modernity* (Louisville, KY: Westminster/John Knox, 2003), 454–56. One can argue from this that taking biblical myths literally may

lead to dogmatism and purposing not to take them seriously or literally leads to sentimentality.

34. Paul Althaus, *The Theology of Martin Luther* (trans. Robert C. Schultz; Philadelphia: Fortress, 1966), 161–68.

35. Gerhard Ebeling, *Luther: An Introduction to His Thought* (trans. R. A. Wilson; Philadelphia: Fortress, 1970), 122.

36. Augustine, *Answer to the Pelagians* (ed. John E. Rotelle; trans. and intro. Roland J. Teske; Hyde Park, New York City: New City, 1997); see also Augustine, *On Free Choice of the Will* (trans. and intro. Thomas Williams; Indianapolis: Hackett Pubg., 1993); Martin Luther, *The Bondage of the Will*, in *Luther's Works*, vol. 33 (ed. Philip S. Watson; Philadelphia: Fortress Press, 1972), 3; John Calvin, *The Institutes of the Christian Religion* (ed. John T. MacNeill; trans. F. L. Battles; Philadelphia: Westminster, 1960); Jacob Arminius, *The Works of Arminius* (vols. 1–2 trans. James Nichols; vol. 3 trans. W. R. Bagnall; Buffalo: Derby, Miller & Orton, 1853).

37. This is clearly exhibited in Godard's commentary throughout *Sympathy for the Devil*. He uses the film as a statement against war, which is the ultimate in inflicting harm on one another.

38. For a clear example of this, see the Neptune mix video of "Sympathy for the Devil" on the 2003 ABKO release of Godard's 1970 film *Sympathy for the Devil*.

39. Here I have in mind the high Christology of Barth, but to other and more important degrees the necessary Christology/anthropology of Feuerbach, *Essence of Christianity*.

40. Ibid., 336.

41. Ibid., xviii.

42. "Mick Jagger: Our Most Underrated Songwriter?" *The New York Observer*, October 2, 2003, 1.

43. John Sandford, *Chosen Prey* (New York: G. P. Putnam's Sons, 2001), 132; Norman, *The Stones*, 313.

44. *Sympathy for the Devil* (produced by Eleni Collard et. al.; directed by Jean-Luc Godard; 101 min.; Cupid Productions, 1970; released on DVD, with Neptune remix music video by ABKCO Music & Records, 2003).

God, the Bad, and the Ugly

The Vi(t)a Negativa *of Nick Cave and P. J. Harvey*

—J. R. C. Cousland

IN THE WORLD OF CONTEMPORARY MUSIC, Nick Cave and Polly Jean (P. J.) Harvey are hardly household names, and it is most unlikely (thankfully!) that the Britneys and Janets will ever cover their songs.[1] Nevertheless, in the course of the last decade or two, they have produced two of the most compelling and challenging of oeuvres on the contemporary musical scene.[2] In the world of the venal, banal, or simply (if unrelentingly) puerile, these two artists have consistently challenged their hearers with some of the more searching and fundamental artistic probings about the human condition that are to be found in the world of popular music today.

I have chosen to consider both artists together for several reasons. They have recorded together and were, for a time, romantically involved.[3] Second, Cave's long-term collaborator, Mick Harvey (no relation to Polly), has been a major contributor to Polly's albums since 1995's *To Bring You My Love*, as instrumentalist, arranger, or producer.[4] Most importantly, however, are the similarities in the way they approach their art. At various points both Cave and Harvey aim to shock or discomfit their listeners, and they adopt what might be described as an "antiaesthetic"—an aesthetic of the grotesque, where the unrighteous and the unlovely are dwelt upon to evoke their alternatives. As in a photographic negative, where the polarities of light and dark are reversed, they "watch the dark" to limn the light.[5]

Both artists rely on representations of a *vita negativa* to establish a kind of *via negativa* in their approach to the divine. In their negativity, the very unloveliness to which they refer is both a challenge to and, ironically, a signal of transcendence and beauty.

The purpose of this essay, therefore, is not simply to expatiate on the work of these two artists (as it is bound to do in any case), but to explore the approaches they have taken. I show how both have used their musical vision to hint at the strategies of transcendence or redemption that they educe from the bricolage of the shattered worlds around them. The anti-aesthetic approach they adopt, or to phrase it differently, the grotesque, has a long and venerable history in literature and in art, if not necessarily in music.[6] One of the best accounts of the rationale underlying the religious uses of the grotesque is that of one of its practitioners, Flannery O'Connor:

> My own feeling is that writers who see by the light of their Christian faith, will have in these times, the sharpest eyes for the grotesque, for the perverse, and for the unacceptable. . . . Redemption is meaningless unless there is cause for it in the actual life we live. . . . The novelist with Christian concerns will find in modern life distortions which are repugnant to him, and his problem will be to make these appear as distortions to an audience which is used to seeing them as natural; and he may well be forced to take ever more violent means to get his vision across to this hostile audience. . . . You have to make your vision apparent by shock—to the hard of hearing you shout, and for the almost blind you draw large and startling figures.[7]

A more recent expositor builds on her evaluation by observing, "The grotesque simultaneously attracts and repels, excites laughter and terror, invites pleasure and disgust."[8] Neither Cave nor Harvey is averse to using shock or violence to mediate their message, though their rationale for this aesthetic varies at different points in their careers. In what follows, the grotesque in the work of both will be examined in some detail, with attention being paid to the bad and the ugly. I begin with Cave, whom I style as an exemplar of "the Bad," and his band of almost two decades—the fittingly named "Bad Seeds." Then I move to P. J. Harvey, the "Ugly," as expressed through the persona on her albums and demeanor on stage, which is that of the ugly and unlovely.

The Bad: Nick Cave

Nick Cave's career falls into two main phases, first with the post-punk band, the Birthday Party, and then with his own band, the Bad Seeds. Cave was born in Australia in 1957, the son of an English teacher and a librarian. From Nick's early years, his father instilled in him a passion for literature by reading to him from Nabokov, Dostoyevsky, and other authors. The Australian music scene of the 1970s together with selected British and American imports helped inform his musical vision.[9] The Birthday Party, having achieved a certain notoriety in Australia, came to England in the early 1980s at the height of the so-called New Romanticism, with a vision very different from that of the gelled-hair and coiffed music of the likes of Spandau Ballet and Duran Duran.[10] They found the entire movement disillusioning, something that made their music even more angular and dissonant. Despite being championed by some distinguished broadcasters (notably the late John Peel) and critics, their music proved to be so starkly uncompromising and unrelenting that it achieved only a succès d'estime, even if it has since become a benchmark for any number of alternative performers.[11]

The band imploded in early 1983, whereupon Cave took up residence in Berlin. He soon assembled a group of musicians around him, including Mick Harvey from the Birthday Party, Thomas Wydler from Die Haut, and Blixa Bargeld, the leader of the avant-garde industrial band Einstürzende Neubauten, who became the nucleus of the Bad Seeds. Over the next few years, their reputation gradually expanded, attracting the notice of the German film director Wim Wenders, among others. Wenders included two performances by the Bad Seeds in his film *Der Himmel über Berlin* (*Wings of Desire*)[12] and included songs by the band in the soundtracks of his later films.[13] Cave also took advantage of the intense artistic and kinetic atmosphere of Berlin to begin a novel *And the Ass Saw the Angel*, which took him five years to write and was published in 1988.[14]

The close of the 1980s marked some major changes in his life. He underwent treatment for his long-standing heroin addiction, and left Berlin to move to Sao Paulo, Brazil, where he married and became a father. In the early nineties this marriage came to an end; he returned to London and embarked on a brief relationship with P. J. Harvey. His album *The Boatman's Call*, probably the starkest and most revealing of all his works, reveals much of his mind-set at the time. While at work on this album, he quickly executed *Murder Ballads*, one of his most lurid albums and one of the most successful (owing part of its success to a duet with pop siren Kylie Minogue). He has since happily remarried and produced several more highly regarded albums.[15] His recent literary endeavors include lectures on the love song, the incarnation, as well as an introduction to the Gospel of Mark.[16]

From the outset of his career, Cave's oeuvre was marked by a desire to challenge his hearers and to push the limits of musical expression. The results were extreme both in terms of their lyrics but also musically: the dissonance of the music was the perfect complement to the tenor of the lyrics. "Dead Joe" proclaims "welcome to the car smash" while the Birthday Party's instrumentals do their best to replicate the screech and cacophonous horror attendant upon a car crash.[17] To cite Reynolds and Press, "The Birthday Party play[ed] a music of dis-ease, nausea and discomfort."[18] A great part of this was designed to express the band's frustration with the musical climate of Britain, and a desire to galvanize a response—any response—from the audience.[19] Cave deplored the passivity and complacency of the audience and used performance as a means of unsettling his hearers with the extremity of his vision. Building on a crumbled romanticism as refracted through figures like Baudelaire and Dowson, Cave constructed images of dissolution and violence to establish his aesthetic. This included directing his scorn on himself; his "Nick the Stripper" is reminiscent of Kafka's "Metamorphosis" in its vivid depiction of self-loathing:

Nick the Stripper
Hideous to the eye . . .
He's a fat little insect . . .
Insect Insect Insect Insect[20]

Other works focused their rancor outward and uneasily explored the aberrant mind-set of criminals, a topic that would continue to fascinate Cave at least as late as 1996's *Murder Ballads*. Songs like "She's Hit," "6" Gold Blade," and "Deep in the Woods" raise the disquieting specters of murder and misogyny.[21] Cave has explained part of it as a reaction to "a certain numbness in the world today," an attempt to provoke a reaction to the horrific.[22] At the same time, aspects of these songs are not without their macabre humor. In "Deep in the Woods," the narrator relates:

I took her from rags right through to stitches
Oh baby, tonight we sleep in different ditches.[23]

The notion of "his" and "hers" ditches, pathetic as it is, also satirizes the middle class and its status quo. Cave has said: "I do have quite a broad sense of humour about things. I'm an Australian, I have an Australian sense of humour, and I like to give that a bit of breathing space as well."[24] He has said much the same about his later album *Murder Ballads*, every song of which describes at least one murder: "I think the reason it is funny is because it is gruesome. It is so relentlessly gruesome that it can't be taken seriously. But there is a very broad, open kind of humour in it as well. It's not all black comedy. Some things are just funny in anyone's language."[25]

Yet, in keeping with the sensibility of the grotesque, he has also acknowledged how repugnant he found the album: "*Murder Ballads* was such a disgusting record to make. . . . It does make you feel kind of unclean to make records like that."[26] And though Cave appears at times to have been beguiled by the romance of the dark and villainous, he recognizes: "It's a prehistoric, romantic notion about things that don't really stand up in today's world. You can't really push that across as a message: the romantic concept of the Bad Man."[27]

It is arguably Cave's aesthetic that led him to saturate himself in the Bible, and the Old Testament in particular. Part of this aesthetic was simply an attraction to the language of the Authorized Version: "I always loved the way it was written. It basically started out as just enjoying the turns of phrases that were used."[28] A characteristic instance can be seen, for example, in the title of his album of cover songs, *Kicking against the Pricks* (1986), which evokes Jesus' reproach to Paul on the road to Damascus (Acts 26:14 KJV). Yet, as is typical for Cave, it was intended to be multivalent; it also recalls the title of Samuel Beckett's *More Pricks than Kicks* (1934), as well as giving voice to Cave's ongoing dissatisfaction with the British musical press.[29] Songs like "The City of Refuge" and "The Mercy Seat" are also redolent of the language of Scripture, but again, Cave frequently adds a twist: the latter song is about a criminal on death row, and the mercy seat is the electric chair:

> And the mercy seat is waiting
> And I think my head is burning
> And in a way I'm yearning
> To be done with all this measuring of truth
> An eye for an eye
> A tooth for a tooth[30]

In addition to the language of Scripture, Cave was drawn to the strange and violent traits of the stories to be found in many of the early books of the Bible. Though Cave does not elaborate, one can readily supply instances (Jephthah in Judg 11, Elisha and the she-bears in 2 Kgs 2, Og in Deut 3, angels sleeping with human women in Gen 6, and so on):

> The Old Testament spoke to that part of me that railed and hissed and spat at the world. I believed in God, but I also believed that God was malign and if the Old Testament was testament to anything, it was testament to that. Evil seemed to live close to the surface of existence within it, you could smell its mad breath, see the yellow smoke curl from its many pages, hear the blood-curdling moans of despair. It was a wonderful, terrible book, and it was sacred scripture.[31]

Here Cave's theological stance can be fruitfully compared with that of the Gnostics or Marcion, in seeking to dismiss the deity of the Hebrew Scriptures as a demiurge and a deceiver. Cave, like the gnostics, is struck by the irony of a deity who claims to have humans' well-being at heart, but seems to manifest a different persona:

> The God of the Old Testament seemed a cruel and rancorous God and I loved the way He would wipe out nations at a whim. I loved the book of Job and marveled over the vain, distrustful God who turned the life of His "perfect and upright" servant into a living hell. Job's friend Eliphaz observed, "Man is born unto trouble, as the sparks fly upward," and those words seemed to my horrid little mind about right. And why wouldn't man be born into trouble, living under the tyranny of such a God. So it was the feeling I got from the Old Testament, of a pitiful humanity suffering beneath a despotic God, that began to leak into my lyric writing. . . . I was a conduit for a God that spoke in a language written in bile and puke.[32]

This God has affinities with the demiurge, Ialdabaoth, in Gnostic literature: "Ialdabaoth and his fellow heavenly 'rulers' are possessive and arrogant and try to dominate all human affairs; their desire for domination leads them to create human sexual lust and the bond of destiny (control by the stars), by which they intend to enslave humanity."[33] Cave is likewise able to describe humans as the playthings of the divine:

You're one microscopic cog in his catastrophic plan,
Designed and directed by his red right hand.[34]

The culmination of this perspective emerges in Cave's novel, *And the Ass Saw the Angel*, the very title of which betrays its indebtedness to the Hebrew Scriptures.[35] It is also indebted to Southern Gothic, a seething roadkill burgoo of Flannery O'Connor, William Faulkner, and Ronald Firbank.[36] The story is set in the anonymous "South" in the mid-twentieth century and concerns the mute Euchrid Eucrow. He lives with his grotesque parents on the marges of a religious sectarian community known as the Ukelites. Euchrid's older brother dies at birth, and Euchrid, the progeny of generations of incest and inbreeding, narrates the sorry events of his life and that of the Ukelite community at large. His parents are grotesque; his mother is a bloated alcoholic, and his father a crazed trapper who stages battles between the animals he captures in his vicious traps. Euchrid develops a passion for the local prostitute Cosey Mo, but shortly after he sleeps with her she is lynched at the instigation of a false, itinerant evangelist named Abie Po. She lives long enough to give birth to a daughter, Beth, and exposes her in the town square. Beth's advent accompanies the end of years of rain, so she is heralded as a divine visitation and adopted by a church elder. Over the years, Euchrid becomes increasingly fascinated with her, and she with him, supposing him to be God. In the end he wounds her at what he believes is divine instigation, and the massed villagers chase him into a swamp, in which he slowly drowns, the novel being the substance of his dying "utterance."

The style of language used by Cave is highly idiosyncratic, what he describes as a "kind of hyper-poetic thought-speak, not meant to be spoken—a mongrel language that was part-Biblical, part-Deep South dialect, part-gutter slang, at times obscenely reverent and at others reverently obscene."[37] On occasion, the work is leavened by the type of black humor just remarked upon above; if nothing else, the sustained horror and squalor are so unrelieved that one is compelled to laugh at the extremity of Cave's vision.

The symbolism also owes much to the biblical tradition and has particular points of contact with apocalyptic imagery. The rain of divine judgment, falling in Ukulore Valley for years after the near-lynching of Cosey Mo and her subsequent death, recalls Noah and the flood.[38] With Euchrid, we find a case of children rising against parents and having them put to death (Mark 13:12); and with the visit of Abie Po we have the appearance of "false messiahs and false prophets" (13:22). The prevalence of crows, even to the name "Eu[good]-Crow," is reminiscent of the carrion-fowl in Revelation, the birds of heaven that are summoned by the angel standing in the sun to "the great supper of God," the "flesh of all" (Rev 19:17–18).[39] That the work begins from the perspective of crows assembling in the valley insinuates a judgmental theme within the work. A related perspective emerges in the song "Black Crow King," which further demonizes a murder of crows by associating them with Christ's murder:

> I am the black crow king
> Keeper of the forgotten corn
> The King! The King!
> I'm the king of nothing at all.
> The hammers are a-talking
> The nails are a-singing
> The thorns are a-crowning him
> The spears are a-sailing
> The crows are a-mocking
> The corn is a-nodding
> The storm is a-rolling[40]

The inhabitants of the Ukulore are under judgment. Their community "raises cane," and it is not much of a stretch to see that they are also "raising Cain," both by their actions and their willingness to allow Euchrid to grow up in their midst. He is a Cain figure in a world where the Abel figure never survives childbirth. The designation "Euchrid" is itself highly ironic: he is by no means a "good anointing" (from the Greek *euchriō*); rather, he is the very antithesis of Christ, the anointed one. As Satan is cast down into hell, so Euchrid ineluctably slips ever deeper toward the nether realms. This insight and Euchrid's ultimate demise suggest that the Ukulore valley and its inhabitants are little more than a circle of hell. There is no genuine affection, no truth, no communication, and no understanding. Nor is there any divine inspiration; whatever "inspiration" is there is malign and delusory. Finally, there is no real humanity; merely cruelty and ignorance and decay. The animals are alienated from the humans, who mistreat them; the humans are alienated from each other and above all from the divine.[41] This alienation produces a total failure to communicate. Cave relates: "Throughout the story, God fills the mute boy with information, loads him up with bad ideas, 'hate inspiration straight from God,' as he calls it, but with no one to talk to and no way to talk, Euchrid, like a blocked pipe, bursts. For me Euchrid is Jesus struck dumb, he is the blocked artist, he is internalised imagination become madness."[42]

Such an extreme vision impelled Cave to consider alternatives: "I was sick and I was disgusted and my God was in a similar condition."[43] As a result Cave turned increasingly to the Christian Scriptures and to the figure of Jesus. His 1990's album *The Good Son* marks something of this transition in its inclusion of the Portuguese "Foi Na Cruz." This transition soon became apparent to his band members. Cave's longtime friend and collaborator Mick Harvey has acutely commented: "Nick's writing can be broken into two parts. In the '80s you could say he was obsessed with the Old Testament. In the '90s, he's obsessed with the New Testament. There's the old fire and brimstone Nick, and the newly humanitarian Nick."[44] Cave's change of perspective can probably be attributed to a variety of factors. One was likely Cave's increased confidence in relationships and communication, precipitated by his marriage and fatherhood.[45] A second factor is his becoming reacquainted with the Gospels:

One day, I met an Anglican vicar and he suggested that I give the Old Testament a rest and read Mark instead. I hadn't read the New Testament at that stage because the New Testament was about Jesus Christ and the Christ I remembered from my choirboy days was that wet, all-loving, etiolated individual that the church proselytised. I spent my pre-teen years singing in the Wangaratta Cathedral Choir and even at that age I recall thinking what a wishy-washy affair the whole thing was. The Anglican Church: it was the decaf of worship and Jesus was their Lord. "Why Mark?" I asked. "Because it's short," he replied. I was willing to give anything a go, so I took the vicar's advice and read it and the Gospel of Mark just swept me up.

Cave's rediscovery of the Gospels prompted a reconsideration of the nature of God, and of Christ. He no longer subscribes to the demiurgic tyrant he saw underlying the Hebrew Scriptures. Though his theology appears to be in something of a developmental process, he appears to regard God as a transcendent being, although one who does not actively intervene in the world. "Into My Arms" from the *Boatman's Call* starts off:

I don't believe in an interventionist God
But I know, darling, that you do

But if I did I would kneel down and ask Him
Not to intervene when it came to you[46]

He has elaborated further on this viewpoint in interviews:

> I don't think that the duty of God is to make people's lives better,
> to change the march of events. God is the highest substance. It is
> impossible for us to understand that substance. People can have
> reason, heart, wishes, give the gift of intercourse to each other but
> they don't have something which is more important. Every person
> lives within the limits of his own passions, his problems. Sometimes
> we can help each other but there are events people's spirits can't
> overcome.[47]

Elsewhere he adds: "For me, believing in God doesn't change life. It is neither an obstacle nor a relief. It has no influence on my behaviour. Believing
has nothing to do with morality, but with freedom and inspiration."[48]

Cave's theology has some quite suggestive affinities with Stoic
thought. The rarified divine Logos is the substance that furnishes the
source of inspiration, but it is up to humans to recognize the divinity of
the Logos and live in accordance with it. When one does live in accordance with the Logos, life becomes reasonable, and one is able to cope
with the vicissitudes of human experience and human suffering. This is
where the figure of Jesus becomes meaningful for Cave: "The life of Christ
as told in the Bible seems to me to be an encrypted, powerful story, practically a metaphor for all the tribulations humans must suffer. I believe the
message of Christ is that we must shake off all those demons that stop us
from reaching our potential."[49]

Christ, in addition to being an exemplar of suffering, also embodies the
spirit of communication:

> God lives within communication. If the world was suddenly to fall
> silent God would deconstruct and die. Jesus Christ himself said, in
> one of His most beautiful quotes, "Where ever two or more are
> gathered together, I am in your midst." He said this because where
> ever two or more are gathered together there is language.[50]

Thus, the importance in being a writer and performer becomes clear.
Being a conduit for divine inspiration, and one who is able to impart this

meaning to others, becomes profoundly significant. Here the love song comes to the fore. In its fusion of darkness and light the love song also helps fuse the human and divine, anthropology with theology:

> We all experience within us what the Portuguese call *saudade*, which translates as an inexplicable longing, an unnamed and enigmatic yearning of the soul, and it is this feeling that lives in the realms of imagination and inspiration and is the breeding ground of the sad song, for the Love Song. The Love Song is the light of God, deep down, blasting up through our wounds. . . . The Love Song exists to fill, with language, the silence between ourselves and God, to decrease the distance between the temporal and the divine.[51]

His increased awareness of the importance of songs has meant that Cave has taken his role as songwriter far more seriously, something that has had a notable influence on the type of songs Cave has produced. From *Boatman's Call* onward, he has aimed for simplicity both lyrically and musically. At times, the spare tunes with keyboard accompaniment are reminiscent of hymns, and with hymns they share a certain timelessness. The lyrics refrain from the prolixity of his earlier work and do not have the feel of being labored; it is as though he is allowing the song to speak itself, rather than trying to speak through the song. What his songs lose in intensity, therefore, they regain through stature. His acknowledged exemplars are Bob Dylan, Leonard Cohen, Neil Young, and Van Morrison, brilliant songsmiths all, and he has become fully their equal in songcraft.[52]

That said, Cave has not totally relinquished his sense of humor, nor his focus on the grotesque. The video of the rollicking fourteen-minute song "Babe, I'm on Fire" features Cave and the Bad Seeds gleefully playing and acting out the dozens of figures mentioned in the song, all of whom proclaim that Cave is "on fire":

> The athlete with his hernia says it
> Picasso with his Guernica says it . . .
> The Chinese herbologist says it
> The Christian apologist says it[53]
> The dog and the frog
> Sitting on a log says
> Babe, I'm on fire
> Babe, I'm on fire

Cave includes other more scabrous images, but on the whole the song is suffused with a spirit of the carnivalesque—the joyous concomitant of the grotesque.

It is safe to say, then, that over the course of his career Cave has moved away from the bad and horrific to a more considered understanding of humans and their relation to God. The lineaments of the bad have ultimately pointed him to the good, and ultimately to God himself. This tendency is most vividly seen in his recent two-album set *Abbatoir Blues/The Lyre of Orpheus*. The opening song of *Abbatoir Blues* is entitled "Get Ready For Love" and is perhaps the most explicitly religious song of Cave's career. The refrain "Praise Him!" adjures others to "praise Him till you've forgotten what you're praising Him for, Then praise Him a little bit more."[54] While there is clearly a humorous undertone here, the song makes a refreshing change from the stolid and plodding hymns of the nineteenth century. His reworking of traditional genres extends to a remake of the Negro spiritual, a song entitled "O children" from *The Lyre of Orpheus*. Complete with a backing chorus featuring the London Community Gospel Choir, he evokes the time-honored trope of the train going to the Kingdom:

> Hey, little train! Wait for me!
> I once was blind but now I see
> Have you left a seat for me?
> Is that such a stretch of the imagination?[55]

Once again, Cave does not relinquish his more visceral perspective on the world of every-day humans, and their romances and fallibilities, but it is these very features that make his observations of the spiritual world so compelling.

The Ugly: P. J. Harvey

Polly Jean Harvey was born in 1969 to a sculptor and quarryman near the village of Yeoville in Somerset (UK). Her parents were blues enthusiasts and her mother organized local weekend blues shows. As a consequence, Harvey was exposed to this influence from an early age: "I was brought up listening to [John Lee] Hooker, to Howlin' Wolf, to Robert Johnson, and a lot of Hendrix and [Captain] Beefheart. So I was exposed to all these very compassionate musicians at a young age, and that's always remained in me and seems to surface more as I get older. I think the way we are as we get older is a result of what we knew when we were children."[56] Elsewhere, she relates: "The blues is in my blood. I grew up listening to blues music, so any record that I've made that hasn't been influenced by it has been a fight to get away from it. Now, I'm no longer trying to smother it. I felt like I could let it run rampage here because the nature of this record [2004's *Uh Huh Her*] is so very homemade."[57]

Not only was she exposed to these blues influences, but also the performers at the blues shows often stayed with the Harveys. They paid for their accommodation by giving the young Polly music lessons on guitar, saxophone, and other instruments. After such an apprenticeship, it is hardly unexpected, therefore, that she should come to perform herself in a variety of bands as a teenager. After a spell in art college, she joined the band Automatic Dlamini, with which she toured Europe. She then assembled her own group PJ Harvey (Stephen Vaughn on bass and Automatic Dlamini alumnus Robert Ellis on drums) and in 1992 released her first album, *Dry*. Despite its appearance on an independent label, it was an immediate success, especially in Britain and North America. It led to a contact with a major record label (Island), and she has followed *Dry* with a spate of highly regarded albums. *Dry* prompted *Rolling Stone* to select her as Best Songwriter and Best New Female Singer of 1992. Her 1995 album, *To Bring You My Love*, was nominated for two Grammies, and *Rolling Stone* and *Spin* magazine both selected her as Artist of the Year. Her fifth album, *Is This Desire?* (1998) was again nominated for a Grammy and also for a Brit Award. And, having been nominated twice before for a Mercury Music Prize (1993, 1995), she won the award in 2001 for *Stories from the City, Stories from the Sea*.[58]

If Nick Cave's approach to his music can be described as grotesque in its fusion of the sacred and profane, and its focus on violence, Harvey's music addresses the issues of sexuality and of beauty and ugliness. Her songs and her albums are calculated to shock through their forefronting of female sexuality.[59] She frankly admits that, in her early albums in particular, "What I wanted to do was shock: I wanted to do something shocking."[60] One way was to portray herself using images she "wouldn't show [her] grandmother,"[61] an example being the back cover of *4 Track Demos* (1993), where a nude and blasé Harvey stands swathed in cellophane. It is the antithesis of the album's front cover, where a lingerie-clad Harvey, heavily made up and with rhinestone sunglasses, postures with a paparazzo's camera slung around her neck. Like Titian's painting *Sacred and Profane Love* (1514) or Prodicus's "Choice of Heracles," the images ask which persona represents the true Harvey, or the quintessential feminine. The paradox, of course, is that even if one chooses the unadorned Harvey on the back over the vamp on the front, we are still dealing with a "packaged" Harvey. She is as much an artistic production as the CD or album, which, of course, is also wrapped in cellophane.[62]

Her reaction to being in the limelight has been similar to that of David Bowie in the 1970s—namely, to create new personae. She has, in effect, focused her artistic gifts into making herself an "art project" and created a range of "PJ's" that range from the elegant to the grotesque.[63] She has said, "I don't want to do anything that's just straight glamorous. . . . It has to have some element of uneasiness or humor."[64] Part of the humor of this process is that she is able to transform herself from the natural beauty she is in ordinary life into someone ugly: an artistic grotesque.[65] Her most recent album *Uh Huh Her* is a case in point, with the cover featuring a quite unflattering photographic self-portrait of Harvey. Inside, several equally unflattering self-portraits show Polly in a range of different guises, none that is especially attractive.

None is the real Polly, and therein lies the humor implicit in her work, just as the personae she has assumed in her videos also confound classification. She has stated: "It's just a very natural move for me to experiment with my looks and see how that affects my demeanour and performance."[66] Another part of her intention, one supposes, as it was with Bowie, is to hide from public scrutiny by taking refuge behind a series of masks.[67] And, finally, as Mavis Bayton has stated, her transformations are deliberately subversive.[68] They raise the questions of identity, which lie at the root of her work, and explore where she fits as a performer, and where modern women performers belong in the conservative and constricting world of popular music.

She has acknowledged that part of this dilemma of sexual identity arises from her tomboy roots:

> As a result of being the only girl in the village, all I had to play with was boys. I thought they were wonderful. I wanted to be just like them. I used to wear trousers and pee backwards, and all, everything that happens to tomboys. I remember really clearly when I went [to] secondary school, standing in the dinner queue and getting told off by the headmaster for not wearing a tie. I said to him, "But I'm a girl, I don't have to wear a tie." And he said, "Oh, sorry." It was at that point, when I used to have trouble going to the girl's loo

without people saying get out, I'm going to have to start looking like a girl and doing girl's things.[69]

Musically, however, she hasn't done "girl's things" so much as reappropriate "men's things" for herself—among them the masculine idioms of the blues. Harvey's tack has been little less than to deconstruct the male ethos underlying the blues. Eschewing the masculine voice, and the arch double entendres so characteristic of that voice—even among traditional female blues singers—she reinvents the idiom with her unblenching femininity and its stark sexuality. For her, femininity and its accompanying sexuality are not to be reduced to a male optic. As Reynold and Press have observed, "Men in Harvey's world are both ludicrous and larger than life; they're bullies with an undeniable power and freedom, a 'birthright' that Polly wouldn't mind usurping. And who can blame her?"[70] But rather than skirt (as it were) around the issue of female sexuality and appropriate the male perspective so stereotypical of the blues genre, she creates a blues-based feminism that confronts sexuality directly. In particular, she skewers the immaturity of "masculine" blues and its latent misogyny.

To do this, she explores the roots of misogyny in Western, Christian culture and its pervasive double standards. Harvey's own background was not particularly religious: "my mother taught us that nature came from God. But we were never encouraged to go to church, we weren't baptized, and my mother didn't believe in that kind of organization."[71] She states elsewhere that her understanding of Christianity and the Bible is a result of deliberate study on her part: "I wanted to find out about religion myself, so I spent a year or so looking into it. There are so many references to the Bible every day that I felt like I was missing out on something, and reading it improved my knowledge and English language."[72] Her songs invoke what amounts to a litany of male-centered responses to female sexuality, emerging from various periods of Western Christendom. The locus classicus is, of course, the Christian interpretations of the Adam-and-Eve narratives. Harvey's satire of this double standard can be found in "Snake," from 1992's *Dry*, where she makes explicit the Miltonic association of the "fall" with female carnality:

"I'll make
You queen of
Eve-
ry thing
No need

For god
No need
For him

"Just take
My hand
You be
My bride
Just take
That fruit
Put it
Inside"

Women are condemned for preferring sexuality to God. In fact, their association with the serpent makes them nothing less than demonic. The same subtext underlies her song "Easy" from *Dry*, where her lover condemns her for not playing the traditional role of being hard to get. She cites his reproach to her—"You call me Devil's gateway"—a charge almost two thousand years old, which originated with Tertullian:

> The sentence of God on this sex of yours lives in this age: the guilt must of necessity live too. *You* are the devil's gateway: *you* are the unsealer of that (forbidden) tree: *you* are the first deserter of the divine law: *you* are she who persuaded him whom the devil was not valiant enough to attack. *You* destroyed so easily God's image, man.[73]

According to Tertullian, women are not even made in God's image. Yet, unjust as it is, this concept proved to be profoundly enduring. Peter Brown observes that "the misogyny to which Tertullian appealed so insistently was, in his opinion, based on unalterable facts of nature: women were seductive."[74] Because of that, women are thereby inherently culpable. The root of all this evil is the female and her sexuality. Women become marginalized by very virtue of being feminine.

Harvey brings this male disgust and distrust with the feminine to the fore in a further song from *Dry*, "Sheela-Na-Gig":

> I've been trying to show you over and over
> Look at these my child-bearing hips
> Look at these my ruby red ruby lips

Look at these my work strong arms and
You've got to see my bottle full of charm
I lay it all at your feet
You turn around and say back to me
He said

Sheela-na-gig, sheela-na-gig
You exhibitionist
Sheela-na-gig, sheela-na-gig
You exhibitionist
. . . .
He said "Wash your breasts, I don't want to be unclean"
He said "Please take those dirty pillows away from me"
He said "Wash your breasts, I don't want to be unclean"
He said "Please take those dirty pillows away from me"[75]

This disgust is seen to be symptomatic of female sexuality: females are ugly and unclean. Harvey's title makes this disgust even more pronounced: the sheela-na-gig was akin to a gargoyle, a statue of a female grotesque who exposed her genitals. These figures were affixed to medieval cathedrals to drive demons away.[76] The apotropaic function of human genitals has a long history,[77] but its particular significance here is that the sheela-na-gig is outside the ambit of the cathedral, outside, in other words, the purview of Christianity. As with the mythical figure of Lilith the mythical first wife of Adam, there is no acceptable place within the conventional orthodox framework for a sexualized female, one who is necessarily beyond the control of masculine authority.[78] As a consequence, women are marginalized and demonized; they are denied a legitimate role in the church, or in the machinery of salvation.[79]

Harvey further suggests that even women who are acknowledged as saints only occupy a marginal position, and that even sainthood is seen as somehow unsatisfactory. In her song "The Wind" from *Is This Desire?* Harvey reflects on St. Catherine of Alexandria:

Catherine liked high places
High up on the hills
. . . .
Here she built a chapel
With her image on the wall

A place where she could rest and
A place where she could wash
    And listen to the wind blow
She dreamt of children's voices
And torture on the wheel
Patron-Saint of nothing
A woman of the hills
She once was a lady
Of pleasure, and high-born
A lady of the city
But now she sits and moans
    And listens to the wind blow
I see her in her chapel
High up on the hill
She must be so lonely
Oh Mother, can't we give
A husband to our Catherine?
A handsome one, a dear
A rich one for the lady
Someone to listen with

Unless the last paragraph is calculated to be ironic, Harvey raises the specter of a wasted life as "Patron-Saint of nothing," where the anchoress has nothing to look forward to apart from her impending martyrdom: "torture on the wheel." And again, it raises the question of how women can be made to fit successfully within the patriarchal framework of Christianity.

As a consequence, much of Harvey's music is the music of the marginalized, those without an idiom to speak to their situation. The sense of marginality extends to the way the music is played. Though her recent album, *Stories from the City, Stories from the Sea*, shows that she is quite capable of producing songs that are melodic and tuneful,[80] she has repeatedly returned to making music that is dark, difficult, and unsettling.[81] She remarks of earlier albums: "[I] experimented with some dreadful sounds on *Is This Desire?* and *To Bring You My Love*—where I was really looking for dark, unsettling, nauseous-making sounds."[82] Nor are these albums exceptional in this regard; her earlier album *Rid of Me* (1993) has aptly been variously described as a "vicious stew of rural blues, with Harvey's voice and guitar sounding almost animalized by the production,"[83] and as "a brilliant miasma of tortured love and fractured fables."[84] Greil Marcus has memorably remarked that Harvey "appeared naked on the cover of her first album, but as record followed record, it was as if a layer of flesh—flesh as a kind of clothing, a body mask that gave the illusion of nakedness— was being removed with every new year, until finally, with *To Bring You My Love*, . . . she appeared on the cover in a glamorous red dress and in sound was exposed down to her bones."[85]

This exposure is particularly evident on the album's title track. She again assumes a marginal persona, this time that of the demonized, romantic, *âme damnée*, who damns herself in order to be with her lover.[86] Here she invokes traditional blues themes. One is particularly reminded of Robert Johnson's seminal blues songs: "Cross Road Blues," "Me and the Devil Blues," and "Hellhound on my Trail." She has also managed to impart some of Howlin' Wolf's menace to her vocals; the result is an entirely fresh deployment of the established blues idiom, totally convincing in its presentation of a *female* damned soul:

> I was born in the desert
> I been down for years
> Jesus, come closer
> I think my time is near
>
> I've lain with the devil
> Cursed god above
> Forsaken heaven
>
> To bring you my love
>
> Forsaken heaven
> Cursed god above
> Lain with the devil
> Bring you my love

"Long Snake Moan" from the same album is, if anything, even more menacing and unsettling. Working in the tradition of Leadbelly's song "Black Snake Moan," Harvey produces a song that retains the sexual subtext, but goes on to transcend it on a number of levels. Barbara O'Dair rightly remarks that the "blues tropes run deep, and the sexual motifs run true—they intersect in all sorts of startling ways, particularly when you consider that the blues she refigures are manmade (there's no Big Mama Thornton on her list)."[87]

You oughta hear my long snake moan!
You oughta see me crawl my moan!

Duck you
Under
Deep salt
Water
In my
Dreaming
You'll be
Drowning
Raise me
Up lord
Call me
Lazarus
Hey lord
Hear me
Make me
My fill

It's my voodoo working

Physical love allows for the possibility of transcendence and rebirth as well as death and drowning. It is unclear whether the line "Call me Lazarus" is intended to invoke Sylvia Plath's "Lady Lazarus."[88]

Dying
Is an art, like everything else
I do it exceptionally well

I do it so it feels like hell

The parallel references to hell may suggest some influence. Whether they do or not, however, the song certainly brings God into the sexual sphere and into what would normally be seen as the realm of the demonic: "It's my voodoo working." Here the voodoo presumably refers to the narrator's sexual allure and her own "power," a power situated in a context of resurrection. What this suggests, as does the paradoxical appeal to Jesus to "come closer" in "To Bring You My Love," is that Harvey has restructured her understanding of the feminine so as to sanctify female sexuality. This seems to be the underlying message of the song "Send His Love to Me," also from *To Bring You My Love*:

> Left alone in desert
> This house becomes a hell
> This love becomes a tether
> This room becomes a cell
>
> How long must I suffer?
> Calling Jesus, please
> Send his love to me[89]

Here Jesus is invoked, almost in the style of courtly love, to bring about the union of the lovers. "His love" in these lines is left deliberately ambiguous and likely refers both to Jesus' love and that of her lover. Divine love and erotic love mirror each other, and the former sanctifies the latter. Moreover, though she is distanced from her lover, she is not cut off from Jesus. In this case her marginalization is not a marginalization from God.[90] Her feminine identity is ultimately rooted in divine acceptance of herself as a female. This seems to be the sense of a further song from *To Bring You My Love*, "Working for the Man."

> In the night I look for love
> Get my strength from the man above
> God of piston, god of steel
> God is here behind the wheel
>
> I'm just . . . working
> For the man
>
> Pretty things get in my . . . car
> Take them flying, it's not far
> Take in handsome, take in me
> Look good in my steel machine
>
> I'm just working
> For the man

Don't you know yet who I am?
Working harder for the man
Go around I'm doing good
Get my strength from the man above

I'm just working
For the man

I'm just doing
What I can

Go around I'm doing good
Go around I'm doing good

If the love that she is looking for is human love (or human and divine love), it seems probable that erotic love is to be regarded as a part of her "working for the man" and part of her "doing good."[91]

If the above inferences holds true, then it can be argued that there is a centripetal movement to Harvey's work. Divine acceptance of her and her sexuality exert a centering influence that pulls her in from the margins. Certainly, the tenor of her recent work has focused more on acceptance and the possibilities of romantic love. And increasingly, as with Cave, humor and not anger now functions as one of the touchstones of her work. Harvey says of two of the songs on her latest album *Uh Huh Her*, "I love the humour in those songs. . . . I find those to be really funny songs but a lot of people I'm talking to seem to be missing out on that, so I end up thinking, 'Oh, I didn't do that very well because it was supposed to be quite a funny song.' People always ask me, 'You're angry. Why are you so angry?' And it's like, 'I'm not angry at all! I'm just having fun! Can't you see I'm having fun?'"[92] In fact, the angriest sounding song on the album, "Who the F***," deftly satirizes her earlier persona of outraged femininity as well as her perennial concerns about beauty and ugliness. Addressed to her hairdresser, it runs:

who the f*** do you think you are

Get your comb out of there
Combing out my hair

I'm not like other girls[93]
You can't straighten my curls

I'm not like other girls
You can't straighten my curls
No!
. . . .
I'm free, you'll see
I'm me, you'll see

Thus, the profound issues of liberty and identity come down to the success of a hairstyle or coiffure. Just how ironic Harvey is being here can be seen when one contrasts these lyrics with the horrific words of *Dry*'s "Man-Size":

Silence my lady head
Get girl out of my head
Douse hair with gasoline
Set it light and set it free

Here freedom only comes with immolation. In her excellent analysis of this song, Judith Peraino asks, "How do we reconcile the horrifying image of dousing hair with gasoline and setting it afire with the accompanying notion of freedom? The shock value of this image is indeed a wake-up call: gender (that is, feminine gender) is inescapable without a willfull acy of violence—here specifically, self-immolation so that the unfettered, ungendered soul can rise phoenix-like from the ashes."[94] The accompanying video is equally ironic and shows Harvey mugging for the camera as if she were a preteen being filmed by one of her school chums. As with Cave's recent video, a carnivalesque tone comes to prevail over the grotesque. Harvey states: "It's ridiculous that they can take this seriously as an angst-ridden, hateful song towards a man . . . It's fun, it's a punk-rock song, it's energy. That song's about jumping up and down. That's all it's about."[95] Though the music retains its marginal feel, it is obvious that some of the dilemmas surrounding Harvey's earlier work have been resolved. The mirror of the divine has led Harvey to reconsider her identity, her sexuality, and the relation of beauty to ugliness.

Conclusion

The foregoing has sought to situate the grotesque in the work of Nick Cave and Polly Jean Harvey in relation to the divine. Their musical evocations of the bad and the ugly do indeed, as Flannery O'Connor suggests, point to the need for redemption in the actual lives that humans lead. As with the paintings of Bosch, Ensor, and Beckmann, the oeuvres of both musicians portray human life and its horrific aspects, but just as deftly point to the transcendent and the divine that lie beyond it.

The focus of both artists upon the evil, the grotesque, and the unlovely in human experience has led both to consider what is implicit in the other side of the grotesque—the beautiful, the divine, and the lovely. Both have come to realize that the humorous, the ugly, and the violent are actually conduits to the divine and transcendent. Their very evocation of the limits of the human condition are some of the strongest suggestions of life beyond these confines.

Notes

1. I do not mean to imply that other artists have adapted or built on their work. One need only mention the haunting version of Nick Cave's "Mercy Seat" by Johnny Cash on *American III: Solitary Man* (2000), or the surprisingly visceral covers of P. J. Harvey's songs by Juliette Lewis in the film *Strange Days*. A Nick Cave song "People Ain't No Good" from *The Boatman's Call* has even made it onto the soundtrack of *Shrek 2* (DVD, directed by Andrew Adamson, Kelly Asbury, and Conrad Vernon [Dreamworks, 2004]). "Cover": "Make a cover version (of a song, etc.)." (Oxford Concise English Dictionary, s.v. "cover.")

2. For a discography of Cave to 1999, see: Maximilian Dax et al., *The Life and Music of Nick Cave: An Illustrated Biography* (trans. Ian Minock; Berlin: Die Gestalten Verlag, 1999), 173; Ian Johnston, *Bad Seed: The Biography of Nick Cave* (London: Abacus, 1996 [1995]), 307–38. His discography is online: http://www.nick-cave.com/_discography_nctbs.php. P. J. Harvey's discography is also online: http://www.pollyharvey.co.uk/. See also James R. Blandford, *P. J. Harvey: Siren Rising* (London/New York/Paris: Omnibus Press, 2004) 159–76.

3. Harvey sings a duet with Cave on "Henry Lee" and sings a verse of "Death Is Not the End," both from *Murder Ballads*. Cave's songs "West Country Girl" and "Black Hair" from *The Boatman's Call* have been interpreted by some as being reflective of his relationship with Harvey. See further Blandford, *Siren*, 93–95.

4. Both Cave and Harvey have also collaborated recently with Marianne Faithfull on her album *Before the Poison*. Apart from playing on the album, they also assumed songwriting duties. Harvey contributed three songs and collaborated on two others; Cave contributed the music to three more songs.

5. Here I allude to the celebrated phrase of Richard Thompson from *Shoot Out the Lights* (song and CD; London: Hannibal, 1982); cf. his 3-CD anthology *Watching the Dark* (London: Hannibal, 1993).

6. For an instructive discussion of the grotesque, see especially Mikhail Bakhtin, *Rabelais and His World* (Boston: Massachusetts Institute of Technology Press, 1968), 1–58. For a brief overview, see Alton Kim Robertson, *The Grotesque Interface: Deformity, Debasement, Dissolution* (Frankfurt: Vervuert, 1996), 1–13; and cf. John R. Clark, *The Modern Satiric Grotesque and Its Traditions* (Lexington: University of Kentucky Press,

1991); Bernard McElroy, *Fiction of the Modern Grotesque* (New York: St. Martin's Press, 1989); Michael J. Meyer, ed., *Literature and the Grotesque* (Amsterdam: Rodopi, 1995).

7. Flannery O'Connor, "The Fiction Writer and His Country" in *Flannery O'Connor: Collected Works* (New York: The Library of America, 1988), 805–6. Cave readily acknowledges the "perverse" strain in his music: "I think there is a certain perversity in my music in that I continue, you know, to eat at the same ball of vomit year after year." Cited in Jim Sullivan, "This Time Back Nick Cave's Dwelling Mainly on Love" (Globe Staff 1998): http://www.nick-cave.com/_interviews.php.

8. Frances K. Barasch, "Theories of the Grotesque," in Irena R. Makaryk, ed., *Encyclopedia of Contemporary Literary Theory: Approaches, Scholars, Terms* (Toronto: University of Toronto Press, 1993), 85.

9. On the literary influence of his father, see "The Flesh Made Word," in Nick Cave, *King Ink II* (London: Black Spring, 1997), 137.

10. The band was not named after the Pinter play, but apparently after Cave's (mis-) recollection of a birthday party in Dostoyevsky's *Brothers Karamazov*; see Johnston, *Bad Seed*, 65.

11. The only post-punk band to approach the discomfort level of the Birthday Party in terms of sheer relentlessness and desperation was Joy Division. For a representative overview, see the 4-CD *Heart and Soul* (1997).

12. *Der Himmel über Berlin* (*Wings of Desire*), DVD, directed by Wim Wenders (Argos Films/Road Movies Filmproduktion/Westdeutscher Rundfunk 1987; Hollywood, CA: MGM/UA Video, 2005).

13. Cave on his own has appeared in several other films including *Ghosts . . . of the Civil Dead*, directed by John Hillcoat (Australia: Correctional Services/Outlaw Values, 1989), and *Johnny Suede*, DVD, directed by Tom DiCillo (Arena/Balthazar Productions/Starr/Vega Film Productions, 1991; Front Row Video, 2001). For a not entirely convincing discussion of Cave's involvement in Wenders's film, see Andrew Murphie, "Sounds at the End of the World as We Know It: Nick Cave, Wim Wenders' *Wings of Desire* and a Deleuze-Guattarian Ecology of Popular Music," *Perfect Beat: The Pacific Journal of Research into Contemporary Music and Popular Culture*, 2 (1996): 9–14.

14. Nick Cave, *And the Ass Saw the Angel* (New York: HarperCollins, 1989).

15. These CDs include *No More Shall We Part* (2001), *Nocturama* (2003), and *Abbatoir Blues/The Lyre of Orpheus* (2004).

16. Two of Cave's lectures, "The Secret Life of the Love Song" (delivered to the Vienna Poetry Festival in 1998) and "The Flesh Made Word" (for BBC Radio 3), have been released as a CD, *The Secret Life of the Love Song* (1999). The text of the latter is also available in Cave, *King Ink II*, 137–42. Nick Cave, "Introduction to the Gospel according to Mark," in *Mark's Gospel* (KJV; Pocket Canon; Edinburgh: Canongate, 1998); online: http://members.fortunecity.com/vanessa77/index700.html.

17. Lyrics from Nick Cave, *King Ink I* (London: Black Spring, 1993), 25.

18. Simon Reynolds and Joy Press, *The Sex Revolts: Gender, Rebellion, and Rock 'n' Roll* (Cambridge: Harvard University Press, 1995), 92.

19. He has said of his attitude at the time: "The way I approached life . . . was fuelled by hatred and rage against things." Cited in Mick Brown, "Cave's New World," *The Age* (Australia), May 31, 1998; online: http://www.nick-cave.com/_interviews.php.

20. Cave, *King Ink I*, 10.

21. On Cave and the issue of misogyny, see Reynolds and Press, *Sex Revolts*,

22. Cited in ibid., 30.

23. Cave, *King Ink I*, 35.

24. Cited in Jonathan King, "Interview" with Nick Cave, from *Rip It Up Magazine* (New Zealand), January 1996; online: http://www.nick-cave.com/_interviews.php.

25. Cited in Michael Dwyer, "Murder He Said," *Rolling Stone* (Australia), November 1995; online: http://www.nick-cave.com/_interviews.php.

26. Cited in King, "Interview."

27. Cited in ibid.

28. Cited in Michael Dwyer, "Interview," *Revue* (Australia), December 1994; online: http://www.nick-cave.com/_interviews.php.

29. Beckett's solipsistic vision appears to inform much of Cave's early work. Birthday Party's *Junkyard* recalls Beckett's fascination with decay and dissolution (broken perambulators and discarded bicycle wheels litter the stage in *Breath*). The physical situation of Winnie in *Happy Days* is the same as that of Euchrid, the protagonist of Cave's novel: both are buried up to their chests, and both deliver largely uninterrupted monologues.

30. Cave, "The Mercy Seat," *King Ink II*, 7.

31. Cave, "Gospel according to Mark."

32. Cave, "The Flesh Made Word," *King Ink II*, 138–39.

33. Bentley Layton, *The Gnostic Scriptures: Ancient Wisdom for the New Age* (New York: Doubleday, 1987), 16.

34. Cave, "Red Right Hand," *King Ink II*, 89.

35. The title is taken from Num 22:23 (KJV). For Cave's wordplay on the title, see Cave, *Ass*, 90. Readings from the novel are available on the CD *And the Ass Saw the Angel* (1999). A further reading can be also found on Gary Lucas's CD *Improve the Shining Hour* (2000), where Lucas provides solo guitar accompaniment.

36. Cave acknowledges the influence of Flannery O'Connor and William Faulkner. Whether he is familiar with Ronald Firbank is unclear, though his fascination with language and his sly humor are certainly reminiscent of Firbank's *Prancing Nigger* (New York: Brentano's, 1924).

37. Cave, *King Ink II*, 141.

38. Cave develops this same theme in "Carny," *King Ink I*, 140–42.

39. Fans of the band Genesis will recognize that the same passage serves as the inspiration for Peter Gabriel's epic "Supper's Ready," on *Foxtrot* (1972).

40. Cave, *King Ink I*, 121. Cf. the lines in "Carny": "And a murder of crows did circle around, / First one, then the others flapping blackly down" (142).

41. Euchrid's experience also recalls Mary Shelley's *Frankenstein* in its depiction of a mute freak victimized by the townsfolk for his unwitting harm of a young girl. The first (1818) manuscript of *Frankenstein* is in Betty T. Bennett and Charles E. Robinson, eds., *The Mary Shelley Reader* (New York: Oxford University Press, 1990).

42. Cave, *King Ink II*, 141.

43. Ibid., 139.

44. Cited in Mick Brown, "Cave's New World."

45. Cave has indicated that "Papa Won't Leave You, Henry," from *Henry's Dream* (1992), is addressed to his son: "Well, the road is long, / And the road is hard, / And many fall by the side, / But Papa won't leave you Henry, / So there ain't no need to cry" (Cave, *King Ink II*, 55).

46. Cave, *King Ink II*, 145.

47. Cited in James McNair, "Nick Cave Interview," *Mojo Magazine* (UK), March 1997; online: http://www.nick-cave.com/_interviews.php.

48. Cited in "Interview" with Cave, in *Telemoustique* (Belgium), 1998; online: http://www.nick-cave.com/_interviews.php. Later in the same interview, however, Cave says: "I try to do my best, like everyone. I try to work with honesty and integrity. I feel it's the only thing that matters in the end. You have to appear intact before God." That is to say, his belief in God does seem to have a bearing on his behavior.

49. Cited in Dax, *Nick Cave*, 149.

50. Cave, *Secret Life of the Love Song*.

51. Ibid., *Secret Life*.

52. See Jonathan Valania, "Let There Be Light," in *Magnet* (UK), Fall 2001, 72. Cave has contributed songs to tribute albums in honor of Neil Young ("Helpless," in *The Bridge: A Tribute to Neil Young* [1989]) and Leonard Cohen ("Tower of Song," in *I'm Your Fan: The Songs of Leonard Cohen* [1991]). It is also likely that his song "Hallelujah" from *No More Shall We Part* is intended to echo Cohen's own "Hallelujah."

53. Cave, sans costume, assumes the role of the "Christian apologist" in the video. If this identification is not ironic, he would still distance himself from organized religion; cf. his song "God Is in This House," in *No More Shall We Part*.

54. *Abbatoir Blues*.

55. *The Lyre of Orpheus*. The second line, of course, cites the song, "Amazing Grace."

56. Cited in Barbara O'Dair, "Polly Jean Harvey," in *Trouble Girls: The Rolling Stone Book of Women in Rock* (ed. Barbara O'Dair; New York: Random House, 1997), 544. For Don Van Vliet's (Captain Beefheart's) continued influence on Harvey, especially as a mentor, see: Blandford, *Siren*, 117–18; Sylvie Simmons, "PJ Harvey Does it Her Way," *Harp Magazine*, October 2004, 81–83.

57. Cited in Martin Turenne, "The Sweet and Lowdown of PJ Harvey," *Exclaim!* May 31, 2004.

58. Harvey is the only artist who has been nominated for the award three times; Blandford, *Siren*, 146.

59. Judith A. Peraino, "Harvey's 'Man-Size Sextet' and the Inaccessible, Inescapable Gender," *Women & Music* 2 (1998), 47–63.

60. Cited in David Cavanagh, "Dark Star," *Q Magazine*, December 2001, 114.

61. Cited in ibid., 114.

62. Harvey's use of the cellophane may deliberately recall an album jacket by the UK band the Undertones, which showed a woman wrapped in butcher's cellophane and strips of bacon.

63. *Q Magazine* (December 2001), 113, celebrated Harvey as Woman of the Year, and also included a series of photos emphasizing her protean transformations over the course of her career.

64. Cited in O'Dair, "Polly Jean Harvey," 546.

65. She remarks: "I actually find wearing make-up like that, sort of smeared around, as extremely beautiful. Maybe that's just my twisted sense of beauty. I'm always attracted to things which are a little bit too much, as you can hear in the music. Certain pieces of music that might seem unsavoury or difficult for some people to listen to, I might find very soothing." Blandford, *Siren*, 84.

66. Cited in ibid., 548.

67. Blandford, *Siren*, 3, 83, 91,126. Mélisse Lafrance, "Is This Desire? (1998)" in Lori Burns and Mélisse Lafrance, *Disruptive Divas: Feminism, Identity & Popular Music* (New York: Routledge, 2002), 178; Simmons, "Her Way," 81.

68. Mavis Bayton, *Frock Rock: Women Performing Popular Music* (Oxford: Oxford University Press, 1998), 113–14.

69. Evelyn McDonnell, "PJ Harvey," *Option* magazine, March/April 1995, 70–71. These experiences may well underlie her recent song "The Pocket Knife" from *Uh Huh Her*:

> Please don't make my wedding dress
> I'm too young to marry yet
> Can you see my pocket knife?
> You can't make me be a wife
>
> Mummy, put your needle down
> How did you feel when you were young?
>
> Flowers I can do without
> I don't wanna be tied down
> White material will stain
> My pocket knife's gotta shiny blade.

The lyrics for this song and others I cite by Harvey, unless otherwise indicated, are online: http://www.pollyharvey.co.uk/. On occasion I have made minor corrections.

70. Reynolds and Press, *The Sex Revolts*, 243.

71. Cited in Cristina Martinez, "Polly's Phonic Spree," *Bust Magazine*, Fall 2004, 54.

72. Blandford, *Siren*, 41. "When recently asked 'do you believe that there's more to us than merely our biological selves? Do we go on?,' she replied cryptically, 'Yeah. I believe there's more'" (Martinez, "Polly's Phonic Spree," 56).

73. Tertullian, *On the Apparel of Women* 1.1, in *The Ante-Nicene Fathers*, vol. 4 (1885; reprint, Edinburgh: T&T Clark, 1994), 14.

74. Peter Brown, *Men, Women, and Sexual Renunciation in Early Christianity* (New York: Columbia University Press, 1988), 81; cf. 77–82.

75. The reference to breasts as "dirty pillows" is from the film *Carrie* (1976).

76. For examples of the sheela-na-gig, see: Margaret Miles. "Carnal Abominations: The Female Body as Grotesque" in James Luther Adams and Wilson Yates, eds., *The Grotesque in Art and Literature: Theological Reflections* (Grand Rapids/Cambridge: Eerdmans, 1997), 97–100; Janetta Rebold Benton, *Holy Terrors: Gargoyles on Medieval Buildings* (New York: Abbeville, 1997).

77. The head of Medusa (the Gorgoneion) used to figure frequently on the antefix or other external parts of the ancient Greek temple and was intended to drive away evil forces. It has been argued by at least one scholar that the Gorgoneion was figurative of the female genitals: see Philip F. Slater, *The Glory of Hera* (Princeton: Princeton University Press, 1968), 319ff.

78. For accounts of Lilith, see Louis Ginzberg, *The Legends of the Jews. Vol 1 From the Creation to Jacob* (Baltimore/London: Johns Hopkins, 1998), 65–66.

79. It is entirely appropriate, therefore, that Harvey's major film role to date is playing Mary Magdalene in Hal Hartley's intriguing film *The Book of Life* (1998).

80. She states that she intended *Stories from the City, Stories from the Sea* to be a "beautiful, sumptuous, lovely piece of work." Cited in Cavanagh, "Dark Star," 108.

81. For a detailed analysis of the way Harvey constructs her music to produce a sense of threat and menace, see Sheila Whiteley's examination of "Rid of Me" (in *Rid of Me* [1993]), in *Women and Popular Music: Sexuality, Identity and Subjectivity* (London: Routledge, 2000), 210–11.

82. Blandford, *Siren*, 134.

83. Colin Larkin, ed., *The Virgin Encyclopedia of Nineties Music* (London: Virgin, 2000), 311.

84. O'Dair, "Polly Jean Harvey," 545.

85. Greil Marcus, *Double Trouble: Bill Clinton and Elvis Presley in a Land of No Alternatives* (New York: Henry Holt, 2000), 139. The same holds true for *Uh Huh Her*, of which Harvey said: "With this record, it's pretty ugly really. Quite an ugly sounding batch of songs. Quite disturbing, quite dark, quite bluesy. At the moment it's feeling good. I just go by how my guts feel." Cited online: http://star-ecentral.com/music/sleeve/notes.asp?file=archives/sleeve/2003/1/29/NewPJHarve&date=1/29/2003. She goes so far, in fact, to describe *Uh Huh Her* as "*The Ugly Album*" ("PJ Harvey," *Oor*, May 2004, 45 [in Dutch].

86. For a comparable Nick Cave song, see "Straight to You," from *Henry's Dream* (1992).

87. O'Dair, "Polly Jean Harvey," 547.

88. Sylvia Plath, *Collected Poems* (ed. Ted Hughes; New York: Harper, 1981), 244–47. The final line, "And I eat men like air," certainly has a Harvey-esque quality to it.

89. In "Taut," on *Is This Desire?* (1998), the narrator muses on her crazed boyfriend and repeatedly utters the refrain "Jesus, Save Me."

90. "This Wicked Tongue," in *Songs from the City, Songs from the Sea* (2000), is a song highlighting pessimistic thoughts and does appear to contemplate this sort of marginalization:

> This wicked tongue says
> God is a million miles away
> This wicked tongue says
> He can't see my day to day

91. Blandford (*Siren*, 81) offers a radical interpretation of this song.

92. Cited in Turenne, "Sweet and Lowdown."

93. One wonders whether this line is designed to echo Michael Jackson's (apt!) self-assessment from *Thriller* (1983): "I'm not like other guys."

94. Peraino, "Harvey's 'Man-Size Sextet,'" 57. To add to the horror, Peraino notes that in the symphonic version of the song ("Man-Size Sextet"), there's a quotation of the music from the shower scene in Alfred Hitchcock's *Psycho* (60).

95. Martinez, "Polly's Phonic Spree," 56.

"Pulling Back the Darkness"

Starbound with Jon Anderson

—Randall Holm

Prelude

WITH OVER TWENTY ALBUMS and collaborative projects recorded in a thirty-five–year period, Jon Anderson, the lead singer Yes, combines a distinctive velvet-like voice that slides its way through an upper register that few dare to emulate,[1] with lyrics that at the best of times can only be described as otherworldly. Identified as one of the pioneers of progressive rock, Anderson early on incorporated the use of synthesizers, symphonic instruments, and other alternative sound effects to accompany the rhythm and tempo of rock music. Thereby he creates a layered tapestry of sound that is intended to be visualized as much as it is heard.

Yes was one of several major rock bands that in the early 1970s[2] succeeded in creating a syncretic genre of music known alternatively to fans as prog-rock, art-rock, symphonic rock, classic rock, and avant rock. In effect, progressive rock attempted to maintain the distinctive rhythm and song form of rock music while experimenting with the fusion of jazz, classical, and other established musical forms. The result was a sound that looked like rock, with extravagant stage performances, and at times sounded like rock, with the relentless beat of the drums and guitar; but somehow it did not quite belong in mainstream rock n' roll. Simple three-minute songs often gave way to twenty-minute opuses replete with a

158

multitude of instrumental soloists, dense lyrics bordering on incomprehensibility, complex harmonies, and chord changes. Rock albums that typically consisted of a series of eight to ten unrelated songs became "concept albums," with a running theme both lyrically and musically throughout. And concerts were as much about the show as the music. Elaborate costumes and the introduction of laser lights were all designed to create an experience of sight as much as sound.

From 1968 to 1978 some of the most popular bands of the time fit under this classification of prog-rock. Yes enjoyed prestigious company with the likes of King Crimson, Genesis, Jethro Tull, and Emerson, Lake and Palmer. At the peak of their popularity, with record sales in the millions, Yes sold out Madison Square Garden in 1977 for seven nights in a row, a feat that has not yet been duplicated by a rock band.

However, to put things into cultural perspective, prog-rock was born into the same generation that birthed bell-bottom jeans, hot pants, shag carpets, and a general splash of over-the-counter psychedelic colors. Anyone over-the-top self-indulgent in a decade that wallowed and celebrated its excesses was blending in with the times.

Nevertheless, not everyone was happy with this evolution of rock music. Detractors began distancing themselves from the perceived pretensions of prog-rockers. Some later said that punk rock emerged in the late 1970s as the necessary answer to prog-rock. Punk rock would be touted as a return to the fundamentals of a garage sound. By the late '70s music critics seized every opportunity to lampoon and vilify prog-rock.[3] *Rolling Stone's Record Guide* would describe Yes as "pointlessly intricate guitar and bass solos, caterwauling keyboards, quasi-mystical lyrics proclaimed in alien falsetto, acid dipped album-cover illustrations: this British group wrote the book on art-rock excess."[4] Indeed by the end of the '70s the prog-rock flame appeared to be all but extinguished, snuffed under the cover of its own excesses.

Today, however, in the midst of a thirty-five–year anniversary tour (2004) and the release of a new compilation album, *The Ultimate YES*,[5] it can be safely concluded that rumors of Yes's demise, and by extension that of prog-rock, were somewhat premature. After thirty-five years with numerous changes in personnel,[6] Yes has braved the winds of change. With a lineup that can boast the best of Yes—guitarist Steve Howe, keyboardist Rick Wakeman, drummer Alan Light, bassist Chris Squire, and vocalist Jon Anderson—Yes is playing to sold-out audiences in both Europe and North America.

I suspect that the study of music for any dilettante like myself is as autobiographical as it is anything else. Music not only evokes memories of particular moments; it also enhances those moments with an interdimensional[7] quality as it transports us back to another time and place. Arguably, this is no more powerful than through the music of our adolescence—music that has undeniable spiritual import as it often transcends any reasonable logic.[8]

As for me, music came of age between 1970 and 1975. Except for an early disdain for country music, I confess I was not too discriminatory in my aural tastes. With album covers safely tucked away from parental eyes, I could be found listening to everything from the schmaltzy Bread, to the big brass sound of Chicago, the earthy sounds of Cream, and ethereal otherworldly ballads of Jethro Tull and Yes.

Currently as a professor of biblical studies and theology, I have had ample time to take a second look at those early memories. In particular, I have been strangely drawn to the oblique lyrics of Jon Anderson, lead singer of Yes. At times bordering on being incomprehensible,[9] Anderson is on a spiritual mission. An indefatigable optimist, humanist, and mystic, Jon Anderson is committed to making "Beetyfol [sic]" music to transform the face of evil "by the one we call Love, Love, Love."[10] In what could only be described as an autobiographical parable, Anderson likens himself to the holder of a *Singing Flame* that works to hold back the darkness. This Flame accompanies his listeners across the lake of forgotten Dreams, leading them around the Caverns of the Dead to a "world where children sing and play, and dream only wonderful dreams; no sadness, no crazy feeling, only the pure joy of living."[11]

In what follows I develop an overall template to assist in understanding the inherent spirituality in Anderson's work. Unfortunately, I have soon discovered that Anderson's spirituality is as oblique as his lyrics. Anderson does not readily fall into any conventional framework. In 1975, after playing a concert at the Las Vegas Convention Center, Anderson was preparing himself to meet Frank Sinatra at Caesars Palace when he for the first time encountered an angel. Apparently the angel appeared as a little girl no more than seven years of age, who told Anderson that he was doing good work and to continue on. Anderson explains: "From that moment, there in Vegas, I met angels. It was a wonderful experience for me. So I didn't meet Frank. But I met God. And it gave me such sustenance over the years, and strength over the years, as to why I do what I do."[12] As unconventional as that may seem, since then

Anderson claims to have spoken with fairies[13] and even some persons close to him who have died.

As a songwriter, Anderson freely dabbles in a wide variety of religious and spiritual writings. In his music one readily finds traces of Christianity, Hinduism, Zen Buddhism, Native American Toltec spirituality, Celtic mythology, and the list can go on. In an interview with *Music Street Journal*, Anderson reiterated his universalistic vision: "We're all spiritual people. Islamic people are spiritual. Buddhists are spiritual, Zen. All the rivers meet in the same ocean. . . . I've read it years ago that Krishna was Christ. Buddha was Christ. Mohammed was Christ. Jesus was Christ."[14]

For inspiration Anderson draws on a number of eclectic sources. Among those who have influenced his music, Anderson acknowledges friend and musician Vangelis, and spiritualists Carlos Casteneda and Paramhansa Yogananda. But without a doubt his greatest influence has come from a woman he met in Hawaii whom he simply calls Divine Mother. It was Divine Mother who taught Anderson how to meditate and discover the awakening of the "third eye."[15]

Jon Anderson is certainly a complex person. His home displays several native Dream Catchers, and when he takes time off he can be found sipping "Dream Tea" while listening to the likes to Strevinsky and Sibelius. He talks about interdimensional energies, our dream potential, the feeling that oneness of being comes from being in balance, the fourth dimension of higher knowledge, and the experience of chakra energy. Commenting on working with such an individual, keyboardist Rick Wakeman adds: "Well, Jon's the only guy I know who's trying to save this planet while living on another one."[16] In a recent interview with Anderson, journalist Alexis Petridis shows that he understands Wakeman's position. He comments: "It's hard not to warm to someone who is willing to let you in on the meaning of life within minutes of meeting you—but his is a rock star from an entirely alien era."[17] Even amid a current revival in spirituality, it is hard to know what to make of Anderson.

Tales from Topographic Oceans

Perhaps the best place to start in this brief analysis of spiritual themes in Anderson's work is 1974, the year of which Homer Simpson quips: "Rock attained perfection. It's a scientific fact." That was the same year Yes, at the height of their popularity, released their sixth album, *Tales from Topographic*

Oceans,[18] a concept album that remains to this day their most controversial venture. For those already enamored by Yes, the album was brave and enlightened as it musically and lyrically explored new territory for a rock group. For those who were either undecided or critical of the prog-rock trend, *Tales* pushed them over the edge of the prog-ocean into a cesspool that by default opened the door to punk. The group itself was divided on the merit of the work. Keyboardist Rick Wakeman left the group at the end of the project. He is on record as saying: "*Tales from Topographic Oceans* is like a woman's padded bra. The cover looks good, . . . but when you peel off the padding there's not a lot there."[19] Even their producer-engineer Eddie Offord apologized: "That album was really a horrific album. . . . That album almost killed me. . . . I think there was a psychological effect of, 'Oh, we're doing a double album; now we can make things twice as long, twice as boring, and twice as drawn out.'"[20] If those closest to the music were unsure of its merits, music critics had a feeding frenzy. *Tales* has been described as mindless noodling, where Yes is at its pretentious and bloated best. Yet, for true Yes fans *Topographic Oceans* remains to this day a slightly flawed virtuoso masterpiece. It is considered a defining moment that has made a major contribution to their longevity.

Coming after the critical and commercial success of their previous release *Close to the Edge*, what could possibly account for such vitriol and passion? On the surface *Topographic Oceans* was a stretch since it consisted of a double LP with only one song on each side. Each song lasted over twenty minutes. In total, the album is over eighty minutes long and should be considered as one song with four movements. By default, *Topographic Ocean* would not fit on any radio billboard that relied on a three- to four-minute attention span.

Structurally the four movements correspond to a footnote on page 83 of Paramhansa Yogananda's *Autobiography of a Yogi*. The titles follow the four-part Shastric scriptures: Shrutis, Suritis, Puranas, and Tantras. Yogananda himself and his Eastern philosophy was no stranger to rock n' roll having achieved a degree of notoriety by previously appearing on the background of the Beatles' *Sgt. Pepper* cover.

My own interest in the album, however, lies in the lyrics as a synthesis of Jon Anderson's spiritual framework. At first blush the lyrics appear as though they are individual words tumbled in a drum and chosen at random. Consider:

As the silence of season on we relive abridge sails afloat
As to call light the soul shall sing of the velvet sailors course on
Shine or moons send me memories trail over days of forgotten tales.

In an almost apologetic tone the bassist Chris Squire reports:

> I used to sing most of the harmonies and half the time I didn't know
> what the hell I was singing about. Jon has always been fairly abstract,
> and I think that explaining it is a difficult thing for him to do. But
> that's the way we worked—Jon was trying to make the vocals part of
> the instrumental tapestry, and that approach was important to us.[21]

If poetry is the fine art of conciseness, then *Tales* is probably poor
poetry. At the risk of reading too much into these lyrics, Anderson seems
to be reaching for something different in *Tales*. Anderson invites listeners
into an expansive drama that reaches as far back as the lost civilization of
Atlantis and moves to some future utopia. The track listing is as follows:

Track listing
1st Movement: Shrutis
The Revealing Science of God (Dance of the Dawn)
2nd Movement: Suritis
The Remembering (High the Memory)
3rd Movement: Puranas
The Ancient (Giants under the Sun)
4th Movement: Tantras
Ritual (Nous Sommes du Soleil [We Are of the Sun])

The Revealing Science of God

The opening movement[22] is aptly entitled "The Revealing Science of
God," as Anderson attempts to fuse together mystery and reason into a
seamless dance. The drama moves from creation into a threatening
wilderness, with the future held out as promise. Listeners may recognize
something of the exodus story being replayed in prose, couched albeit in
Eastern philosophy. In this opening movement we witness in succession
the "Dawn of light, thought, our power and love," which though presenting promise, appear to be vulnerable to potential sabotage. Light is

threatened by forgetfulness, thought is undermined by disjointed memories, power is corrupted by misused passion. Love seems to suffer from a wrongheaded desire to follow only "tunes of a different age," where "different" presumably refers to a destructive age.

Rhetorically Anderson asks: "What happened to this song we once knew so well / . . . What happened to wonders we once knew so well / Did we forget what happened surely we can tell." Evidently despite a "future poised with the splendor" something has happened that threatens the promise—a promised place beyond war and violence to both land and people. In these first few stanzas Anderson holds promise and jeopardy in a sharp tension. Over the "tallest rainbow" and "sunshower seasons" stands a "raped forest" and "warland seekers."

However, before leaving the "Revelation," Anderson is quick to offer us a hint of salvation in the form of a living tradition:

And through the rhythm of moving slowly
Sent through the rhythm work out the story
Move over glory to sons of old fighters past
Young Christians see it from the beginning
Old people feel it, that's what they're saying
. . . .
Past present movers moments we'll process the future.

Anderson's prose reminds me of Edmund Burke's definition of tradition: a "partnership in all science, all art, every virtue (that) becomes a partnership between not only those who are living, but [also] between those who are living, those who are dead, and those who are to be born."[23] Or, to put it in the words of theologian Jaroslav Pelikan, the future promised land is only attainable as humanity reassesses and appropriates "the living tradition of the dead and not the dead tradition of the living,"[24] which inexorably leads to war, rape, and pillage of both land and humanity.

The Remembering (High the Memory)

The second movement[25] picks up the previous theme and addresses the need for discernment. Since so many stories and voices vie for our attention as we "stand on hills of long forgotten yesterdays," and since each of these stories can be subjected to myriad interpretations, "alternate ways and tunes," how can anyone know which tune we should sing? For

Anderson, the answer does not appear to be an either/or but a both/and. At this point he is more concerned with process than message. The point is to listen and sing:

> We dream as we dream! Dream as one
> And I do think very well
> That the song might take you silently.

In effect he says, sail away with your thoughts, expand your mind:

> Don the cap and close your eyes
> Imagine all the glorious challenge
> . . . .
> Remember to sail the skies
> Distant suns
> Will we reach
> Winds allow
> Other skylines
> Other skylines to hold you.

For Anderson, here lies the "Topographic Ocean": a vast expanse of experiences, ideas, beliefs, and even previous lives,[26] which generally lie beneath the naked eye, but which all flow eventually into a common river of consciousness.

It is in this state—when we can see, hear, and witness the lost stories of other civilizations and individuals—that we can learn from the past and move to a better future:

> All the dying cried before you
> Relayer
> We've rejoiced in all their meaning
> Relayer
> We advance we retrace our stories
> . . . .
> All the passion spent on one cross
> Relayer
> Sail the futile wars they suffer
> Relayer
> We advance we retrace our story, fail safe now

In Anderson's vision, death, pain, and destruction have collaborated together, sometimes in the name of religion, and by default are pointing us in the direction of alternative tunes and a new rainbow. Remembering reconnects us with the ancient people in the hope that we all become aware of our heritage as tribal people and take care of this planet for the sake of our souls, our ancient ones, and our future children.[27]

The Ancient (Giants under the Sun)

The third movement[28] delves further into the past, pointing to lost civilizations whom Anderson believes have left behind "immense treasures of knowledge." Lyrically, the piece appears to serve as an interlude to set up the final movement. Rhetorically, with all this knowledge both lost and found, it asks:

> Where does reason stop and killing just take over
> Does a lamb cry out before we shoot it dead
> Are there many more in comfort understanding
> Is the movement in the head[29]

It is here that Anderson's vision stumbles, as I point out later in greater detail. Anderson recognizes the unreasonable nature of evil. But he still holds out the hope that proper enlightenment can change this destructive cycle. I submit, however, that Anderson fails to compensate for a heart that may be corrupt to begin with.

Ritual (Nous Sommes Du Soleil)

The final movement[30] returns to the sublime optimism Anderson has portrayed throughout his work.

> Surely daybreaks cross our path
> . . . .
> Hurry home as love is true
> Will help us through the night

With Anderson, there seems to be something of an already/not yet dichotomy that is often reflected in Christian theology.

Catch as we look and use the passions that flow
As we try we continue
We receive all we venture to give
. . . .
We won't tender our song clearer
Till we sail
Then I will be there
As clearer companions

In the meantime,

Hold me my love, hold me today, call me round
Travel we say, wander we choose, love tune
Lay upon me, hold me around lasting hours
We love when we play

To his credit, Anderson is not a reincarnated flower child of the '60s. As optimistic as he is, Anderson is acutely aware that "Life seems like a / Fight," evil abounds. However, to coin a Bible-based biblical adage, where evil abounds, in Anderson's world love abounds greater still (cf. Rom 5). Love is the cure. Only through love do changes come.

Postlude

Twenty-two years after composing *Topographic Tales*, Anderson returns to this drama in a short story entitled "The Forgotten Star: A Story of Love, Peace and Forgiveness."[31] A little less ethereal than *Topographic Tales*, the story begins with a boy sobbing at the sight of a homeless family sleeping in their cardboard home during the Christmas season. For Anderson, this symbolizes in particular the failure of religion as a faith in form only, which ignores the general plight of people and their environment. The boy is encountered by a girl who has come back from the year 2020—a time, we are told, when the stars have long disappeared and people have forgotten the true meaning of Christmas. Moving in interdimensional time, she takes the boy on a journey to search for the seven points of the "Star of Love." They travel to the jungles of the Amazon, where indigenous children are singing "This Glowing Earth"[32] and receive the first star piece. From there they dive into the ocean and visit the lost city of Atlantis, where sea nymphs singing "Under the Sun"[33] give the couple the next piece. Subsequent pieces are found in Kauai among tree fairies singing "I'll Find My Way Home,"[34] in the air among doves and eagles singing "Change we Must,"[35] in the desert among Bedouin children singing "Take the Water to the Mountain,"[36] and on the mountains among children of shepherds singing "Where Were You."[37] Finally, they are visited by true angels, who give them the final star piece: "Ave Verum"[38] is sung, and the angels explain the true meaning of Christmas:

> You are Christ inside. Krishna was a Christ. Mohammed was a Christ. Buddha was a Christ. Jesus was a Christ. You are the Gift of Life. You are the Gift of love. You have the power within to give the Christ love everyday. You see the world as you want to. Whether you know or not, Christ is always here, always with us and so is Christmas. You don't need presents. You don't need trees, lights or snow. You only need Love / love for yourself. Then you can love others.[39]

For all his spiritual talk, Anderson has little time for religion that he believes gets in the way of true freedom. We are all spiritual people, he says, and we do not need to go any farther than our own selves to find the truth. In an age when musicians and in particular those often associated with rock music stand out because of their destructive behavior, it is refreshing to know that some take their work seriously as an opportunity to make this world a better place. It is easy to sympathize with what Anderson is trying to do and for that matter why critics either love him or despise him for his pretensions. Anderson envisions a world where all the streams of life, however muddy they may be, will one day converge into a river of love. However, missing from Anderson's anthropology is any acknowledgement of the depths of human depravity. Anderson would create a climate for people to find themselves and discover the goodness already within. He even laments the loss of civilizations and a crumbling ecology, but he fails to fully appreciate the lostness of the human condition that has precipitated such conditions. To someone who is lost, dreaming, and/or meditating will at best only confirm their lostness. Anderson would then have us unravel the onion of our life and discover our true meaning. But what happens if one unravels the onion and finds nothing there?

We live in a vast world, a world that Anderson wants to expand to lost civilizations and other dimensions beyond our ability to fully grasp or see.

Anderson does not hesitate to take his listening audience beyond our immediate horizon into a space of interdimensional energies, fairies, angels, aliens, and the like. In the end, however, he underestimates the human condition and its ability to save itself. Anderson may need to revisit the need for some sort of mediator who can redeem the human condition. By itself, love will not always conquer, even in a room thick with sage burning and swirling in charka colors. But, Yes, Anderson is fun to listen to.

Notes

1. As one of the most distinct voices in rock music, Jon Anderson is acquired taste. For those who love his voice, Anderson can do no wrong. On the other hand, those who dislike it fall over each other in similes to describe their disdain. Jackson Griffith writes: "It didn't help that Anderson sang those lyrics in a fey ethereal voice that sounded like a boys choir of hobbits after Frodo stole Galadriel's secret elven mushroom stash and fed it to them in the recording studio." *Sacramento News and Review*, November 20, 2003; online: www.newsreview.com/issues/sacto/2003-11-20/arts.asp (accessed May 3, 2004).

2. It is generally assumed that prog-rock in its genesis spanned the years 1968–78.

3. Griffith, ibid.: "Admitting you have an appetite for any kind of prog is an invitation to a metaphorical bum's rush, at least from people who value the compression and brevity of the prevailing punk-rock aesthetic."

4. As quoted by David Womack, "Yes," *San Francisco Music Chronicle*; online: http://www.crecon.com/davidwomack/yes-rockandroll.htm (accessed June 1, 2004).

5. Yes, *The Ultimate Yes—35th Anniversary Collection* (Elektra/Rhino US, 2004).

6. In thirty-five years, Yes has gone through too many personnel changes to list them. The only constant in these years has been Chris Squire, the bassist. Ironically, their changes have not been too "progressive" since many of the key members such as Jon Anderson and Rick Wakeman have left only to return again.

7. Apologies to Jon Anderson for shamelessly borrowing one of his key concepts. See Jon Anderson, "The Forgotten Star," online: http://www.jonanderson.com/story_forgottenstar.html (accessed April 1, 2004).

8. What else could explain some of my colleagues in biblical studies behaving like maudlin groupies the moment a KISS or Metallica concert announces that it is coming to town?

9. Everyone seems to have a favorite oblique line that defies any sense of logic. For example:

> A seasoned witch could call you from the depths of your disgrace
> And rearrange your liver to the solid mental grace
> And achieve it all with music that came quickly from afar
> Then taste the fruit of man recorded losing all against the hour.

From Yes, "The Solid Time of Change," *Close to the Edge* (LP Atlantic Records, September 1972).

10. Jon Anderson, "The Singing Flame," online: http://www.jonanderson.com/story_singingflame.html (accessed March 5, 2004).

11. Ibid.

12. Doug Elfman, "Yes Singer Finds Vegas Spiritual Experience," *Las Vegas Review Journal*, April 20, 2004; online: http://www.reviewjournal.com/lvrj_home/2004/Apr-20-Tue-2004/living/23614263.html (accessed June 1, 2004).

13. "Fairies live in a parallel faster dimension than ours. It's right parallel, and it's actually where lasers comes from, the laser phosphorus energy." Anderson believes that these fairies are responsible for sending us the laser beam: "They said, Hey! You can have it back." Because we used to have it, as you know, in Lemoria and Atlantis, in those days. And they've given it back, and look what we're using it for. We're using it for all sort of magical things. Healing, . . . you know we make our music, . . . laser sound reproduction is coming, no more speakers. But that's the future. That's the fourth dimension, which we are slowly moving into." Quoted by Elizabeth Gips, "Keys to Ascension—An Interview with Jon Anderson," KKUP-91.3 FM Radio, Cupertino, CA; online: http://yesinthepress.com/1996/may/may27_96.html (accessed May 12, 2004).

14. Jon Anderson, "Interview with Jon Anderson of Yes," *Music Street Journal*, no. 33 (October 1, 2001); online: http://www.musicstreetjournal.com/jonandersoninterview.htm (accessed April 1, 2004).

15. Based on a book by Vera Stanley Alder, *Finding of the "Third Eye"* (1938; rev. ed., 1968; London: Century, 1987). Anderson describes the "third eye" as some sort of radio antenna that presumably gives him insight into hidden truths.

16. Tom Roland, "The Sonic World of Yes Is Still in Lush Orbit," *Orange County Register*, July 29, 2001; online: http://wwwyesinthepress.com/2001/jul/jul29_01.html (accessed May 28, 2004).

17. Alexis Petridis, "The Idea Is to Unravel the Onion," *The Guardian*, July 30, 2003; online: http://guardian.co.uk/petridis (accessed April 5, 2004).

18. Yes, *Tales from Topographic Oceans*, LP (Atlantic, 1974).

19. Rick Wakeman in an interview, in *Yesstories: Yes in Their Own Words* (compiled by Tim Morse; New York: St. Martin's Press, 1996), 45.

20. Eddie Offord in an interview, in *Yesstories*, 45.

21. Quoted by Brett Milano, "Topogaphic Rock: Reconsidering Prog in Light of Reissued Yes," *The Boston Phoenix*, September 26, 2003; online: http://www.boston-phoenix.com/boston/music/top/documents/03179848.asp (accessed April 1, 2004).

22. Each of the movements is accompanied by liner notes meant to explain that movement's overall thrust. "Shrutis: The Revealing Science of God can be seen as an everopening flower in which simple truths emerge examining the complexities and magic of the past and how we should not forget the song that has been left to us to hear. The knowledge of God is a search, constant and clear." Anderson liner notes, *Tales from Topographic Oceans*.

23. Edmund Burke, *Reflections on the Revolution in France* (ed. Conor Cruise O'Brien; New York: Penguin English Library, 1982), 194–95.

24. Jaroslav Pelikan, *The Vindication of Tradition* (New Haven: Yale University Press, 1984), 65.

25. "Suritis: The Remembering. All our thoughts, impressions, knowledge, fears, have been developing for millions of years. What we can relate to is our own past, our own life, our own history. Here, it is especially Rick's keyboards that bring alive the ebb and flow and depth of our mind's eye: the topographic ocean. Hopefully we should appreciate that given points in time are not so significant as the nature of what is impressed on the mind, and how it is retained and used." Anderson liner notes, *Tales from Topographic Oceans*.

26. Anderson writes: "Like a dreamer all our lives are only lost begotten changes." Is this a cryptic reference to reincarnation? Elsewhere, Anderson credits Constantine in the third century as being responsible for removing all the information on reincarnation from the Bible "just to keep us unorganized." Gips, "An Interview with Jon Anderson."

27. The idea of a tribal people is a notion that reappears frequently in interviews with Anderson. He is loath to explain the term except to say: "I was Chinese once; I was Negro once; I was American Indian once; I was aborigine. I've been everybody. We have all been tribal people." Gips, "An interview with Jon Anderson."

28. "Puranas: The Ancient probes still further into the past beyond the point of remembering. Here Steve's guitar is pivotal in sharpening reflection on the beauties and treasures of lost civilisations, Indian, Chinese, central American, Atlantean. These and other people left an immense treasure of knowledge." Anderson liner notes, *Tales from Topographic Oceans.*

29. "Head" in Anderson's world is problematic. In a song entitled "Changes" Anderson quips: "For some reason you're questioning why / I always believe it gets better / One difference between you and I / You're heart is inside your head." Yes, "Changes," "9012Live—the Solos," video EP (Atco Music, 1985).

30. "Tantras: The ritual seven notes of freedom to learn and to know the ritual of life. Life is a fight between sources of evil and pure love. Alan and Chris present and relay the struggle out of which come a positive source. Nous sommes du soleil. We are of the sun. We can see." Anderson liner notes, *Tales of Topographic Oceans.*

31. Jon Anderson, "The Forgotten Star: A Story of Love, Peace and Forgiveness," online: http://www.jonanderson.com/story_forgottenstar.html (accessed February 10, 2004).

32. Jon Anderson, "Forest of Fire," *Three Ships*, LP (Elektra, 1985).

33. Yes, *Tales of Topographic Oceans.*

34. Jon and Vangelis, "I'll Find My Way Home," *I'll Find My Way Home*, LP (Polydor, 1981).

35. Jon Anderson, "Change We Must," *Change We Must*, CD (Angel, 1994).

36. Yes, "Take the Water to the Mountain," *Union Album*, CD (Arista, 1991).

37. Jon Anderson, "Where Were You," *Three Ships*, LP (Elektra, 1985).

38. Jon Anderson, "Ave Verum," written by Mozart, *Toltec*, CD (High Street, 1996).

39. Anderson, "The Forgotten Star."

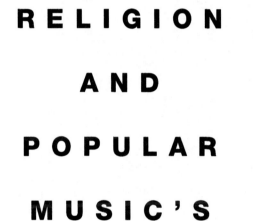

Section Three

RELIGION

AND

POPULAR

MUSIC'S

AUDIENCES

"God's Smiling on You and He's Frowning Too"

Rap and the Problem of Evil

—Angela M. Nelson

Theodicy and Humanocentric Theism

SOME AFRICAN-AMERICAN SONG LYRICS illustrate a unique African-American conceptualization of a theological problem in Judeo-Christian belief: theodicy. From the Greek words *theos* (God) and *dike* (justice), "theodicy" is the term for the propositional answers to the question or problem of evil. Theodicy is the defense or justification of God's justice and righteousness in the face of evil's existence in the world. Human beings posit different theodicies in an attempt to explain how a good God permits evil in the world.[1] African-American gospel music heralds the "harder the cross / brighter the crown" theodicy, which means one's suffering on earth pays off incrementally in heaven. Blues emphasizes the "reap what you sow" theodicy,[2] which means suffering is brought on by one's own misdeeds. In the context of this study, I am interested in secular theodicies. I will draw on thought of black theological thinkers William R. Jones, in his book *Is God a White Racist?* and Jon Michael Spencer, in his essay on the theodicy of the blues.

Spencer especially influenced my resolve that theodicies do in fact exist in rap. In an essay titled "God in Secular Music Culture: The Theodicy of the Blues as the Paradigm of Proof," Spencer demonstrates that early blues singers reflected on both the cause of evil and the nature of suffering. They

175

developed various theodicies addressing these "ultimate concerns."[3] Spencer identifies two blues theodicies to demonstrate that the ethos of the blues is in fact religious: the "reap what you sow" and "work of the devil" theodicies. The "reap what you sow" theodicy, the most typical of the blues theodicies, explains the suffering of "blues people" as derived from their living a life of reckless abandon—gambling, drinking, drug use, sexual promiscuity, and so forth.[4] The "work of the devil" theodicy made the devil a convenient means of explaining the existence of certain kinds of suffering in the lives of blues people.[5] In other words, blues people often blamed the devil for wreaking havoc in their lives.

As Spencer argues and demonstrates through analyzing blues texts, blues people, to the surprise of some scholars, unquestionably reflect on the cause of evil and the nature of human suffering. Indeed, for many African-Americans, an understanding of the cause and nature of suffering in their present and historical lives has framed most of their verbal discourse. For this reason, a black theodicy—one that not only exonerates and justifies God's purpose and works in the face of evil, but also determines the cause of black suffering or oppression[6]—has been central to the black experience in and beyond America. African-American music has been a major medium for the documentation of black theodicean reflection upon suffering, and today rap is one such medium.

As already mentioned, theodicy is a concept that operates in Western monotheism. Except for Judaism, it is almost entirely a Christian concern that dates back at least to the writings of the fifth-century theologian Augustine.[7] Traditional Christian belief in God describes the "ultimate reality" as the unique infinite, the uncreated, the eternal personal Spirit absolute in goodness and power.[8] The problem of theodicy is in acknowledging the goodness and power of God in a world with moral and natural evil.[9] The problem, as theodicist John Hick details it, is this: (1) If God is perfectly good, he must want to abolish all evil. (2) If God is unlimitedly powerful, he must be able to abolish all evil. (3) But evil exists. Therefore, either God is not perfectly good or his power is limited.[10] A theodicy, then, comprises the vindication of God in an evil-stricken world. The theodicy problem is a major concern of theologians across the world, but it is not my intention to give any further detailed exposition of the endless discourse it has aroused. My task here is to demonstrate the interrelatedness of the theodicy problem to the black experience in America and the existence of secular theodicy in African-American popular and folk music, particularly rap from the late 1980s and early 1990s.

The traditional definition of theodicy may seem to fall outside the periphery of black secular music (or any secular music for that matter) since it involves expressly the vindication of God. Rap appears to be centered on the ultimacy of human beings rather than God. If this is true, it seems to question the assumption that rap can be examined in a theodicean framework. However, rap can be examined in this framework if one embraces the notion of secular humanism or humanocentric theism. "Humanocentric theism" is a concept developed by theologian William R. Jones in response to the implied purpose and definition of black theology as a theology of liberation. Liberation assumes that human beings are oppressed in some manner and are suffering to some degree. African-Americans still wear the "stripes" of almost 250 years of enslavement in America. The lingering effects exist in the areas of education, housing, employment, health care, and law. Jones insists that we need to give special attention to black oppression and suffering. He also suggests that black theologians should embrace new models for treating black suffering and openly illustrate that God is not, in fact, a white racist, who willingly allows black people to suffer under white oppression.[11]

Jones contends that theodicy must be the controlling element in a black theology of liberation. Yet he demonstrates that it was already an implied and explicitly stated concern of leading black theologians James Cone, Joseph Washington, Albert Cleage, Major Jones, and J. Deotis Roberts because of their collective dialogues about black oppression and suffering.[12] Jones's theodicy, or humanocentric theism, and secular humanism both advocate the functional ultimacy of human beings. Human beings must act as if they were the ultimate valuators or ultimate agents in human history, or both. Humanocentric theism puts the responsibility for human actions and evil upon human beings. It removes God's overruling sovereignty from human history. In this way, Jones points out, God's responsibility for the crimes and errors of human history—Auschwitz, Native American genocide, the European slave trade—is reduced if not effectively eliminated.[13]

Humanocentric theism is based on thought from the writings of existentialist philosophers Martin Buber, Jean-Paul Sartre, and Albert Camus, and theologians Harvey Cox and Erich Fromm.[14] Although these scholars are not of African descent and have little personal knowledge of the black experience in America, they are significant to Jones's thesis because of their affirmation of the freedom of human beings to make choices that are best for them and in keeping with God's will. Human beings portray

God's will and purpose for them by exercising human freedom, their freedom to choose. Human beings then become cocreators of human existence. In this respect, racism—probably the most oppressive circumstance for people of African descent—is traced to human rather than divine forces; God is not a white racist.[15] Therefore, the theodicies of such black secular music forms as rap can and should be interpreted under the rubric of humanocentric theism. No doubt, most (if not all) rappers would agree. I propose that rap has at least two secular or humanocentric theodicies that resolve the problem of black suffering without permitting the position that God is a white racist. I term these the "white supremacy" and "slave mentality" theodicies.

White Supremacy and Slave Mentality Theodicies

The white supremacy theodicy posited by rappers is derived from the blatant forms of European (white) dominance over nonwhite populations. "White supremacy" refers to the attitudes, ideologies, and policies associated with "white domination."[16] Although white supremacy was a primary factor in the enslavement system in America and in white-black relations in the Republic of South Africa, white supremacy as an institutionalization of written and unwritten policies in America did not fully come into being until the period of Reconstruction. Recognizing the economic, political, and educational gains of newly freed blacks following the Civil War, southern whites aggressively began campaigns to make African-Americans chattel, even though slavery was abolished. White supremacist acts included legislation that disenfranchised blacks, allowed rampant violence against blacks (fueled by the reorganization of the Ku Klux Klan in 1915), and enacted a series of Jim Crow laws and Black Codes similar to the old slave codes. These actions advanced the sharecropping system, which kept most black sharecroppers in debt, bound to the land, and bound to white landowners.[17]

The most developed form of white supremacy recently existed in the Republic of South Africa, with its color bars, apartheid, and citizenship rights restricted to privileged group members characterized by light skin pigmentation.[18] The latter feature has been experienced in America to a lesser degree; however, color bars and racial segregation have been blatantly practiced and are only now showing concrete signs of being eliminated. Historian George M. Fredrickson states that white supremacy also suggests systematic and self-conscious efforts to make a person's race (or color) a qualification for membership in the dominant community.[19] Although white America shows evidence of a systematic exclusion of African-Americans, the sum of its efforts has not necessarily been self-conscious or government sanctioned. In fact, compared to South Africa's once well-devised policies, it almost seems coincidental that America has such a racist and discriminatory history. Nevertheless, the main concern here is that many whites, or people of European descent, have attitudes and ideologies that do not permit African-Americans to realize freedom. These attitudes and ideologies comprise what is called "white supremacy."

In rap music, African-American females and males express a theodicy that says the choices, values, and resulting actions of white Americans are the direct cause of the oppression and suffering of African-Americans. Consequently, black enslavement in North America was not an evil sent by the good Lord or a God who was a white racist. Instead, it was a circumstance created and augmented through decisions made by white people who also happened to have opposing worldviews on the meaning of humanity.

White American views on black humanity have affected and continue to affect African-Americans emotionally, mentally, physically, and socially. What results is a theodicy closely related to the white supremacy theodicy, one that places the perpetuation of black suffering squarely on the shoulders of African-Americans themselves: the slave mentality theodicy. "Slave mentality" refers to the residuals of slavery in the psyche of African-Americans. Amiri Baraka describes "slave mentality" as the mental adjustments slaves made during over two hundred years of slavery, the "marks" left by bending to the will of the white oppressor.[20] He further adds that a slave mentality encompasses some blacks accepting the superiority of the white oppressor and an accompanying contempt for other black people who do not possess the "refined" characteristics of the oppressor.[21]

In a more detailed description of this concept, William Jones comments on slave mentality while discussing theodicy, oppression, and quietism. His conclusion is that theodicies that say African-Americans are God's chosen vessels and that their suffering is God's means of disciplining them for his divine task are in fact "enslaving beliefs":

At the base of oppression lies a complex of beliefs that define the role and status of the oppressor and the oppressed, and this complex of beliefs legitimates both. The oppressed, in part, are oppressed precisely because they buy, or are indoctrinated to accept, a set of beliefs that negate those attitudes and actions necessary for liberation. Accordingly, the purpose and first step of liberation is to effect a radical conversion of the mind of the oppressed, to free his mind from those destructive and enslaving beliefs that stifle the movement toward liberation.[22]

In other words, Jones contends that slave mentality also entails the oppressed accepting the goals and outcomes of the oppressor as equally profitable and advantageous for themselves. The slave mentality theodicy, which is humanocentric, puts the responsibility for continued black oppression and suffering upon African-Americans who are unable or refuse to realize that they carry the "scars" of the slavery experience in both their social and mental lives.[23]

Adding tremendously to the scholarship on slave mentalities is clinical psychologist Na'im Akbar. In his book *Chains and Images of Psychological Slavery*, Akbar says that slavery was a "severe psychological and social shock to the minds of African-Americans."[24] He then outlines nine areas in which the "slave mentality" is present in African-American social and mental life: (1) attitudes toward work; (2) mixed attitudes toward material objects and property; (3) disrespect of African-American leadership; (4) overwhelming tendency to become "clowns" or entertainers; (5) sense of inferiority; (6) disunited communities; (7) women choosing to become "breeders" and men seeking to prove their manhood through physical exploits, sexual exploits, or deviation; (8) excessive consciousness of skin color; and (9) psychological confusion from racial, religious, and symbolic imagery.[25]

African-American rappers comment on several of the manifest forms of slave mentality that Akbar describes. Many rappers believe, in general, that African-Americans are failing to make the best possible decisions for the lives and livelihood of themselves, their families, their communities, and their race. For example, in her rap entitled "Cappucino," female rapper MC Lyte tells the story of a girl named Berry, who would not listen to a social worker's warning about a notorious crack dealer. Lyte said Berry would not listen just as so many others do not listen to warnings about potential dangers to their lives.[26] In "Not Wit a Dealer," MC Lyte warns her friend Cecelia to stay away from a crack dealer named Born Supreme. Cecelia tells MC Lyte: "Girl, I love him, he treats me so good, he gets much respect in my neighborhood." Again, MC Lyte tells us that Cecelia would not listen because she, like so many other black females, loves her man even more than herself.[27] Rappers such as MC Lyte believe that African-Americans are not living out God's divine decrees by discerning between good and evil, and by identifying societal elements that systematically hinder their racial progress. A slave mentality prevents African-Americans from attaining this liberation.

To summarize, the white supremacy theodicy, in view of humanocentric theism, says that ungodly decisions made by people of European origin in the past and present continue to result in black oppression and suffering. The slave mentality theodicy says that the residuals of white supremacy—especially from slavery—have left scars on the mental psyches of African-Americans, causing perpetual self-inflicted black oppression and suffering. Both theodicies are nonbiblical and noneschatological; rappers neither draw life narratives from Sacred Scripture nor find it feasible or comforting to expect a possible future reward at the end of time.

What makes the slave mentality theodicy a great burden to African-Americans, to emphasize the crucial point, is that it causes passivity or quietism (the refusal to undertake corrective action),[28] so much so that the slave mentality theodicy resembles otherworldiness. This otherworldliness is what Benjamin E. Mays terms "compensatory beliefs,"[29] which enable African-Americans to endure hardship, suffer pain, and withstand maladjustment. But such beliefs do not necessarily motivate them to eliminate the source of these ailments.[30] The slave mentality, indeed, prevents African-Americans from desiring to liberate themselves; however, this part is not precisely a compensatory belief. The important difference is that, since African-Americans have "enslaving beliefs" passed down through the generations over centuries, in some cases they do not recognize hardship, pain, and maladjustment. In other words, the psychic and social maladjustments of slavery are complete to the extent that some African-Americans today do not even recognize that they do not have the essential tools—such as education in African and African-American history—to eliminate the source of the ailments they suffer. The source of the ills they suffer, as rappers repeatedly point out, has been a racist ideology. Until African-Americans reach the state of awareness that rappers are questing for the masses, the slave mentality theodicy will continue to be a self-inflicted evil that is perhaps even more enduring than actual enslavement.

Accompanying the notions of the white supremacy and slave mentality theodicies are African-American conceptions of God and Satan and the nature of black suffering. Although there may be tremendous textual differences between the conceptions of these, in black sacred and secular music there still remains the past of slavery, which connects sacred and secular forms of music. Molefi Asante contends that in order to understand the role of vocal expressiveness within African-American communities, one must recognize slavery and *nommo* (the generative and dynamic quality of vocal expression).[31] Because of the shared historical experience of enslavement, African-Americans both in the sacred (church) and secular (nonchurch) context usually have the same concrete ideas about God and Satan and the circumstances of suffering. This fine line of what is sacred (and of God) and is not (and of Satan) is present even in rap music.

Conceptions of God and Satan

Jon Michael Spencer states that blues was ideologically "oppugnant."[32] One of the attitudes and ideologies that blues oppugned, or opposed, was Jim Crow ethics: the systematic discrimination, segregation, and oppression of people of color based on race. This particular oppugnancy is overwhelmingly evident in rap. Rappers view Jim Crow ethics as playing an influential part in the continual bombardment of black self-worth, self-esteem, and self-affirmation. Segregation, endorsed by Jim Crow ethics, was a successful breeding ground for white fears about blacks and their supposed inferiority. White disdain for blackness—both its color and its disposition—culminated in the highest code of separation, which was to prevent the "mongrelization" of the white race through so-called miscegenation. An excerpt from Mississippi Senator Theodore Bilbo's book *Take Your Choice: Separation or Mongrelization* (1947) is typical of white sentiment, not only in the past but also in the present, as the horrific killing of a black man in Jasper, Texas suggests. Bilbo says: "I'd rather see civilization blotted out with the atomic bomb than to see it slowly but surely destroyed in the maelstrom of miscegenation, interbreeding, intermarriage, and mongrelization."[33] Bilbo's preference for an atomic bomb is absurd and irrational, but it serves to illustrate the intensity with which many white Americans despised black people. It demonstrates that racism and white superiority complexes are entirely subjective and emotional decisions, based on a misreading of history.

Rappers Public Enemy comments on the problems of racism, white supremacist ideology, and the fear of so-called miscegenation in their rap "Pollywanacraka."[34] The title "Pollywanacraka" is a pun on a familiar phrase often spoken by parakeets in television and film ("Polly wants a cracker") and also a pejorative reference made by African-Americans about whites, especially economically poor ones—"crakas," or "crackers."

The term derives its meaning from the skin color of people of European descent and (Saltine) crackers. Chuck D, leader of Public Enemy, tells black people that they should not hate any "brother or sister" who is united with someone of another race. He argues, "No man is God," and "God . . . put us all here" in the first place. Chuck D says the system of white supremacy and the white fear of "mongrelization" have "no wisdom," and that "the devil" split the races by convincing black and white people that "White is good, Black is bad, and Black and White is still too bad."

While commenting on white supremacist ideology and slave mentality, Chuck D also shares his conceptions of God and the "devil." In saying, "No man is God," and that it was "God who put us all here," he implies that he has a fundamental belief in the omnipotence of God and belief in God as the infinite and sole creator of the universe. The concept of so-called miscegenation cannot be God's creation, since God is and possesses wisdom. Whites perceive so-called miscegenation to be the mixing of two distinct human species or races, as the Latin derivation of this word suggests. "Misce" comes from *miscere*, which means "to mix"; "genation" comes from *genus*, which means "species" or "genes": hence, "to mix species." Nevertheless, while there are many animal and plant species, there is only one living human species, Homo sapiens sapiens.[35] There are no distinct or different human species; all persons are human—period! "Miscegenation" therefore is a misnomer, only supporting the fact that, as Chuck D maintains, white supremacist ideologies are illogical and irrational.

Since "miscegenation" is not a concept related to God, it consequently falls within the domain of Satan's ideation. Public Enemy says "the devil" split the races in pairs with this lie of mixing races. Satan, or "the devil," taught all people that the union of two whites is good, that blacks are bad, and that the "mixture" of white and black persons is even worse. Rap group Public Enemy portrays Satan as an adversary who has no good in him. His evil ways have caused black people and white people to despise black-white relationships and caused people of white cultures especially to have contempt for white-black sexual unions. Basically, Chuck D's (Public Enemy's) conceptions of God and Satan are traditional and consistent with such older African-American portrayals found in spirituals, folktales, and legends.

Grandmaster Flash and the Furious Five offer a traditional conception of God as all-knowing (omniscient), all-powerful (omnipotent), and all-present (omnipresent) in their rap entitled "The Message." Lead MC, Melle Mel, speaks of the omniscience and omnipresence of God when referring to a black inner-city youth: "God's smiling on you and He's frowning too, / 'Cause only God knows what you go through."[36] The power and presence of God is assumed by the mere fact that Melle Mel says God is "smiling and frowning" on this African-American teenager. God must be all-powerful and all-knowing if he is "everywhere and nowhere present" to see and know what this person is "going through."

Similarly, Kool Moe Dee comments on the omniscient, or all-knowing, character of God in his rap "Knowledge Is King."[37] Kool Moe Dee says the "knowledge of God" (Christ or Allah) will teach African-Americans that money and fame are only temporary gains. He says the "knowledge of God" will give subliminal messages that free all human beings from the "criminal acts of the devil." Kool Moe Dee perceives the "acts of the devil" to be self-ambition, greed, ignorance, sexual promiscuity, and "slave mentality." Clearly, he sees knowledge as power and God as knowledge. The knowledge of God will prevent human beings from falling into the traps of Satan, particularly African-Americans making inappropriate decisions or choices at the expense of their own liberation. The acts of Satan, contends Kool Moe Dee, will continue to keep African-Americans oppressed if they do not obtain knowledge of God.

In a vein of thought similar to Kool Moe Dee, rappers 7A3 conceive of Satan as representing ignorance, physical violence, and the prevention of human liberation. They say people who are living with "Lucifer" need to quit this relationship. 7A3 says the issue of "ultimate concern" today is peace between the races, sexes, and classes of people who constitute America. They say cohabiting with Satan will not assist Americans in obtaining these goals.[38]

Conceptions of the Nature of Black Suffering

As shown above, the texts of African-American rappers illustrate their essentially traditional conceptions of God and Satan. While they reflect on the cause of black suffering with the white supremacy and slave mentality theodicies, they also reflect upon the essential character or nature of black suffering. An example is the frequently misquoted and misunderstood verses of Public Enemy's "Welcome to the Terrordome": "Apology made to who ever pleases / Still they got me like Jesus."[39] A conception of the nature of black suffering is implied in the clause "They got me like Jesus." Based on descriptions in the Bible, the crucifixion of Jesus was excruciating but a necessary fulfillment of Old Testament prophecy. The nature of Jesus' suffering was that he had to endure cursings and violent physical reactions to his claim of being the Messiah. The significance here is that Jesus suffered horribly before he died. African-Americans have also endured a chronic suffering that seems just as unsubstantiated as that of Jesus. Rappers Public Enemy are saying that white American culture has still "got African-Americans like Jesus" in that African-Americans are enduring oppression and discrimination simply because of their culture and darker skin pigmentation.

James Cone, documenting "ultimate concerns" of black spirituals almost twenty years before Public Enemy's release, finds similarly that enslaved African-Americans identified personally with Jesus. They believed he could save them from the oppression of slavery because he himself had suffered, died, and yet overcame death. Cone says:

> They were impressed by the Passion because they too had been rejected, beaten, shot without a chance to say a word in defense of their humanity. In Jesus' death black slaves saw themselves, and they unleashed their imagination, describing what they felt and saw. . . . His death was a symbol of their suffering, trials, and tribulations in an unfriendly world. They knew the agony of rejection and the pain of hanging from a tree. . . . Because black slaves knew the significance of the pain and shame of Jesus' death on the cross, they found themselves by his side. . . . If Jesus was not alone in his suffering, they were not alone in their slavery. Jesus was with them![40]

Thus, eighteenth- and nineteenth-century African-Americans were using essentially the same rhetorical language as late twentieth-century African-Americans regarding the nature of their suffering in American society. The reason for the continuity of conception and language is the single experience of slavery and its residual effects. We can conclude, then, that the social, economic, and political contexts of African-American life have remained relatively the same, thus allowing a theological discourse surrounding the nature of suffering to stay alive. Cultural, social, economic, and political contexts are important in ascertaining an understanding of African-American music.

Another perspective on the nature of black suffering is illustrated in Naughty by Nature's brief case study of a young black male in a ghetto in their rap entitled "Ghetto Bastard (Everything's Gonna Be Alright)."[41] The protagonist, who has the point of view of Naughty by Nature's principal MC, Treach, recounts his life while growing up in the projects. Each stanza tells stories of suffering because of personal, familial, and especially, societal constraints. In his introductory stanza, Treach tells us he never knew his father, and that this explains why he is always angry. His mother was not able to keep him at home because she had too many mouths to feed; therefore, he had to "wander the streets." To express this despair and apparent sense of hopelessness, Treach revises a common "floating verse" in blues lyrics: "If not for bad luck, I would have none." In all of this, Treach cannot understand why he has had to suffer or what it means to his life in the present. As he continues, he speaks about contemplating suicide: "Sometimes I wish I could afford a pistol then though, / And stop the hell I would and ended things a while ago." Midway into his narration, Treach says that even while his neighborhood dictates a life of drug pushing and alcoholic intoxication and has caused him to consider suicide, he feels there must be a better way of life. He proclaims: "Hell no, I say there's gotta be a better way." He also decides that one way he can combat this reality is to "never gamble in any game" that he cannot play. In other words, he will not get involved in any activity that, within himself, he knows he cannot win. Even with his apparent resolve, the memories of suffering resurface and Treach asks, "How will I do or how will I make it?" And he answers, "I won't, that's how! Why me, huh?" Responding to all of Treach's questions of "Why me?" is a chorus of black women who reply, "Everything's gonna be alright."

In the last stanza of Treach's autobiographical account, he tells of his suffering but also illustrates how he responds to people who perpetually attack his self-worth. Treach's suffering is symptomatic of America's social ills. The only real hope that can be ascertained from his monologue is the reply by the chorus of black women: "Everything's gonna be alright." This refrain and specifically the use of black women portray the mandatory role and traditional response of African-American women in African-American culture, especially in the black church. This role and response has been to build up their broken families and their broken men by affirming their fundamental humanity. Although Treach emphatically warns naive curiosity seekers to stay out of the ghetto, his story ends with a dialogue between himself ("Why me, huh?") and the chorus of black women ("Alright, alright").

The nature of Treach's suffering has been unsubstantiated, one with no logical answers as to the purpose of its occurrence since his suffering is the result of America's long history of systematic discrimination against black people on the basis of race. Treach's story is a microcosm of black suffering as a whole and illustrates clearly that African-Americans, whether they are Saturday revelers or Sunday worshippers or both,[42] are reflecting on the nature of their suffering and devising resolutions to their oppression through song.

My analysis of theodicy in rap has drawn on thought by black theological thinkers: William R. Jones in his book *Is God a White Racist?* and Jon Michael Spencer in his essay on the theodicy of the blues. African-American rappers express concerns about evil in a world created by a good God, in the form of theodicean discourse, or theodicy. Theodicy, as specifically used in this study, examines the provisional means by which rappers exonerate and justify God's seeming inactivity in the face of evil, as well as determining the cause and nature of black oppression and suffering. Using William Jones's concept of "humanocentric theism," I found two secular theodicies in rap: the white supremacy theodicy and the slave mentality theodicy. These theodicies reconcile the tension between African-Americans' belief in an all-powerful good God and their actual suffering in the world. In other words, it is not God's fault that certain people, out of their free will, choose to oppress others, and that as a result certain other people have developed an enslaving mentality. Both sets of people work to perpetuate evil in the lives of African-Americans. I have also shown that the expression of the white supremacy and the slave mentality theodicies are evident in the rapper's traditional conceptions of God and Satan and in how they relate stories of the nature of black suffering.

Notes

1. John Hick, *Evil and the God of Love* (San Francisco: Harper & Row, 1978), 6.

2. Jon Michael Spencer, "God in Secular Music Culture: The Theodicy of the Blues as the Paradigm of Proof," *Black Sacred Music* 3, no. 2 (Fall 1989): 25, 34.

3. Ibid., 17–18.

4. Ibid., 27.

5. Ibid., 25.

6. William Jones, *Is God a White Racist?* (Garden City, NY: Anchor, 1973), xviii.

7. Hick, *Evil*, 3.

8. Ibid., 5.

9. Ibid., 12: "Moral evil is evil that we human beings originate: cruel, unjust, vicious, and perverse thoughts and deeds. Natural evil is the evil that originates independently of human actions: in disease bacilli, earthquakes, storms, droughts, tornadoes, etc."

10. Ibid., 5.

11. W. Jones, *White Racist?* xiii–xxii.

12. Ibid., 72–78.

13. Ibid., xxii.

14. See Martin Buber, *Tales of the Hasidim* (trans. Olga Marx; 2 vols.; New York: Schocken, 1947–48); idem, *The Eclipse of God: Studies in the Relation between Religion and Philosophy* (New York: Harper, 1952); Albert Camus, *The Plague* (trans. Stuart Gilbert; New York: Knopf, 1948); idem, *The Rebel* (trans. Anthony Bower; New York: Knopf, 1954); Harvey G. Cox, *The Secular City: Secularization and Urbanization in Theological*

Perspective (rev. ed.; New York: Macmillan, 1966); Erich Fromm, *You Shall Be as Gods: A Radical Interpretation of the Old Testament and Its Tradition* (New York: Holt, Rinehart & Winston, 1966); and Jean-Paul Sartre, *Anti-Semite and Jew* (trans. George J. Becker; New York: Schocken Books, 1948).

15. W. Jones, *White Racist?* 185–95.

16. George M. Fredrickson, *White Supremacy: A Comparative Study in American and South African History* (New York: Oxford University Press, 1981), xi.

17. James A. Banks, *Teaching Strategies for Ethnic Studies* (Boston: Allyn & Bacon, 1991), 204–5.

18. Fredrickson, *White Supremacy*, xi.

19. Ibid.

20. LeRoi Jones (Amiri Baraka), *Blues People: The Negro Experience in White America and the Music That Developed from It* (New York: Morrow Quill, 1963), 57.

21. Ibid., 59.

22. W. Jones, *White Racist?* 41.

23. Na'im Akbar, *Chains and Images of Psychological Slavery* (Jersey City, NJ: New Mind Productions, 1984), 7.

24. Ibid.

25. Ibid., 9, 12, 15, 19, 20, 23, 30, 31, 38–42.

26. MC Lyte, "Cappucino," *Eyes on This* (New York: First Priority Records, distributed by Atlantic Recording, 1989).

27. Ibid., "Not Wit a Dealer."

28. W. Jones, *White Racist?* 44.

29. Cited in ibid., 40.

30. Ibid., 40–41.

31. Molefi Kete Asante, *The Afrocentric Idea* (Philadelphia: Temple University Press, 1987), 93.

32. Jon Michael Spencer, *Protest and Praise: Sacred Music of Black Religion* (Minneapolis: Fortress, 1990), 115.

33. Theodore Gilmore Bilbo, *Take Your Choice: Separation or Mongrelization* (Poplarville, MS: Dream House Pubg., 1947), 105.

34. Public Enemy, "Pollywanacraka," *Fear of a Black Planet* (New York: Def Jam Recordings, 1990).

35. See Acts 17:26.

36. Grandmaster Flash and the Furious Five, "The Message," *The Message* (Englewood, NJ: Sugarhill Records, 1982).

37. Kool Moe Dee, "Knowledge Is King," *Knowledge Is King* (New York: Jive/Zomba Records, 1989).

38. 7A3, "Lucifer," *Coolin' in Cali* (London: Geffen Records, 1988).

39. Public Enemy, "Welcome to the Terrordome," *Fear of a Black Planet*.

40. James Cone, *The Spirituals and The Blues: An Interpretation* (San Francisco: Harper & Row, 1972), 52–54.

41. Naughty by Nature, "Ghetto Bastard (Everything's Gonna Be Alright)," *Naughty by Nature* (New York: Tommy Boy Music, 1991).

42. Albert Murray, *Stomping the Blues* (New York: Da Capo, 1982), 27, 42.

Transcendent Trancer

The Scholar and the Rave

—Tim Olaveson

Raving is not something that can be experienced vicariously.[1]
—Jimi Fritz

Those who write about the rave rarely solicit the voices and experiences of people who actually go to raves.[2]
—Scott Hutson

I define a rave as a gathering of people for the purpose of extended listening and dancing to electronic music. Raves fall into one of three types:

1. large-scale events (with more than one thousand participants) held in large, open spaces or buildings not regularly used as nightclubs;
2. medium-sized events with attendance between three hundred and one thousand participants held in impromptu, informally advertised and decorated spaces; or
3. events characterized as "intimate" with attendance of less than three hundred participants, held in informal impromptu spaces, sometimes referred to as "private parties," with little or no advertising other than word of mouth.

This definition retains the distinction that ravers themselves usually draw between raves and after-hours club events. Though at one time large numbers characterized raves, it is really the temporary and impromptu nature and lack of rigid social mores that differentiate raves from other events.

We can trace the history of rave culture[3] and its roots in 1980's house, garage, and techno, and 1970's acid rock, Northern soul, and disco. And we can consider the rapid globalization of the rave phenomenon and electronic music culture. Hence, it is a remarkable fact that academic commentators have been relatively silent on it until the last five or six years. With the exception of a few sparse social analyses of rave in the early 1990s,[4] virtually nothing scholarly was written on it until the end of the millennium, when it appears that "the academic community has woken up to the presence of this ubiquitous (sub-)culture."[5] Since 1997, an accelerating number of social-scientific studies of the rave phenomenon have appeared, primarily in the fields of sociology and cultural studies.

In this chapter I briefly survey several of the key themes in these studies. In concurrence with Scott Hutson,[6] I then argue that while these studies have raised some interesting questions and provided some plausible initial conclusions, they ultimately present superficial analyses about rave. Moreover, most of them exclude a wide and crucial range of data intrinsic to a more emically informed understanding and analysis of rave, especially *the rave experience*. Reasons for this superficiality and these exclusions include failures to privilege the voices of those who rave, to take informants seriously, and to obtain direct, bodily knowledge of the rave experience. Much previous research on rave culture and the rave experience has lacked an experiential approach. At the conclusion to the chapter, I outline some facets of such an approach, which I employed during three years of fieldwork in the central Canadian rave scene.

Social Scientific Approaches to the Study of Rave

Rave as Moral Panic

In "Raves, Risks and the Ecstasy Panic," Sean Hier refreshes an old model in the sociology of deviance. He demonstrates how the events of 1999–2000 in the rave community in Toronto, Ontario, precipitated a "moral panic . . . through the construction of a discourse centred on the dangers and risks associated with Ecstasy use."[7] However, paralleling the argument made by Sarah Thornton in her now-classic study of electronic music cultures, *Club Cultures*,[8] Hier contests and problematizes the traditional employment of the moral panic model. Using the Toronto rave scene as a case study, he illustrates how Toronto's rave communities successfully subverted the moralizing discourse in mainstream media through engaging with alternate media outlets. Thereby they demonstrated the relational aspect of governance and the agency of social actors in "moralized political projects."[9] For example, Hier notes that "the actions of [Mayor] Mel Lastman and [Police Chief] Julian Fantino were singled out for interrogation by supporters of the rave communities as threatening to push raves underground, concomitantly escalating the risks involved with raving in Toronto."[10] As a result, on August 2, 2000, city council voted 50 to 4 in favor of sanctioning raves in city spaces.

Chas Critcher[11] also claims that the moral panic framework does in fact approximate the social and governmental reaction to rave culture in Britain, but he suggests a less unitary narrative on three fronts. First, there were actually three separate but interrelated moral panics—about New Age travelers, raves, and Ecstasy use. Second, the precise identities of the folk devils were far from settled; ravers themselves were usually portrayed as victims, promoters were sometimes targeted, and universally vilified were drug dealers. And finally, Critcher suggests that the media coverage was not as monolithic as has been suggested. Quoting McDermott and others, he states that broadcast media were more balanced in their coverage and actually forestalled the development of the panic.[12] In contrast to Critcher but along the same grounds as he outlines, however, Sarah Thornton and Angela McRobbie[13] favor either a radical revision of the moral panic model—if it is to convincingly apply to the dynamics and history of rave culture—or a rejection of it altogether in such an analysis.

Rave as Ecstatic Disappearance

Probably no other article has been cited or quoted more often in academic and journalistic pieces on rave culture than Antonio Melechi's "The Ecstasy of Disappearance,"[14] which appears as a chapter in Steve Redhead's *Rave Off: Politics and Deviance in Contemporary Youth Culture.*[15] Although brief and somewhat disjointed, "The Ecstasy of Disappearance" has been interpreted by many as an insightful analysis of the essence of the rave experience.

Melechi outlines a brief history of the birth of acid house on the island of Ibiza and how young tourists imported acid house culture to England.

He then suggests that although the concept of "the tourist gaze" is useful in analyses of traditional types of tourism, it is inapt in this case. This is because the Balearic holiday and British acid house itself comprise a spectacular disappearance, a disaccumulation of self and culture. "To understand the pleasures of the dance floor we must move to a different logic of tourism where one comes to hide from the spectre of a former self (Britain and San Antonio) to disaccumulate culture and disappear under the dry ice and into the body."[16] Hence, there is nothing left at which to gaze; or at the very least, the body has moved "to a different plane of pleasures" than the traditional "phallic domain of visibility where female absence is reflected."[17] Melechi compares rave to Baudrillard's America: both represent "a seductive absence and enticing void where one can partake in the Ecstasy of disappearance."[18] For Melechi, the spaces of acid house

> represent a fantasy of liberation, an escape from identity. A place where nobody is but everybody belongs. . . . This is the enigmatic void of Acid House: where the invisible hide and the mute prefer silence, where the Ecstasy of disappearance resists the imperative to reveal one's self.[19]

Unfortunately, Melechi's rather depressing interpretation of the rave as an empty, superficial, and ultimately meaningless void would proceed to directly and indirectly inform a host of other readings of rave as just another symptom of the postmodern, just another cultural product that is all style and no substance. For example, echoing and quoting Melechi, Josephine Leask characterizes the clubbing experience as anything but human, as "a journey and an arrival at a spiritual void."[20] Similarly, in the same volume as Melechi, Hillegonda Rietveld writes that

> To try and find a depth beneath the aesthetic of the rave-event is like trying to deflate a bouncy castle (a favourite feature at open air raves): all that can be found is air and an affirmation of a Thatcherite enterprise culture, leaving its shape, the representation of the dream of "love," hope and happiness, deflated in the process.[21]

This statement is especially surprising coming from Rietveld, whose former membership in seminal new wave/house group Quando Quango, current status as a house DJ, and meticulously researched doctoral thesis on the house movement[22] clearly evince her passion for electronic music and its culture.[23]

Rave as Subcultural Capital

Sarah Thornton was the first scholar to treat the idea of rave culture and its manifestations as subcultural capital, adapting Bourdieu's term. In "Moral Panic, the Media and British Rave Culture,"[24] and especially in her widely cited doctoral thesis, published as *Club Cultures*,[25] Thornton brought an early and fresh insight to some of the cultural and social dynamics underlying the rave scene.

One of Thornton's insights is a more nuanced and mature examination of the media's relationship with rave cultures. Contrary to the previously one-sided analysis of ravers as victimized by the mass media through the tabloids' overblown stories of drug overdoses and rampant adolescent sex-capades, Thornton demonstrates ravers' agency in utilizing alternative media to construct their own discourse about their culture. In particular, Thornton highlights the vital role that niche media such as rave flyers and "zines" played in the British acid house and rave cultures of 1988–94, an analysis that still applies to many Canadian rave scenes today. Thornton also highlights how even negative portrayals of rave in mass media serve to construct and develop the culture in various ways. In both works Thornton's central project is describing the process by which subcultures like rave develop and define themselves against an "other," which in this case is mass culture or "the mainstream." "More than fashionable or trendy, underground sounds and styles are 'authentic,' and pitted against the mass-produced and mass-consumed."[26] Thornton goes on to describe the various techniques that members of rave cultures use to protect their subcultural capital from going mainstream, such as white labels and the word-of-mouth advertising of raves.

Jerrentrup[27] presents a similar, yet more simplistic argument for "techno" culture in Germany, claiming that it has been "mainstreamed" and is in decline.[28] Despite the obvious falsity of the latter statement (Germany is still one of the most vibrant and productive locations for electronic music culture in the world), Jerrentrup does offer some acute observations that also hold true for North American rave culture, such as

1. Big capital and extramusical commerce has invaded techno culture: cigarette companies sponsor tours with techno musicians, and travel bureaus organize trips to raves.
2. Techno music has become a part of our everyday listening environment, played in shopping spaces, reception areas, elevators, and warehouses.
3. Techno is now established as a musical genre in large chain stores.

4. Techno discotheques have permeated the world.
5. Techno DJs and producers are now superstars.

Taking a decidedly economic perspective, Smith and Maughan also theorize about the process by which rave and dance cultures accumulate and distribute cultural (and material) capital. Refreshingly, they begin with the following statement: "Young people, therefore, should not just be seen as a group that threatens the social order and needs to be 'dealt with,' or as consumers of forms of postmodern culture, but as individuals and members of collectives which are at the forefront of creating a new culture and economy."[29] From this statement it is clear that the authors depart from the well-worn paths in the study of subcultures.

Smith and Maughan sum up their argument thus:

> It is our contention that the music industry takes a basically Fordist structure, and that the music scene coming out of the dance culture takes a post-Fordist structure. This can principally be seen in the huge number of micro-labels, the use of new technology which reduces the costs of production, a cultural aesthetic that embraces this diversity and the sounds that can be made from the technology, and an underground culture which generates space for the micro-labels and restricts the domination of the major music corporations.[30]

Brown,[31] Gibson,[32] Goodwin,[33] Hesmondhalgh,[34] and Reynolds[35] similarly discuss the shifts in the cultural, material, and political dynamics of production and consumption that have accompanied the acid house and rave explosions. These shifts come through such techniques and innovations as digital music production, sampling, white labels, microlabels, flyers, Web-based communication and promotion, and the deliberate eschewing of the "star system."

Rave as Resistance: Variations on a(n) (Old) Theme

It took several years before academics earnestly turned their attention to the exploding subcultures of acid house and rave. Nevertheless, it predictably took them little time to apply the familiar "subculture as resistance" model to these subcultures, inspired by such classic works as *Resistance through Rituals*[36] and *Subculture.*[37] The broader "rave as resistance" argument has taken three more-specific forms, centering around the notions of space, sex and gender, and "clubcultures."

Temporary Autonomous Zones

Several authors have analyzed the spaces and places of rave. Several in particular have drawn upon anarcho-mystic philosopher Hakim Bey's idea of the Temporary Autonomous Zone. Chris Gibson, for example, highlights how previous musical scenes' (such as rock and "indie") mythologization of fixed locations with rich traditions is in contrast to idealized rave, which "occupies space momentarily, before such industry narratives are solidified. . . . This radical sense of spatial *fluidity* is perhaps most vividly accounted for in the works of left-anarchist Hakim Bey, whose essay on the Temporary Autonomous Zone (TAZ) has been influential in shaping a radical rave practice in NSW [New South Wales]."[38] Gibson further highlights Bey's advocacy of the use of the Internet in establishing TAZs, as well as the way this has been taken up by electronic music communities in Australia (and in fact in rave communities the world over).

Similarly, Tim Jordan argues—based on the work of Gilles Deleuze and Felix Guattari—that rave is an example of a postmodern revolutionary movement. Paradoxically, however, rave can be considered a *politically indifferent* revolutionary movement because its only aim is the continued production of the "collectively lived present."[39] Also drawing upon Deleuze and Guattari, among others, Drew Hemment argues that *ekstasis*—the raison d'être of the house (rave) movement—embodies a temporary suspension of our humanity, specifically the puritan self that thwarts and holds desire in suspense:

> In dance the body stands forth and becomes ecstatic. If the self is a sedimentation of a certain stable alignment of forces, the ecstatic body sets those forces loose. . . . The self that is "lost" on the dance floor is neither abstract nor eternal, but the historical product of a puritan heritage—and this heritage is in crisis. Amidst a generalized loss of meaning, the modern subject is cut adrift, disorientated and unsure.[40]

With Gibson and others, Hemment significantly recognizes that much of the panicked reaction by authorities to the early raves and warehouse parties during the acid house explosion derived not from their illegality or danger to participants. Instead, the panic came because they were opening up an unstructured physical (and social) space, free from "the lack of a clear regulative framework."[41]

Sex, Gender, and Rave

As arguably *the* major youth cultural phenomenon and, as some have claimed, revolutionary movement of the twentieth century, it is to be expected that issues of sex and gender in rave culture would be treated by scholars. However, as Maria Pini noted in 1997, "With the notable exception of Angela McRobbie's 'Shut Up and Dance' (1994), none of the existing academic works on this scene, or on clubbing more generally, seriously address the position of girls and women within rave."[42] The essay written by McRobbie that Pini refers to was one of the first pieces of true academic writing on rave. McRobbie first treated gender issues in the piece to which Pini refers, a chapter in *Postmodernism and Popular Culture*, which McRobbie edited.[43]

McRobbie's work on rave "is characterized by optimistic descriptions of the ways that 1990s youth seek and use 'pleasure' as a symbolic escape from the social tensions of their times."[44] At certain points she seems to be reaching beyond her grasp in her reading of some of rave's practices—either that or she simply overinterprets them, as when she claims that pacifiers, whistles, and popsicles are a way for female ravers to symbolically seal off their bodies from sexual advances. Her analysis may ultimately be superficial, yet she does present some noteworthy and interesting conclusions. For example, McRobbie highlights a paradox: The androgyny and ritualized safety of the rave open up new sociosexual spaces for women to explore their bodies without the expectation of sexual attention. Nevertheless, raves are also another cultural phenomenon in which the means of production are controlled predominantly by males; most DJs are male, and most promotion companies are owned and/or operated by males.[45] In addition, McRobbie observes the particularly gendered way in which dance, the principal medium of social expression and relationship in rave, departs from previous youth subcultures: "Dance is where girls were always found in subcultures. It was their only entitlement. Now in rave it becomes the motivating force for the entire subculture."[46] In previous subcultures dance was viewed as a particularly feminine form of embodiment, and ideals of "coolness" and subcultural style for men involved remaining aloof and in control. But in rave, "losing it" and abandoning oneself to the dance is acceptable and encouraged for both sexes.

Pini echoes many of the conclusions reached by McRobbie concerning the paradoxically simultaneous novel and traditional relationship between women and rave as subculture. In Pini's view, "Rave represents an undoing of the traditional cultural associations between dancing, drugged, 'dressed-up' woman and sexual invitation, and as such opens up a new space for the exploration of new forms of identity and pleasure."[47] Unfortunately, Pini's focus on gender analysis inevitably leads to a misunderstanding, similar to McRobbie's, of not only some of the most fundamental *technologies* of rave, but also of its *teleologies*—she views it primarily as a practice whose ultimate aim is the pursuit of pleasure. Thus, she concludes that rave is "possibly best understood as a non-phallic form of pleasure."[48] While the field of sexuality inevitably comprises a part of the social dynamics at work at a rave—contrary to Pini's and McRobbie's dominant reading of the rave as a space of hotly contested and constructed gendered identities—sometimes a cigar is just a cigar.

The ultimate methodological shortcoming and intrinsic error in Pini's treatment of the rave epitomizes the problem with so many of the other analyses in the cultural studies literature. Using the "notion of 'textuality,'" Pini states: "My particular reading, then, aims to elucidate the stories or 'texts' through which women experience rave."[49] Despite its current popularity as an interpretive framework, the concept of textuality is probably the worst possible investigative tool for any sustained and substantial analysis of rave, and particularly of the rave experience. With such a body-centered, fleshly, ephemeral practice, "instead of inventing nonsensical rhetorical devices [like] Pini's 'text of excitement' . . . in an inept attempt to flatten and 'textualize' an immensely contoured, sensual, and intense experience like raving, the experience itself should be the object of study."[50]

Clubcultures?

In 1993, Steve Redhead, then of the Manchester Institute for Popular Culture, edited the first book-length scholarly publication on rave culture, *Rave Off: Politics and Deviance in Contemporary Youth Culture*.[51] *Rave Off* was largely exploratory and from a purely textual approach had a cobbled-together, haphazard appearance. However, being the first book to seriously treat the already outdated subcultures of acid house and rave, *Rave Off* is cited widely in rave studies. Redhead's work on "clubcultures" has gone on to found an entire school of "clubcultural studies."

Redhead takes the theoretical construct and object of Sarah Thornton's 1995 book *Club Cultures* and reifies it in *Subcultures to Clubcultures: An Introduction to Popular Cultural Studies*[52] and in *The Clubcultures Reader: Readings in Popular Cultural Studies*.[53] In these works, Redhead argues for the abandonment of the outdated, classic notion of subculture (and the "subculture as resistance" model) in favor of what he calls "clubculture" or post-subculture. This is characterized by a dissolution of the line between the subcultural and the mainstream, an erosion of meaning and authenticity, and a nostalgia for styles/forms of the past.[54] As I discuss below, the entire concept of "clubcultures" is suspect for many reasons. The thesis that all cultural practices falling outside mainstream culture are in some way "clubcultures" betrays a tunnel vision and an Anglo-centrism bordering on the absurd. Not all contemporary practices occur in or revolve around clubs or the clubbing experience. Moreover, as others have noted, the *Clubcultures Reader* doesn't even really deal with clubcultures per se.[55]

Falling within the "clubcultures" school of cultural studies and yet tremendously more nuanced and researched is Ben Malbon's *Clubbing: Dancing, Ecstasy and Vitality*.[56] In many ways *Clubbing* is a turning point in the study of rave cultures. Rather than just the stylistic elements of rave and club settings and their habitués, *Clubbing* attends to the actual physical experience of clubbing and raving as a serious object of academic study. Malbon's basic thesis is that clubbing is an essentially apolitical practice through which social actors "lose themselves" in order to paradoxically "find themselves." They explore the self and form identities through highly embodied "playful vitality." Malbon draws upon Maffesoli's concepts of neotribes and unicity and Turner's *communitas* in his attempt to map the clubbing experience, ultimately abandoning both in favor of his own term "playful vitality." Though I have several problems with the way he uses and dismisses these theories,[57] Malbon's serious and detailed attention to the experience of clubbing itself and his lack of trepidation in exploring its ephemeral side warrant praise.

The only multiyear, sociologically oriented study of rave culture in Canada to date whose results have been published is Brian Wilson's "The Canadian Rave Scene and Five Theses on Youth Resistance"[58] (only a study of the Toronto rave scene). Wilson remains within the "resistance" model of analysis, employing and modifying recent theoretical projects such as those of McRobbie, Thornton, and Malbon. Specifically, Wilson posits "five theses of youth resistance" within the rave scene: (1) Rave is a form of symbolic "purposeful-tactical" resistance. (2) Rave is a form of "adaptive-reactive" resistance. (3) Rave is a form of "trivial" resistance. (4) Rave is a form of self-aware or oblivious nonresistance. (5) Rave culture actively supports reproduction of the dominant culture. While hardly breaking new theoretical ground, Wilson's study of the Canadian rave scene is nonetheless an important contribution to rave studies in at least three ways.

First, it is the only such *Canadian* study. Second, Wilson actually attended rave and club events himself and sought the opinions and experiences of real ravers. And third, he both summarizes and furthers current sociological theories on rave.

Rave as the New Tribes

Aside from the notion of resistance, another of the most popular ways of framing raves and the communities they engender (both real and virtual) in the sociological literature has been as "tribes" or "neotribes." This derives from Michel Maffesoli's "sociology of sociality," especially his *The Time of the Tribes: The Decline of Individualism in Mass Society*.[59] In this work Maffesoli uses the concept of the tribe to describe the microgroupings characteristic of social identities in the increasingly consumer-oriented societies of late modernity. Modern tribes or neotribes "foreground the immediate and the affectual and are marked more by their practices and spacings of inclusion and exclusion and their shared styles than by more formalized memberships and contractual codes of behaviour."[60] Also more important than formal membership in neotribes such as rave are shared notions and priorities of emotionality, community, atmosphere, and especially ephemerality. The notion of membership in a particular tribe is less important than the fluid movement between different tribes. Quoting Maffesoli, Halfacree and Kitchin write that neotribes are places "where people gather together to 'bathe in the affectual ambience' . . . in their search for community and belonging, the loss of which is the leitmotif of the postmodern condition."[61]

In their discussion of the world-renowned indie music and rave community Madchester, Halfacree and Kitchin draw attention to place as a central feature of the neotribal collective. In particular, they claim that "only by producing a distinct space can a neo-tribe survive."[62] With regard to Madchester, they observe:

> Even with the establishment of a sound and varied infrastructure which went beyond music (for example, Joe Bloggs fashions), Madchester was pronounced "dead" by 1991–2. Madchester ultimately failed to produce the space required for its music, with its hedonistic immaturity, and the failure to link the music sufficiently with broader aspects of everyday life and experience. In this light Madchester can be compared unfavourably with other neo-tribal

groupings, such as "New Age" travelers, who appear to display a more developed sense of identity.[63]

However, Halfacree and Kitchin also suggest that Madchester's demise was in part a function of its attempt at subverting "an intensely capitalist music business."[64] Additional studies applying Michel Maffesoli's theory to dance cultures with varying degrees of precision include those of St. John,[65] Bennett,[66] Roberts,[67] and Klein.[68] For example, Klein offers a simplistic blanket analysis seemingly intended to cover the entire spectrum of rave musics and their developments. Thus, he states that the whole of techno/house was developed by black American urban teenagers as a response to high unemployment and bleak futures, and that local techno scenes in Europe are formally known as "tribes" and have adopted "the original Black subculture."[69] House's and techno's (two separate and distinct genres/movements) histories are far more complex than this. Though I do not have firsthand knowledge of the European techno scene(s), it is highly unlikely that all or even many local scenes and dance communities explicitly call themselves "tribes." As far as adopting "the original Black subculture," whatever that may be, many of my informants and acquaintances during research on the central Canadian rave scene have stated that if anything, the matter is quite the contrary. Rave and dance culture seems to be far more progressive and widespread in Europe than in North America. In genres such as epic or progressive trance, European artists make virtually all the music currently played at North American raves.

Rave as Revolution

While there have been countless comparisons between rave and the American counterculture of the 1960s, most commentators are quick to point out one of their fundamental differences: rave's apolitical character. For example, Langlois wrote the following in 1992:

> The ideology of the House phenomenon does not propose an alternative lifestyle to mainstream culture, neither could it be described as a cathartic outburst from socially frustrated sections of society. What House does sometimes generate is a transient but powerful experience of shared sensual over-stimulation. It provides colour, excitement and a sense of community for a generation with few obvious causes to follow.[70]

In contrast to this, we need the fundamental recognition that dancing at a rave is at root a political action in that it simultaneously signifies and reifies a form of being-in-one's-body antithetical to the dominant discourses of embodiment in most developed nations. More specifically, some scholars have reported on particular segments or pockets of dance culture with overtly political ends and/or methods. For example, in a fascinating and award-winning essay, Stephanie Marlin-Curiel describes how in 1999 young nationalists organized a rave in South Africa with the specific goal of "redefining Afrikaner identity in the wake of Apartheid's demise."[71] Held in a barn in Melkbosstrand, forty minutes from Cape Town, Transmissie was the first in a planned series of parties aimed at spreading the message that it was time for Afrikaners to reclaim their personal and cultural identity.[72]

The political and cultural significance of these emerging neo- or "techno-tribes" forms the basis for another body of literature on "postrave" electronic music cultures, sometimes called "doof" cultures—an onomatopoeic reference to the sound of the archetypal 4/4 bass drumbeat underlying most forms of techno and trance (see Murray[73] and Strong[74] for histories of doof). Edited by Graham St. John, *FreeNRG: Notes from the Edge of the Dance Floor*[75] deals primarily with Australian doof cultures. It especially focuses on their relationship with and appropriation of the techniques of other subcultural groups such as DIY (Do-It-Yourself) cultures,[76] sound systems,[77] environmentalist groups,[78] "travelers," New Agers, the Situationiste Internationale (SI),[79] and direct-action protest groups.[80] In the opening chapter, St. John argues that—contra Melechi and others who critique rave and postrave cultures for their ultimate emptiness and futility at instigating real change—such cultures are in fact involved in generating meaningful social experience leading to cultural and political change:

Politically engaged techno-propagandists, digital artists like Strong, the members of Subvertigo, Organarchy or Labrats, are "techno-rebels" whose "rebellion" is not equivalent to a refusal of meaning, their multi-mediations not denoting *withdrawal.* . . . Articulated with community and direct action contexts, these "works" are efforts at disseminating alternative values and practices. Following Balliger, these "oppositional music practices," attempt to "generate social relationships and experience which can form the basis of a new cultural sensibility and, in fact, are involved in the struggle for a new culture." By contrast to the near monolithic "rave"—thought

to propose no "new meanings capable of renewing the configura-
tions of contemporary community" and where demand for "a shared
present" conveys "an imperative not to give in to the future"—such
interventions appropriate technology in order to "reclaim the future."[81]

The Need for a New Approach to Studying the Rave Experience

In an apt quotation, Hollands sums up some of the shortcomings of recent
studies of youth cultures like rave:

> Recent studies of youth cultures have been pre-occupied with more
> post-modern "readings" of styles (Muggleton, 1997, 2000), lifestyles
> (Miles, 2000), club-cultures (Thornton, 1995; Redhead, 1997), and
> "neo-tribal" patterns of activity (Bennett, 2000), and have often
> failed to address questions of inequality and spatial separation
> among different consumption groupings.[82]

Such postmodern readings, he continues, are heavily "textualized" and

> end up in discussions about endless chains of signification, com-
> peting generational multicultures, or decentred subjectivities
> (Cohen and Ainley, 2000). At best, attempts are made to show
> what these hybrid youth cultures say about our so-called post-
> modern society and culture—usually in the form of reaffirming its
> existence, thereby masquerading as both "evidence" and "cause"
> simultaneously.[83]

The work of several scholars of rave and clubcultures that I summarized above—including Redhead, Melechi, McRobbie, (the early)
Rietveld, Luckmann, and Pini—focuses on just such semiological readings of taste and style, decentered subjectivity, and absence of meaning.
There is little question that rave is a decidedly postmodern practice and
phenomenon, as many of these analyses amply demonstrate. And yet I
cannot help but agree with Hollands's statement that postmodern analyses of postmodern (sub)cultural formations often appear to accomplish little more than a feting of the latter, as well as a rationalization of the world
in which we currently live. Andrew Goodwin, writing in 1989, already
makes much the same point:

By conflating postmodernism as *theory* and as *condition*, the former finds itself with a vested interest in promoting the latter, if not morally and/or politically, then as a cultural form of far greater significance than the evidence often suggests.[84]

Other scholars of rave and dance-based cultures have begun to similarly problematize the epistemological foundations of the extant work on them. David Muggleton, coeditor of the recently released *Post-Subcultures Reader*[85] and himself firmly rooted in this school, nevertheless wrote in 1997: "What is now required is an approach where the subjective meanings and perceptions of the subculturalists themselves constitute the first, privileged level of analysis."[86] Brian Wilson echoes this when he states that "[post-subcultural] theories remain underdeveloped and particularly abstract until evaluated through an analysis of the meanings that youth give to their activities, and the various contexts of youth behaviour."[87] And about the "clubcultures" school of research headed by Steve Redhead,[88] Hollands poignantly writes: "Despite continued reference to keeping alive a tradition of ethnography, Redhead's work provides very little room for the actual voices and actions of young people engaged in clubcultures."[89] Finally, Scott Hutson, one of the handful of scholars to have performed real fieldwork among ravers before the turn of the millennium, observed in 1999: "Once the surfaces [of rave] are interpreted as meaningless simulacra, postmodernists often stop interpreting. . . . Those who write about the rave rarely solicit the voices and experiences of people who actually go to raves."[90]

The cautions expressed by Hollands, Muggleton, Wilson, and Hutson can be boiled down to one important notion. The danger with postmodern theorizing *on the postmodern*, as with any form of social theorizing, is that the act of theorizing can eventually lead one far astray from the actual, lived experiences of the subjects or groups about which one theorizes. This is particularly true in the case of rapidly changing and fluidly constituted social entities such as raves and rave communities. Such theorizing can lose all attachment to social reality and become an end in itself. In other words, the postmodernist and post-structuralist obsession with decentered subjectivities, endless meaningless surfaces, and fractured social experience often precludes them from verifying such notions by speaking to the real people purportedly caught up in them.

Thus, Clifford Geertz writes about the notion of lived experience: "Without it, or something like it, cultural analyses seem to float several feet above their human ground."[91] To date much of the sociological scholarship on rave adds to our understanding of this significant turn-of-the-millennium social movement. Nevertheless, a substantial amount of it does in fact float above the actual experiences and stories of its subjects. It is concerned more with advancing postmodern theory at the expense of real and thorough examination of data on and about ravers themselves—what they think, who they are, what they get from raving, and most important for me, why they rave. After examining the majority of the sociological and cultural studies literature on rave, one therefore is left asking several questions:

> Do we really understand rave culture? Why have people from globally diverse cultural and socioeconomic backgrounds embraced rave so enthusiastically? What is it about the rave experience that attracts people, especially youth? More importantly, what does it feel like, what does it *mean*, to rave?[92]

Rave as Religion

An increasing number of recent rave studies have begun asking these questions. The answers have been surprising and have contradicted several of the earlier conclusions drawn by postmodern and post-structuralist analyses that typically dismissed rave as simply a form of meaningless hedonism. These earlier studies saw rave as another ultimately insignificant example in a growing list of shallow and superficial leisure activities pursued by a generation bored and disenfranchised by their generally meaningless postmodern existence. But recent studies have demonstrated that, rather than empty hedonism, raving is actually a highly meaningful, even spiritual practice for many participants.[93] My own fieldwork in the central Canadian rave communities of Toronto, Ottawa, Montreal, and Quebec City revealed similar conclusions.[94] Not only was raving a vital, serious, and highly meaningful part of several of my informants' lives, for some it was also a spiritual practice. Moreover, raving became an important and meaningful part of my life. This is because I became a raver myself.

Before doing so, I too was initially skeptical about the religious language with which participants framed their experiences, and about the numerous tales of conversion. I too saw little possibility of uncovering a depth beneath what appeared to be merely a nighttime leisure activity, albeit one taken to a new level of sophistication and seriousness. After reading the literature, however, I soon realized that I still didn't really know what happened at a rave, or what it meant or felt like to rave. I thus decided on an experiential approach to studying the rave experience in central Canada. As Takahashi and I wrote in "Music, Dance and Raving Bodies," such an approach is crucial in any serious inquiry into the rave experience. The opening quotations to this chapter say it best: to truly understand rave, you have to experience it. In the remainder of the chapter, I outline a few components of the methodology I employed to arrive at my conclusions—experiential anthropology—which I argue should inform any study of the religious dimensions of popular music, whenever possible.

Experiential Anthropology, Radical Empiricism, and Anthropological Praxis

> As a first step, however, anthropologists can begin to take their informants seriously and to entertain the idea that an informant's account may be more than a "text" to be analyzed.[95]

Experiential anthropology as a methodological stance involves a shift away from the text, and is "removed from the textualist lock-in."[96] This is in contrast to much postmodern and post-structural social research, such as the rave research studies summarized above, which are "rarely informed from direct ethnographic fieldwork, or for that matter from the actual practice of any phenomenology."[97] Related to this is the important insight by Laughlin and McManus that the writings of Jacques Derrida, which inspired the post-structuralist movement, betray an obvious ethnocentrism in their almost complete concern with the written word. In other words, post-structuralism glosses over the tremendously rich, vibrant, and yet nonliterate meaning and symbol systems of oral cultures.

Several previous studies of rave have taken the flattening and textualizing of the immensely corporeal and sensuous experience of raving as their jumping-off point, rather than exploring the visceral, carnal nature of the rave experience itself, whether through informants' accounts or direct, personal experience. While textualizing lived experience— abridging the practical activities of real persons—is the "unfortunate end game"[98] of anthropological or any other social research, employing such a methodological strategy compresses and squeezes out the "juicy bits" of such experience from the finished account *at the outset*. An apt analogy belying the deficiency of such a strategy exists in modern techniques of digital music file compression. Bits (literally) of information are systematically and permanently eliminated from the original, CD-quality song to shrink and contain it in the new MP3 or other format, leaving an imperfect copy.

Contrary to postmodern and post-structural research, the thrust of experiential anthropology is to focus on the *lived experience* of real people engaged in the practicalities of their daily lives. As opposed to most ethnographies of the nineteenth and early twentieth centuries, as well as to much current research, the polestar of the experiential anthropologist is not the construction of the others' *worldview*, but rather the entrance into their *lifeworld*.[99] In fact, as Goulet and Young remind us, anthropologists' informants often insist that rather than the logocentric, cognitive approach to learning by which most Western-trained anthropologists are enculturated, an experiential approach is essential. Only thus can they gain a true understanding of local accounts and such things as dreams and visions,[100] or in this case, the nonrational, carnal, ecstatic practice of raving.

Empathetic, sincere, and deep sharing in the lifeworld of one's informants is thus a crucial component in an experiential anthropology. Of course, even an experientially focused anthropology suffers from the intractable epistemological problem inherent in any ethnographic study: the reader cannot share directly in the ethnographer's experience in the field and must ultimately "take the ethnographer's word for it."[101]

> However, and especially so for cultural practices focused on techniques of embodied knowing, the ethnographer's process of interpretation can only be strengthened by getting as close as possible to the actual experience had by her informants. Moreover, irrespective of the extent to which the anthropologist's experience approximates that of her informants, such an experience-near (Geertz 1976; Wikan 1991) methodology will at least locate the researcher in a position to ask relevant and "appropriate" questions (Given 1993:93), and thus limit the potential for misrepresentation.[102]

Flying in the face of the century-old taboo against "going native," a fieldworker employing an experiential methodology "surrenders himself" to the culture[103] with the intent of becoming "one of them," with the recognition that he must eventually come back.[104] Proponents of the experiential method argue that only by experiencing another culture in full, empathetic participation can the anthropologist speak with any authority about the experience of its members. Calling for a reexamination of methodological praxis *in the field* rather than *at the writing desk*, Poewe urges: "If the ethnographic other experiences something, so can, indeed should, the anthropologist."[105]

In recent years, William James's concept of radical empiricism, of including the widest possible range of human experience within scientific investigation and treating one's own experience as primary data, has entered discussions of method in anthropology.[106] A radically empirical approach privileges not only textual data, but in fact any and all data captured in the field, including the experiences of the anthropologist, be they "ordinary" (fishing, cooking, sipping coffee with an informant) or "extraordinary" (dreaming, meditating, entering a trance state). Moreover, radical empiricism in anthropology

> is rooted in the recognition that not only are the notepad and the tape recorder tools of the anthropologist in the field, but [also] *the entire person of the anthropologist is a research tool.* Viewed from a non-dualistic understanding of consciousness and the structuring of experience in the lifeworld, the anthropologist, when doing experiential fieldwork, is herself embodied knowledge.[107]

The radically empirical anthropologist takes up Poewe's call to experience everything possible that her informants do. In effect, *she becomes her own informant.*[108] Unfortunately, Western-trained ethnographers are generally enculturated in monophasic cultures,[109] which not only do not privilege extraordinary experiences such as the transcendental experiences often had by ravers, but in fact pathologize them. Laughlin and others declare:

> The failure of modern Western culture to prepare individuals for an easy, fearless exploration of alternate phases of consciousness has the unfortunate consequence for science of not equipping most ethnographers with the experiential and conceptual material requisite for sophisticated research into the religious practices of other cultures (see Evans-Pritchard 1965:17, 87).[110]

An important component in a radically empirical investigation of transpersonal experiences such as raving is an emphasis on corporeal, sensuous data: data inscribed upon and collected through human bodies. "The body" has recently become a popular topic not only in anthropology but also the social sciences generally. Related to experiential ethnographies have been anthropologies of the senses[111] and anthropologies of the body.[112]

These anthropologies highlight such pertinent methodological issues as non-Western cultures' alternative schemas for privileging the senses and information gathered through them, and the necessity of anthropologists' raising their awareness of their own cultures' schemas. As Bryan Turner points out in "The Body in Western Society: Social Theory and its Perspectives," an anthropology of the body was being formulated as long ago as Mary Douglas's work on pollution taboos, and in fact really began with Mauss's conception of *habitus* and "body techniques."[113] As in any scientific paradigm, it simply took a backseat to the most popular epistemology of the day. In the first half of the twentieth century this was functionalism, structural-functionalism, and structuralism. In the last half, it was structuralism, post-structuralism, and postmodernism. Contrary to the latter's focus on language and texts, a body-centered, radically empirical method calls for

> a rigorous attention to phenomenology, and awareness not only of cognitive experience in the field, but also data which is collected *through the body* of the anthropologist. It also entails awareness of the preconditioned, intentional, and constructed basis of perception, and of how this necessarily impacts the experience of the anthropologist in the field, and the data gathered.[114]

Practicing anthropology of the senses in an ethnography of the rave experience is especially important due to rave's highly embodied, carnal, and multisensory nature. As Saldanha points out about the Anjuna goa trance scene, and as was the case in central Canadian raves, "you can *smell* the dancing."[115]

A final methodological component of an experiential anthropology is the requirement by the researcher to suspend disbelief and take his informants seriously. Again, while this may seem a non sequitur in the same way that full and empathetic participation in a host culture's lifeworld may seem, its simplicity is deceptive. In their introduction to *Being Changed by Cross-Cultural Encounters*, David Young and Jean-Guy Goulet highlight this as perhaps the most crucial commitment of a truly experiential method, as well as the one most often broken:

> The emic (inside) reality of one's informants is frequently viewed as something which may be intensely interesting—even eminently reasonable (given the premises upon which the system is constructed).

But emic views are not considered as serious alternatives to Western scientific conceptions of reality. In other words, one's informants are not taken seriously.[116]

In the same volume, several authors espousing the experiential method describe how they too struggled with seriously committing to their informants' models of reality, and for good reason. To do so means nothing less than altering one's worldview and ontology (hence, the title of the book), a profound and disquieting experience for anyone. And yet, once they did so, explanations and accounts offered by their informants began to make sense on a different level. A new and deeper understanding developed, as the anthropologists' experiences began to be modeled and even perceived with their host cultures' categories and values.

Conclusion

While presenting some initially plausible and interesting conclusions, the majority of postmodern and post-structural studies of rave culture could only take their investigation of the phenomenon so far. The reason for this lies in methodologies based virtually completely on the notion of textuality. Despite some relevant insights, Maria Pini's 1997 piece on women and rave took this to absurd lengths, with its "text of excitement."[117]

More recent work on rave as a religious practice, most of which has been built upon actual fieldwork and direct experience of the phenomenon by the researcher, has demonstrated that rave cultures do have depths beyond their "meaningless glittering surfaces." To get to those depths, however, involves a number of commitments by the researcher that together form part of the wider methodological approach known as experiential anthropology. I have outlined just a few of these commitments here. After employing them during a three-year study of the rave experience in central Canada, I too found that raving is deeply meaningful, even spiritual for many participants. And importantly, I sometimes found it so myself, such as on the night of my first rave in Toronto in 2000:

The feeling, the experience was indescribable. I kept saying over and over "I can't believe it." "I can't believe it." That was the only way I could describe how intense, how out-of-this-world it was. . . . It was the most intense, incredible experience of my life. I've never felt so euphoric, so exhilarated, so empathetic. It changed my life.[118]

Notes

1. Jimi Fritz, *Rave Culture: An Insider's Overview* (Canada: Small Fry Press, 1999), 199.

2. Scott Hutson, "Technoshamanism: Spiritual Healing in the Rave Subculture," *Popular Music and Society* 23, no. 3 (Fall 1999): 53–77, esp. 60.

3. Because the primary focus of this chapter is on methodological issues in rave studies, rather than providing a background or description of rave, I assume a basic familiarity with the phenomenon. For further description and information, readers can consult Melanie Takahashi's chapter in this volume, "Spirituality through the Science of Sound," and competent histories of rave such as B. Brewster and F. Broughton, *Last Night a DJ Saved My Life: The History of the Disc Jockey* (New York: Grove, 2000); M. Collin, *Altered State: The Story of Ecstasy Culture and Acid House* (London: Serpent's Tail, 1997); J. Fritz, *Rave Culture*; S. Garratt, *Adventures in Wonderland: A Decade of Club Culture* (London: Headline, 1998); T. McCall, *This Is Not a Rave: In the Shadow of a Subculture* (Toronto: Insomniac Press, 2001); K. B. Reighley, *Looking for the Perfect Beat: The Art and Culture of the DJ* (New York: Pocket Books, 2000); S. Reynolds, *Generation Ecstasy* (New York: Routledge, 1999); H. Rietveld, *This Is Our House: House Music, Cultural Spaces, and Technologies* (Aldershot: Ashgate, 1998); M. Silcott, *Rave America: New School Dancescapes* (Toronto: ECW, 1999); S. Thornton, *Club Cultures* (Cambridge: Polity, 1995).

4. A. McRobbie, "Shut Up and Dance: Youth Culture and Changing Modes of Femininity," in *Postmodernism and Popular Culture* (ed. A. McRobbie; London: Routledge, 1994); S. Redhead, ed., *Rave Off: Politics and Deviance in Contemporary Youth Culture* (Aldershot: Avebury, 1993); S. Thornton, "Moral Panic, the Media and British Rave Culture," in *Microphone Fiends: Youth Music and Youth Culture* (ed. A. Ross and T. Rose; New York: Routledge, 1994).

5. M. Takahashi and T. Olaveson, "Music, Dance and Raving Bodies: Raving as Spirituality in the Central Canadian Rave Scene," *Journal of Ritual Studies* 17, no. 2 (2003): 72–96. See also C. Critcher, "'Still Raving': Social Reaction to Ecstasy," *Leisure Studies* 19, no. 3 (2000): 145–62; Reynolds, *Generation Ecstasy*.

6. S. Hutson, "The Rave: Spiritual Healing in Modern Western Subcultures," *Anthropological Quarterly* 73, no. 1 (2000): 35–49.

7. S. P. Hier, "Raves, Risks and the Ecstasy Panic: A Case Study in the Subversive Nature of Moral Regulation," *Canadian Journal of Sociology* 27, no. 1 (2002): 33–57.

8. Thornton, *Club Cultures*; idem, "Moral Panic."

9. Hier, "Raves, Risks."

10. Ibid.

11. See Critcher, "'Still Raving.'"

12. Ibid., 153.

13. A. McRobbie and S. Thornton, "Rethinking 'Moral Panic' for Multi-Mediated Social Worlds," *British Journal of Sociology* 46, no. 4 (1995): 559–74; Thornton, *Club Cultures*; Thornton, "Moral Panic."

14. A. Melechi, "The Ecstasy of Disappearance," in *Rave Off* (ed. Redhead).

15. Redhead, ed., *Rave Off*.

16. Melechi, "The Ecstasy of Disappearance," 32.

17. Ibid., 33.

18. Ibid., 32.

19. Ibid., 37–38.

20. J. Leask, "Club Culture: The Body in the Bubble," *Dance Theatre Journal* 12, no. 4 (1996): 38.

21. Rietveld, *Our House*. "Living the Dream," in *Rave Off* (ed. Redhead), 57. See also D. Hemment, "E Is for Ekstasis," *New Formations* 31 (1997): 23–38; T. Jordan, "Collective Bodies: Raving and the Politics of Gilles Deleuze and Felix Guattari," *Body and Society* 1, no. 1 (1995): 125–44; A. Vitukhnovskaya, "The Crest of a Rave (the Russian Youth Culture)," *Index on Censorship* 25, no. 3 (1996).

22. Rietveld, *Our House*.

23. I suspect that the cynicism and postmodern reading of rave in Rietveld's article was perhaps subtly coerced, originating in the environment that it did—a seminar led by Steve Redhead at the Manchester Institute for Popular Culture.

24. Thornton, "Moral Panic."

25. Thornton, *Club Cultures*.

26. Thornton, "Moral Panic," 177. See also D. Hesmondhalgh, "The British Dance Music Industry—a Case Study of Independent Cultural Production," *British Journal of Sociology* 49, no. 2 (1998): 234–51.

27. A. Jerrentrup, "Techno Music: Its Special Characteristics and Didactic Perspectives," *World of Music* 42, no. 1 (2000): 65–82.

28. See also S. Verhagen et al., "Fast on 200 Beats Per Minute: The Youth Culture of Gabbers in the Netherlands," *Youth and Society* 32, no. 2 (2000): 147–64.

29. R. J. Smith and T. Maughan, "Youth Culture and the Making of the Post-Fordist Economy: Dance Music in Contemporary Britain," *Journal of Youth Studies* 1, no. 2 (1998): 211–28, esp. 212.

30. Ibid. See also P. Chatterton and R. Hollands, "Theorising Urban Playscapes: Producing, Regulating and Consuming Youthful Nightlife City Spaces," *Urban Studies* 39, no. 1 (2002): 95–116; R. Hollands, "Divisions in the Dark: Youth Cultures, Transitions and Segmented Consumption Spaces in the Night-Time Economy," *Journal of Youth Studies* 5, no. 2 (2002): 153–73.

31. A. Brown, "Let's All Have a Disco? Football, Popular Music and Democratization," in *The Clubcultures Reader: Readings in Popular Cultural Studies* (ed. S. Redhead, Derek Wynne, and Justin O'Connor; Malden, MA: Blackwell, 1997).

32. C. Gibson, "Appropriating the Means of Production: Dance Music Industries and Contested Digital Space," in *FreeNRG: Notes from the Edge of the Dance Floor* (ed. Graham St. John; Altona, Australia: Common Ground, 2001); C. Gibson, "Subversive Sites: Rave Culture, Spatial Politics and the Internet in Sydney, Australia," *Area* 31, no. 1 (1999): 19–33.

33. A. Goodwin, "Sample and Hold: Pop Music in the Digital Age of Reproduction," *Critical Quarterly* 30, no. 3 (1988): 34–49.

34. Hesmondhalgh, "British Dance Music Industry."

35. Reynolds, *Generation Ecstasy*.

36. S. Hall and T. Jefferson, *Resistance through Rituals: Youth Subcultures in Post-War Britain* (London: Unwin Hyman, 1976).

37. D. Hebdige, *Subculture: The Meaning of Style* (London: Routledge, 1979).

38. Gibson, "Subversive Sites," 22.

39. Jordan, "Collective Bodies," 139.

40. Hemment, "E Is for Ekstasis," 25–26.

41. Ibid., 33. See also J. Gilbert, "Soundtrack to an Uncivil Society: Rave Culture, the Criminal Justice Act and the Politics of Modernity," *New Formations* 31 (Spring/Summer 1997): 5–22; S. Luckman, "Practice Random Acts: Reclaiming the Streets of Australia," in

FreeNRG (ed. St. John), 205–21; G. St. John, "Alternative Cultural Heterotopia and the Liminoid Body: Beyond Turner at ConFest," *The Australian Journal of Anthropology* 12, no. 1 (2001): 47–66; D. Tramacchi, "Chaos Engines: Doofs, Psychedelics, and Religious Experience," in *FreeNRG* (ed. St. John).

42. M. Pini, "Women and the Early British Rave Scene," in *Back to Reality? Social Experience and Cultural Studies* (ed. A. McRobbie; Manchester: Manchester University Press, 1997), 153.

43. McRobbie, "Shut Up and Dance."

44. B. Wilson, "The Canadian Rave Scene and Five Theses on Youth Resistance," *Canadian Journal of Sociology/Cahiers canadiens de sociologie* 27, no. 3 (2002): 373–412, esp. 379.

45. Pini, "Women"; G. St. John, "Doof! Australian Post-Rave Culture," in *FreeNRG* (ed. St John), 9–36.

46. McRobbie, "Shut Up and Dance," 169.

47. Pini, "Women," 155.

48. Ibid., 167.

49. Ibid., 155.

50. Takahashi and Olaveson, "Music, Dance," 90.

51. Redhead, ed., *Rave Off.*

52. S. Redhead, *Subcultures to Clubcultures: An Introduction to Popular Cultural Studies* (Malden, MA: Blackwell, 1997).

53. Redhead et al., eds., *Clubcultures Reader.*

54. D. Muggleton, "The Post-Subculturalist," in *Clubcultures Reader* (ed. Redhead et al.).

55. A. Bennett, "Researching Youth Culture and Popular Music: A Methodological Critique," *British Journal of Sociology* 53, no. 3 (2002): 451–66.

56. B. Malbon, *Clubbing: Dancing, Ecstasy and Vitality* (London: Routledge, 1999).

57. T. Olaveson, "'Connectedness' and the Rave Experience: Rave as New Religious Movement?" in *Rave Culture and Religion* (ed. Graham St. John; London: Routledge, 2004), 88.

58. Wilson, "Canadian Rave Scene."

59. M. Maffesoli, *The Time of the Tribes: The Decline of Individualism in Mass Society* (trans. Don Smith; London: Sage, 1996).

60. Malbon, *Clubbing*, 57.

61. K. H. Halfacree and R. M. Kitchin, "Madchester Rave On—Placing the Fragments of Popular Music," *Area* 28, no. 1 (1996): 47–55, esp. 48.

62. Ibid., 52.

63. Ibid.

64. Ibid.

65. St. John, "Doof!"

66. A. Bennett, "Subcultures or Neo-Tribes? Rethinking the Relationship between Youth, Style and Musical Taste," *Sociology* 33, no. 3 (1999): 599–617.

67. K. Roberts, "Same Activities, Different Meanings: British Youth Cultures in the 1990s," *Leisure Studies* 16, no. 1 (1997): 1–16.

68. G. Klein, "The Subversive Mainstream: Hiphop and Techno, New Dance and the Music Scene in the Clubs and on the Streets," *Ballett International* (special issue) (1999).

69. Ibid., 21, 24.

70. T. Langlois, "Can You Feel It? DJs and House Music Culture in the UK," *Popular Music* 11, no. 2 (1992): 229–38, esp. 237.

71. S. Marlin-Curiel, "Rave New World—Trance-Mission, Trance-Nationalism, and Trance-scendence in the 'New' South Africa," *TDR/The Drama Review: The Journal of Performance Studies* 45, no. 3 (2001): 149–68, esp. 150.

72. Ibid., 151.

73. E. Murray, "Sound Systems and Australian DIY Culture: Folk Music for the Dot Com Generation," in *FreeNRG* (ed. St. John).

74. P. Strong, "Doofstory: Sydney Park to the Desert," in *FreeNRG* (ed. St. John).

75. G. St. John, ed., *FreeNRG*.

76. K. Iveson and S. Scalmer, "Carnival at Crown Casino: S11 as Party and Protest," in *FreeNRG* (ed. St. John); Murray, "Sound Systems."

77. Murray, "Sound Systems."

78. G. St. John, "Techno Terra-ism: Feral Systems and Sound Futures," in *FreeNRG* (ed. St. John).

79. Luckman, "Random Acts."

80. Ibid.; Iveson and Scalmer, "Carnival"; St. John, "Techno Terra-ism"; Strong, "Doofstory."

81. St. John, "Doof!" 20.

82. Hollands, "Divisions," 154.

83. Ibid., 158.

84. Goodwin, "Sample and Hold," 49.

85. D. Muggleton and R. Weinzierl, eds., *The Post-Subcultures Reader* (Oxford: Berg, 2003).

86. Muggleton, "The Post-Subculturalist," 201.

87. Wilson, "Canadian Rave Scene," 38; see also Bennett, "Researching Youth Culture."

88. Redhead et al., eds., *Clubcultures Reader*.

89. Hollands, "Divisions," 156.

90. S. Hutson, "Technoshamanism," 60.

91. C. Geertz, "Making Experiences, Authoring Selves," in *The Anthropology of Experience* (ed. Victor Turner and E. M. Bruner; Urbana: University of Illinois Press, 1986), 373–80, esp. 374.

92. Takahashi and Olaveson, "Music, Dance," 73.

93. M. Corsten, "Ecstasy as 'This Worldly Path to Salvation': The Techno Youth Scene as a Proto-Religious Collective," in *Alternative Religions among European Youth* (ed. L. Tomasi; Aldershot: Ashgate, 1999); Hutson, "The Rave"; idem, "Technoshamanism"; Malbon, *Clubbing*; St. John, ed., *Rave Culture and Religion*; Takahashi and Olaveson, "Music, Dance"; Tramacchi, "Chaos Engines"; D. Tramacchi, "Field Tripping: Psychedelic *Communitas* and Ritual in the Australian Bush," *Journal of Contemporary Religion* 15, no. 2 (2000): 201–13.

94. Olaveson, "'Connectedness' and the Rave Experience."

95. D. E. Young and J.-G. Goulet, "Introduction," in *Being Changed by Cross-Cultural Encounters: The Anthropology of Extraordinary Experience* (ed. D. E. Young and J.-G. Goulet; Peterborough, Ont., Canada: Broadview, 1994), 12.

96. K. Poewe, "Writing Culture and Writing Fieldwork: The Proliferation of Experimental and Experiential Ethnographies," *Ethnos* 61, no. 3–4 (1996): 177–206, esp. 181.

97. C. D. Laughlin and J. McManus, "The Relevance of the Radical Empiricism of William James to the Anthropology of Consciousness," *Anthropology of Consciousness* 6, no. 3 (1995): 34–46, esp. 39. See also C. D. Laughlin, "Psychic Energy and Transpersonal Experience: A Biogenetic Structural Account of the Tibetan Dumo Yoga Practice," in

Being Changed (ed. Young and Goulet); idem, "Transpersonal Anthropology: Some Methodological Issues," *Western Canadian Anthropology* 5 (1988): 29–60.

98. Takahashi and Olaveson, "Music, Dance," 90.

99. M. Jackson, "Phenomenology, Radical Empiricism, and Anthropological Critique," in *Things as They Are: New Directions in Phenomenological Anthropology* (ed. M. Jackson; Bloomington: Indiana University Press, 1996), 1–50.

100. J.-G. Goulet and D. E. Young, "Theoretical and Methodological Issues," in *Being Changed* (ed. Young and Goulet).

101. J. R. Manyoni, "The Anthropologist as Stranger: The Sociology of Fieldwork," in *A Different Drummer: Readings in Anthropology with a Canadian Perspective* (ed. Bruce A. Cox, Jacques Chevalier, and Valda Blundell; Ottawa: Carleton University Press, 1990), 10.

102. Takahashi and Olaveson, "Music, Dance," 74–75.

103. Poewe, "Writing Culture," 196.

104. Goulet and Young, "Theoretical and Methodological Issues," 309; G. Lindquist, "Travelling by the Other's Cognitive Maps, or Going Native and Coming Back," *Ethnos* 60, no. 1–2 (1995): 5–40. It is important to recognize, however, that "becoming one of them," experiencing everything one's informants do, is not always possible, as a female colleague once pointed out to me in relation to research I was conducting on men's healing groups (Laura Cohen, personal communication, 1997).

105. Poewe, "Writing Culture," 190.

106. M. Jackson, *Paths toward a Clearing: Radical Empiricism and Ethnographic Inquiry* (Bloomington: Indiana University Press, 1989); idem, "Phenomenology"; Laughlin and McManus, "Relevance."

107. Takahashi and Olaveson, "Music, Dance," 75; emphasis in original.

108. On this, see E. M. Bruner, "Experience and Its Expressions," in *The Anthropology of Experience* (ed. Victor Turner; Urbana: University of Illinois Press, 1986), 3–32, esp. 23; J.-G. Goulet, "Dreams and Visions in Other Lifeworlds," in *Being Changed* (ed. Young and Goulet), 19; S. Szostak-Pierce, "Even Furthur [*sic*]: The Power of Subcultural Style in Techno Culture," in *Appearance and Power* (ed. Kirk P. Johnson and Sharon J. Lennon; New York: Berg, 1999), 141–51, esp. 144; idem is in the rave context itself.

109. C. D. Laughlin Jr., J. McManus, and E. G. d'Aquili, *Brain, Symbol, and Experience: Toward a Neurophenomenology of Consciousness* (New York: Columbia University Press, 1990).

110. Ibid., 155.

111. D. Howes, ed., *The Varieties of Sensory Experience: A Sourcebook in the Anthropology of the Senses* (Toronto: University of Toronto Press, 1991); P. Stoller, *The Taste of Ethnographic Things: The Senses in Anthropology* (Philadelphia: University of Pennsylvania Press, 1989).

112. J. Benthall and T. Polhemus, *The Body as a Medium of Expression* (London: E. P. Dutton, 1975); J. Blacking, *The Anthropology of the Body* (London: Academic Press, 1977); S. Coakley, *Religion and the Body* (Cambridge: Cambridge University Press, 1998).

113. B. Turner, "The Body in Western Society: Social Theory and Its Perspectives," in *Religion and the Body* (ed. Sarah Coakley; Cambridge: Cambridge University Press, 1997).

114. Takahashi and Olaveson, "Music, Dance," 75; see also Jackson, "Phenomenology"; Laughlin, "Transpersonal Anthropology"; Lindquist, "Travelling."

115. A. Saldanha, "Music Tourism and Factions of Bodies in Goa," *Tourist Studies* 2, no. 1 (2002): 43–62, esp. 52, with emphasis in original.

116. Young and Goulet, "Introduction," 10. See also Evans-Pritchard, *Theories of Primitive Religion* (Oxford: Clarendon, 1965), 121; Hutson, "The Rave," 37.

117. Pini, "Women."

118. Fieldnotes from *Freakin' 2000*, October 2000.

Under the Shadow of the Almighty

*Fan Reception of Some Religious Aspects in the Work and
Career of the Irish Popular Musician Sinéad O'Connor*

—Andreas Häger

THIS ESSAY DEALS WITH SOME ISSUES of religion and popular music in relation to one particular artist, the Irish singer Sinéad O'Connor. After briefly
introducing the artist and giving some examples of religious aspects of her
work, the main part of the chapter continues with an analysis of fan
response. From a mailing list devoted to Sinéad O'Connor, I analyze the fan
discussion of two significant events in her career. These events are her
appearance on the television program *Saturday Night Live* in October 1992,
where on live television she tore a picture of Pope John Paul to pieces; and
her ordination as a priest in an independent Catholic church in April 1999.

I aim to use this discussion of O'Connor's work, some events in her
career, and the fans' response to these events to explore two topics that, in
my opinion, should be central to the whole discussion of religious aspects
of and influences in mainstream popular music. The first of these topics is
the criticism of established religion, particularly of institutional
Christianity, that is quite central to much of the religious commentary
produced by pop artists. In Sinéad's case, a central theme in her commentary on religion has been a sometimes very harsh criticism of the Roman
Catholic Church. The second topic is the syncretistic or "pick and mix"
quality of the use of religious references in popular culture. This is also
quite evident in the work of Sinéad, as will be exemplified shortly. The fact
that the fans of Sinéad also comment on these aspects show that they are
of importance in the reception of the artist and her work.

Sinéad O'Connor was born in 1966 in Dublin, Ireland. In 1987 she released her first record, which she produced herself. The first single from the second album, a cover of the Prince song "Nothing Compares 2 U," released in 1990, was a big award-winning hit. Sinéad O'Connor became a major recording star. Two years later, she purged herself of the main stream pop star image, musically by releasing a record of jazz evergreens, and image-wise by tearing up a picture of the pope on live television. This can be seen as one of several examples when her actions and utterances have earned her a reputation of being quite controversial. Another example is her ordination as a priest in 1999. In the summer of 2003, Sinéad declared that her career as a recording artist and public figure had come to an end.[1]

Religious Aspects in Sinéad's Work

Throughout her career Sinéad O'Connor has used biblical quotes or traditional Christian texts on her records. On her first record a passage from Ps 91 is read in Irish, and reproduced in English in the CD booklet.[2] The same Psalm, slightly paraphrased, has provided the title for her latest album, *She Who Dwells in The Secret Place of the Most High Shall Abide under the Shadow of the Almighty.*[3] Her second album opens with the "Serenity Prayer."[4] Traditional Christian songs recorded by Sinéad include "Kyrie Eleison"[5] and "Regina Caeli,"[6] the lyrics either used by themselves or in combination with elements from other sources.

The examples in the previous paragraph were all from the (Judeo-) Christian tradition. As mentioned above, however, Sinéad uses references not only from this tradition, but also from several different religious traditions. For example, in her recording of "Kyrie Eleison" to a traditional church melody, the song is accompanied by a Rastafarian Nyabinghi-style drumbeat, and the text of the "Kyrie" is interlaced with shouts of "Jah Rastafari," "down goes Babylon," and so on. Some of the other examples of syncretism in her lyrics are from this same record, as in the chorus of the song "Dancing Lessons." She sings, "May the good Lord guide us and may the goddess dance beside us." Then as a newly ordained priest, she calls herself "a strong independent pagan woman" in the song "Daddy I'm Fine."

A special example of syncretism in Sinéad O'Connor's lyrics is the song "Brigidine Diana." It is a tribute to Princess Diana and is included in the album *She Who Dwells. . . .* The lyrics include references to the three traditions most often used by Sinéad: Christianity, paganism, and Rastafarianism. But the most striking feature of the song is the manner in which the late princess herself is described. The song compares her to the

Virgin Mary and addresses her: "Full of grace are you." "Blessed are you among women." The first verse states that "the Goddess is with you," but in the third and final verse, the title "goddess" is used in addressing Princess Diana. The name "Brigidine" in the title of the song can also possibly be a reference to the Irish-Celtic goddess Brigid, with whom Diana then would be associated. In all, the lyrics of "Brigidine Diana" may be seen as an indication of the very independent and creative approach Sinéad takes to religion, not only mixing different religious traditions, but also even trying to create new deities.[7]

Sinéad O'Connor's criticism of established religion is especially directed at the Roman Catholic Church. The most obvious and strident example of this is the previously mentioned appearance on *Saturday Night Live* (*SNL*) in October 1992. During a live performance of the Bob Marley song "War,"[8] she took a picture of Pope John Paul II, tore it to pieces, and shouted out: "Fight the real enemy" (*SNL*, October 3, 1992). At the time she also voiced strong criticism against the Roman Catholic Church in interviews.[9]

There are also a few examples of explicit criticism of established religion in Sinéad's recordings. Perhaps the clearest example from her lyrics is from the song "Petit Poulet," included on the EP *Gospel Oak*[10]:

There isn't any answer in religion
Don't believe one who says there is

The song was written as a reaction to the genocide in Rwanda. I will return to this song and this passage (below).

The album released just before Sinéad's appearance on *SNL* is concluded by a speech (not listed as an individual number on the record). The tone of the speech may be summed up in the sentence "The war has started now and truth will win." Sinéad places herself on the side of truth. The war is fought against "the enemies of God," those who "assassinated" Jesus Christ. To find out who did this "dirty deed," she says, "Look at the one wearing the collar":

Then or now, there's only ever been one liar,
and that's the Holy Roman Empire.[11]

She thus accuses the Roman Catholic Church—or the Roman Empire that she sees as its predecessor—and the priests with their collars, of actually crucifying Jesus Christ. In the same speech she also says that the church "told us lies to keep us away from God." To my mind, these statements contain at least as strong a criticism of the church and of institutional religion as tearing the pope's picture, and yet—hardly surprisingly—without causing the same reaction. I now consider the reaction to this *SNL* incident.

The Fan Discussions

"Jump in the River" is the name of a song from Sinéad O'Connor's first album, and also the name of a mailing list devoted to discussion of this artist, her life, and her work. It has been functioning since 1990, and there is an archive of the whole discussion available online also for nonmembers.[12] In this central part of the article, I present and discuss some quotes from the discussion on this mailing list during two months, October 1992 and April 1999. In these two time periods, a great portion of the fan discussion is devoted to Sinéad's *SNL* appearance in 1992, and her ordination as a priest in 1999.

The Appearance on *SNL*

The fan reaction to the "pope tearing incident," as Sinéad's appearance on *SNL* has been called, was quite strong. The first mail of October 1992 just exclaims: "WOW. Any comments?"[13] I will not attempt to summarize the whole discussion, and not even the whole discussion on religion. The quotes reproduced are comments in relation to the criticism of the Roman Catholic Church as evident in Sinéad's performance, as well as to elements of syncretism.

Most (but not all) of the members of the mailing list were supportive of Sinéad and her action on *SNL*, as in this comment:

> I've seen enough of the damage that the Catholic church has done
> to cheer any attempt to knock the Pope off his throne. That throne
> sits on the backs of the poor, and on the backs of women.

Many list members also try to explain or justify her action in different ways. One fan remembers: "Sinéad has said in interviews that she was abused as a child and blamed the Catholic church for it."[14] Several comments also emphasize a distinction between church, believers, and Christianity. One list member says: "She attacked the Roman Catholic church but not Roman catholics (she is one herself)." Another states:

Sinéad's beef with the Pope is not one against Christianity or God, because I have her recently quoted as believing in God, but I also have read a lot about how she thinks Catholicism is destroying people.

As could be expected, the fans observe and react to the criticism of religion in Sinéad's performance on *SNL*. Perhaps less self-evident is the strong support—especially in comparison to the much more critical discussion on the ordination a few years later (see below). It is also clear that the fans take the action seriously, as something that needs to be analyzed and explained, either by referring to Sinéad's personal biography and psychology, or by conducting what could be described as theological discussions on the nature of the church.

The song Sinéad O'Connor was performing when she tore the pope's picture was "War," by Bob Marley, based on a speech by Haile Selassie. She wore a necklace with a Star of David around her neck, and a red-gold-green flag as a shawl around her shoulders. These references to Rastafarianism and Judaism are also noticed and discussed by the fans. One fan comments:

> That she was wearing a flag in the Rastafarian colors . . . would square with the speech she used when tearing up the Pope's picture. . . . Does anyone know if Sinéad is flitering [*sic*] with Rastafarianism these days, or was it just a one-off?[15]

One fan also interpreted the Star of David as part of "the Rastafarian aspect of her performance," but another list member disagrees:

> Surely some mistake? The Star of David is a Jewish symbol, whereas someone on the list said that the flag which Sinéad wore on *SNL* (and the speech she repeated) were Rastafarian. . . . I'm not sure that there is any particular link between these two "religions," though at the back of my mind there is something about the Ethiopian Rastafarians claiming to be the lost tribe of Israel—can anyone comment?

The fans who comment on the Rastafarian theme seem for the most part to easily accept that Sinéad may be a Rastafarian, at least on short term. One fan, however, comments that this is quite unlikely, joking that the singer with her shaved head "hasn't really got the hairstyle for it, has she?" No one discusses how the possible Rastafarianism may relate to the observations that Sinéad is a Christian and a Roman Catholic, which had been contributed to the list just a few days earlier. The connection between the clear Rastafarian elements—the flag and the song lyrics—and the Star of David, most often associated with Judaism, did cause some discussion. One fan sees the star as an obvious part of Rastafarianism, but another participant on the list emphasizes that it "is a Jewish symbol," yet still wonders about the connection between the two religious traditions.[16]

Ordination as a Priest

Sinéad O'Connor's ordination as a priest is the second major religious event in her career that I explore through the discussion on the "Jump in the River" mailing list. She was ordained as a priest in a small independent Catholic church—the Latin Tridentine church—in April 1999.[17] This event, rather unusual in the career of an international recording artist, provoked quite a vigorous reaction from the fans on the mailing list. If the support for their favorite singer was almost unanimous after the *SNL* performance in 1992, the fans are much more divided on the issue of Sinéad's ordination.

Several fans conclude that Sinéad must have mental problems and that this would explain her actions. They use words such as "demented" or "simply mentally ill and unstable," and conduct a long discussion on a suggested diagnosis: bipolar disorder. Some try to deal with the event by laughing at it; one fan even suggested that Sinéad might become pope someday. There are also many jokes relating to her name as a priest, Mother Bernadette Marie. One list member comments on the ordination:

> It makes me laugh. . . . True, I would feel different if she did something like that in the religion to which I belong.[18]

Others see the ordination as positive: "I for one am always happy when a lapsed Catholic returns to the faith." Some even see it as logical:

> Sinead's wanting to become a priest is really in perfect keeping with her litany of proclamations and spiritual inclination right from the start.

Several of the negative reactions are based on a comparison between Sinéad's decision to become a priest, and her previous statements on religion in general and on Catholicism in particular. One fan relates the ordination to the *SNL* appearance:

> If you feel that you understand an artist when they do something like tear up a picture of the pope because they are fighting organized religion! Then, how do you expect a person to understand when you go ahead and join that same religion? It is just hypocritical!!!!

Many fans are apparently unaware that the church in which Sinéad has been ordained is not the Roman Catholic Church. Others emphasize this difference, as one fan who believes—or at least hopes—that the ordination is a bluff and a strategic move in Sinéad's attempts to criticize religion:

> She will use this to bring to everyone's attention the corrupt nature of these bizarre sects led by people who take money for confessions and prey on the weak and vulnerable. We can only hope.

Many fans also discuss the above-quoted song "Petit Poulet"—released less than two years before the ordination—and its statement that "there isn't any answer in religion." One fan comments:

> I find it hard to believe that she has forgotten that she said this. I am also inclined to think that this action is another manifestation of her despair of late, or indeed an attempt to discredit the Catholic Church.

Another fan comments on the relation between the song "Petit Poulet," the genocide in Rwanda, and the general question of the meaning of suffering:

> We don't always know why human suffering occurs, but that doesn't mean that religion doesn't answer any questions. It has answered a lot of questions for me, but not all of them. Even though I'm a very religious person, quite often there are issues in my life to which I must simply sing to myself those very lines, "There isn't any answer in religion."

This discussion on how Sinéad O'Connor's work criticizes established religion shows that the fans take her comments and actions quite seriously. Some of them think they take her criticism more seriously than Sinéad herself does. In their interpretation, she has changed her mind on the matter in a "hypocritical" fashion. Many fans also discuss possibilities for reconciling her ordination with previous events in her career, to create a consistent biography, or indeed to emphasize a break in the continuity. One fan sees the ordination as a continuation of Sinéad's previous spiritual interests, while others see it as a hoax that actually is part of her criticism of institutional Christianity. The psychological explanations used also in the discussion on the *SNL* appearance are a central topic in the discussion on Sinéad's ordination.

It is interesting to note the significance of the two short lines from "Petit Poulet" that say there is no "answer in religion." To me, these lines are perhaps the clearest example of criticism of religion in Sinéad's lyrics, and some of the fans on the "Jump in the River" mailing list feel the same. These lines are used as an important clue in interpreting all of Sinéad's career and work. I base such a judgment regarding the significance of this quote and its criticism of religion on the observation that no list member mentions any of the many examples of Christian reference in Sinéad's previous work. The closest thing to an exception is the above-quoted vague comment on her "spiritual inclination." Since Sinéad's lyrics have many more references to Christianity than criticism of religion, it would have been easier to see the ordination as a logical step than as a disruptive event. But it seems that the Christian themes are less important and less obvious to the fans than the criticism of religion. The significance of this theme and the fans' readiness to interpret Sinéad's words and actions as criticism of religion are striking also in the statement that her ordination as a priest may actually be a form of criticism of the church. The quote on the issue of suffering is interesting in the way this fan tries to integrate the criticism of religion into a Christian worldview.

The theme of syncretism is not very central to the discussion on Sinéad's ordination, but a few e-mails touch on it. No one mentions the Rastafarian themes commented on above, or the references to goddess worship on the album *Universal Mother*. One fan, however, recalls hearing Sinéad once claiming to be "a trained medium" and asks:

Does anyone else find it curious that she's both a medium and a priest?

There is one answer to this question, from a fan who says that Sinéad in concerts "has often dedicated songs to the dead among the audience":

To be both a medium and a catholic priest can be reconciled. On one hand she is embracing the ceremonies and trappings of the formal religion of catholicism. Yet, she remains personally and spiritually enlightened and welcomes those that seek to contact their departed loved ones through her ability to channel their spirits.

The interpretation dominating the discussion on "Jump in the River" is that Sinéad, through the ordination, has declared quite strongly—and much too strongly, according to many of the fans—that she is a Christian. In spite of this, the syncretistic elements in Sinéad's work and career are still relevant to some of the fans. But the fact that this discussion is relatively limited, in comparison to the comments relating to criticism of religion, may be interpreted as an indication that the latter theme is more important to the fans. Some have their own negative experiences with Christianity, and some explicitly with the (Roman) Catholic Church; such can therefore relate to Sinéad's criticism of the church. The various other religious or spiritual traditions that she expresses an interest in are perhaps too unfamiliar and exotic to many of her fans and therefore difficult for them to relate to.

Concluding Remarks

Sinéad O'Connor is a recording artist who throughout her career has referred to Christian material and even included traditional Christian lyrics in her songs. This tendency, backed up by the fact that she is an ordained priest, could be used to argue that she should be called a "Christian artist," and also that her music is "Christian music." On the other hand, it is also evident that there are many elements in her work and career that make such a clear-cut definition very difficult. In my opinion, these elements—notably the strong criticism of established religion and the elements of syncretism discussed in this article—set her far apart from "contemporary Christian music" in a strict sense. They also make it difficult to claim that her music is Christian in the sense of proclaiming a Christian message.

Furthermore, the observation that even a priest who sings "Kyrie Eleison" can be difficult to pin down as performing "Christian" music shows how difficult it is to make such claims regarding mainstream pop artists in general. There may be clear religious, and even clear Christian, influences in the work of an artist. These features may be quite consistent throughout a career. Nevertheless, it is not easy to claim that the artist and his or her work are part of a Christian "symbolic universe," to use a concept from Berger and Luckmann.[19] And it is all the more difficult to do so on the basis of a few examples from an artist's production, such as Andrew Greeley[20]—to use one example of many from theological discussions on popular culture—tends to do in his discussion of Madonna's "Like a Prayer."[21] I view such attempts as failures to accept not only the independence and competence of the artist, but also the pluralistic character of today's society.

To many artists, the demonstration of independence is a conscious process central to their whole work, and Sinéad O'Connor can serve as a clear example of such an artist. One may well argue that it is not in spite of Christian elements in her life and work but because she has these Christian features that she wants to show her relative independence from this tradition and the institutions carrying it. She does the latter by tearing up a picture of the pope, or singing of "Jah" and "the Goddess." And, more importantly, this not only shows that she herself strives to be an independent individual; it also appeals strongly to fans who identify with her striving for independence.

A quote from one member on the "Jump in the River" mailing list sums up the discussion well:

> One of the things I think she despises the most is predictability. To tear up the picture of the Pope and then a few years later be ordained as a Catholic Priest, is just her way of saying: "You think you have me figured out??"

And the answer of many of the fans seems to be "no." They have not "figured out" their idol, and that is why she continues to interest them. And perhaps they hope that they also, by supporting such a complex artist and person as Sinéad O'Connor in all her sometimes unpredictable actions, may seem a little more unpredictable and more interesting to a postmodern society.

Notes

1. Biographical information on Sinéad O'Connor can be found in Dermott Hayes, *Sinéad O'Connor: So Different* (London: Omnibus Press, 1991), and on several websites, such as online: http://www.angelfire.com/music4/sineadoconnor/.

2. Sinéad O'Connor, *The Lion and the Cobra* (sound recording; London: Chrysalis, 1987).

3. Sinéad O'Connor, *She Who Dwells in The Secret Place of the Most High Shall Abide under the Shadow of the Almighty* (sound recording; Dublin: Hummingbird Records, 2003).

4. Sinéad O'Connor, *I Do Not Want What I Haven't Got* (sound recording; Ensign/Chrysalis, 1990).

5. Sinéad O'Connor, *Faith and Courage* (sound recording; New York: Atlantic Records, 2000).

6. *She Who Dwells in the Secret Place....*

7. It must be noted that Sinéad O'Connor is not the only one contributing to a form of deification of Princess Diana. Cf. Sven-Erik Klinkmann, *Populära fantasier: Från Diana till Bayou Country* (Vasa, Sweden: Scriptum, 2002).

8. Bob Marley and the Wailers, *Rebel Music* (sound recording; New York: Tuff Gong, 1986).

9. Alan Light, "Sinéad Speaks," *Rolling Stone*, October 29, 1992: 50–53, 80.

10. Sinéad O'Connor, *Gospel Oak EP* (sound recording; London: Chrysalis, 1997).

11. Sinéad O'Connor, *Am I Not Your Girl?* (sound recording; London: Ensign/Chrysalis, 1992).

12. *Jump in the River* archives (http://www.postmodern.com/~mcb/jitr/), accessed May 21, 2004.

13. This and other quotes from comments on the *SNL* appearence are from *Jump in the River* archives, October 1992.

14. Cf. Phil Sutcliffe, "This Time It's Personal," *Q Magazine*, September 1994.

15. "Flitering with" is likely intended to mean "flirting with." Another possible association is that Sinéad is "flitt(er)ing" through or by Rastafarianism.

16. Sinéad O'Connor also uses the Star of David in the cover art on some of her records. See *Universal Mother* (sound recording; London: Ensign, 1994), and *Gospel Oak EP*. The symbol is also used within Rastafarianism (as mentioned e.g. on http://www.jamaicans.com/culture/rasta/ganja.htm and http://www.bbc.co.uk/birmingham/faith/rastafarian.shtml.

17. Georg Sederskog, "Sinéad O'Connor prästvigd," *Dagens Nyheter*, April 28, 1999.

18. This and other quotes from comments on the ordination are brought from *Jump in the River* archives, April 1999; online: http://www.postmodern.com/~mcb/jitr/.

19. Peter Berger and Thomas Luckmann, *The Social Construction of Reality: A Treatise in the Sociology of Knowledge* (London: Penguin, 1966; reprinted 1971).

20. Andrew Greeley, "Like a Catholic: Madonna's Challenge to Her Church," in Adam Sexton, ed., *Desperately Seeking Madonna: In Search of the Meaning of the World's Most Famous Woman* (New York: Delta, 1993), 96–100.

21. Andreas Häger, "Like a Prophet: On Christian Interpretations of a Madonna Video," in Tore Ahlbäck, ed., *Dance, Music, Art and Religion* (Åbo, Finland: The Donner Institute for Research in Religious and Cultural Study, 1996), 151–74.

Planet Rock

Black Socioreligious Movements and Early 1980s Electro

—Thomas Nesbit

IN THE EARLY 1980S, a new genre called "electronic funk" or simply "electro" evolved out of pioneering hip-hop and funk records of the late 1970s. While electro could be mistaken as a vapid genre due to its futuristic synthesizer riffs, detached robotic vocals, and choppy drum machine beats, a political current nevertheless flows within some of its most memorable songs. When listening to tracks such as Afrika Bambaataa and Soulsonic Force's *Planet Rock*,[1] we can detect the influence of black socioreligious movements on both the lyrics and sounds of early 1980s electro.[2] The Nation of Islam (NOI) promoted the idea that blacks not only come from outer space, but also will return there in the future. Furthermore, many electro pioneers received variations of such NOI ideology directly through Bambaataa's Universal Zulu Nation (UZN), an inner-city mission organization whose tenets are based on the teachings of Elijah Muhammad, Malcolm X, Louis Farrakhan, and Clarence 13X. In this essay, I examine the UZN and reinterpret electro's most famous single—Bambaataa's "Planet Rock"—to show the incalculable influence that black socioreligious movements had on electro through the popularity and influence of this pivotal song.

Although by no means the first electro record, Bambaataa's *Planet Rock* is the definitive example of the genre.[3] First released in May 1982, the track embodies many of the themes and influences present in most electro songs

from this early period. As hip-hop critic David Toop writes, "All the electro boogie records that flew in the *Planet Rock* slipstream used a variant on
imagery drawn from computer games, video, cartoons, sci-fi and hip-hop
slanguage."[4] The title and album cover alone transport us to a faraway
place even before we place the needle onto the groove. Thinking of *Planet
Rock* within its cultural context, we are reminded of *Star Wars* and other
popular science fiction of the time.[5] In one interview, Bambaataa hints at
how *Star Wars* is an inspiration for him:

> People are going to experimenting 'cause computers take you to a
> whole different world, a cyber-world along with the regular instru-
> ments that you've been (using). You see it in these movies, STAR
> WARS and all that with the bar scene with aliens and humans and
> electronic music.[6]

Examining the album cover confirms the connection as we see "Afrika
Bambaataa and Soulsonic Force" printed in bold graphics that recall the
opening of George Lucas's films. The appellation "Force" itself echoes the
essence that drives Luke Skywalker through his intergalactic journey.
The graphics have a comic-book feel to them, thereby creating a scene in
which the depicted group is transformed into black superheroes.

The cover to Bambaataa's *Renegades of Funk*[7] offers an even more
explicit example of appropriating comic-book imagery. As David Toop
shows us, early hip-hop culture, especially graffiti artists, were influenced
by comic books. In addition, he points out how early electro artists were
inspired by the once-popular cartoon "The Smurfs." Some examples are
Electric Power Band's "Pappa Smerf,"[8] Tyrone Brunson's "The Smurf,"[9]
The Micronawts' "Letzmurph Acrossdasurf,"[10] Special Request's "Salsa
Smurf,"[11] and Spyder D's "Smerphies Dance,"[12] records all released around
the time of *Planet Rock*. What Toop does not address, however, is why
minorities were drawn to these characters. Once we see the Smurfs as a "colored" and "alien" group oppressed by a larger-than-life white male named
Gargamel, we can then see why black artists immortalized them in song.

To return to the cover of *Planet Rock*, we find dark records hovering
over Earth like flying saucers, as if they are to beam down a message from
beyond. Looking at the members themselves, we see them dressed in
futuristic black-and-silver clothing that parodies costumes of old. In their
live shows, Bambaataa and Soulsonic Force would often dress just as
extravagantly on stage, obviously influenced by the excesses of George

Clinton's Parliament/Funkadelic.[13] Sometimes their dress would be a fusion of futuristic attire and traditional African wear, a mélange that William Eric Perkins describes in some detail:

> Carved African walking sticks, elaborate wildlife headdresses (strikingly similar to those worn by the Mardi Gras Indian tribes of New Orleans), and the infamous "Zulu" beads (a black beaded necklace featuring a black medallion carved with a figurine that resembles an African masthead with the smile face) made a bold fashion statement. Bambaataa and his crew would also, on occasion, dye their hair punk orange, purple, and pea green.[14]

In both their live performances and album covers, we see a symbolic attempt on the part of Bambaataa to write the Blacks back into history, to include the accounts of African glory that were systematically erased by white slave owners. One could even argue, as Mark Sinker did in *Loving the Alien*, that by casting themselves as aliens to the Earth, Blacks are not only explicitly saying they are alienated but are also remixing the idea that Africans were once abducted by white aliens. Playfully distorting the history of an oppressive Eurocentric culture, along with misusing its technological achievements, is a popular trend that can be identified in many representative works of early electro.

Once we put the record on, we can identify even more traditional electro motifs. Its opening lyrics are inspirational, creating images of a free future. Consider this excerpt from the opening verses, for example: "Just start to chase your dreams / Up out your seats, make your body sway / . . . Come play the game, our world is free." The futuristic feel, however, is best perceived through the song's instrumentation. Hand in hand with the influence of science fiction's visuals, we can hear the influence of video games.[15] The bleeps and buzzes are reminiscent of countless early 1980s arcade games, a conscious misuse of the Roland TR-808 drum machine's capabilities.[16] But the robotic vocals, courtesy of the vocoder, mirror the first talking video games of the early 1980s. With the vocoder, Bambaataa was able to create vocals that not only sound futuristic, but also purge any traces of accent. We can see this act as a symbolic yearning for a future in which people cannot be discriminated against due to the way they speak. The assumed cyborg armor that comes with the robotic voice also masks skin color, thereby saving the oppressed from further hate crime.

An alternate description of this phenomenon comes from Tricia Rose's musings on the robot motif:

What Afrika Bambaataa and hip-hoppers like him saw in Kraftwerk's use of the robot was an understanding of themselves as *already having been robots*. Adopting "the robot" reflected a response to an existing condition: namely, that they were labor for capitalism, that they had very little value as people in this society. By taking on the robotic stance, one is "playing with the robot." It's like wearing body armor that identifies you as an alien if it's always on anyway, in some symbolic sense, perhaps you could master the wearing of this guise in order to use it *against* your interpolations.[17]

Her reading does not necessarily challenge my own if we look at this act as similar to Bambaataa's attire; the artists wear costumes representing pivotal movements in white rule to express themselves as superheroes.

Planet Rock's melodies are derived from multiple sources, but its appropriation of Kraftwerk's 1977 hit *Trans-Europe Express*[18] has to be the most noteworthy.[19] Although some rap mythology tells the story that Bambaataa was the first to introduce Kraftwerk to a black audience, Bambaataa states in an interview that many Blacks were already listening to the German band by 1977:

> Kraftwerk—I don't think they even knew how big they were among the black masses back in '77 when they came out with *Trans-Europe Express*. When that came out I thought that was one of the best and weirdest records I ever heard in my life. . . . Everybody just went crazy off of that. I guess they found out when they came over and did a performance at the Ritz how big they was [were]. They had four encores and people would not let them leave.[20]

Many critics have tried to account for why Kraftwerk and European synthpop in general were so influential on Bambaataa and other electro pioneers, such as Juan Atkins of Cybotron in Detroit. In an interview, Tricia Rose argues that Kraftwerk's image "demonstrated a mastery over technology, and mastery over technology engenders a degree of awe, particularly in black folks whose access to technology is limited."[21] Although their persona and stage presence certainly cast Kraftwerk atop the industrial world by virtue of pure acceptance, there is much more evidence that Bambaataa and other pioneers were more taken by Kraftwerk's music than by its image. Somewhat tritely, Julian Jonker argues that, at least for those in the Motor City, "the European music sounded as alien as they felt in the industrial heartland of the USA." While alienation may have been a factor, the fact that Kraftwerk sounded *alien* most likely had more to do with the appeal. Kraftwerk's success among the black community is dependent on a yearning for an authentically extraterrestrial music since the early work of Sun Ra, Lee "Scratch" Perry, and especially George Clinton. While these black expressions were mostly derivative of not-so-distant funk, jazz, and reggae, Kraftwerk and Euro synthpop represented something truly unfamiliar. For Bambaataa and others, it must have felt as if the mothership had finally landed.

In perhaps a reversal of slavery and the present social ills that they had experienced as a people, Bambaataa's takeover of Kraftwerk represented a "big payback," a reassertion of power over the products of Aryan culture. Being the first all-black electronic band was also a source of pride for Bambaataa, something we gather as he says, "I was really heavy into Kraftwerk and Yellow Magic Orchestra and I wanted to be the first black group to release a record with no band, just electronic instruments."[22] Even more interesting than its appearance on *Planet Rock* is the way *Trans-Europe Express* was used in Bambaataa's DJ sets. Toop tells us that "Bambaataa was overlaying speeches by Malcolm X and other Nation of Islam ministers or Martin Luther King" while the record was playing.[23] The UZN's website confirms this, adding that he would also use Farrakhan's speeches ("Afrika"). By playing Malcolm X and other NOI ministers over *Trans-Europe Express*, Bambaataa was symbolically putting the Blacks back into an all-white history. This gesture also captures the direct connection between electro and black socioreligious movements.

In addition to Black Muslim teachings, there is some evidence that Rastafarian ideology was present in the South Bronx, influencing hip-hop pioneers like Bambaataa and Kool DJ Herc. Herc himself was from Kingston, Jamaica, and it was through this legend that hip-hop turntabling began.[24] Bambaataa chronicles Herc's early DJing attempts by telling us that "[Herc] knew that a lot of American blacks were not getting into the reggae of his country. He took the same thing that they was doing—toasting—and did it with American records, Latin or records with beats."[25] If Herc imported the music and DJ culture of Jamaica when settling in the Bronx, it seems likely that he also brought Rastafarian teachings into the early hip-hop scenes, influencing figures like Bambaataa. We can imagine a fourteen-year-old Bambaataa gazing wide-eyed at Herc as he learns of Marcus Garvey's prophecy that redemption will come from an African King.[26] Hearing of the 1950s Jamaican Back to Africa attempts probably helped inspire a young Kevin Donovan to change his name into Afrika Bambaataa in the mid-1970s.

There is also evidence that Afrika Bambaataa may have modeled himself after the mysterious NOI prophet W. D. Fard, the man who began the Black Muslim movement after his arrival in Detroit. Black Muslim scholar C. Eric Lincoln documents Fard's enigmatic ways, such as announcing himself to the Detroit Police as "the Supreme Ruler of the Universe," a statement that does not seem too far outside of Bambaataa's comfort range. But it is Fard's own account of his origins that parallels the story of the electro sensation. Sister Carrie Mohammad recalls the Muslim prophet saying, "My name is W. D. Fard, and I come from the Holy City of Mecca. More about myself I will not tell you yet, for the time has not yet come. I am your brother. You have not yet seen me in my royal robes."[27] Jazzy Jay, DJ of Bambaataa's Soulsonic Force, tells us in the recent documentary *Scratch* that the UZN started with the idea that Bambaataa went to Africa, saw how blacks were living, and wanted to start something similar back home.[28] Moreover, Lincoln tells us of the NOI leader Elijah Muhammad's prophecy that Allah will return to America, an image that truly complements Bambaataa's myth.[29] This fusion of Fard's mythology with Garvey's and Muhammad's visions is an important example of how deeply Bambaataa was impacted by the legends surrounding black socioreligious movements.

It is in the doctrines and practices of the UZN that we can most directly see the effect of these movements on Bambaataa. In his book *Hip Hop America*, Nelson George aptly describes the UZN as "a collective of DJs, breakers, graffiti artists, and homeboys that filled the fraternal role gangs play in urban culture while deemphasizing crime and fighting."[30] Bambaataa was in fact a member of the Black Spades gang, which died out the same year he founded the UZN: 1973. There is good reason to believe that Bambaataa was prompted to create the UZN by the legacy of black community outreach organizations such as Father Divine's Peace Mission Movement.[31] Father Divine's adamancy for ending racial division is reflected in some ideas expressed in an early version of "The Beliefs of the Universal Zulu Nation," a document written by Asaad Allah (Bambaataa's pseudonym) sometime in the 1990s.[32] Under the heading "What Is the Universal Zulu Nation," he answers (in part): "Zulu Nation members discourage divisions and want to see peace and unity on the planet earth with all races" (Allah). The community action pulse continues in the section entitled "What Is the Mission of the Universal Zulu Nation?"

As we are dedicated to improving and uplifting ourselves and our communities, all Zulu Nation members should be involved in some activity that is positive and gives back to the community. Hip-hop music is our vehicle of expression. We can learn to write, produce, market, promote, publish, perform and televise our own music, for our own people (Allah).

The separatism entailed in such statements not only contradicts his yearn for unity among the races but also hints at the influence of Black Nationalist ideas promoted by the NOI.

Throughout the years, Bambaataa has adamantly expressed how influential NOI ministers molded him. When asked, "What motivated you to do something different?" in an outtake interview in the documentary *Scratch*, Bambaataa replied, "Hearing a lot of the teachings of the most honorable Elijah Mohammad." In another, Bambaataa attests to the motivational qualities of NOI thought by admitting, "When I'm crazy depressed I stick in one of my Minister Farrakhan tapes and he just gets that spirit in you and makes you jump up and become a warrior" ("Warlocks").[33] While those two statements were made recently, Toop documents Bambaataa's attitudes around the time *Planet Rock* was recorded: "So Martin Luther King was the thing that was happening because he was fighting for civil rights, but Malcolm X was more on the aggressive side. Myself, I was more on the Malcolm X way of thinking."[34] Later Bambaataa adds:

Then when gangs was fading out I decided to get into the Nation of Islam. It put a big change on me. It got me to respect people even though they might not like us because we was [*sic*] Muslims. The Nation of Islam was doing things that America had been trying to for a while—taking people from the streets like junkies and prostitutes and cleaning them up. Rehabilitating them like the jail system wasn't doing.[35]

It seems evident that Bambaataa was doing something much more political than playing Malcolm X speeches over Kraftwerk tunes; he was creating an inner-city social organization founded on the basic principles of the NOI.

Black Muslim thought, along with the ideology of the Five Percenters, is interwoven throughout the most current version of "The Beliefs of the Universal Zulu Nation" and "The Wisdom and Understanding of the Fifteen Beliefs of the Universal Zulu Nation." Under the second belief,

Bambaataa[36] states that Amazulu (members of the UZN) "believe in the Holy Bible and the Glorious Qur'an," but adds in the third belief "that the Bible has been tampered with and must be reinterpreted." In "The Wisdom and Understanding" section, a sort of midrash on "The Beliefs," Bambaataa explains how the Christian Bible has been distorted: "White people, in preaching and teaching White Supremacy, took the Scriptures of the Prophets of God and rearranged them to push for White Supremacy." He continues by linking white people to devils:

> White people have been blessed to rule just like other People of Color have been blessed to rule sometime in history, but when you do not rule in justice, and rule in superiority over others because of color or thoughts that "I am better than you," then you become an evil or Satan, the Devil Him or Herself. Evil overcomes you and you become a Devil His or Herself, that is why the Bible must be reinterpreted so that Mankind will not be snared by the falsehood that has been added to it.[37]

These statements are practically a rephrasing of the teachings of the Black Muslim leader Elijah Muhammad. Two examples from the late 1950s make the link undeniable: "The human beast—the serpent, the dragon, the devil, and Satan—all mean one and the same; the people or race known as the white or Caucasian race, sometimes called the European race." "Since by nature they were created liars and murderers, they are the enemies of truth and righteousness, and the enemies of those who seek the truth."[38] Although Bambaataa's statements do not explicitly render whites as devils, there is an apparent connection between his thoughts and those of Elijah Muhammad.

Black Futurism also appears in various guises within the words of the UZN's declaration, but nowhere is it as startling as the allusion to the Black Muslim legend of Yakub.[39] Bambaataa could be rekindling images of ancient kingdoms when he writes: "People of Color have been blessed to rule sometime in history." Nevertheless, he most likely had Elijah Muhammad's idea of Original Man in mind, a myth that creates a history in place of the one destroyed by whites in the slave trade. Lincoln tells us more about Muhammad's idea of Original Man: "Original Man is, by declaration of Allah himself, 'none other than Black Man.' Black Man is the first and last: creator of the universe and the primogenitor of all other races—including the white race, for which Black Man used 'a special method of birth control.'"[40] The birth control refers to the central story in NOI mythology, which tells of how Original Man was in power until just over six thousand years ago. At this time, the black scientist Yakub rebelled against Allah and created white people. These experiments eventually resulted in slavery by the morally and physically inferior white man.[41] Lincoln tells us how Muhammad believed the white devils were to rule six thousand years, a period that ended in 1914.[42] Lincoln adds, however, that there was to be a grace period of seventy years, after which Allah's chosen ones will once again rule. The proximity of the grace period's end to the rise of Bambaataa's electro music does not appear to be coincidental.

If Blacks were to come back into power in 1984, we can read Bambaataa's *Planet Rock* as a harbinger released two years before the event. With this interpretation, the lyrics take on a new resonance, promoting an ideology that is not as simple as the "let's party" attitude that some hip-hop authorities read in the lyrics.[43] The album cover art also radiates new meaning, especially when we learn that "a fiery battle was to take place in the sky" during these final days before Blacks were to resume their rule.[44] Flying saucer–like records become throwing stars projected toward Earth by the Asiatic Bambaataa, who is dressed in an outfit that recalls portrayals of Genghis Khan. *Planet Rock* as an album thus is both a weapon used to slice white supremacy in two and a joyous noise that praises the end of the devils' rule.

This should not suggest that Bambaataa is racist. A cursory look at the most famous members of the UZN, along with an examination of UZN chapters throughout the world, are a testament that his circle is a far cry from a "Blacks only" organization. Many members of the break-dancing group Rock Steady Crew, all members of the UZN, are Latino; DJ Q-Bert, another member, is Filipino; and UZN chapters in Belgium and Norway are not predominately black. Bambaataa has often said, as in the outtake interview from *Scratch*, that hip-hop is a "raceless" culture; it is the lyrics and incidentals that give it its racial flavor. It appears that Bambaataa has tried to promote racial harmony in his music and actions, trying to emphasize the "liars" connotation of Elijah Muhammad's expression "devils" instead of grouping all whites under the blanket term.

The influence of Black Muslim ideology can be perceived in Bambaataa's music and lifestyle. By incorporating sci-fi themes, video game sounds, and comic-book graphics into his music, Bambaataa's *Planet Rock* exhibits the seemingly uncontroversial characteristics of other electro expressions of the early 1980s. Embedded within the title track and its album cover, however, are the links to NOI and other black socioreligious movements, connections that become transparent once we examine the beliefs and practices of Bambaataa's UZN. The NOI myths—such as Yakub's creation of Whites and the promise of future redemption for Blacks after the six-thousand-year rule—were probably instrumental in creating and sustaining the obsession with intergalactic origin and destination. They also fostered the interrelationship between backward and forward looking in the black consciousness. Although sci-fi and other popular genres of the early 1980s helped Black Futurism to grow from its 1970s origins, decades-old stories dispersed by black socioreligious organizations allowed Blacks to imagine a brighter future than one filled with sustained oppression.

Notes

1. Afrika Bambaataa and Soulsonic Force, *Planet Rock: The Album* (sound recording; New York: Tommy Boy, 1986).
2. The link between urban black socioreligious movements and hip-hop in general has been practically overlooked in most informed scholarship. Ernest Allen Jr. (in his essay "Making the Strong Survive: The Contours and Contradictions of Message Rap," in *Droppin' Science: Critical Essays on Rap Music and Hip Hop Culture* [ed. William Eric Perkins; Philadelphia: Temple University Press, 1996], 159–91) is the first person to strongly develop the connections between Nation of Islam and rap, but he does not consider Afrika Bambaataa or any other hip-hop pioneers. Although he acknowledges that what he calls "message rap" (politically informed rap) has its roots with The Last Poets and Gil Scott-Heron, he bypasses the early days of hip-hop to discuss the gangsta rap trend of the late 1980s. One of the most valuable insights he has concerns the influence of NOI dissenters "the Five Percenters," a group formed when Clarence 13X was expelled from NOI. Allen describes them as follows: "Doctrinally rooted in the early, 'secret' writings of NOI founder W. D. Fard but committed to a relativization of male divinity, the Five Percenters proffered additional metaphysical novelties in the form of a Supreme Alphabet and Supreme Mathematics" (166). While this group mostly influenced hip-hop in the late 1980s on through the Wu-Tang Clan of the 1990s, some of their thought appears in the doctrines of Bambaataa's UZN. Under the tenth Belief of the UZN, Bambaataa states, "We believe that life, creation, everything is based on mathematics." One cannot begin to fathom the amount of influence this idea must have had on creating the ultra precise rhythms of electro tracks like Bambaataa's own *Planet Rock*.
3. See British DJ Greg Wilson's "Electro-Funk" article for more information on pre-*Planet Rock* electro; online: http://www.jahsonic.com/Electro.html.
4. David Toop, *The Rap Attack: African Jive to New York Hip Hop* (Boston: South End, 1984), 148.
5. For more connections between electro and science fiction, see Mark Dery's "Black to the Future: Interviews with Samuel D. Delany, Greg Tate, and Tricia Rose," in *Flame Wars: The Discourse of Cyberculture* (ed. Mark Dery; Durham, NC: Duke University Press,

1994), 179–222; and David Toop's *The Rap Attack* (1984); idem, *Rap Attack 2: African Rap to Global Hip Hop* (London: Serpent's Tail, 1994); idem, *Rap Attack 3: African Rap to Global Hip Hop* (3d rev. ed.; London: Serpent's Tail, 2000).

6. Jason Gross, publisher of *Perfect Sound Forever*, "Afrika Bambaataa: Article/Interview," pt. 2, online: http://www.furious.com/perfect/afrikabambaataa2.html.

7. Afrika Bambaataa and Soulsonic Force, *Renegades of Funk* (sound recording; New York: Tommy Boy, 1984).

8. Electric Power Band, "Pappa Smerf" (sound recording; Peekskill, NY: Bee Pee, 1983).

9. Tyrone Brunson, "The Smurf" (sound recording; New York: Epic, 1982).

10. The Micronawts, "Letzmurph Acrossdasurf" (sound recording; New York: Tuff City, 1982).

11. Special Request, "Salsa Smurf" (sound recording; New York: Tommy Boy, 1983).

12. Spyder-D, "Smerphies Dance" (sound recording; New York: Telestar Cassettes, 1983).

13. The movie *Beat Street* (MGM, 1984), in which Soulsonic Force and Bambaataa-affiliated group Shango perform at the Roxy, provides the most accessible glimpse into Bambaataa's stage show.

14. Perkins, ed., *Droppin' Science*, 13.

15. Toop once again details many early electro records that were heavily influenced by video games: The Jonzun Crew's "Pack Jam (Look Out for the OVC)," The Packman's "I'm the Packman (Eat Everything I Can)," Arcade Funk's "Search and Destroy," Warp 9's "Nunk," Reggie Griffin's "Mirda Rock," and Tilt's "Arkade Funk" (*Rap Attack*, 146–49).

16. Jonker calls this misuse an example of "black secret technology," a term he "samples" from a record title by A Guy Called Gerald. Although Jonker does not adequately explain his spin on the term, it is helpful to see black secret technology as a way to assert power over traditionally oppressive white technological gadgets. In an interview, Delany also points out the origins of scratching and sampling as "a specific *miss-use* and conscientious *desecration* of the artifacts of technology and the entertainment media" (Dery, "Black to the Future," 193).

17. Ibid., 213–14.

18. Kraftwerk, *Trans-Europe Express* (sound recording; New York: Capitol Records, 1977).

19. Toop lists many sources for *Planet Rock*'s inspiration in *Rap Attack* (130–31). Some recent scholars and critics, such as Perkins, erroneously state that Bambaataa sampled Kraftwerk in the track, but it was keyboardist John Robie, according to Toop, who played the riff (*Rap Attack*, 131).

20. Quoted in ibid., 130.

21. Dery, "Black to the Future," 212.

22. Perkins, ed., *Droppin' Science*, 12.

23. Toop, *Rap Attack*, 130.

24. There are some authoritative and many not-so-authoritative sources that immortalize Kool DJ Herc's position as a hip-hop pioneer, but few tell us about his links to Jamaica. Perkins links Herc's DJ style with the "Yard Culture" of Kingston, describing it as follows: "Yard DJs brought huge speakers and turntables to the slums, where they rapped over the simple bass lines and the ska and reggae beats to create a style uniquely Jamaican" (*Droppin' Science* [ed. Perkins], 6). Future hip-hop scholarship could profit from following Perkins lead.

25. Toop, *Rap Attack*, 69.

26. For more information, see Barry Chevannes, *Social Origins of the Rastafari Movement* (Mona, Kingston, Jamaica: Institute of Social and Economic Research, University of the West Indies, 1978).

27. C. Eric Lincoln, *The Black Muslims in America* (Grand Rapids: Eerdmans, 1993), 12.

28. Another source tells "it was the British film *Zulu* which gave [Bambaataa] the idea in the early 1960s to form the Zulu Nation" (Toop, *Rap Attack*, 156–57). If we take both legends into consideration, we see the electro ethos in action, with technology somehow transporting viewers to a faraway place. In this example, the television or movie screen serves as a portal to Africa for Bambaataa.

29. Lincoln, *Black Muslims*, 68.

30. Nelson George, *Hip Hop America* (New York: Viking, 1998), 18.

31. See Robert Weisbrot's "Father Divine's Peace Mission Movement" (*America's Alternative Religions* [ed. Timothy Miller; Albany, NY: SUNY Press, 1995], 285–90) for a fantastic overview of this organization's history.

32. This document by Asaad Allah, "The Universal Zulu Nation" (online: http://www.globaldarkness.com/articles/universal_zulu_nation.htm), is apparently the predecessor of "The Beliefs of the Universal Zulu Nation" and "The Wisdom and Understanding of the Fifteen Beliefs of the Universal Zulu Nation," statements posted on The Universal Zulu Nation's website (online: http://www.zulunation.com/hip_hop_history_2.htm).

33. "Afrika Bambaataa: Warlocks, Witches, Aliens & Microchips," interview in *Fly*, Jan 10, 2003; online at http://www.fly.co.uk/afrika.htm.

34. Toop, *Rap Attack*, 158.

35. Ibid., 159.

36. Although the document is presented as authorless on the Web page, it seems safe to assume Bambaataa wrote it since he is the leader of the UZN and the author of an earlier draft (see Allah, "Universal Zulu Nation").

37. Within this statement is also a hint of the NOI's understanding of history, an invaluable source of inspiration for Black Futurism (see below).

38. Quoted in Lincoln, *Black Muslims*, 72–73.

39. Some parts of the document reflect electro's predilection for things related to *Star Wars* and sci-fi in general; thus, Bambaataa refers to God as "The Force" thirteen times. Other sections suggest the existence of extraterrestrial life forms. Take the exegesis of the Belief 11, for example: "Everyone must have the same (Equal) Justice all over the Planet so-called Earth, and if someday we do meet Aliens from another planet, then the whole Universe must be ruled with equal justice for all" (online: http://www.hiphopcity.com/zulu_nation/wisdom.shtml). In interviews, Bambaataa is much more open about his belief in other planets within our solar system and extraterrestrial life-forms. Discussing the future of hip-hop in the documentary *Scratch*, Bambaataa says, "I just hope to see it be intergalactic since we are all trying to be intergalactic humans. We are trying to get to Mars and Jupiter and all that so I'm ready to see it on all our other planets in the solar system. Not the nine planets but the 12 or 13 that's out there."

40. Lincoln, *Black Muslims*, 71, where he also documents Elijah Muhammad's belief that blacks were "descendents of the Asian Black Nation and of the tribe of Shabazz." The legend of Shabazz and black Asians was appropriated by the Five Percenters and has subsequently been retold in hip-hop culture from the mid 1980s through today.

41. Timothy Miller (*America's Alternative Religions* [ed. T. Miller]) relates a similar story told by F. S. Cherry's "Church of God" in which the first people were black and the "first white person was Gehazi, whose complexion resulted from a curse" (278–79). It seems as though such stories were commonly used to account for differences in skin color.

42. Lincoln, *Black Muslims*, 73.

43. Perkins's work is perhaps the best example of this oversight. He writes, "[Bambaataa's] music ideology as expressed in *Planet Rock* was really quite simple—to encourage the fun life and a 'funky good time'" (12). Later he reemphasizes that the song is "lyrically simple" (*Droppin' Science* [ed. Perkins], 13).

44. Allen, "Making the Strong Survive," 164. Miller tells us of a similar apocalyptic vision promoted by the Black Jewish group Rabbi Matthew and the Commandment Keepers: "Matthew taught themes familiar in black Judaism and Islam—that the temporary ascendancy of whites was nearly over; the end of white domination and the restoration of the true Israelites would come with a devastating atomic war in the year 2000" (Miller, *America's Alternative Religions* [ed. T. Miller], 279).

Spirituality through the Science of Sound

The DJ as Technoshaman in Rave Culture

—Melanie Takahashi

DEE JAYS ARE POWER FREAKS! I feel a huge amount of responsibility in this role. If you sense the need to cast yourself in this directing, controlling, position, then try and do it in a clear minded way, without unconsciously projecting too many personal agendas through the prime time of these trance-dance, altered state, sacred spaces. The dancers put themselves in your hands to take them on a journey, it's like psychic surgery. It's important to understand the dynamic of raising this energy in the body and psyche, through progressing the various levels of intensity in the music, to make a spiraling progression.

—DJ Ray Castle[1]

AN OVERWHELMING RHYTHMIC BASS LINE, colored spotlights, lasers, and fractal projections pulsating in time to the music, the penetrating scents of Vicks VapoRub, incense and perspiration, a crowded room full of trance-dancing bodies, and the ingestion of psychoactive substances—these are just some of the displays characteristic of the all-night dance parties referred to as raves. When combined, these elements are specifically designed to promote feelings of connectedness, spirituality, and a state of what participants refer to as "ecstasy."[2] At the heart of these proceedings one encounters the individual responsible for the success or failure of the event: the DJ. Using equipment to manipulate the rhythm, sound, and lighting, the DJ guides individuals through a psychological journey where the dance floor transcends its function as a space for leisure activity. For many, this is a sacred arena for transformation, healing, and spirituality; the dance floor is a "pseudo church"; and the DJ is a revered figure whose role borders the divine.

The music genre "techno" is often referred to by its subcultural habitués as "the sound of one world shrinking." Described by Merchant and McDonald as "the most vibrant, popular and visible cultural expression of young people,"[3] the subculture referred to as "rave," or "technoculture," has become a significant global youth phenomenon.[4] Techno music, predominantly rhythmic, has dismantled linguistic and geographical boundaries such that rave-style events can be found on every continent,[5] and the burgeoning community of international travelers who orient their destinations around rave parties is supporting a growing tourist industry.[6]

The curious relationship between popular music and religious experience is no more apparent than in technoculture. A small body of recent publications on raves reflects the growing recognition by scholars that the rave scene provides a spiritual outlet for many contemporary youth.[7] Although the DJ's position within this culture as a spiritual leader and guide has been recognized,[8] little attention has been focused on the specific nature of the DJ's role. Poschardt contends that the DJ's tendency toward "laconic autism" has made him a difficult object of inquiry that has "remained untouched by academic study."[9] Similarly, Fikentscher observes that the DJ's "gradual rise in the hierarchy of the music industry has not been accompanied by a corresponding growth in the academic literature."[10]

Based on four years of fieldwork in the central Canadian rave scene, this chapter explores the art and science behind the DJ's craft, focusing on the music and the procedures used by the DJ in triggering altered state/s of consciousness (ASC) in participants. To understand the dynamics underlying the DJ's techniques, I refer to the work of ethnomusicologist Gilbert Rouget and his delineation of how music serves to socialize trance in the ritual context. Recognizing that raves share many common features with possession rituals—rhythmic stimuli, prolonged dancing, sleep deprivation, fasting, and the aspect of performance—I explore the techniques employed cross-culturally by instrumentalists of possession rituals.[11] Similar to instrumentalists in possession rituals, the techno DJ is a musician and expert in knowing how music works. In comparing his role to instrumentalists of ceremonial possession, we see how the DJ's technical expertise and crowd skills operate as trance-inducing cues among rave participants, thereby shedding some light on the variety of transpersonal encounters that have been reported at raves.

The DJ's Ascension:
From Music Selector to Technoshaman

An influential figure in popular culture, the DJ has been depicted as a cultural broker and creator of culture as he[12] directs youth trends through his choice of music. Drawing on Bourdieu's concept of cultural capital, Thornton employs the term subcultural capital to refer to "hipness" or "being in the know" in relation to youth club cultures.[13] For Thornton, "being in the know" translates into economic capital, and this is the driving force behind power and hierarchy in club cultures. As one who embodies and determines degrees of "hipness," the DJ profits financially by having the greatest access to and ownership of subcultural capital.[14] In the rave context the economic potential of the DJ has been taken to an even higher level as the DJ's career now includes studio work that can entail record-producing and songwriting. Fikentscher argues that this move has transformed the DJ from "cult figure to cultural hero."[15] The DJ's elevated status is partially a reflection of his economic potential. But the DJ's association with the underground, a morally and legally ambivalent sphere of society linked with antiestablishment, has also allowed him to replace guitarists and the leaders of rock-and-roll bands as the social and musical role model for today's youth.[16]

Historically, the DJ has been an elusive and marginal figure whose ability to work without restriction has contributed to his quasi-outlaw title. In the quest for exposing others to the newest underground sounds, pirate radio[17] and underground raves afford DJs the opportunity to air music from new genres that have yet to acquire categorical titles, and play songs that have been banned from regular programming.[18] Unlike other artists, the DJ is not dependent or subservient to the record industry, and this guarantees him a certain amount of respect, particularly from the youth population.

In rave culture, the DJ's ability to interact with, read, and take the dancers on what they refer to as an "ecstatic" journey has also been recognized, and his influence has expanded to include the spiritual sphere. The

DJ was once an anonymous figure hidden away behind the DJ booth. With his status being elevated to such monumental heights, he has seen his role expanded beyond the traditional role of music selector to include technician, performer, artist, producer, musician, and most recently technoshaman. In tandem with this transforming role, a cult of the DJ has since emerged: thousands of youths will gather at a rave event to be guided through a spiritual quest under the direction of a technoshaman. Ravers themselves are cognizant of this responsibility and refer to DJs as kings, leaders, gurus, priests, and gods. Much like spiritual gurus, rave DJs tour internationally and ravers will often travel great distances to hear their favorite DJs perform. DJ booths at raves are frequently designed to resemble altars. The DJ's role as spiritual leader is also reflected in the phenomenon witnessed at events where the entire crowd of dancers face in his direction, sometimes displaying signs of reverence and devotion, such as prostration, chanting, and adoration.[19] For these reasons DJs have sometimes been referred to as "shamans" or "technoshamans."[20]

The DJ as Artist and Instrumentalist

Much of the DJ's elevated status and recent success have to do with the artistic license and technological innovations in music production that afford today's DJs with limitless opportunities for creative development. Prior to the 1970s, the DJ profession involved playing one record after the other, and the DJ was regarded as a technician rather than an artist. According to Poschardt, the style of DJ-ing that emerged out of the disco era provided the "crucial breakthrough to an artistic use of turntables and records."[21] Today, DJ-ing is considered an art form, and the turntable is regarded as an instrument where the DJ spontaneously produces new sounds for the crowd. Among the DJs I interviewed, many felt that the creative process of what they call "turntabling" provides them the means to express themselves through their music. Regarding the turntable as an instrument explains why most DJs prefer to work with vinyl despite the invention of the record's modern-day counterparts: the compact disc and MP3. For most, it is the hands-on aspect of the turntable that establishes it as an instrument, rather than a piece of equipment, and it is the physical element that makes the turntable appealing:

> I enjoy playing vinyl a lot more simply because it's a lot more hands-on. It has a lot more of the traditional aspect, but it's also a

lot more fun for me because I can manipulate stuff with my hands. I actually get to use my hands to feel so I have more control over the music. (Casey)[22]

A paradoxical art form, the DJ then is a metamusician whose performance is based on prerecorded music. The profession thus questions the traditional notion of the live performance and, as Poschardt states, "questions the traditional concept of the artist, blows it apart and reestablishes it in overhauled form."[23] An emblematic figure of the postmodern era, the DJ has been likened to a writer, an editor, and even a weaver of mosaics and tapestries. This is largely due to the techniques of mixing,[24] remixing,[25] and sampling[26]—procedures that make each performance spontaneous, unique, unexpected and thus "live" rather than merely prerecorded.

The ability to create and sample an infinite array of sounds also redefines the boundaries of artistic freedom. For this reason the following individual sees techno as the ultimate musical form:

You're not limited to six strings and twenty-one frets like you are on the guitar. Think of having an instrument that can make any sound you want. You are only limited by your imagination. (Greg)

Authorship and performer identity are of less concern in technoculture, and many musicians will release records using a number of pseudonyms to generate confusion over their identities.[27] Additionally, the lack of vocals combined with the techniques of sampling, mixing, and remixing makes dance tracks[28] generally anonymous; the original producers and composers are often so far removed from the various tracks that the DJ ultimately receives the credit for the performance. The use of the term "set," referring to the DJ's total performance, also reinforces the DJ's "authorship" over the music. A DJ is evaluated according to his "set," which comprises the complete ensemble of tracks. Listening to a track implies recognizing the original artist and producer of the music, whereas dancing to a "set" acknowledges the DJ as the principal artist.[29] At the same time, in electronic music culture the boundaries between artist, producer, and DJ have become blurred since in addition to sampling and remixing the works of others, many DJs record and produce their own tracks, often through their own record labels.[30]

A Symbiotic Performance:
The DJ's Relationship with the Dancers

In considering the relationship between music and religious experience, it is often assumed that the music on its own right is responsible for eliciting an altered state of consciousness. In his cross-cultural analysis of the music accompanying trance rituals, Rouget observes features in possession music that are employed universally as a means of triggering trance. These universal features may prompt an individual to be more susceptible to an altered state. Nevertheless, Rouget emphasizes that the music cannot be stripped of its context; the music is effective only when it is familiar to the participant. In this way music serves to socialize trance rather than to trigger it. In framing possession trance as a learned process, Rouget highlights the intricate dynamic established between instrumentalists and dancers as part of the socializing process. In possession, the notion of performance is central to the ritual as instrumentalists perform for an audience.[31]

Irrespective of an individual's familiarity with the music, the trance state is induced only within the ritual space in the presence of others. Ravers listen to technomusic at home, and some have commented that certain tracks of music can elicit ASC similar to the ones experienced at raves.[32] Yet, most would agree that the experience of listening to technomusic at home in no way compares to how music is experienced at raves. What is absent outside of the rave locale is the interpersonal relationship established between the DJ and the participants. On the subject of possession rituals, Rouget emphasizes the importance of the connection between the instrumentalists and the dancers. "To induce trance in a particular person the priests and musicians establish a special relationship with him, 'surround' him, make him the object of their 'solicitude,' address themselves to him in an exclusive way, and become at the same time very attentive to what he himself is feeling."[33]

At raves, an intimate and symbiotic relationship between the DJ and his participants is a prerequisite for trance induction. The dancers' ability to achieve an "ecstatic" state is quite dependent on the DJ's stage presence, his proficiency in intuitively "reading" and responding to the crowd, and his ability to form a temporary bond with the dancers. Without these skills, the mere techniques of trance induction are generally inadequate for eliciting the sought-after "ecstatic" state. Most DJs would agree that mastery over the techniques of mixing, remixing, and sampling are useless if the DJ is unable to connect with the crowd.

Participants also recognize certain qualities in a DJ that are conducive to creating this special bond. A DJ who favors the musical tastes of the participants over his own is a valued trait. In contrast, some DJs go to events with a rigid preselected play list and refuse to alter their selections to accommodate the dancers' responses; ravers refer to such DJs as selfish and have little patience for them:

> I don't understand those DJs that are playing to an empty floor. One minute it's packed and then the next it's sparse. What's going on in a DJ's head that they just don't see? A good DJ will be able to read the crowd and be able to pull tracks out of their little record box based on how the crowd is reacting instead of saying, "Okay, this is my set: next it's this track, next it's this track, screw everyone else." (Sue)

The active role of the crowd in shaping the mood and atmosphere of the party also encourages a more spontaneous approach. Recognizing this, some DJs feel they need a crowd and perform best during a live set. DJs who give the tastes of the crowd priority over their own are also considered to be humble. This quality is admired and considered a precondition in becoming a "people's DJ."[34] Ravers often mention cues indicating a DJ's humbleness: gestures suggesting appreciation and gratitude toward the crowd, such as bowing, clapping, eye contact, and smiling.[35] These gestures also play an important role in breaking the artist-spectator barrier, and this strengthens and reifies the connection between the DJ and the dancers. When ravers discuss their favorite DJs, they name their interpersonal qualities more often than their technical skill or musical style:

> His being a part of the crowd, that was nice. . . . I like to see his smile to see him smile and be happy and dance on stage. (Mike)

One informant recounted how his favorite DJ is notorious for jumping out of the DJ booth and joining the participants on the dance floor. Breaking the barrier between artist and participant is another reason why DJ booths are centrally located at raves. It is important that the DJ see the dancers so he can respond to them. It is equally important for the participants to be in close physical proximity to the DJ, so that his personality and presence are able to come through.

All these factors are conducive to breaking the barrier between the DJ and the dancers. The communication that occurs between the two is much more than the music, lyrics, and the dance movements, or what Rouget refers to as the "level of the code."[36] In reference to possession rituals, Rouget argues that communication is established "at the personal level, the emotional level of direct person-to-person relationships."[37] The active role of the dancers also reinforces the dismantling of the barrier between the performer and audience. This is where the concept of the feedback loop between the DJ and the participants is relevant. As DJ Spooky puts it:

> The DJ-audience relationship is like a symbiosis, you know, it's like a biological structure, you know, I mean, it's like you are sending out information and pulses that the crowd in a way then sends back to you, and like you're like a focal point of the energy of these gathered people.[38]

This is why most individuals in the electronic music scene refrain from using the term "audience" and prefer the term "crowd" or "participant." They say that terms such as "audience" and "spectator" imply a distinct separation between the DJ and the dancers, and at raves the two should operate as one unit. The dancers must therefore give constant feedback to the DJ, which the DJ in turn responds to and builds from, and this explains why dancers generally face the DJ at raves.[39]

There is also an emotional element involved in this symbiotic relationship, and most ravers acknowledge that the DJ is responsible for the emotions of the crowd of dancers. They also recognize that the DJ's emotional state can be transmitted to the crowd through his music, and this consequently impacts the affective condition of the dancers:

> He is the music man, he decides what you're going to feel that night. I would imagine that if a DJ isn't feeling particularly well, it will show up and you'll feel it. (Greg)

A DJ's seeming lack of enthusiasm, his failure to make eye contact, smile, or dance—these are indicators suggesting that he isn't having a good time, and this has consequences on the crowd. One DJ has put this simply:

> If I'm not having fun, they're not having fun, and this is why essentially I come excited, so they can feed off that immediately. (Casey)

While the crowd is sensitive to these nonverbal indicators of the DJ's affective state, the DJ's mental state can also influence his choice of music, and this too will impact the experience of the dancers. There is a strong correlation between genres of rave music and affect at an event.[40] For example, certain analysts blame "terrorcore"[41] and "industrial hardcore"[42] for bringing out aggressive and negative emotional states in some individuals. Bold, militant rhythmic patterns, sounds of machinery, people screaming, and vocals with coarse language—these are the kinds of sounds attributed to some electronic music styles. In contrast, "trance"[43] and "happy hardcore"[44] are characterized by warm melodies and positive lyrics that are recognized for bringing out such feelings as love, a sense of well-being, and connectedness:

> When you go to a happy hardcore rave, everybody knows the tunes. There's always classics that are played in every happy hardcore party, and everybody will have a big smile, and everybody will look like a little Care Bear. Everybody will smile and run and jump everywhere. (Will)

Thus, depending on his mood, the DJ can choose tracks with vocals and melodies that accentuate positive themes, or tracks with sounds and lyrics that concentrate on darker subjects. This is where a participant's sense of trust in the DJ is so important. Evident in the following raver's statement is a sense of fear associated with the DJ's level of control over one's experience:

> I realized that the DJ had POWER over me. I was basically prostituting for the DJ: I was a slave to what he had (the promise of the climax), and he was flexing his power and tweaking with me to see how much I could stretch myself out for it. It really scared me. . . . I think some DJs definitely hold the power of a cult in their turntables and in their speakers, and it's really not something that I want to get down on my knees for. Just a thought, I'm not bagging here. I still think rave is one of the best things the 20th century has to offer, but I think that if left unchecked, it could turn on us.[45]

At raves, the trance state is very much dependent on the individuals' willingness to let go and trust the DJ in allowing him to guide the nature of their experience:

> [DJ] Tiësto's kind of cute, maybe in a gay way, so it was a bit sexy to think that Tiësto the babe was controlling me. I wanted to be

under his control, under his spell. I trusted him, the way you would let go of your senses in certain moments of supposed passion. (Kate)

One DJ regards the dancers as having a responsibility to meet him halfway: "As long as they are open for a while and let themselves go, they have the opportunity to feel things the way I intended them to."[46] Here again, the similarities between possession rituals and rave are apparent. Rouget characterizes the relation of the possessee to the musicians as "the submission of the former to the latter."[47] The following description of the *ndop* ceremony (the healing ceremony of the Wolof of Senegal) highlights many of these striking resemblances including the instrumentalist's ability to observe and respond to the dancers' movements, and the bond established between the two:

> In fact, a close interpersonal relationship develops at this point between drummer and possessee. The drummer takes charge of her, so to speak. Keeping very close to her, never leaving her side, concentrating on her slightest movements, incessantly observing her behavior in order to: speed up the tempo, or, on the contrary, relax it; select the necessary types of beat; and adjust the intensity of the stroke. Communicating the rhythm of the dance to her, he holds the possessed woman in his sway and leads her into the ever more violent whirlwind of his music. But if he is able to lead her in this way, and finally guide her where he wishes, it is because he has been able to establish a close understanding with her. It is because he can follow her that he is able to dominate her and impose his will upon her. He is the master of the game, but within a dialogue. He speaks music and she replies dance.[48]

The theme of submission is also apparent in possession ceremonies in relation to spirit beings that possess cult members. In the case of Haitian voodoo, for example, Bourguignon highlights extreme passivity as one of the prerequisites to trance induction:

> However, one aspect of submission-dominance seems of importance in relations to possession trance: the person, as we have seen, is said to be "mounted" by the spirit, to be his "horse." The personality of the individual, one of his souls called "gros bon ange [large good angel]," is displaced and the body is taken over by the spirit.

In other words, there is total subjection to the spirit and total sub-mission to him (or her). The spirit, as a powerful superhuman entity, can do as he pleases, both with the horse he has mounted and with other human beings present. We thus have an expression of extreme passivity in this interpretation of possession trance.[49]

At raves, references to the power of music in directing the body are remi-niscent of possession's horse-and-rider metaphor. According to Sylvan, these accounts of submitting to the music "suggest a trance state very simi-lar to possession, in which the music becomes the rider and the body becomes the horse, but without reference to any specific possessing spirit."[50] The high volume of the music also reinforces the power of the DJ and the theme of submitting to the bass. According to Fikentscher, the high volume ensures the authority of the DJ as the music establishes "absolute priority over other acoustic phenomena: conversation, hand-clapping, foot-stomping, yelling, whistling."[51] The notion of submission is also reflected in some ravers' attitudes toward drugs. "First-timers" are often prepared ahead of time to avoid fighting the effects of the drug as this can often result in a bad trip and minimize the positive benefits:

> You need to be ready to give yourself away to the buzz that you gave yourself since normal ceases to exist once you've swallowed the pill. It is the only way to fly, to appreciate the buzz; you're not doing it so everything can stay normal. (Greg)

Some ravers feel that the onset of nausea frequently experienced with MDMA[52] ingestion is a physical reaction to the psychological attempt at fighting the drug. It is commonly acknowledged that, once an individual comes to accept the new reality, the nausea will pass.

In the rave locale, the DJ is equally influenced by the emotions of the crowd, where participant feedback is transmitted at the visceral level. I have observed participants demonstrating their admiration for a DJ by whistling or repeatedly chanting his name. Yet, for the most part, crowd feedback is nonverbal. Occurring as sets of coordinated body techniques that all ravers seem to intuitively know and all DJs, no matter what their country of origin, can follow, these moves are acquired at the corporal level. Most ravers seem to be unconscious or unaware of these movements. From an observer's point of view, the responses to the DJ are well coordi-nated. When I first started attending raves, I thought the dancers were performing a predetermined pattern of steps because the movements were surprisingly ordered, synchronized, and even predictable.[53] Fikentscher calls the sum of individual dancing bodies the "collective performance," wherein the bodies of the dancers can potentially unite to form "one musical instrument."[54] As McCall suggests, this process is mediated by dancers' observation of subconscious cues:

> People are helping each other dance without knowing it, feeding off the collective anticipation for that moment of synergy where it feels like utter madness: cheers, claps, whistles, hands in the air. Suddenly everyone is dancing in unison.[55]

When the dancers are "in sync" with one another, the boundaries between individuals seem to vanish as the crowd appears to function as one organism.[56] This process of synchronization, known to insiders as "phase locking," also encompasses the entry into a collective psychic space. Referring to the crowd as a "sea of dancers" is another commonly used description that suggests the merging of dancers into one:

> Crazy you know, like fifteen [or] twenty thousand people and the underworld is spinning and you look at these people and it's like a sea, it's like a literal sea of people moving together as one. (Kurt)

Rather than being informed by thought and intentionality, learning seems to take place at the corporal level as seasoned ravers appear unaware of these patterns and insist that there are no steps or "choreography" at a rave. As dancers increase their exposure to the music and learn the nuances of the communication, these movements become intuitive. As one raver says:

> You'll only have that communication when you've danced a lot or when you can really appreciate the intricacies of electronic music. (Kurt)

This is not to say that rave dancing is coordinated or by any means restricted. On the contrary, the freedom to dance any style without being judged is what attracts many individuals to the scene. The coordinated movements being referred to are intermittent, occurring only during certain intervals in response to specific changes in the music. These gestures are actually learned bodily responses to what are the DJ's trance induction techniques.[57] As dancers become increasingly familiar with the music, they memorize the melodic and rhythmic structures built into each specific track and can precisely coordinate their movements to subtle changes in the music.[58] When these familiar segments of music are introduced during the DJ's climactic build-up, the dancers not only anticipate the DJ's manipulation of the music, but familiarity and the emotional connection to specific tracks also fuel the fervor:

So at first you don't know what's going on, you don't know, and slowly especially as it becomes familiar to you, you hear a track and you hear it again and you'll recognize it. And then you remember where the bass drops, you remember where it climaxes and what's going to happen next. And so it becomes much more emotional because you have emotionality tied to it. But yeah, it takes some getting used to, it takes some time to sit back and listen to it, and listen to the layers, and yeah, pay attention to what it's doing to your feelings and especially what it's doing to your body so you can move to it. (Sue)

In the case of raves, Rouget's point that trance is a socialized scripted process is evident, as is the critical role of music in socializing altered mind states.[59] The divide between an experienced and inexperienced dancer becomes quite apparent when one is observing novices. Dancers unfamiliar with tracks and the structure of a DJ's set will often look confused, hesitate, stop, and/or look to others for guidance.[60] The movements are often disjointed and lack the ease and flow of the veterans.

The Science of Sound: Trance Induction at Raves

In *Music and Trance*, Rouget emphasizes that rituals of possession are embedded within rich cultural traditions, in which trance is a learned and culturally patterned process.[61] It is the possessee's ability to identify emotionally with the music and dancing as signifiers of cultural knowledge that enables him to enter the trance state. Translated into the media of cultural theater, "Priests become impresarios, mediums are actors; musicians form orchestras; spirit recitations become scripts that are central to the drama of the expression of culturally specific themes."[62] In rave culture, it can be said that the impresarios are the event promoters, the dancers become the actors, the DJs become the orchestra, and the music serves as the script. What is unclear in these musical scripts, however, are the story lines that narrate these culturally specific themes. Although some have characterized rave as a culture void of meaning and content,[63] raves are actually the antithesis of empty. They are pregnant with symbols wherein cultural themes collide and overlap with one another. Symbols specific to rave such as happy-face logos and glowsticks, intermingle with painted mandalas, alien and UFO imagery, and representations of the Buddha and numerous Hindu deities. An event can begin with a smudging ceremony, the reading of a poem or prayer, a yoga class, a guided meditation, a collective ingestion of the "holy sacrament" (MDMA), or a group recitation of the Om mantra. As an open system, rave culture operates at a metacultural level, welcoming and encouraging cross-pollination with other symbol systems,[64] including the revival of symbols from the ancient past. This is where rave departs from ceremonial possession. No clear and consistent single body of narrative binds the complex symbol traditions together in such a way that the symbols can operate in concert with one another. Although raves are emotionally charged events, the music and dance movements are not rooted in one specific cultural tradition and thus do not anchor the component parts of the music. A DJ's set is comprised of varying fragments of melody and rhythm, sampled from a variety of cultural sources and music genres. An individual reports one consequence of this sampling: "You don't have a very clear feeling anymore, that's what's happening with the music, you know it's just all spliced up, it's all watered down and I mean it's a kind of dried up old feeling."[65]

Nevertheless, there is an inherent power in technomusic as reports of extraordinary states of consciousness evoked by the music are numerous. This is where the universal agents involved in trance induction are paramount. DJs have not only utilized these mechanisms to induce trance among participants, but technology in sound and music production have also given artists the means to refine these practices into a science of precision. To an extent, these technological advancements may compensate for the lack of coherent cultural signifiers, because DJs have access to a range of equipment that is clearly absent in ceremonial possession. Reynolds attributes the "DJ-godstar phenomenon" to MDMA use, suggesting that the overwhelming emotions that the drug elicits often get transferred to the DJ.[66] However, in appreciating the DJ's developing aptitude for music and crowd interaction, it is more plausible to argue that the "godstar" phenomenon has more do to with the DJ's accuracy in technique. After all, some ravers who worship DJs and hold them in high regard have never taken MDMA. Electronic music producers are creating works intended to elicit specific states in the brain, and advancements in sound and visual effects at raves create the optimal listening environment for these tracks. These features—combined with the DJ's proficiency in track selection, crowd interaction, and the learning on the part of participants in recognizing and responding to the DJ's cues—account for the ASC that people are reporting. Thus, raves achieve such ASC even though they lack the sophisticated scripted process of initiation observed in ceremonial possession.

Many DJs as well as experienced rave participants have developed their senses in such a way that they perceive technomusic differently than those who have never been exposed to it. This shift in musical perception is a learned by-product of repeatedly exposing the auditory system to new stimuli, and this transition is a critical step in socializing ASC induction. Ravers are fanatical about sound quality and give tremendous attention to such details as the equipment used, the positioning of speakers, and the settings of equalizers. The tones, frequencies, and beats of electronic music are designed by producers and further refined by DJs to target the body in precise ways. Electronic music is intended to be physically experienced. This is evinced by many veterans of the rave scene describing the music as having a three-dimensional quality that transcends the traditional way music is perceived.[67] In reference to this attribute, one raver describes the music as being

> all around you rather than just going in your ears, the music is being absorbed by your body because it's energy. (Kurt)

This three-dimensional aspect of rave music is partially a result of surround-sound[68] reproduction that most club and rave venues now house. This technology allows the listener to become a part of the music as the sound appears to resonate from all points surrounding the listener. Such music creates movement in the composition and a perception that surpasses the auditory to involve kinesthetic and spatial perception:

> I think the music just really really embraces you, it completely surrounds you. . . . It's sort of a cushion around you with all these different effects. (Sue)

Surround sound has also provided a number of creative opportunities for musicians as new parameters—such as the location of sound, its trajectory, and its direction—can be incorporated into compositions.[69] Some DJs who mix in surround sound have noted that they can integrate a greater number of sounds without obtaining the muffled result that often occurs in stereo sound. With these enhanced capabilities, artists can incorporate complex textures into their works. At the same time, it is increasingly possible for the listener to detect these subtle nuances of sound and detail that would otherwise go unnoticed in mono and stereo formats.

Laser, lighting, and visual technology are additional features of the rave environment that enhance the overall physical experience of electronic music. There are software programs, for example, that allow users to input audio tracks into computers running a fractal-generating program. The overall effect is the projection of fractal patterns on screens that move in time with the music. The recent rise of the VJ (video-jockey) profession reflects the important role of visual effects at raves. Similar to music and the art of DJ-ing, VJs can sample and mix various forms of imagery that can range from fractals to film loops, digital animations, and live recordings. These visual projections are further enhanced by lighting equipment referred to as "intelligent lighting fixtures," moving lights in patterns projected through different-colored filters. Similarly, computer programs can also transform lasers into shapes, patterns, and even logos. VJs and lighting technicians will often work with DJs to create tension and excitement in the crowd by running these systems during peak moments at an event.

Although not all DJs refer to themselves as technoshamans, most are aware of how music can operate as a catalyst for an ASC. In fact, many individuals involved in the electronic music scene are interested in consciousness expansion through psychoactives, yoga, meditation, and various New Age practices. It therefore is not surprising that some DJs have researched the perception of sound and its relationship to various brain states and ASC. Computer technology has provided the DJ with the power to fully control the means of perception at raves. With the computer's capacity to create sounds that cannot be produced in the natural environment, and to present melodies and rhythms so rapid and complex that they go beyond the human ability for performance, our perceptual systems are being exposed to completely new stimuli. The intentional experimentation with sound on the part of music producers may account for the emotional and physiological responses that technomusic has been found to elicit in the laboratory.[70]

Some electronic musicians are even experimenting with sounds that go beyond the human auditory range. Fritz argues that sounds vibrating through the body without being heard "may be partly responsible for the powerful emotional response people have when listening to rave music."[71] DJs are thus experimenting with these technological innovations to create the optimal listening experience and brain state. For example, Mike Adamzek, a DJ/artist uses brain-scan equipment to test various drumming patterns in an effort to create an ideal "state of mind and connect it with the heart."[72] One artist who refers to himself as DJ EEG chose his stage name because "I was interested in the positive effects of alpha waves on the psyche."[73] Similarly, DJ BT has an electrode brain-scan machine called a "dual hemisphere electro encephalograph" that records brain-wave activity. BT wears this headset and records his own brain states while he listens to music to test the relationship between musical stimuli and mind state. Eventually he hopes to use this headset, to coordinate additional sensorial elements with the music, to induce specific brain states among participants:

> I eventually want to use this headset to control lighting rigs, to control visual imagery, to control sensor sweeps. . . . It's more about learning how to use it if you know what I mean, it's like experimenting and training certain brain states.[74]

This DJ has also researched auditory and photic driving in indigenous cultures and is cognizant of the theta waves these driving mechanisms produce in the brain. He recognizes that these driving mechanisms are present in club and rave culture:

> I've done a lot of research on photic and auditory driving, which are two really interesting naturally occurring things that happen in loads of different indigenous music. It's continual stimuli of a certain frequency and it's always very small frequencies, and what people do is they entrain to that particular brain state. If they're being stimulated with either by photic flashing or by auditory sound . . . I mean this goes back to indigenous rituals performed by the shaman in the Peruvian Amazon and stuff. They would beat a drum at a certain number of wave cycles per second. Usually four to six wave cycles per second or something . . . which is in brain state, . . . theta brain state which is the very creative brain, and then they'd have someone else while the shaman was beating the drum, flaming or fanning the flames on a fire at the same time, at the same speed, and people would all eventually entrain in this brain state. In modern

club culture, and in seeing modern club events and modern rave events and things like that, you're seeing people entrain into the same brain state. You've got strobes, you have lighting that everyone's taking in, you have big time photic driving, the music is auditory driving.[75]

While the majority of DJs are not necessarily versed in the scientific literature on trance states, or use scientific language to describe what they do, there is an underlying intuitive knowledge of what works with the crowd at raves. Listeners can expect to hear certain tracks at events that all DJs play, and different DJs will consistently employ the same techniques to stimulate the crowd. Rouget observes that an interruption in the music's flow is used cross-culturally to induce trance. The acceleration of tempo, an increase in volume (crescendo), the use of polyrhythm, rhythmic changes such as syncopation, and even a brief cessation of the music—such catalysts are techniques that interrupt the music's flow, triggering trance.[76] Rouget notes that most possession ceremonies begin slowly, gradually intensifying throughout the evening with the onset of possession being the climax of the event.[77] The methods, implemented by instrumentalists in interrupting the music's flow, function to intensify the sound and atmosphere of the possession rituals. With electronic music, the idea of tension and release is a built-in characteristic of all classifications of rave music.

The notion of peak experience and climax is also a central part of the rave, and this is one of the reasons for the extended hours of events. Ravers are well aware of the fact that the peak hours for raving generally occur between 2:00 and 6:00 a.m. Knowing this, drug ingestion is precalculated so that the drug's effects will peak during these hours. Headliner DJs are normally slotted to spin over this period, and as the evening progresses, the music gradually becomes harder, faster, and louder. Coinciding with the music, the visual effects are often more intense and spectacular during this period as well. Since possession is not the ultimate objective for participants at raves, there is no singular climax point of the event. Instead, the process is built around a series of tension-building episodes, which are resolved, with each subsequent cycle of tension and release being more intense than the previous one:

I will start off very very down temp, pick it up, throw it back down a little bit. Pick it up, throw it back just a little bit, and then jack it right through the roof. (Casey)

While the sets of headliner DJs are the climatic foci of the event, preceding and proceeding DJs perform tension-building sets that are juxtaposed within the larger framework of the peak experience; each track within the set follows the same thematic pattern. With the average set being two to three hours, a DJ will frequently start playing tracks with slower tempos, gradually increasing the beat per minute (BPM) range. DJs refer to this as "peaking the floor." As well-known DJ Frankie Knuckles put it, peaking the floor creates a churchlike environment.[78] This is why the metaphor of "the journey" is so often used to describe the rave experience. The music's constant cycle of tension and release is accompanied by a range of emotion and bodily sensations that MDNA only heightens. I interviewed one DJ who organizes his "story line" according to the following parameters:

From what I have to say a set for a DJ is like a story. Like all stories the beginning has to be catchy, relatively simple beated/plotted for the dancer/reader to enjoy. After the first hours, move on after the crowd is fullish, and the energy is high. The music is no longer the same, now it is like an "anthem" and the tribal instincts of people kick in because there's so many in the crowd. Now is the time to put something hard, to sort of satisfy them for what they have been waiting for—loud floor thumping hard bangs. This is the part of the story where the intro is over, and the characters are beginning to shape in our minds. . . . At the end it comes back to simple beats again, not as trippy as the beginning, but much harder, but simple—not so synthy—music. That you can remember, dance to, . . . and by this time he's playing something that's pretty popular too, . . . and alternate that with something hard again. If that is not really hard, . . . and sometimes you just wind up begging for more. You are now the DJ's slave. Additionally, like all interesting stories, sets must have surprises, . . . the odd old favorite, the sudden climax, . . . the sudden hard beats you never expected. (Kayleb)

Some describe the music as being sexually charged and compare the cathartic properties of the anticipated bass to reaching orgasm. One way the DJ builds tension in the crowd is by leaving out the percussive elements and/or removing all musical inputs (including visual and lighting displays), with the exception of a vocal or synthesizer line. Gradually the DJ will reintroduce the musical components one at a time, with the bass being the last element added. Before the bass is introduced the DJ will often further increase the tension by accelerating the music, increasing its volume, and raising the pitch.[79] The DJ's equipment offers technical opportunities that are unavailable to acoustic instrumentalists. For example, a DJ can increase the tempo to a rate that exceeds human performance ability, and the volume of sound can clearly exceed the range of an acoustic instrument. Although Rouget[80] does not mention an increase in pitch as a possible provocation of trance, this is likely due to the fact that increases in pitch have not been observed ethnographically because acoustic instruments are unable to perform this.

When the bass is finally introduced, it is often accompanied with a synchronized display of lasers and fractal projections, as well as overlapping rhythmic patterns presented in syncopated time. While the bass is "being dropped,"[81] DJs may at this point strategically introduce a well-known rave anthem.[82] Hence, accompanying the adrenaline of the anticipated beat is a flood of emotions elicited from the memory of past rave experiences, which these songs carry with them:

> A skilful DJ will be able to bring different levels around and especially when it's a song that you recognize and you really like, and you can associate it with a past experience and he's got some other mix on it. You know he's got some crazy scratching or top fit or something, and you're like "wow where did this come from" and then like you can just all of a sudden you'll remember. You'll hear a line and you'll be like "this is that song" and the moment you're like "this is that song" you don't hear that scratching part that's new anymore. You're just pulled backward to this other time and it's the most extraordinary feeling. (Kurt)

At this point a surge of energy is released by the dancers, who exhibit their approval and gratitude by jumping up and down, screaming, whistling, and shouting. The introduction of the bass is consistently the sought-out resolution, and it is here that the sexual metaphors of the music are particularly evident:

> The DJ will play with me. Like he'll go to give me and then he'll be like "oh no" and I'll just be like, . . . and he can tell like we'll have eye contact even and I can tell that he's keeping it from me and I'll be like "give it to me give it to me" and he'll be like "no

no" and I'll be "come on drop it in" you know, . . . fallin' on my ass or something like that. When it [the bass] finally drops I'll be rushing so hard. (Kurt)

A similar sentiment is expressed in the following account:

The music was reaching a crescendo, rising higher and higher, building until the entire house was screaming and jumping up and down in a frenzy of near complete body consciousness. The mind was no longer important and the body was merely a receiver for the music. Suddenly, the music stops, for a split-second, and then BAM! It's back harder and faster than ever, now freeing the minds and spirits of the dancers in an ecstatic explosion of joy. It was like a hive-mind having an orgasm.[83]

Visible in these accounts is a similar kind of psychological manipulation that often occurs in possession rituals.[84] DJs will intentionally withhold the bass from the dancers, or torment them further by indicating cues that the bass is coming, but instead the DJ will extend the vocal line, thus prolonging the dropping of the bass. As Reynolds states: "Rave music has always been structured around the delay of climax" and the anticipation of a "plateau of bliss that can be neither exceeded nor released."[85] For one DJ, removing the percussive elements and adding a well-known vocal line serves to unify the crowd and seize their attention, so they can be taken to a higher level of consciousness. Once this occurs, he teases the crowd with the anticipation of the beat:

Stuff like ole-ole . . . or Sweet Surrender by Sarah McLachlan . . . or trancey tunes . . . and then plain synths with no percussion, drums or beats . . . that gets you to feel the music in a collective way with the rest of the crowd. Basically at this point you're at union with the crowd, the DJ, the producer, the floor and your inner self. You reach a new point since you can feel the absence of the drums. The tune is "dancey" but there's no drum for you to catch your anatomy into so you're eagerly waiting for that beat as you're being teased every second. Every second before the drum begins adds to your tease, and you reach another level, probably because of your increased sense of anticipation. It gets even wilder inside you when you hear the buildup of a drum begin and then the buildup finishes with those hard kicks, thuds coming in and everyone bouncing. You reach a next level: you get high. (Kayleb)

In addition to being aware of these tension-building procedures, a good DJ must be able to intuit when and how to resolve the tension, which is referred to as "pacing." As Fikentscher observes, pacing is very much dependent on performance time[86] as well as the overall structure of the DJ lineup. At one event I attended, some informants felt the DJ was too extreme and sudden in using these techniques. Mike, for example was annoyed with the DJ because "he was bringing it high and dropping it [the bass] like sirens and that was totally killing it." Knowing how much tension an audience can handle and resolving the tension at the appropriate time is underscored in the following raver's statement:

Like they have to know how long you can keep it at 155 beats per minute and if you slow it down too fast too quickly it just screws everybody up and they leave the dance floor or they just stand there scratching their heads. I mean music is all about creating tension and resolving tension and a really good DJ especially with this technomusic can create tension, but there's a point where you create too much tension. Like that drumbeat that goes "cho cho cho." You can only do that for so long before someone goes "get this drum beat over with." But if you do it just right you'll get people right at the height of the tension, and then you resolve it and people go crazy. And the DJs that can feel the tension in the crowd and resolve it appropriately can just keep you going for hours and hours. (Eric)

This chapter has examined the role of the electronic music DJ and how the DJ's profession has evolved into an art form as well as a science. Technology has played a pivotal role in shaping the development of rave culture. At its core, the music that binds this global culture together is created, exchanged, performed, and experienced through computer-mediated technology. It is probable that rave culture could continue to thrive without the clandestine venues, the stylistic preferences, and even the drugs. Throughout my fieldwork, I have already observed regional changes in rave accoutrements, clothing, drug preference, and venue locations. What has remained consistent is the culture's total dependence on technology and the rapid thrust toward technological advancement. According to Wilson, "a reverence to and celebration of technology, and an implicit and explicit belief in 'progress through technology'" is one of the underlying doctrines of rave culture.[87] Raves would be crippled without technology; this reinforces a point made by Reynolds: Rave music is not about "what the music 'means' but [about] how it works."[88] As Sylvan says, part of what makes these "hybridized forms of popular religiosity" so attractive is that the "depth of 'content and substance' tends to be sacrificed in favor of breadth and 'intensity of transmission.'"[89]

The techno DJ is indeed an expert in knowing how electronic music works, and his method of transmission is intense. In drawing parallels between the DJ and the role of instrumentalists in possession ceremonies, it is apparent that music plays a critical role in eliciting ASC among participants at raves. The DJ's expansive knowledge of repertoire, his technical prowess at the turntable, his onstage charismatic presence, his success in earning the dancers' trust, and his uncanny ability to interact with, read, and manipulate the crowd—these have awarded him the power to take his dancers on an "ecstatic" journey. To quote an informant: "For the duration of his set the DJ is god . . . or pretty darn close" (Greg).

Notes

1. Graham St. John, ed., *FreeNRG: Notes from the Edge of the Dancefloor* (Altona, Australia: Common Ground, 2001), 161.

2. In this paper, "ecstasy" and "trance" are referred to according to the emic perspective. While it is clear that ravers are experiencing altered states of consciousness at raves, a discussion concerning the precise nature of these states goes beyond the scope of this essay.

3. J. Merchant and R. McDonald, "Youth and the Rave Culture, Ecstasy and Health," *Youth and Policy* 45 (1994): 16–48, esp. 16.

4. Since its emergence in the late 1980s, the rave scene has undergone a fragmentation from one "unified" scene to several subscenes. The more general terms "technoculture" or "electronic music culture" are increasingly being used by participants as umbrella terms that include all the proliferations of electronic music. Some participants are reluctant to use the term "rave" due to the negative media attention focused on rave events. These newer labels are also favored for shifting the focus away from drugs, instead giving priority to the music. According to most ravers, the music is the most fundamental aspect of the culture and the primary reason for attending events (see M. Takahashi and T. Olaveson, "Music, Dance and Raving Bodies: Raving as Spirituality in the Central Canadian Rave Scene," *Journal of Ritual Studies* 17, no. 2 [2003]: 72–96).

5. Yes, even Antarctica; online: http://donegal.uchicago.edu/antarctica/rave.html.

6. In *Rave Culture: An Insider's Overview,* Jimi Fritz cites eighty-two countries where rave culture is "alive and well" (Victoria, BC: Smallfry Press, 1999, 236–52), and this number is undoubtedly growing. In Goa, a popular international party location for enthusiasts of "psytrance" music, the number of tourists during the winter months surpasses the local population of Goans (Arun Saldanha, "Music, Tourism, and Factions of Bodies in Goa," *Tourist Studies* 2, no. 1 [2002]: 45).

7. T. Becker and R. Woebs, "Back to the Future: Hearing, Rituality and Techno," *World of Music* 41, no. 1 (1999): 59–71; M. Corsten, "Ecstasy as 'This-Worldly Path to Salvation': The Techno Youth Scene as a Proto-Religious Collective," in *Alternative Religions among European Youth* (ed. L. Tamasi; Aldershot, UK: Ashgate, 1999); G. Fournier, "Rave, intensité et quîte de sense," *Religiologiques* 24 (2001): 71–80; F. Gauthier, "Consumation: La religiosité des raves," *Religiologiques* 24 (2001): 175–97; S. Hutson, "Technoshamanism: Spiritual Healing in the Rave Subculture," *Popular Music and Society* 23, no. 3 (Fall 1999): 53–77; idem, "The Rave: Spiritual Healing in Modern Western Subcultures," *Anthropological Quarterly* 73, no. 1 (2000): 35–49; G. St. John, "Doof! Australian Post-Rave Culture," in *FreeNRG* (ed. St. John); idem, "Techno Millennium: Dance, Ecology and Future Primitives," in *Rave Culture and Religion* (ed. G. St. John; London: Routledge, 2004); R. Sylvan, *Traces of the Spirit: The Religious Dimensions of Popular Music* (New York: New York University Press, 2002); Takahashi and Olaveson, "Music, Dance."

8. Hutson, "Technoshamism"; D. K. Hill, "Mobile Anarchy: The House Movement, Shamanism and Community," in *Psychedelics Reimagined* (ed. T. Lyttle; New York: Autonomedia, 1999); D. Green, "Technoshamanism: Cyber-Sorcery and Schizophrenia," *The Spiritual Supermarket: Religious Pluralism in the Twenty-First Century* (International Conference of CESNUR [Centro Studi Sulle Nuova Religioni/Center for Studies on New Religions], 2001), online: http://www.cesnur.org/2001/london2001/green.htm; Sylvan, *Traces of the Spirit.*

9. U. Poschardt, *DJ-Culture* (London: Quartet Books, 1998), 17.

10. Kai Fikentscher, *"You Better Work!" Underground Dance Music in New York City* (Hanover, NH: University Press of New England, 2000), 33.

11. Gilbert Rouget, *Music and Trance: A Theory of the Relations between Music and Possession* (trans. B. Biebuyck; Chicago: University of Chicago Press, 1985), makes a distinction between shamanism and possession. He argues that there are two main ways of managing trance: a scripted or programmed method associated with possession trance, and a nonscripted one associated with shamanism.

12. Most DJs are male. The low representation of women at the level of music promotion and production in the rave scene has been widely noted. See A. McRobbie, "Shut Up and Dance: Youth Culture and Changing Modes of Femininity," in *Postmodernism and Popular Culture* (ed. A. McRobbie; London: Routledge, 1994); M. Pini, "Women and the Early British Rave Scene," in *Back to Reality? Social Experience and Cultural Studies* (ed. A. McRobbie; Manchester: Manchester University Press, 1997); S. Reynolds, *Generation Ecstasy* (New York: Routledge, 1999), 274; B. Brewster and F. Broughton, *Last Night a DJ Saved My Life: The History of the Disc Jockey* (New York: Grove, 1999), 376–77. McRobbie cites that 90 percent of DJs are male (1994, 171). In the New York City scene, Fikentscher (*"You Better Work!"*) observes that male DJs outnumber female DJs by a ratio greater than 10:1. Similarly, from the events I attended during fieldwork, less than 1 percent of the DJs were female.

13. S. Thornton, *Club Cultures: Music, Media and Subcultural Capital* (Cambridge, UK: Polity, 1995), 11.

14. Ibid., 12. The DJ's access to subcultural capital is not a recent phenomenon; the bribes accepted by the DJs to promote records resulting in the payola scandals of the 1950s are just one example of the power and influence occupied historically by the DJ.

15. Fikentscher, *"You Better Work!"* 54.

16. T. Langlois, "Can You Feel It? DJs and House Music Culture in the UK," *Popular Music* 11, no. 2 (1992): 234–38, esp. 234.

17. A pirate radio station is unlicensed and illegal, defying the broadcasting laws of its country.

18. Brewster and Broughton, *Last Night a DJ Saved My Life*, 278–79.

19. Takahashi and Olaveson, "Music, Dance," 86.

20. Hutson ("The Rave," 38) cites Fraser Clark, the editor of the underground music magazine *Evolution*, as the individual to first describe the DJ as a "technoshaman." See Hutson, "The Rave"; idem, "Technoshamanism"; Eugene ENRG and R. Castle, "Psychic Sonics: Tribadelic Dance Trance-Formation," in *FreeNRG* (ed. St. John); S. Reynolds, "Rave Culture: Living Dream or Living Death?" in *The Clubcultures Reader: Readings in Popular Cultural Studies* (ed. S. Redhead; Malden: Blackwell, 1998), 35, 151, 216, 275; M. Silcott, *Rave America: New School Dancescapes* (Toronto: ECW, 1999), 58–59; Melanie Takahashi, "Theater in Search of Storyline: The Role of the 'Technoshaman' in Rave Culture" (PhD diss., University of Ottawa, 2004).

21. Poschardt, *DJ-Culture*, 32.

22. To protect the anonymity of my informants, I have used pseudonyms and removed personal data that could identify individuals.

23. Poschardt, *DJ-Culture*, 15–16.

24. This refers to seamlessly combining two records together.

25. This refers to altering and therefore reinterpreting an existing song.

26. This consists of inserting any sound, musical passage, or rhythm into an existing song at any desired point.

27. David Hesmondhalgh, "The British Dance Music Industry: A Case Study of Independent Cultural Production," *British Journal of Sociology* 49 (1998): 234–51, esp. 238; see also D. Hemment, "E Is for Ekstasis," *New Formations* 31 (1997): 37.

28. In reference to musical selections, DJs and ravers prefer to use the term "track" instead of "song."

29. Benjamin S. Thomassen (2002), online: http:// www.chikinsandowichi.com/data/culture/dj/job.html (accessed December 19, 2002).

30. R. J. Smith and T. Maughan, "Youth Culture and the Making of the Post-Fordist Economy: Dance Music in Contemporary Britain," *Journal of Youth Studies* 1, no. 2 (1998): 211–28, esp. 222–23.

31. G. Rouget, *Music and Trance*; idem, "Music and Possession Trance," in *The Anthropology of the Body* (ed. J. Blacking; London: Academic Press, 1977).

32. Melanie Takahashi, "The Natural High: Altered States, Flashbacks and Neural Tuning at Raves," in *Rave Culture and Religion* (ed. G. St. John).

33. Rouget, *Music and Trance*, 112.

34. See also Brewster and Broughton, *Last Night a DJ Saved My Life*, 11–12.

35. In contrast, Reynolds suggests that successful DJs must also carry with them a certain amount of arrogance, and a disposition that favors leadership and authority ("Rave Culture," 275). Considering the DJ's role as music educator, a DJ has to take risks by exposing the crowd to new sounds, sometimes at the expense of playing exactly what the crowd wants to hear (1999, 274).

36. Rouget, *Music and Trance*, 113.

37. Ibid.

38. Jon Reiss, director, *Better Living through Circuitry* [documentary DVD] (Studio K7/Cleopatra, 1999).

39. M. Gerard, "Selecting Ritual: DJs, Dancers and Liminality in Underground Dance Music," in *Rave Culture and Religion* (ed. St. John), 175, observing that in the Toronto scene, failing to observe this convention (by dancing together in a group facing

each other) is an indicator of "novice status." Circle dancing is common among mainstream club-goers, where the grouping together of females, for example, serves to discourage males from making unwanted advances (181).

40. A correlation between drug choice and music genre has also been suggested. Ravers will often select drugs that complement the music's emotional attributes as well as the beat per minute range. LSD has been named as the drug of choice among "psytrance" ravers (Reynolds, "Rave Culture," 176), crystal methamphetamine is associated with "hardcore" (see B. Wilson, "The Canadian Rave Scene and Five Theses on Youth Resistance," *Canadian Journal of Sociology* 27, no. 3 [2002]: 373–412, esp. 393), and cannabis with "jungle" and "hip-hop" (T. R. Weber, "Raving in Toronto: Peace, Love, Unity and Respect in Transition," *Journal of Youth Studies* 2, no. 3 [1999]: 317–36, esp. 327). W. Pedersen and A. Skrondal ("Ecstasy and New Patterns of Drug Use: A Normal Population Study," *Addiction* 94, no. 11 [1999]: 1695–1706) found MDMA (3,4-methylenedioxymethamphetamine) use to be highest among "house" and "techno" rave-goers.

41. "Terrorcore" is a branch of "hardcore" featuring a beat per minute range exceeding 160. It is intended to be the antithesis of the uplifting positive tone of "happy hardcore" and is thus characterized by darker melodies, bass lines, and vocals. "Terrorcore" is also commonly referred to as "speedcore," "darkcore," "extremecore," "doomcore," "demoncore," and "deathcore."

42. Another derivative of "hardcore" or "industrial hardcore" is rhythmically fast but is distinct from other "hardcore" genres for sampling sounds of machinery.

43. "Trance" is characterized by its continuous 4/4 rhythm, which is said to have a hypnotic effect on the listener. This music genre is also reported to be emotional and uplifting.

44. Like "hardcore," "happy hardcore" has an elevated beat per minute range, typically exceeding 160. The music often includes samples of music from cartoons, female or cartoon character vocals, piano riffs, and a strong 4-beat kick drum. The stuffed animal kiddy backpacks, beaded jewelry, body glitter, and pacifiers are the stylistic features associated with this subscene of raving.

45. Online: http://www.hyperreal.org/raves/spirt/technoshaminism/Techno_Orgasm.html (accessed December 7, 2000); cited in Takahashi and Olaveson, "Music, Dance," 86.

46. Heiko Laux, in *Raw Music Material: The Fifty Most Famous Electronic Music DJs of the World* (ed. Walter Huegli with Martin Jaeggi; Zurich: Scalo, 2002).

47. Rouget, *Music and Trance*, 112.

48. Ibid.

49. Erika Bourguignon, *Possession* (San Francisco: Chandler & Sharp, 1976), 40.

50. Sylvan, *Traces of the Spirit*, 129.

51. Fikentscher, *"You Better Work!"* 85.

52. Commonly referred to by ravers as "Ecstasy," "E," and "XTC," MDMA is the drug most often associated with the rave scene. In a collaborative study of the central Canadian rave scene in which I participated, it was found that while a variety of substances were reported at raves, MDMA was the most frequently reported substance at 67 percent, followed by cannabis at 64 percent and crystal methamphetamine or "speed" at 34 percent (see Takahashi and Olaveson, "Music, Dance").

53. Tara McCall, *This Is Not a Rave* (Toronto: Insomniac Press, 2001), 95.

54. Fikentscher, *"You Better Work!"* 58–59.

55. McCall, *This Is Not a Rave*, 93; see also Fikentscher, *"You Better Work!"* 80–81. The dancers relate to each other but communication occurs at an embodied subconscious level. There is no verbal interaction taking place. In order for the symbiotic relationship to occur

between the DJ and the dancers, the dancers need to operate as one. It is the paradox of "dancing alone among a crowd"—turning inward, yet being a part of a group at the same time.

56. McCall, *This Is Not a Rave*, 95.

57. Gerard ("Selecting Ritual") also remarks on the proficiency of dancers in the Toronto scene by comparing the movements of novice dancers to the more experienced ones. While I have called these movements learned bodily responses to trance induction techniques, Gerard refers to similar displays as responses to the DJ's "techniques of liminality." Although Gerard employs a slightly different lexicon, the DJ's techniques result in transformative experiences that both "liminality" and ASCs are reported to produce.

58. Some ravers acknowledged using psychoactives to help them with their dancing. One informant felt that MDMA helped him to relax, thereby enabling him to dance with total abandon, free from the constraints of worrying about how others might "evaluate" his moves. This kind of freedom gives dancers the opportunity to block out external inputs and focus directly on the music so that the dancing naturally becomes more precise. The tendency for psychoactives to enhance and heighten the senses is also said to work well for music interpretation. In reference to Psytrance music, one informant reported that "on LSD I feel like I just plug into the music and just all of my moves are just bang on, like I feel like I've become this instrument and everything is right on time, right when it's supposed to be and you're really high off that sort of precision" (Andy).

59. Rouget, *Music and Trance*. This point is reiterated throughout chapters 1 and 2.

60. Gerard, "Selecting Ritual," 178.

61. Rouget, *Music and Trance*. This point is reiterated throughout chapters 1 and 2.

62. P. Stoller, *Embodying Colonial Memories: Spirit Possession, Power and the Hauka in West Africa* (New York: Routledge, 1985).

63. Reynolds, "Rave Culture"; A. Melechi, "The Ecstasy of Disappearance," in *Rave Off: Politics and Deviance in Contemporary Youth Culture* (ed. S. Redhead; Aldershot, UK: Avebury, 1993); H. Reitveld, "Living the Dream," in *Rave Off* (ed. Redhead).

64. The appropriation of a traditional Balinese musical group into the San Francisco rave scene is one such example; see G. A. Fatone, "*Gamelan*, Techno-Primitivism, and the San Francisco Rave Scene," in *Rave Culture and Religion* (ed. St. John).

65. Deblekha Guin, "Sampling Goa," *IDEAS* (Canadian Broadcasting Corporation Radio One, May 19, 2000).

66. Reynolds, *Generation Ecstasy*, 275.

67. See also Fritz, *Rave Culture*, 76.

68. This refers to any recording, playback, or amplification system that utilizes more than two speakers positioned around rather than in front of the listener.

69. G. Galloway, "Young Teens Embracing Ecstasy Drug," *Globe and Mail*, October 27, 2003, A1; online: http://www.ovenguard.com/omnicetera/issue2/vance.html (accessed October 21, 2003).

70. Listening to "techno" has been correlated with an increase in heart rate and systolic blood pressure, alterations in levels of neurotransmitters and peptides and hormonal reactions, in addition to changes in affective states; see G. Gerra et al., "Neuroendocrine Responses of Healthy Volunteers to 'Techno-Music'" Relationships with Personality Traits and Emotional State," *International Journal of Psyhophysiology* 28 (1998): 99–111.

71. Fritz, *Rave Culture*, 78.

72. Online: http://www.spiritweb.org/Spirit/techno-shamanism.html (accessed December 7, 2000).

73. Online: http://www.emeraldreels.com/monte-interview.html (accessed June 10, 2003).

74. Reiss, *Better Living*.

75. DJ "BT" in ibid.

76. Rouget, *Music and Trance*, 80–84.

77. Ibid.

78. Fikentscher, *"You Better Work!"* 42.

79. Sylvan, *Traces of the Spirit*, 128, 138.

80. Rouget, *Music and Trance*.

81. "Dropping the bass" refers to the DJ adding in the rhythm (bass) after it has been withheld from the dancers.

82. Ravers use the term "anthem" to refer to a popular or "classic" track.

83. Online: http://www.chikinsandowichi.com/data/culture/voices/shaman.html (accessed December 19, 2002).

84. Rouget, *Music and Trance*, 180.

85. S. Reynolds, "Generation E," *Artform* (February 1994): 54–56, esp. 56.

86. Fikentscher, *"You Better Work!"* 84.

87. Wilson, "Canadian Rave Scene," 386.

88. Reynolds, *Generation Ecstasy*, 9.

89. Sylvan, *Traces of the Spirit*, 220.

Jesus, Mama, and the Constraints on Salvific Love in Contemporary Country Music[*]

—Maxine L. Grossman

FLIPPING UP AND DOWN THE RADIO DIAL in fall 2000, fans of Top 40 country music could count on one guarantee: before too long they were certain to hear John Michael Montgomery's massive hit, "The Little Girl."[1] Unusual for both its explicitly Christian message and its harsh portrait of life outside the realm of Christian salvation, the ballad nevertheless gained a secure foothold on secular country radio, standing at number 1 on the charts for three weeks in a row.[2] The song tells the story of a little girl's journey from a world of sin and suffering (the absence of Christ in her life is marked by her parents' violent marriage, substance abuse, and eventual death by murder-suicide) to a world of faith and salvation (marked by a new family, a new stability, and an introduction to the Christian gospel). By the end of the song the little girl's new family has introduced her to Sunday school, where she surprises the listener by recognizing a picture of Jesus on the cross. The girl explains that she has met this man before, and

* This essay was previously published in the *Journal of the American Academy of Religion* 70, no. 1 (2002): 83–115, and is adapted here with permission. It grew out of a paper given in a session of the Religion and Popular Culture Group of the AAR at the 2000 Annual Meeting in Nashville. I am grateful for the responses I received there. I am also grateful to Susan Oehler, Lucy H. Allen, and Philip Vandermeer for bibliographic advice; to the staff of the University of Maryland Music Library for their help; and to the anonymous reader at *JAAR*, whose critiques made this a better essay. I owe a debt of gratitude to Hayim Lapin, Mark Ching, Marilyn Henick, Laura Trivers, Nan Enstad, and Carole and Jake Dorn for their insights and engagement. I apologize to Laura for "ruining the music" for her.

she is certain that his suffering on the cross was only temporary because he was with her at her parents' house, sheltering her from their violence at the time that they died. For the innocent and the trusting, it turns out, salvation in Christ is always already a given.

As the phenomenon of "The Little Girl" suggests, themes of religious salvation are not alien to the world of country music. A discussion of contemporary popular country music, in fact, finds it permeated with religious themes and sensibilities. But the religion of country music—the religious world created in its lyrics and in listeners' interpretations of them—presents the dynamics of salvation in terms of a highly stylized and conventionalized model. Close analysis of some recent country song lyrics reveals a subtle homeostasis. Although country music lays claim to an "unchanging" values system grounded in patriotism, sincerity, and an implicitly Protestant Christian sensibility, the lyrics of country songs reflect the absorption and incorporation of new and alternative models for faith and identity construction. A complex dynamic allows some themes and images to be absorbed into the religious discourse of the music and domesticated within it, while a number of more "threatening" categories (including race, sexuality, and non-Christian religion) are left strictly to the imagination of the listener. What results is a commercially successful secular music with an implicit—and ultimately hegemonically Christian—religious message.

The purpose of this essay is to unpack one set of religious dynamics in contemporary country music, specifically the language and conventions of salvation. I begin with a discussion of identity construction in country music lyrics,[3] identifying the basic values that such lyrics imply. The centrality of religion in this values system warrants a further discussion of the components of country music religion (love of home and family, love for a God who can be understood in intimate familial terms, and above all, the search for salvation) and the articulation of this religious sensibility in one specific country song form. This, in turn, opens space for a discussion of changing dynamics in the presentation of religion in country music and an assessment of the boundaries between religious discourse and an unspoken category of things that stand "outside the true."

Jesus and John Wayne: On Identity, Values, and Self-Construction

In the stories they tell and the situations they describe, country songs are best known for providing, as one expert puts it, "a more direct and personal expression of the current, the everyday, and the mundane."[4] Tied to this valuation of the everyday is the assertion that country music is sincere: the songs describe real experiences and real emotions, and the singers are expected to be "real" themselves.[5] Richard Peterson has described this dynamic as a "fabrication of authenticity," observing that commercial country music, from its origins in the 1920s, has worked consistently to construct "the image of the country artist as open, down-home, and utterly conventional."[6] The world of country music, then, like any other discourse, has what Foucault might identify as its "regime of truth, its 'general politics' of truth."[7] This discursive structure shapes the sorts of assumptions songwriters, singers, and listeners will make and the standards they will use to distinguish between truth and falsehood, between the "real" and concepts that stand "outside the true" of the country music world.[8]

Certain themes appear central to this discursive world, including home, family, religion, love, and death.[9] The everyday experiences and emotions of working-class life dominate the scene.[10] Suffering, strife, and the potential for redemption from pain are also central motifs,[11] and humor—in theme or wording—often lightens the more painful of accounts. For fans who say, "My life is like a country song," the implication is that pain, heartache, and misery abound, but the hope remains that salvation and laughter are within reach. Given this discursive frame, we might ask what sort of values system is at work within it.

The country-rock group Confederate Railroad provides a surprisingly comprehensive introduction to the values that underlie the discursive world of country songwriting. Self-identified as a "tougher-than-leather Southern rock band," the group expresses an interest in "championing the working man and espousing down-home values, while keeping their humor and Southern Rock roots intact."[12] From their tight blue jeans and cowboy boots to their mullet haircuts (short on top, long in back) and their predilection for Confederate flag regalia, the members of the group embody a stereotypical, tender-and-tough masculine "country" ethos. Carving a path between enthusiastic tackiness and outright offense,[13] the group has produced songs that range from ironic observations on country music culture ("Redneck Romeo," "Trashy Women") to more serious descriptions of suffering in the world ("Hunger Pains") and country family values ("Daddy Never Was the Cadillac Kind"). Through their willingness to paint themselves in highly stereotypical terms, the men of Confederate Railroad generate examples of the very stereotypes under consideration.

In "She Never Cried" the implicit values of the country music world are made explicit in reverse, through the description of a (soon to be ex-) girlfriend who lacks them all. A decent woman, indeed, a decent person of whatever gender, would know enough to cry at the end of *Old Yeller*. Decent people stand up for the national anthem; they recognize the innate artistic merits of John Wayne movies, and they understand—and have experienced—personal salvation through baptism (with a country sensibility) in the blood of the Lamb. Hints of indecency include a fondness for Barry Manilow and (at least in women) a tendency toward crass speech or behavior. But the real cutoff, the sign that this man's girlfriend is beyond all hope of redemption, is that she would dare to "cuss" in front of his mama. In this, the song argues, lies the ultimate affront to the country values system.

Other songs in the group's repertoire add to our understanding of country music values and identity. From "Daddy Never Was the Cadillac Kind," for example, we learn to value substance over style, rather than the reverse. Parents must toil to provide for their children, the song suggests; only when those children grow to maturity will they come to see that what really matters are the basic necessities, not the frills. Love, dedication, and a sense of humor make life worth living, according to this song. Other lessons include the importance of self-reliance ("Roll the Dice"), compassion ("Hunger Pains"), and Southern pride ("I Am Just a Rebel").

The example provided by this group is admittedly extreme, and the hypertrophied redneck pride expressed in their music is certainly more than a little bit tongue-in-cheek. Nevertheless, the beliefs and behaviors described in their music suggest some of the normative values of country discourse. A representative summary of those values might include the view that life and love are painful but that redemption is always possible; the belief that intangibles (love, respect, faith) matter more than material success; a sense of "right and wrong" and of appropriate sexual standards, family relationships, and gender norms that tend toward the socially conservative;[14] a high degree of patriotic pride, sometimes tempered by a regional or rural chauvinism or a general distrust of government authority; and—first, last, and always—an emphasis on sincerity, honesty, and authenticity above all else.[15] Certainly complex, and at times internally self-contradictory, this value system provides contemporary country music with an implicitly religious outlook on music and life.

Jesus and Mama: The Value of Salvific Love

My analysis of religion in country music, following especially on the arguments of Curtis Ellison,[16] is tied up in the concepts of salvation and transformation.[17] If country songs are about suffering and broken hearts, they are also about the relief of suffering through redemptive love. Ellison, observing the historical and artistic connections between gospel music and secular country, argues that just as the gospel tradition is grounded in the salvation of the sinner through the love of Jesus Christ, so does secular country music imagine a man's salvation through the love of a good woman.[18] Building on this important observation, I would add that salvific love in country music can take any of a number of forms: the parent-child bond, the connection of spouses or lovers, or a more generalized love of all humanity. Salvific love, even in secular country music, can also be associated with an explicit connection to God or Jesus. But this religious connection too is expressed in intensely human terms. The God who loves humankind does so for "family" reasons; God loves in the way that Daddy and Mama love. And salvation through Jesus is associated with the Jesus who suffered on the cross and was redeemed; rarely do we find reference to a high Christology of Christ as King.

The dynamic of salvific love, as expressed in the discourse of contemporary country music, is grounded in several basic assumptions. The first, consistent with the dominant Protestant tradition in which so much of this music has been written,[19] is that the human condition is one of imperfection. Humans are sinful, and on account of their sins and imperfections, they suffer. Sometimes this suffering is innocent (the child in "The Little Girl" did not ask to be born into a troubled family), and sometimes it arises from a person's own actions (cheating on a lover, stealing from strangers, lying to oneself). The suffering may be material (jail time, for example), but more often it is spiritual (the heartache of losing the person one has hurt just one time too often). As Frye Gaillard describes it, the religious sensibility that defines country music is "the human and imperfect grappling with the human and imperfect condition."[20]

The second basic assumption of this religious discourse is that the only solution to the sufferings of the human condition comes through a personal transformation. Such a change of state may be effected as a one-time radical break from past transgression. In this case, the love of God (or Mama or a good woman or man) allows one to "see the light" and mend one's ways, to be "baptized" by the spirit—of God, or love, or God as love. But the transformation may also take place over time and in multiple stages. Just as some repentant sinners answer the altar call again and again, so also do some figures in country songs experience their transformations as a series of small victories, offset by painful failures.

A third assumption, at least as important as the first two, is that the salvific transformation occurs only when a connection is made. The connection may occur between lovers, but it also may occur in the love that a parent feels when considering a child or the love that an adult feels in looking back on his or her parents and grandparents. The connection can take the form of empathy: by recognizing the suffering of other people or by reaching out to alleviate their pain, an individual can experience this same sense of connection. At still another level the connection may be entirely internal, taking the form of a sort of "aha!" moment. Here an individual realizes that in fact love is real or that one's place in the world does matter—to God or Mama, if to nobody else.

Connection is not enough to account for the transformative quality of this religious experience. In addition, the connection must involve some element of sacrifice. Just as the cross provides the gospel tradition with a symbol of the ultimate divine sacrifice (that God would take on human form, and human suffering, to redeem the sins of human beings), so does the secular country music tradition identify a host of sacrificial symbols, both human and divine. Legions of long-suffering wives remain faithful to their wandering husbands in country songs, just as countless parents "sacrifice unselfishly" (in a phrase common enough to country lyrics to be outside the realm of copyright permission). Poverty, illness, and other challenges build more than character in country songs (although they do that, too); through such challenges people make the connections and experience the transformations that define their religious experience in the first place.

And there is more to say about the religious world of country music. The place of "Mama" in this discourse is especially notable. Clearly, a mother's love may have a salvific quality (she suffers, she is eternally faithful to her children, and she always wants to make the connection that allows them to transform themselves), but Mama is more than just another family member in the country music world. As the members of Confederate Railroad demonstrate in "She Never Cried," offending Mama is the one permanent taboo. Another of their songs, "Jesus and Mama," takes the message one step further. In that song, a repentant sinner looks back on his life of misdeeds: the car theft, the affairs with other men's wives, the inability to settle down and have a family of his own. Ultimately he realizes that, through it all, there were two who kept faith in him: Jesus and his mama. In the song's telling chorus, which expands on the old Sunday school standard "Jesus Loves Me," Mama's love is put on par with that of Jesus, and the affirmation for this love appears in the familiar refrain "This I know."

These examples suggest that Mama's role in the country music pantheon is singular. Her love is salvific, as other loves might be, but her place in the world is far above that of mere mortals. As Philip Vandermeer puts it, in a slightly different context, the image of mothers in country music "has not only been sanctified (in a human sense), but also sacralized and deified."[21] Mama has a place by the throne of Jesus, and her salvific powers are at least as great as his own.[22]

If Mama is elevated in country music to the level of a god, the situation for Daddy is a bit more complicated. On the one hand, his sacrifices and hard work, and the lessons that he tries to teach (which sometimes do not sink in until after he is gone), certainly fit the mold of salvific love. But his gender shapes the way in which that salvific message is experienced. First, for reasons that are equal parts Romantic and Freudian, the pedestal that country music constructs for Daddy is not quite as high as the one that Mama occupies. Second, a theological category for a divine figure of masculine gender already exists in the religious discourse of this music. Rather than inventing a place for Daddy in the divine pantheon, that is, country music has the task of figuring out how to map him onto the already (omni)present Father, God.

The result of this theological bricolage goes in two directions. The first—that Daddy's love and sacrifice lead his children from sin to salvation—fits the standard of salvific human love that we have seen before. What is new is a reverse dynamic, through which God himself is to be understood not as the Father—distant, high, and mighty—but, rather, as a Daddy, whose mercy toward his children mitigates the justice he dispenses. Just as Daddies are stern but patient and always willing to give their children a second chance, so also does God provide an ever-present source of intimate paternal wisdom, firm guidance, and gentle understanding.

If God is the stern but deeply loving father, the Jesus of country music appears as an even more intimate and immanent divinity. The tendency in country music is to emphasize the human aspects of Jesus, focusing on his role as a man, whose actions might be emulated and whose sufferings might be familiar to an average person. His salvific love is expressed most clearly in the crucifixion, and that image plays a central role in country music references to Jesus, with the resurrection as another common theme. Jesus looks with mercy on "his children" because their suffering resembles his own, but the power that he brings is more personal than transcendent.

Consider, for example, the image of Jesus in "The Little Girl." The first verse of the song mentions him only abstractly (the parents of the little girl fail to expose her to "his" name and "his" word), and he then disappears until the final verse. In that verse the little girl describes Jesus as a "man" and offers a humanistic account of the basic tenets of Christian theology: a man in a picture hangs on a cross. (The little girl does not ask why, but perhaps this merely reflects her innate empathy for someone who has suffered as badly as she has suffered.) Somehow, his suffering is ended, and he gets up off the cross. She knows the truth of this account because the same man has come to her and sheltered her in her time of greatest need. Interestingly, the Jesus portrayed in this song is not strong enough to make "sinners" change their ways or to protect them from themselves; all he can do is shield the innocent from the violence of others' sins.

An additional observation should be made with regard to the gendering of salvation in this music. Although many country songs are written from a feminine perspective, and some are written with a gender-balanced schema,[23] the majority of contemporary country songs tend to look at the world from a masculine perspective. This should not be surprising, given the continuing majority presence of men as country artists and songwriters,[24] but it does contribute to the complicated gendering of intimacy and salvation in the music. If salvific love can come from masculine figures (God, Jesus, Daddy) or feminine ones (Mama, the proverbial "good woman"), then it follows that the discursive category of masculinity in country music includes a significant place for same-gender intimacy[25] and not only for cross-gender (heterosexual) love. Unlike rap music and other forms of pop, which may express intensely homophobic sensibilities, country songs rarely display any explicit homophobia. They regularly include images of men welling up with tears out of love for other men (admittedly, these men are usually their fathers or grandfathers, but the image is still male-male).

What makes this same-gender intimacy possible, I think, is country music's basic discursive assumption that sexual attraction is exclusive to relationships that men have with women. Because the discourse of country music allows for no comprehension of same-gender sexuality[26] or makes no room for it, there is little threat implicit in a man's expression of love or affection for another man. And the same is true for intimacy between women, who are stereotyped as loving and nurturing in a way that makes such intimacy even more appropriate.[27] The absence of homophobia, in other words, stems not from acceptance or tolerance but from the erasure of homosexuality itself. Only recently have any explicitly gay or lesbian images made their way into country music, and the most obvious recent example lends credence to this argument. Riffing off the novelty song "She Thinks My Tractor's Sexy" (by Kenny Chesney),[28] a country parodist sings "My Cellmate Thinks I'm Sexy," with the implication that homosexuality—when confronted explicitly—is incomplete without its inevitable other half: the male anxiety about it.[29]

As this discussion suggests, the religious sensibility of country music follows a consistent but complicated pattern. Salvation is the living core of religion, but salvation can stem from any sort of transformative love experience as long as it offers connection and requires sacrifice. Mamas, Daddies, and grandparents all offer a love that proves salvific but whose efficacy is only fully realized (in both senses of the word) when the children become parents themselves. Partners and spouses may offer such love, although again it is by loving back—and not merely being loved—that characters achieve their religious transformations. God and Jesus, too, in their roles as parent, lover, or friend, provide a locus for religious transformation through the divine promise of loving and being loved in return. Salvific love thus serves as a motif for religious expressions in country music that are both diverse and highly conventional.

Conventions of Completeness: Filling the Music's "Religious Space"

Like conventional views of the world, conventional song structures and forms also shape country lyrics. Prominent among these is the verse-chorus song type, in which a series of verses provides the narrative of the song and a chorus sums up the song's essential message.[30] Many verse-chorus country songs fit a commonplace three-verse structure, in which a first verse sets the scene, a second verse expands or extends the narrative, and a third verse offers a reinterpretation of the narrative or a transformation of its basic message. In this model the convention of the third-verse transformation provides the context for exactly the sort of religious message we would expect to find in a country song. In this message emotional or spiritual connections, often combined with an element of sacrifice, provide for an individual change of state or identity. Three-verse songs thus offer fruitful ground for discussing the development of religious imagery in contemporary country music, the flexibility of that category, and the boundaries for religious expression in this discursive world.

Like country music more generally, three-verse country songs are highly conventional in their structure and content.[31] Narrative structure, for example, tends to fit one of two basic patterns. In the first pattern, the song concentrates on a single individual, locating him or her first in childhood or adolescence (verse 1), then in adulthood (v. 2), and finally in the context of some life-changing experience (v. 3).[32] A second pattern introduces a variety of characters, rather than a single individual, but presents them in a gender-balanced succession. For example, the song may describe a man or boy (v. 1), and then a woman or girl (v. 2) before concluding with a description of a married couple or humanity more generally (v. 3).[33]

Whatever the pattern of the narrative, it is the chorus that holds the song together and distills its most fundamental message.[34] As songwriter Holly Tashian has observed, in an interview with Cecilia Tichi, "If you're writing a song, you're telling a story that funnels down and it makes its point—bam!—and there's your chorus. . . . You've been showing this story, with examples, and then in the chorus you tell it: '*This* is what I'm trying to say.'"[35] The repetition of the chorus after each verse reinforces the message of the song while generalizing outward from the concrete examples of the verses. At times, slight changes in the wording of the chorus may be introduced to lend specific ties to the narrative of each verse. More significantly, the *sense* of the chorus is altered in the course of the song, especially after the third verse. This verse regularly recasts the narrative of the song or reconsiders its basic premise. In this way "the chorus can function in the same song as an extension of the story in one place and later as an ironic commentary on what has transpired."[36] At times, the chorus itself conveys an explicitly religious message.[37]

An example of a song that fits the first pattern is Steve Wariner's "Holes in the Floor of Heaven." In the first verse the main character is a little boy trying to celebrate his eighth birthday even though his grandmother has just died. He is full of sorrow, and a sudden rainstorm seems to match his mood until his mother tenderly explains (in the chorus of the song) that those tears are his grandmother's, falling through the "holes in the floor of heaven." The boy finds comfort in this country aphorism and in the knowledge that whenever he misses his grandma, he can look to the rain for an emotional connection with her. The second verse follows this pattern, with a rather elliptical reference to the same character as an adult: having met and married his true love, he is sad to be left alone after her apparently untimely death. Again, the chorus provides a message of comfort, implicit in the falling rain. The last verse finds the man celebrating his daughter's wedding, which he does with a sense of loss until a light rain again begins to fall and his daughter reminds him that the family is all together in their celebration.

An example of the second pattern can be found in Reba McIntire's "What Do You Say?" In verse 1 a little boy sees an adult bookstore from the car window and asks his father what it is. Dad shifts the conversation to sports, leading into a chorus that asks rhetorically: "What do you say" when there is no good answer? "What do you say" in an impossible situation? In the second verse a teenaged girl finds herself drunk and out of control at a party and decides to do what her mother has always told her she could do in such a situation: call home. Her mother dutifully comes to pick her up and skips the lecture, at least for the moment, as the chorus again asks rhetorically, Just what *are* you supposed to say in that sort of situation? In the third verse a man sits at his wife's bedside, holding her hand and trying to think of something to say when she tells him she is ready to die. Again, as the chorus reminds us, the situation is impossible, and there are simply no words to answer such a statement.

Although the patterns differ in their basic structures (the first is a linear narrative, and the second is a sort of balance of parallels), they share a common sensibility with regard to the value of wholeness or completeness. Each tells a story that can be understood as complete, either because it has a beginning, a middle, and an end or because it is equally applicable to men, women, and the world in general.[38] The logic of this formula is that while they tell stories that are often highly specific (in their verses), these songs also provide a "universal" insight into the human condition (particularly through the third verse/final chorus combination).[39]

The desire for universality of meaning generates a diverse specificity of narrative, so that almost any relationship or pattern of relationships can serve to structure a three-verse song. The song may trace a single relationship (father-daughter, mother-son, husband-wife, etc.) through three successive stages,[40] or it may highlight one character's experience of three different but parallel relationships (a man and his father, the same man and his son, the man and God).[41] The song may also work through stereotyped categories to present an intentionally universalistic message about "humanity"—bravery in everyday life (the soldier, the mother), human struggle (a homeless man, a crack-addicted baby)—culminating in a third-verse moment of transformative redemption (the cross, the salvific love of Jesus).[42]

The physical setting of the third-verse "scene" often fits into a recognizable mold: the explicitly religious (church, cemetery), the secularized version of the same (hospital room, deathbed), or its idealized rendering (dream sequence, heaven). Weddings, funerals, births, deaths, and spiritual renewals all fit into this third-verse "religious space." Interestingly, perhaps because of the importance of perceptions of universality, there is a tendency to avoid explicit or heavy-handed Christian language in this religious space. The point is not that a Christian *message* is avoided but rather that the expression of that message tends to be more subtle than it could be: God is reduced to "a voice" in heaven[43]; the entirety of Christian evangelism is boiled down to a reminder of "the cross."[44] Anyone in search of Christian truths will find them in the music's religious spaces, but—importantly—for those who might resist explicit evangelizing, an overbearing Christian agenda is rarely visible. "The Little Girl," in other words, is an exception that proves the rule.

Textual Production and Perceptions of Religious Imagery

Up to this point the discussion has been framed in terms of the world constructed within the lyrics of country songs, and in the next section we will return to that discursive context. But in between (and again in the final section of this chapter) it is useful to make a foray outside the text, to ask how country songwriters and performers—and the industry more generally—understand the place of religion in country music.

We might first observe that throughout its history, commercial country music has been defined by what it is *not*: gospel, church music, or (in recent years) Christian pop.[45] Even so, the earliest training ground for many country singers is the church, and hymns and gospel songs historically have provided a common pool of shared knowledge for country artists. The religious core of commercial country music dates back to its founding generation; the Carter family, for example, included a significant number of Christian tunes in their repertoire and tended to sing both secular and religious songs with the same intonations and stylings, which erased many of the differences of content.[46] Hank Williams, in the next musical generation, wrote and sang Christian as well as secular songs.[47] And the famed "Sun recordings" (a 1956 jam session involving Carl Perkins, Jerry Lee Lewis, Johnny Cash, and the newly famous Elvis Presley) included a variety of gospel songs, reflecting the common religious heritage of the four singers.[48]

Contemporary country artists, too, reveal their Christian roots in a variety of ways. The most ubiquitous—while the least explicitly religious—is the "Christmas album," usually a mix of sacred and secular tunes released in the fall for the "holiday" season. On a less universalist front, some secular country artists also choose to release gospel records. The recent cross-fertilization of popular music industries has allowed both secular and "Christian contemporary" singers to make "crossover" hits. Christian singer Amy Grant occasionally finds her way onto the secular country chart. A whole host of secular country singers have gained ground in Christian radio. And the Christian Country Music Association (CCMA) includes a category for "mainstream country artist of the year" at its annual awards event.[49] In their public personas (through television interviews, official websites, and authorized biographies) secular country singers routinely attribute their success—or their survival in the face of tribulation—to their faith in Jesus and their strong Christian values. Country concerts often end on a religious note, as Curtis Ellison has well documented,[50] and albums, too, may end with such a feature.

Even if the sensibility of country music is Christian, the fact remains that the industry presents itself as secular. This presentation, in part, reflects the desire to be "universal" and "American," rather than particularist. Underlying both the desire for universality and the claim to secular status is the basic issue of commercial success and niche marketing. The popularity of country music has varied considerably in the seventy-five years of its history as a commercial genre,[51] peaking most recently in the "hat acts" of the early to mid-1990s. Yet, most people perceive country music as a genre that is more marginal than mainstream.[52] With its origins in the rural American South, commercial country has been scorned as "hillbilly" music (an official category in the catalogs of recordings from the 1920s and later). The association of country music with the rural (and urban) working class has further underscored the distance between country and "high" culture.[53] Marginalization may breed the perception of authenticity, but from an economic perspective attaining the mainstream yields a greater profit.

For country artists and music promoters, the appeal of the Christian music audience represents a similar, and perhaps more extreme, tension.

Recent attention has demonstrated the vast economic power of the Christian popular culture consumer (whose taste extends beyond country to rock music, videos, books, and movies), but at a certain level the Christian entertainment industry remains still culturally marginal.[54] Thus, while country artists may be happy to see their music climb both Christian and secular charts, and although they may be happy to accept awards from the CCMA, being labeled a "Christian" singer brings with it the risk of being doubly marginalized. The standard for widespread success remains that of secular country radio play and album and single sales.[55]

Consider, for example, John Michael Montgomery's description of the popularity of "The Little Girl" and his assessment of the song's message:

> It's the kind of song that hits deep-down emotions. It's nice that radio is taking a chance and playing this record because it's a very powerful song with a powerful message. And the melody is infectious. I strive to find songs like this. Obviously, "The Little Girl" is the epitome of putting you right in the action. It makes people feel they're a part of that song and they react in all sorts of ways. I love the kind of song that tells a deep story like this and has an immediate reaction.[56]

Montgomery's description—found on his official website—is remarkably circumspect. He pays the most extensive attention to the immediacy of the song: it puts his listeners into the action, allows them to feel "part of" the song, tells a "deep story," and generates an "immediate reaction." Only sandwiched between references to the "deep-down emotions" that the song evokes and its "infectious" melody do we find reference to the religious sentiments so explicit in the song itself. Here Montgomery avoids Christian terminology, leaving it to his audience to figure out for themselves what sort of "powerful message" his song might convey. Similarly, his assumption that "radio is taking a chance" in playing "The Little Girl" demonstrates the real economic risk at stake in releasing Christian popular music to a secular audience. It also shows the extent to which the secular country music industry is at pains to hide the hegemonic Christian sensibilities with which it is permeated. After all, Montgomery is not a first-time struggling country singer. And the success of his song—its fourteen-week climb to number 1 and three-week stay at that spot on the charts—would not have been possible without the support of a massive marketing and distribution campaign by his label. But the desire to reach a mainstream audience—and to speak in universalist terms—contributes to a smoothing over of explicitly Christian messages in favor of a Christian-compatible religiosity with universalist pretensions.

Expanding the Boundaries of Country Music Religion

Turning back to the discursive space of the three-verse song, we can find evidence for a complicated negotiation of religious motifs and messages. Country music has been described as "conservative" in tendency, but this conservatism is not reflected in an unwillingness to be open to new things. In fact, the intense valuation of "relevance" ("country music is about real life") requires that songwriters and artists constantly experiment with new forms and introduce new motifs and images into the music.[57] What makes country music conservative is what the industry *does* with the novel elements it absorbs. First, although country music embraces widely, it also holds on tight: novelties that quickly pass out of fashion in other popular music styles may become central elements in a country context.[58] Second, and specifically with regard to song lyrics, new material is not only absorbed but also processed to fit within existing discursive frames. Lyrical and formal conventions serve to domesticate the potentially problematic new images in the music.

Two recent country hits provide examples of the power of lyrical conventions to absorb and reconfigure spiritual motifs that might otherwise have seemed out of place. The songs—Mark Wills's "Don't Laugh at Me" and Tim McGraw's "One of These Days (You're Gonna Love Me)"—work within modified three-verse formats. But they replace the expected religious motifs of their third verses with aphorisms more appropriate to a contemporary self-help manual or an introductory therapy session. The message of these two songs is one of self-love and self-interest, which should run contrary to the country music value of "connection." However, the stylistic and lyrical conventions of these songs actually smooth over the dissonance of their messages, thus resulting in a perception of "compatibility" with normative country music religion.

The first two verses of Wills's song present a series of stereotypical social outcasts, beginning with geeky schoolkids and moving on to unwed mothers and a homeless man. In place of the third verse, and before the final repetition of the chorus (in the space we have come to view as religious), we find a series of short, declarative, first-person statements listing a variety of personal disabilities. The view of the verselet is that we *all* have our shortcomings and that we all deserve equal respect from the people around us: "I'm fat, I'm thin, I'm short, I'm tall; / I'm deaf, I'm blind; hey, aren't we all?" The solution to individual isolation is not connection with others (as the standard country message might have it) but recognition that everyone is equally alone in the world. This message seems, at first glance, to contradict many of the basic assumptions of country religion as we have come to understand it. But the song itself became a number 1 hit, which suggests that listeners (and the industry insiders who promoted the song in the first place) did not interpret it as subversive to their shared values system. Rather, in the image of collective isolation and individual self-actualization, listeners were able to find another version of the music's normative presentation of shared religious transformation.

McGraw's contribution, another number 1 hit, also clothes contemporary values in conventional terms. The first two verses of his song introduce a narrator who is cruel toward a classmate (v. 1) and unkind to his high school girlfriend (v. 2). The refrain asserts that he will someday come to his senses and realize what a rotten person he has been ("One of these days, you're gonna love me"). The third verse finds the man in church, standing, as the church choir begins to sing. Every possible cue is present—the setting, the swelling chords of the music. We have every reason to expect that there can be only one possible outcome to this song: Jesus will appear to the narrator and say to him, "One of these days, you're gonna love Me." And the narrator will, and his personal transformation will follow. The song is a setup. It is not Jesus or God or even Mama who fills the religious space. Rather, the narrator concludes that one of these days, he is going to love *himself*. Here, as in the previous example, the primary message is one of self-love, self-focus, and interiorization. And yet, because those self-directed emotions are articulated in terms of connection and relationship, they too can be understood in fundamentally religious terms.

Mark Wills and Tim McGraw made hits out of songs that play a bit with the religious conventions of country music. Other artists have pushed the envelope further—which raises the question of just how flexible country discourse is. How much can the music absorb and still maintain its claim to "universality" and "unchanging, solid values"? Two additional songs point to the potential for the absorption of novelties while raising the question of what, if any, concepts and claims are "outside the true" of the country music world.

The first song, Sawyer Brown's "800 Pound Jesus," is more silly than challenging, but it is interesting to see how it was interpreted in the industry.[59]

The song describes a man who buys an enormous concrete statue of Jesus at a yard sale and sets it up in front of his house. Life turns bad—he loses his job, his best friend, and his girlfriend all at once—and he decides to hang himself from the tree beside the statue. But his suicide is a failure, and he winds up falling into Jesus' arms, whereupon he says his thanks, plants some flowers, and gives his Lord some ceramic sheep. Notably, although this song could have played as a comic piece, the members of Sawyer Brown consider it a serious "message" song, a sort of winking take on "What a Friend We Have in Jesus." Although only a moderate success on the secular charts (the song peaked at number 40 after a fifteen-week climb), "800 Pound Jesus" went on to win both "Song of the Year" and "Video of the Year" at the 2000 CCMAs.[60] Serious enough to be celebrated by the Christian country music group, it was apparently neither outrageous enough to cause controversy nor charming enough to win widespread praise in secular country circles.

In contrast, and perhaps surprisingly, Diamond Rio's surreal single "It's All in Your Head" peaked at number 15 (after thirteen weeks on the country charts)[61] and won praise and awards for an accompanying video starring actor Martin Sheen.[62] Sung in rapid-fire fashion and layered with internal rhymes, alliteration, and assonance, the song tells a boy's story of his family: Mama was an unwed mother who died young; Daddy was a street preacher who met his death in a failure of the spirit. The strangeness of the song—and its curious power—lies in its take on religious experience. Daddy is a preacher but not of the mainstream sort. He preaches in the local bars, is not above seducing young women, and offers a melange of baptism in the Spirit, conspiracy theory (Elvis lives! The moon shot was faked!), and snake handling (which is where he ultimately meets his end). The chorus subversively claims that truth is only a matter of interpretation and that all people are responsible to seek out their own versions of it and thus their own versions of salvation. Interpretation, salvation, and heaven itself, the song claims, are all a matter of one's personal mind-set.[63]

The popularity of Diamond Rio's song is really somewhat remarkable. Even with significant backing from the song's producers and significant airplay on commercial country radio, a song that equates Christianity with conspiracy theory and urges individuals to invent their own religious reality seems, at first glance, just too "edgy" for the conservative discourse of country music. And yet this song had fairly significant mainstream success: though not a breakaway hit like Montgomery's, it climbed more than twice as high as Sawyer Brown's song, in less time.

Several possibilities suggest themselves as explanations for the success of the song. First, and from a purely aesthetic perspective, the song *sounds* good. Its complicated beat and slip-sliding speed lyrics demand attention, and the words are just strange enough to sustain interest. That alone may be enough to make a song popular (who, besides a tortured academic, listens to all the words, anyway?). But two other points are worth mentioning. The first offers a reconsideration of the song's view of religion. I have suggested that mainstream Christians might take offense at the song's equation of charismatic Christianity with conspiracy theory. But it is entirely possible that mainstream Christians (charismatic or otherwise) might view the preacher of the song not as a representative of their own Christianity but rather as something else entirely, something "other," with which they need not identify themselves. In other words, because his is a religion of ranting and raving rather than of relationship and redemption, the street preacher's message need not qualify as country music religion at all. In this case, it may serve perfectly well as entertainment. A second possibility—assuming again that no one really thinks about the words of the song—is that listeners might hear the whole strange story, including the statement that truth is no more than what one makes it, and fixate instead on the chorus's more benign statement. In this interpretation, heaven is a state of mind and individuals are responsible for finding their own paths to salvation. This, at least, is a reasonable country music message.

The relative commercial and popular success of "It's All in Your Head" suggests that the discourse of country music—for all its conservatism—is actually remarkably open to new, unusual, or controversial religious messages. If self-help strategies, jokey Jesus tunes, and Elvis-sighting street preachers can all make their way into the religious mix, we might ask if there is any boundary to the discourse at all. Is there no image, no message, that country music religion cannot either embrace or manipulate into acceptable form?

Outside "the True": Discourse and Diversity

In fact, there are a number of social issues that country song lyrics cannot, will not, or do not address. But songwriters eliminate the need to address many of those issues by creating a world in which they do not exist. The imagined world of country music, for example, contains little racial, ethnic, or interreligious conflict because it contains no races, ethnicities, or religions (other than the one that has been the subject of this essay).

Human diversity—and, hence, human conflict—is articulated instead in differences between rich and poor; urban, rural, and (increasingly) suburban; age and youth; education and common sense.[64] Ethnic diversity is exhausted with the appearance of the occasional Native American, and religious diversity is limited to those who are and those who are not. The discursive world of country lyrics, in other words, is remarkably stylized when compared with the worlds outside the music, occupied by the people who produce and distribute it and the people who listen to it as well.

In this chapter I have suggested that country music locates religious significance in salvific love of many sorts. But—as in the cases of race, ethnicity, and religious diversity—one set of intimate relationships has been shown to be outside "the true" of country music religion. Country lyrics make no place for gay or lesbian sexuality; it is not salvific because it does not exist. In the rest of the essay, the question that I would like to address is what happens to the noncategory of sexuality when we turn from a discussion of country lyrics to a discussion of the less stylized and infinitely more complicated discursive worlds of country music producers and their audiences.

The attitude toward nonheterosexual sexuality in Nashville appears, at least superficially, to reflect the tendency of the music: whenever possible, just make it go away. This is not to say that individuals—or even the industry as a whole—express explicit homophobic perspectives (though some do), or that the Nashville scene is completely closed to anyone who is not heterosexual.[65] Rather, my point is that the public and "official" discourse of the industry assumes and imposes a normative heterosexuality that shapes the composition, production, and promotion of songs, as well as the construction of country artists' public personae. Homophobia, in the community as in the lyrics of country songs, is rarely expressed because homosexuality is rarely acknowledged in the first place.[66]

I have mentioned (above) that the one recent reference to male homosexuality in a country lyric was from a parody song, "My Cellmate Thinks I'm Sexy."[67] The song pokes fun at singers Kenny Chesney and Tim McGraw, who were arrested while on a concert tour on charges of assorted hijinks, including disturbing the peace and stealing a horse. The song lightheartedly chides them for their charmingly boyish, if illegal, behavior. It is notable, however, that no such parody song was written a few years earlier when relative newcomer Ty Herndon was arrested on charges of indecent exposure and drug possession (2.49 grams of methamphetamine) after he allegedly approached a male police officer in a public park and began masturbating in front of him.[68]

What followed the arrest illustrates the power of discursive norms to shape interpretations. From the same set of events three separate narratives were generated, each with its own criteria for "truth." The first is that of the police report, with its allegation of a crime committed and a suspect apprehended. The second is found in the legal records of the case. Following his release on bail, Herndon checked himself into a drug and alcohol rehabilitation center. He ultimately pleaded guilty to felony drug possession (for which he received five years of probation plus a $1,000 fine and 200 hours of community service).[69] According to a *Billboard* news brief, "Prosecutors decided not to pursue the indecent exposure charge."[70] The third and most interesting narrative is the one constructed by Herndon and his management in the days (and then years) after the arrest. Unlike the police narrative—with details "outside the true" of country music— Herndon's narrative makes sense within the realm of country discourse and uses standard motifs of honesty and masculinity to do so. Immediately following the arrest, Herndon admitted to suffering from "personal problems," and he voluntarily entered a rehab program. But he also left telephone messages with friends assuring them that the other police charges were "a bunch of bullshit" and stating, "I'll tell you what the moral of this story is. Don't pull off the road and take a leak in the woods."[71] Herndon's statement is *not* an explanation of the police charges or a defense against them. Instead, it replaces one purported reality with another. The police charges are impossible, according to this latter reality, because men do not solicit other men for sex in public parks; they do, however, stop by the side of the road to relieve themselves.

A year later a follow-up article refers to the drug and indecent exposure charges but reports that "the latter charges were soon dropped."[72] The tone of the article is upbeat overall, and one source praises Herndon for his honesty toward friends and fans. Herndon himself remarks on the support he received from country radio: "I credit the fact that I've been so honest with those guys. . . . I think if I had tried to cover up what happened, that would have destroyed me."[73] In highlighting his need for honesty, Herndon reiterates that most central of country music values. More recently, the official Ty Herndon website lists "the worst time of my life" as "five weeks in rehab," and the "accomplishment I'm proudest of" as "four and a half years of sobriety."[74] The narrative that Herndon and his management choose to present is one that fits with standard norms in the country world (where suffering and human failings can take the form of drug and alcohol abuse, run-ins with the law, and other "personal problems"), rather than one that stands outside that norm.[75]

A notable exception to this erasure of homosexuality appears in Garth Brooks's gospel-style song "We Shall Be Free." The song takes a global view of human salvation, arguing that people will not be free from suffering until violence, injustice, and hatred disappear from the earth; until the hungry are fed and the environment is cleansed; and until people are free to speak, worship, and love as they wish. For all its high-mindedness, the song sparked a remarkable reaction among listeners and industry insiders. In liner notes to a later compilation that includes the song, Brooks comments:

> "We Shall Be Free" is definitely and easily the most controversial song I have ever done. A song of love, a song of tolerance from someone who claims not to be a prophet but just an ordinary man. I never thought there would be any problems with this song. Sometimes the roads we take do not turn out to be the roads we envisioned them to be. All I can say about "We Shall Be Free" is that I will stand by every line of this song as long as I live. I am very proud of it. . . . I hope you enjoy it and see it for what it was meant to be.[76]

It is interesting to speculate on just why a gospel-style song about justice might be controversial in a country context. Implicit references to racism and sexism may contribute to audiences' discomfort; the pro-environmentalist stance may also be an issue. But Brooks's description of his song—like John Michael Montgomery's description of "The Little Girl"—is telling in its ambiguities. What Brooks chooses *not* to say in describing this song says as much as what he does say.

Describing "We Shall Be Free" as "a song of love," Brooks (like Herndon in his use of "honesty") underscores a central country music motif. But he follows this statement with a clarification, that this is "a song of tolerance." The use of the key word *tolerance* suggests, I believe, that the controversy Brooks has raised is not one connected to sexism or racism. In contemporary America's public discourse, one does not "tolerate" the presence of women or minorities. Such an attitude, in most public circles, would be decried as a continuation of inappropriate sexism or racism. In contrast, gays and lesbians are—at least in some public conversations— "tolerated" for their "sexual preference" or "alternate lifestyles." In referring to "tolerance," then, Brooks implicitly acknowledges that sexual orientation is the subject of the controversy over the song. Brooks promises to "stand by every line" of his song and hopes that people will "see it for what it was meant to be." All this implies that he continues to hold an antiho-mophobic view. But in his construction of the message—failing to mention homosexuality explicitly and plugging for "tolerance" as much as love—Brooks ultimately argues not that "gay is good" but merely that people should be allowed to be whatever they are.[77]

It seems fair to say that, at least in the discourse of country lyrics and in the official comments of the music industry, an overwhelmingly heterosexual norm dominates. In the world of the audience, however, a different dynamic may apply. With regard to literature, Michel de Certeau has commented that the audience's experience of a text "makes the text habitable, like a rented apartment. It transforms another person's property into a space borrowed for a moment by a transient."[78] The transient listener of the country song—for the period in which the song plays, on the radio or in one's head—becomes the occupant of that song. We are the singer, or we are the one being sung to; the song is about us, or it is for us, or it tells a truth in which we can find a (temporary) home. For the time that the song is ours, we are free to say exactly what it is about, without regard for what the song's producers might want us to think. Or we are free to wonder. I remember the first time I heard Garth Brooks's gospel tune. I spent the second half of the song fixated on the "free to love" line, half hearing the rest of the words and half engaging in a running conversation with myself: "Does he mean that the way I'd mean that? Or does he mean love whomever you want as in Hatfield and McCoy? Does he mean interracial love—but there's already a line in the song about race—does he *mean* that?" My own first "rental" of the song was not about claims of "freedom" but, rather, about the nature of Brooks's take on "love."

Whatever songwriters, singers, and producers think they are doing, the anecdotal evidence suggests that the songs themselves are open to a remarkable range of interpretations. A sampling of recent country hits suggests that easily one-third to one-half (and in some cases as many as eight out of ten) are completely ambiguous with regard to gender and could just as easily be "inhabited" by a gay or lesbian listener as by a listener with heterosexual assumptions.[79] The majority of these songs are love songs—"Why Not Me," "If There Hadn't Been You," "Don't Toss Us Away," "Cross My Broken Heart"—which are notable for the intimate world they create. Focusing on the love that "I" give to "you" or the joy that "you" give to "me," these songs limit themselves to images of hearts, minds, souls, and bodies, with occasional references to "people" outside the relationship. To the extent that a listener's particular sexuality does not limit his or her ability to feel passion, jealousy, joy, or sorrow, the "universaliz-ing" tendencies of these songs leave them open to personal interpretation.

Another significant proportion of the selected songs appear to imply a heterosexual relationship only because of the gender of the singer.[80] For example, in Billy Dean's "Tryin' to Hide a Fire in the Dark," the main character sings to his partner ("you") about his recent infidelity, wonder-ing why the partner has not yet caught on to the presence of the other woman. Because the singer is male, at least one of the two relationships must be heterosexual, but a female singer could cover this song meaning-fully (and sing it to either a male or a female lover) without changing a word. Similarly, when Suzy Bogguss covers Patsy Montana's country classic "I Want to Be a Cowboy's Sweetheart," the song is heterosexual only because Bogguss (like Montana before her) sings as a woman. But there is no word or expression in the song that prevents a gay male lis-tener from identifying with the song's main character and sharing the desire to head west with a cowboy of his own. This sort of potential for complexity is exploited, notably, in the final scene of the movie *The Crying Game*, when a male character promises to wait for his male lover to get out of prison while, in the background, Lyle Lovett sings a cover of "Stand by Your Man."

All told, significantly fewer than half the songs under consideration make explicit reference to heterosexual relationships or present a picture that makes sense only in a heterosexual context.[81] Among these, many are songs that introduce specific characters and tell their stories in specific detail, like some of the three-verse songs discussed above. And while some explicitly heterosexual songs offer a wholly positive view of love relation-ships ("Two of a Kind, Workin' on a Full House"), others ("Papa Loved Mama," "The Thunder Rolls") have less happy endings. Homosexuality is never explicit in country music and must be imagined by the listener, but heterosexuality, when it is explicit, is not always pretty.

A number of purely technical elements contribute to this convention. One is a matter of country music business. Because a high percentage of country songs are written by one person (or team) and sung by another, there is a tendency to write songs that can be made to fit, with minimal tailoring, any singer who might want to release them.[82] At the same time, the construction of country singers as sincere and "real" requires that they sing songs that feel and sound personal. First-person songs and songs sung "to" their audiences ("you") contribute to the sense of direct connec-tion between singer and listener and also to the sense that the singer has a genuine message to convey. Finally, because a country song must be "complete," it must also be consistent. A regular pattern of characters is necessary to give the song its proper shape. Sometimes, in the interest of a desire for immediacy, the actors are named, described, and contextualized. But at other times the desire for universality requires that those actors appear in the most general of terms: "I" and "you," but also "he," "she," "a heart," "a person," "someone," "whoever." In many of these cases the gendering of sexuality is much in the control of the listener, who may internalize and inhabit a song in any way she or he chooses.

Saying that country songs are open to queer readings is only meaningful if gay and lesbian people are actually listening to country music. And, in fact, statistics and anecdotal evidence both indicate that this is the case.[83] The sweeping success of country music in the early 1990s and the rise in popularity among urban and suburban audiences included many gay and lesbian listeners.[84] Country music nights and line dancing were popular at gay clubs in this period, and the music has continued to attract gay and lesbian listeners even as the boom has slowed.[85] The manager of one gay country-Western bar observed that "a lot of men who come here relate very closely to the music. They bond with the fact that [country is] openly emotional, and yet extremely masculine."[86] In listening to country songs, gay and lesbian audiences adopt and inhabit the music in ways that embrace all of country music's central religious conventions: connection, sacrifice, and, ultimately, transformation.

Conclusions

Country singers and songwriters have a relationship with their listeners that amounts to a sacred trust.[87] Theirs is the power and the responsibility to speak "the truth" of country music. They recount pain, remember shame, and offer promise of the salvation that listeners have come to expect in the music. But the boundaries on "truth" in country music are permeable. A singer today can incorporate self-help messages (just as mainstream churches do) and can offer a winking portrayal of religion on a popular scope. There are, in fact, only two sorts of boundaries restricting religious expression in country music.

The first boundary on religious expression lies in the requirement that singers not *explicitly* contradict the implicit values of the music by speaking directly of issues that lie "outside the true" of country discourse. Songs may speak *to* gay and lesbian listeners, but they cannot speak *about* them.

Non-Christian listeners, too, may find themselves in the music, but they cannot expect to be addressed in clear and specific terms. Racial and ethnic minorities also remain all but invisible in the music and the world it creates.[88] But if the musical discourse forbids explicit reference to religions that are not American, white, and nominally Christian, it also stands against music with an overly explicit Christian message. This is the second boundary on religious expression in country music, and—as the examples discussed above have shown—it is a boundary that the industry is sometimes ready to cross. The world of country music is a Christian world, and the religion of country music is equally Christian. But the country music message is one with universalist pretensions, and so, even with a Christian subtext, the religion of country music necessarily presents its truths as universal truths.

Notes

1. John Michael Montgomery, "The Little Girl," in *Brand New Me* (WEA/Atlantic [WEA Corp.], 2000). Scholarly analysis of popular music quickly runs into the problem of copyright. Rather than seeking copyright permission from the multiple owners of each song discussed in this article, I have chosen to paraphrase the relevant song lyrics. Much of the rhythm and multilayered nuance of the music is lost in this approach, and I encourage readers who are unfamiliar with these songs to track them down. Lyrics and some recordings are available on the Internet, either on the artists' official websites or on unofficial fan sites; the viscerally twang-averse have the option of reading the lyrics rather than actually listening to the songs themselves. For additional discussion of music copyright issues, see Cecelia Tichi, *High Lonesome: The American Culture of Country Music* (Chapel Hill, NC: University of North Carolina Press, 1994), xiii. In idem, ed., *Reading Country Music* (Durham, NC: Duke University Press, 1994), lyrics are quoted without copyright permission under a standard of fair use (3).

2. "Hot Country Singles and Tracks," *Billboard*, November 4, 2000, 40; idem, November 4, 2000, 38; idem, November 11, 2000, 40. Charts "are compiled from a national sample of retail store, mass merchant, and internet sales reports collected, compiled, and provided by SoundScan," according to the notice that tops each *Billboard* chart.

3. I should identify two limits on this study: First, my discussion focuses on song lyrics and the discursive world they construct. A more comprehensive study would take into account the "production of culture" of the country music industry and also the world of country fans, who not only consume the music but also produce a culture of fandom of their own, through fan clubs, Web pages, and concert attendance. See Curtis W. Ellison, *Country Music Culture: From Hard Times to Heaven* (Jackson, MS: University Press of Mississippi, 1995); Erika Doss, *Elvis Culture: Fans, Faith and Image* (Lawrence, KS: University Press of Kansas, 1999); and, for a theory framing consumer production of culture, Michel de Certeau, *The Practice of Everyday Life* (Berkeley, CA: University of California Press, 1984). Second, the discussion focuses on recent, highly popular (Top 40) country music, rather than the classic periods of country (e.g., 1920s–30s) or its more

visible icons (e.g., Hank Williams, Emmylou Harris). Often dismissed as "trash" (even by scholars of country music!), contemporary commercial country provides fertile ground for analysis of religion in a popular, economically driven realm.

4. Dorothy Horstman, *Sing Your Heart Out, Country Boy* (rev. and expanded ed.; Nashville: Country Music Foundation Press, 1996), xix.

5. Nicholas Dawidoff, *In the Country of Country: People and Places in American Music* (New York: Pantheon Books, 1997), 18–19; Curtis W. Ellison, "Keeping Faith: Evangelical Performance in Country Music," in Tichi, ed., *Reading Country Music*, 121–52; idem, *Country Music Culture*, 591; Horstman, *Sing Your Heart Out*, 71; Jimmie N. Rogers, *The Country Music Message, Revisited* (Fayetteville, AR: University of Arkansas Press, 1989), 17.

6. Richard A. Peterson, *Creating Country Music: Fabricating Authenticity* (Chicago: University of Chicago Press, 1997), 130. On the construction of country music as "natural," see also Tichi, *High Lonesome*, 201–76. On the contradictions implicit in country music and the attempts to erase those contradictions, see David Sanjek, "Blue Moon of Kentucky Rising over the Mystery Train: The Complex Construction of Country Music," in Tichi, ed., *Reading Country Music*, 22–44. The most comprehensive presentation of the history of commercial country music, including its constructions of naturalness, continues to be found in Bill C. Malone, *Country Music, U.S. A.* (rev. ed.; Austin: University of Texas Press, 1985).

7. Michel Foucault, "Truth and Power," in *Foucault Reader* (ed. Paul Rabinow; New York: Pantheon Books, 1984), 51–75, esp. 73.

8. Ibid., 73; Michel Foucault, *The Archaeology of Knowledge and the Discourse on Language* (trans. A. M. Sheridan Smith; New York: Pantheon Books, 1972).

9. Horstman, *Sing Your Heart Out*, xii–xv; Rogers, *The Country Music Message, Revisited*, ix–x.

10. Mary A. Bufwack and Robert K. Oermann, *Finding Her Voice: The Saga of Women in Country Music* (New York: Crown Publishers, 1993), ix–x; Tex Sample, *White Soul: Country Music, the Church, and Working Americans* (Nashville: Abingdon, 1996), 70–77.

11. Ellison, *Country Music Culture*, 270.

12. This quotation is taken from the group's official website (itself a reflection of sophisticated marketing choices, clothed in a "down-home" sensibility) Online: http://www.confederaterailroad.net/front.html, accessed Jan. 23, 2001.

13. In the song "I Hate Rap," for example, rappers are accused of crassness and a lack of creativity, but the subject of race is studiously avoided. On the stereotyped "whiteness" of country music, see D. Sanjek, "Blue Moon," 30–35.

14. "Justice" and gender intersect problematically in country lyrics. For example, as T. Walter Herbert observes, "Killing 'bad' women and sex with 'good' women become paired means of saving a man's soul"; idem, "'The Voice of Woe': Willie Nelson and Evangelical Spirituality," in Tichi, ed., *Reading Country Music*, 338–49, esp. 344.

15. For the association of these values specifically with Western and working-class images (the cowboy, the mountaineer), see Bill C. Malone, *Singing Cowboys and Musical Mountaineers: Southern Culture and the Roots of Country Music* (Athens, GA: University of Georgia Press, 1993), 89–95, 113–15.

16. Ellison, "Keeping Faith"; idem, *Country Music Culture*.

17. See also Sample, *White Soul*, 102–6. Ellison ("Keeping Faith" and *Country Music Culture*) provides analysis of song lyrics and performances but also of the central role of fandom in constructing a country music "culture." I will return to some of these points in my concluding discussion.

18. Ellison, *Country Music Culture*, 118–19.

19. Frye Gaillard, *Watermelon Wine: The Spirit of Country Music* (New York: St. Martin's Press, 1978), 118–19; Horstman, *Sing Your Heart Out*, xix; Philip Roy Vandermeer, "Religious Ideals, Musical Style, and Cultural Meaning in the Gospel Songs of Hank Williams" (PhD diss., University of Maryland School of Music, 1999).

20. Gaillard, *Watermelon Wine*, 127.

21. Vandermeer, "Religious Ideals," 175–76.

22. The origins of mothers' divinization in popular music extend back to the nineteenth century. In both secular and gospel music traditions, "mother songs" and "mother hymns" gained a popularity that extended well into contemporary popular music. See ibid., 171–74; Bufwack and Oermann, *Finding Her Voice*, 15; Vandermeer, "Religious Ideals," 171–74.

23. The gender-balanced song pattern (discussed further below) consists of a series of verses (or sections of verses) that describe male and female characters in parallel situations, often with the same chorus commenting on each situation.

24. Bufwack and Oermann, *Finding Her Voice*; Rogers, *Country Music Message*, 61.

25. See also Herbert, "'Voice of Woe.'"

26. A theoretical frame for discussing the discursive limits imposed on understandings of sexuality can be found in Judith Butler, *Bodies That Matter: On the Discursive Limits of "Sex"* (New York: Routledge, 1993), 20–23. See also idem, *Gender Trouble: Feminism and the Subversion of Identity* (New York: Routledge, 1990), 1–34; Eve Kosofsky Sedgwick, *Epistemology of the Closet* (Berkeley: University of California Press, 1990), 1–63; and Michel Foucault, *The History of Sexuality* (3 vols.; New York: Random House, 1985–86).

27. A recent exception is the Dixie Chicks' "Good-Bye, Earl," in *Fly* (Monument Records, Sony Music Distribution [Distn.], 2000), which generated public controversy with its description of two childhood friends who conspire to kill one's abusive husband and then live happily (and unrepentantly) ever after, together. It is not clear whether this song was controversial only for its display of unremorseful husband killing (itself a gender issue) or also for the picture of two women living alone together.

28. Kenny Chesny, "She Thinks My Tractor's Sexy," in *Everywhere We Go* (BMG/BNA Entertainment, BMG Distn., 1999).

29. Cledus T. Judd, "My Cellmate Thinks I'm Sexy," *Just Another Day in Parodies* (Monument Records, Sony Music Distn., 2000). Judd, a country parodist along the order of pop musician "Weird Al" Yankovic, released this song following Chesny's arrest on a disorderly conduct charge. See further discussion below.

30. The origins of this verse-chorus form are complex. Influences include the Anglo-Celtic ballad tradition (for narrative conventions and forms), Christian hymnody and the gospel song tradition (for their use of verse-chorus structures), and especially the Tin Pan Alley songwriting style, which may have been the most significant influence on commercial country music by the early twentieth century. The situation is complicated by the fact that Tin Pan Alley also influenced the commercial development of gospel songwriting and popular folk music in the early decades of the twentieth century. On the commercial and creative interrelationship of these varied songwriting styles, see Daniel Kingman, *American Music: A Panorama* (New York: Schirmer Books, 1998), 162–67; Charles Hamm, *Music in the New World* (New York: W. W. Norton, 1983), 355–69, 463–70, 497; and Malone, *Singing Cowboys*, 43–60. On the efforts of folklorists and settlement school workers to identify a purely British ballad tradition in American music, in the years before country's commercial nascence, see Bufwack and Oermann, *Finding Her Voice*, 2–16; and Malone, *Country Music, U.S.A.*, 27–28, 428; idem, *Singing Cowboys*.

31. In addition to three-verse songs that fit the conventional pattern perfectly, I will also consider several songs that play beyond this pattern by truncating the third verse or even removing it completely.

32. Songs that fit this pattern include Bob Carlisle, "Butterfly Kisses," in *Butterfly Kisses (Shades of Grace)* (Diadem Music Group, 1997); Confederate Railroad, "Jesus and Mama," in *Confederate Railroad* (WEA/Atlantic [WEA Corp.], 1992); idem, "Three Verses," in *Notorious* (WEA/Atlantic [WEA Corp.], 1994); Billy Dean, "Daddy's Will," in *Billy Dean* (EMD/Capitol, EMI Music Distn., 1991); Patty Loveless, "How Can I Help You Say Goodbye," in *Only What I Feel* (Sony/Columbia, Sony Music Distn., 1993); Tim McGraw, "Don't Take the Girl," in *Not a Moment too Soon* (WEA/Atlantic/Curb [WEA Corp.], 1994); Collin Raye, "One Boy, One Girl," in *I Think about You* (Sony/Columbia, Sony Music Distn., 1995); George Strait, "Love without End, Amen," in *Livin' It Up* (Uni/MCA, Universal Music Distn., 1990); idem, "The Best Day," in *Latest Greatest Straitest Hits* (Uni/MCA/Nashville, Universal Music Distn., 2000); and Steve Wariner, "Holes in the Floor of Heaven," in *Burnin' the Roadhouse Down* (EMD/Capitol, EMI Music Distn., 1998).

33. Songs that fit this pattern include Billy Dean, "You Don't Count the Cost," in *Greatest Hits* (EMD/Capitol, EMI Music Distn., 1994); Reba McEntire, "What Do You Say," in *So Good Together* (Uni/MCA/Nashville, Universal Music Distn., 1999); Tim McGraw, "One of These Days (You're Gonna Love Me)," in *Everywhere* (WEA/Atlantic/Curb [WEA Corp.], 1997); Collin Raye, "What If Jesus Came Back Like That?" in *I Think about You* (Sony/Columbia, Sony Music Distn., 1995); Pam Tillis, "'Till All the Lonely's Gone," in *Sweetheart's Dance* (BMG/Arista, BMG Music Distn., 1994); and Mark Wills, "Don't Laugh at Me," in *Wish You Were Here* (Uni/Polygram Pop/Jazz, Universal Music Distn., 1998).

34. Roger D. Abrahams and George Foss, *Anglo-American Folksong Style* (Englewood Cliffs, NJ: Prentice-Hall, 1968), 66–68.

35. Tichi, *High Lonesome*, 7.

36. Abrahams and Foss, *Anglo-American Folksong*, 66; Allen Forte, *The American Popular Ballad of the Golden Era, 1924–1950* (Princeton: Princeton University Press, 1995); Hamm, *Music in the New World*, 355–61, 369.

37. Wills, "Don't Laugh at Me"; Raye, "What If Jesus?"

38. The patterns also may mesh with one another, presenting (for example) verses focused on a young boy, an adolescent girl, and an elderly couple (McEntire, "What Do You Say"); or verses that describe a male singer in the 1950s, a female singer in the song's present day, and Jesus, in eternal and universal time (Tillis, "'Till All the Lonely's Gone.").

39. Stylistic elements that contribute to a specificity of narrative include detailed references to dates, times, and ages (which set the scene in each verse); references to specific physical locations and objects (which work to the same end); and the use of personal names and descriptions of characters (rather than general ones). Appeals to universality include generalized presentations of humanity (more often in choruses but occasionally in verses as well) and grammatical structures that draw the listener into the narrative (questions, use of second-person pronouns). Wordplay and double entendre ("What do you say?" to mean both "What can one say?" and "Don't you agree with me?") are also common.

40. Examples include relationships between a father and his daughter (Carlisle, "Butterfly Kisses"), a father and his son (Strait, "The Best Day"), a mother and her daughter (Loveless, "How Can I Help You Say Goodbye"), and a husband-wife pairing (McGraw, "Don't Take the Girl").

41. Examples include Strait, "Love without End, Amen"; Wariner, "Holes in the Floor of Heaven"; and Dean, "Daddy's Will."

42. Consider Dean, "You Don't Count"; and Raye, "What If Jesus?"

43. Strait, "Love without End."

44. Dean, "You Don't Count."

45. *Billboard* maintains separate charts for country, gospel, and contemporary Christian music. The country chart is published each week; gospel and contemporary Christian charts appear every other week.

46. Ellison, *Country Music Culture*, 28–32; Malone, *Country Music, U.S.A.*, 65–68.

47. Vandermeer, "Religious Ideals," 47–71, 209–13.

48. Ellison, "Keeping Faith," 148–49; Nick Tosches, *Hellfire* (New York: Delacorte, 1982; New York: Grove, 1998), 115–16.

49. Deborah Evans Price, "Laverne Tripp, Fox Brothers Win at CCMA Awards," *Billboard*, November 11, 2000, 41, 94.

50. Ellison, "Keeping Faith"; idem, *Country Music Culture*, xiii.

51. Country Music Foundation, *Country: The Music and the Musicians: From the Beginnings to the '90s* (New York: Abbeville, 1994); Malone, *Country Music, U.S.A.*; Robert K. Oermann, *A Century of Country: An Illustrated History of Country Music* (New York: TV Books, 1999); Russell Sanjek, *Pennies from Heaven: The American Popular Music Business in the Twentieth Century* (updated by David Sanjek; New York: Da Capo, 1996).

52. Bruce Feiler, "Gone Country: The Voice of Suburban America," *New Republic*, February 5, 1996, 19–24; Tichi (*High Lonesome*, 1) argues against this marginalization, declaring that "country music is emphatically national music. It belongs not solely to the locales to which folklorists and historians of music have assigned it, like the Texas honkytonk, the Louisiana bayou, or the Appalachian hollow." A number of scholars have traced the spread of commercial country music from its roots in the American Southeast in the 1920s to the Southwest in the years during and after the Great Depression, and the development of the genre as a national music in the decades following; see Bufwack and Oermann, *Finding Her Voice*, 161–63; Malone, *Country Music, U.S.A.*; Sample, *White Soul*, 176–86. The economic success and cultural mainstreaming of commercial country music in the 1990s led Tichi (*High Lonesome*, 1–2) to the apt observation that this genre "has gone suburban to become the new pop music with mass appeal." But this mainstreaming is best understood as one example of a dynamic that has accompanied the industry from its earliest years.

53. Sample, *White Soul*, 12–14.

54. "Contemporary Christian Music: A *Billboard* Artists and Music Expanded Section," *Billboard*, April 30, 1994, 35–47; "The *Billboard* Spotlight on Contemporary Christian," *Billboard*, April 29, 1995, 33–41; Carrie Borzillo, "SoundScan's Hard Facts Support Christian's Competitive Edge," *Billboard*, April 27, 1996, 34, 38; Deborah Evans Price, "With Media Exposure and Chart Success, Contemporary Christian Artists Are Baptized into the Mainstream," *Billboard*, April 27, 1996, 34–36.

55. In contrast, any singer who self-identifies as "Christian contemporary" is in the position of seeking a niche market while choosing whether or not to pursue an accompanying mainstream crossover.

56. John Michael Montgomery, online: http://www.johnmichael.com/Disocgr/08/08.html, accessed Jan. 23, 2001.

57. Peterson, *Creating Country Music*, 33–36.

58. Tin Pan Alley song forms from the mid-twentieth century continue to dominate songwriting practices in Nashville today; the brief mainstream fads of Swiss yodeling and

Hawaiian steel guitar shaped country music for decades afterward, and the latter also continues to be influential today.

59. Sawyer Brown, "800 Pound Jesus," in *Drive Me Wild* (WEA/Atlantic/Curb [WEA Corp.], 1999).

60. Price, "Laverne Tripp."

61. Diamond Rio, "It's All in Your Head," in *Diamond Rio IV* (BMG/Arista, BMG Music Distn., 1996).

62. "Hot Country Singles and Tracks," *Billboard*, November 16, 1996, 37.

63. The video, a minimovie with Martin Sheen as the street preacher, ends on a shocking note. In the final scenes, after the father's death, the narrator attempts suicide by throwing himself off a building. The picture then cuts away to a room in a mental institution, occupied by a doctor (also played by Sheen) and a young man in a straitjacket. Sheen tells a visitor that the young man has not spoken since he entered the hospital as a little boy and that there is no way of knowing what is going on "in his head." See online: http://www.accessnashville.com/real media/diamond.htm, video accessed Jan. 25, 2001.

64. Consequently, social class and economic status are extremely important forces in the world of country music, although I have not been able to address them significantly in this article. Tex Sample has dealt extensively with issues of class, religion, and country music (*White Soul*) and also with the specific issue of religion and class in contemporary American oral culture, as in *Ministry in an Oral Culture: Living with Will Rogers, Uncle Remus, and Minnie Pearl* (Louisville: Westminster/John Knox, 1994). On country as working-class music, see Sample, *White Soul*, 13–14; and Bufwack and Oermann, *Finding Her Voice*, ix–x. The suburbanization of country music during its most recent spike in popularity (in the early to mid-1990s) suggests that their analysis must be adjusted for the presence of more middle- and upper-middle-class listeners in this working-class world.

65. Phyllis Stark, "Gays See Gains in Country Radio: Acceptance Growing among Staffers, Audience," *Billboard*, February 8, 1997, 68–69. A number of country stars have expressed antihomophobic sentiments in interviews and public settings, if not in their music or "official" publications (see further discussion of Garth Brooks, below). Lesbian singer k. d. lang got her start in country music, but she remained guarded about her sexuality until after switching musical formats.

66. Stark (ibid., 69) observes that "even in San Francisco, . . . [country station] KSAN has supported the Gay Pride Parade with off-air marketing but has never mentioned it on the air."

67. Judd, "My Cellmate Thinks I'm Sexy."

68. "Ty Herndon Sentenced," *Billboard*, July 29, 1995, 26; Chet Flippo, "Herndon's Label, Management Firm Stand by Their Man," *Billboard*, July 1, 1995, 14; Deborah Evans Price, "Herndon Is 'Living' with Honesty: Epic Artist Bounces Back from '95 Arrest," *Billboard*, July 13, 1996, 34, 36.

69. "Ty Herndon Sentenced."

70. Ibid.

71. Flippo, "Herndon's Label."

72. Price, "Herndon is 'Living' with Honesty," 34.

73. Ibid., 36.

74. See online: http://www.tyherndon.com/qa.html, accessed Jan. 21, 2001.

75. Interestingly, in an interview with the *Calgary Sun*, Herndon apparently addressed the question of his sexuality directly, commenting that he and his wife "certainly have relationships in our lives with people who are gay," but that he himself is not gay; reported by

David Veitch, "Ty Herndon Says: I'm Not Gay," *Calgary Sun* (n.d.; online: http://www.canoe.ca/JamMusicArtistsH/herndon_ty.html, accessed Jan. 25, 2001).

76. Garth Brooks, "We Shall Be Free," in *The Hits* (EMD/Capitol, EMI Music Distn., 1998), liner notes.

77. Brooks has addressed the issue more explicitly outside of "official Nashville," telling a *New York Times* reporter that his understanding of "family values" means a happy, healthy family, whether "a set of parents are black and white, or two people of the same sex, or if one man or one woman acts as the parent" (Ellison, *Country Music Culture*, 259).

78. De Certeau, *Practice of Everyday Life*, xxi.

79. I have considered a series of "greatest hits" albums that were offered in the mid-1990s by the BMG music club: Suzy Bogguss, *Greatest Hits* (EMD/Capitol, EMI Music Distn., 1994); Garth Brooks, *The Hits* (EMD/Capitol, EMI Music Distn., 1998); Dean, *Greatest Hits*; The Judds, *Number One Hits* (RCA/Curb Records, BMG Music Distn., 1994); Patty Loveless, *Greatest Hits* (Uni/MCA; Universal Music Distn., 1993). These examples reflect a double filtration, first because the songs were hits on country radio as single releases, and second because the after-the-fact collections were deemed marketable enough to be selected and promoted by BMG. A more comprehensive approach, like that taken by Rogers (who uses the fifty most popular songs of each year from 1960 to 1987), is a desideratum. However, the results of this brief study are so overwhelming as to be worth reporting in themselves. Numbers of gender-ambiguous songs range from six songs out of eighteen (Brooks, *The Hits*) and five out of twelve (The Judds, *Number One Hits*) to seven out of ten (Bogguss, *Greatest Hits*; Loveless, *Greatest Hits*) and eight out of ten (Dean, *Greatest Hits*).

80. Here the range is from one out of ten (Loveless, *Greatest Hits*), to two out of twelve (The Judds, *Number One Hits*), two out of ten (Bogguss, *Greatest Hits*; Dean, Greatest Hits, 1994), and five out of eighteen (Brooks, *The Hits*).

81. Dean's *Greatest Hits* contains *no* explicitly heterosexual songs, *Greatest Hits* of Bogguss contains one, *Greatest Hits* of Loveless contains two, and *Number One Hits* of The Judds contains five. Brooks, *The Hits*, contains seven, including a number of story songs, which are necessarily explicitly gendered.

82. At least one example from the songs under consideration here was released by a woman but sounds as though it was written for a male singer. In "On Down the Line" (in *Greatest Hits*), Patty Loveless sings of owing debts to the government, the landlord, and "the man," but of promising her love to Jesus and "you." Two points suggests that the narrator is supposed to be a man. First, the singer's debts are owed to a series of (implicitly) masculine creditors, which may imply a balanced male-male relationship between the singer and the creditors. Second, the singer acknowledges receiving salvific love from Jesus and a lover, and country convention suggests that salvation most often comes from Jesus and a good *woman*.

83. Debbie Holley and Larry Flick, "Country Music Is Striking Chord with Gay Community," *Billboard*, July 25, 1992, 1, 22, 27; Stark, "Gays See Gains."

84. Holley and Flick, "Gay Community," 1.

85. According to a 1996 market survey, 41 percent of gay and lesbian respondents purchased a contemporary country album that year; the only categories to rank higher among gay and lesbian audiences were contemporary pop/vocal and Broadway/TV soundtrack (Stark, "Gays See Gains," 68).

86. Holley and Flick, "Gay Community," 22.

87. Ellison, *Country Music Culture*, 59.

88. An exception to this generalization can be found in the success of a number of African-American country artists, such as Deford Bailey (of Grand Ole Opry fame) and, more recently, Charlie Pride. Scholars have explored the interrelationship of "white" country music and "black" blues and jazz and the influence of African-American artists on country music. Examples are Barbara Ching, *Wrong's What I Do Best: Hard Country Music and Contemporary Culture* (New York: Oxford University Press, 2001), 30–31, 141n15; Sample, *White Soul*, 106–8; and D. Sanjek, "Blue Moon." However, a discussion of the place of race in the lyrics of country music and in the rhetoric of the industry is overdue. Few, if any, contemporary country song lyrics explicitly mention race; a recent exception is Chely Wright's "Single White Female," in *Single White Female* (Uni/MCI/Nashville, Universal Music Distn., 1999). But even this song mentions race only in the stylized context of a newspaper personal advertisement. It is particularly interesting to ask how changes in the industry, the economy, and the listening audience will affect changes in the discourse of the industry and the music (Stark, "Gays See Gains").

LIST OF
CONTRIBUTORS

Cousland, J. R. C. PhD. Associate Professor, Classical, Near Eastern, and
Religious Studies, University of British Columbia

Froese, Brian. PhD. Assistant Professor of History, Canadian Mennonite
University (Winnepeg, Manitoba), beginning January 1, 2006

Gilmour, Michael J. PhD. Associate Professor of New Testament,
Providence College (Manitoba)

Grossman, Maxine L. PhD. Assistant Professor of Jewish Studies,
University of Maryland

Häger, Andreas. PhD. Senior Lecturer, Department of Sociology, Åbo
Akademi University (Finland)

Holm, Randall. PhD. Associate Professor of Biblical Studies, Providence
College, (Manitoba)

Kessler, Anna. PhD (Philosophy), University of Alberta

Knight, James. PhD cand. (New Testament), Toronto School of Theology.
Instructor of Biblical Studies, Tyndale University College and Seminary

Maoz, Daniel. PhD. Lecturer of Jewish Studies, Department of Religion,
University of Waterloo, Ontario.

Martens, Paul. PhD cand. (Theology), University of Notre Dame

McDaniel, Karl J. PhD cand. (New Testament), McGill University.

Nelson, Angela M. PhD. Associate Professor, Department of Popular
Culture, Bowling Green State University (Ohio)

Nesbit, Thomas. PhD Visiting Lecturer, Department of English and American Studies, Charles University, Prague.
Olaveson, Tim. PhD (Religious Studies), University of Ottawa
Penner, Harold. PhD cand. (Philosophy of Religion), McGill University
Takahashi, Melanie. PhD (Religious Studies), Heritage College

INDEX